T3-AJK-493

Institute for Research on Public Policy

Institut de recherche en politiques publiques

Founded in 1972, the Institute for Research on Public Policy is an independent, national, nonprofit organization.

IRPP seeks to improve public policy in Canada by generating research, providing insight and sparking debate that will contribute to the public policy decision-making process and strengthen the quality of the public policy decisions made by Canadian governments, citizens, institutions and organizations.

IRPP's independence is assured by an endowment fund, to which federal and provincial governments and the private sector have contributed.

The Canadian Institute for Research on Regional Development, located on the campus of the Université de Moncton, was established in 1983. It is an independent, nonprofit organization governed by a board of directors. Through its research, publication and conferences programs, it seeks to encourage continuing research into questions relating to regional development.

The institute views the study of regional development from a broad perspective and encourages a multidisciplinary approach including economics, economic geography, political science, public policy and sociology.

The institute's goals are twofold:

1. To act as a catalyst in promoting informed public debate on regional development issues.
2. To make available to all interested parties objective information and data pertaining to the study of regional development.

Scholars with an interest in undertaking research on regional development issues are invited to contact the institute. Our Web site is: www.umoncton.ca/icrdr

Institute for Research on Public Policy

Institut de recherche en politiques publiques

Fondé en 1972, l'Institut de recherche en politiques publiques (IRPP) est un organisme canadien, indépendant et sans but lucratif.

L'IRPP cherche à améliorer les politiques publiques canadiennes en encourageant la recherche, en mettant de l'avant de nouvelles perspectives et en suscitant des débats qui contribueront au processus décisionnel en matière de politiques publiques et qui rehausseront la qualité des décisions que prennent les gouvernements, les citoyens, les institutions et les organismes canadiens.

L'indépendance de l'IRPP est assurée par un fonds de dotation, auquel ont souscrit le gouvernement fédéral, les gouvernements provinciaux et le secteur privé.

L'Institut canadien de recherche sur le développement régional a été créé en 1983 et est établi sur le campus de l'Université de Moncton. Organisme indépendant et sans but lucratif, il est régi par un conseil d'administration. Son mandat est de promouvoir la recherche sur les questions relatives au développement régional dans le cadre notamment de programmes de recherche, de publication et de conférences.

L'Institut envisage l'étude du développement régional dans une perspective très large et souhaite favoriser une approche pluridisciplinaire, incluant l'économie, la géographie économique, la science politique, les politiques publiques et la sociologie.

Les objectifs de l'Institut sont les suivants :

1. susciter un débat public éclairé sur le développement régional;
2. rendre accessibles des informations et des données objectives à ce sujet.

Tout spécialiste intéressé à entreprendre des recherches sur les questions de développement régional est invité à communiquer avec l'Institut. Son site Internet est à l'adresse suivante : www.umoncton.ca/icrdr

The Art of the State

Governance in a World Without Frontiers

Thomas J. Courchene and
Donald J. Savoie, editors

Printed in Canada
Dépôt légal 2003

National Library of Canada
Bibliothèque nationale du Québec

CANADIAN CATALOGUING IN PUBLICATION DATA

The art of the state : governance in a world without frontiers / Thomas J. Courchene, Donald J. Savoie, editors.

(Governance)
Papers originally presented at Château Montebello, Oct. 2001
Includes bibliographical references.
ISBN 0-88645-196-5

1. State, The. 2. Political science. 3. Globalization. 4. International economic relations. 5. Canada—Politics and government—1993–. I. Courchene, Thomas J., 1940– II. Savoie, Donald J., 1947– III. Institute for Research on Public Policy IV. Series: Governance (Montréal, Quebec)
JZ1318.A77 2003 320.1 C2002-905228-9

Suzanne Ostiguy McIntyre
VICE PRESIDENT, OPERATIONS

COPY EDITOR
Marilyn Banting

COVER DESIGN AND INTERIOR PRODUCTION
Schumacher Design

COVER ILLUSTRATION
Normand Cousineau

PUBLISHED BY
The Institute for Research on Public Policy (IRPP)
l'Institut de recherche en politiques publiques
1470 Peel Street, Suite 200
Montreal, Quebec H3A 1T1

GOVERNANCE IN A WORLD WITHOUT FRONTIERS IS THE INAUGURAL VOLUME IN *THE Art of the State* series of conferences and proceedings sponsored jointly by the Institute for Research on Public Policy (IRPP) and the Canadian Institute for Research in Regional Development (CIRRD). Central to the conference and volume planning process were the generosity and insight of IRPP President Hugh Segal and Vice President Research France St-Hilaire. We are most grateful for their valuable input and encouragement.

Many people have played key roles in bringing this governance volume to fruition and it is a pleasure for us to recognize their contribution. First and foremost, we thank the authors and discussants for their presentations at the Chateau Montebello conference in October of 2001 and for their timely completion of their written papers, which appear in this volume. It is also a pleasure to acknowledge the constructive role played by the conference participants in providing commentary on the various papers. Their edited comments are also included in the proceedings.

The IRPP played the oversight and managerial role for this project. In this regard, the following people merit our thanks: Suzanne Lambert for organizing the conference in Montebello, Suzanne Ostiguy McIntyre for managing and coordinating the production of the book, Marilyn Banting for copy-editing and proofreading the manuscript, Chantal Létourneau for production assistance and Jenny Schumacher of Schumacher Design for the desktop publishing and cover concept.

As editors, our job was made easier thanks to the professional assistance we received from Sharon Alton of Queen's School of Policy Studies and Ginette Benoit of CIRRD.

As a matter of protocol, we were quite pleased with ourselves when we came up with *The Art of the State* title for the conference series only to realize that this was also the subtitle of a recent book edited by Robert Young, *Stretching the Federation: The Art of the State in Canada*. We thank Bob for giving his blessing to this title for our series.

Thomas J. Courchene and Donald J. Savoie

Introduction

CANADIANS HAVE WITNESSED THE END OF CERTAINTY. INDEED, IT HAS NOW BECOME trite to write that the pace of change in society has accelerated dramatically in recent years. It is apparent, even to the most casual observer, that traditional public policy solutions no longer work. In Canada, the national economy is withering away at the edges as regional economies begin the process of disengaging from each other and forging new relations with their neighbours to the south.

Not surprisingly, therefore, the Canadian federation is undergoing important changes, albeit by stealth rather than by constitutional reform. Canadians are far more pragmatic today than they were 40 years ago, but public opinion surveys suggest that they have less confidence in government as a problem-solving mechanism for society. Protecting jurisdiction and turf only makes sense to the current generation of politicians who came of age when federal-provincial conflicts over constitutional reform and when Ottawa's spending power dominated the national media. The next generation of politicians will have come of age in the new economy, seeing endless potential for both government and the private sector in the cybernetic revolution. They will likely have very little interest in old federal-provincial conflicts preferring to focus on how to make things work, and how to strike new collaborative mechanisms between regions.

Indeed, the issues today are even different from those associated with the not-so-distant Charlottetown Accord, the last major rethink of our institutions. They include the rise of multi-level governance because the dominant issues now require it; the search for new public policy instruments because existing ones are being discarded (e.g., tariffs); dealing with the mobility of capital and the impact of international markets on fiscal and monetary policies because trade barriers continue to fall, and so on. Quite apart from the above, we now need to explore how to make representative democracy work better and how to gain a better understanding of the growing trend toward decentralization and its implications.

There is also a growing populist demand for greater public participation as a means of solving problems and making the outcomes of the political process more equal. The sense here is that the leadership of government has lost touch with the people and has appropriated power and benefits for itself. Beyond the demands for mass political participation there are also increasing demands for participation at lower levels of policy-making. It appears that many citizens are not pleased with the representation their views are receiving through political parties, elections and legislatures and they want to have more direct influence over policies.

These demands for popular participation present some paradoxical pressures on governments attempting to be more efficient and more responsive to the market. On the one hand, government officials are frequently being told to be decisive, entrepreneurial and responsive to market signals. On the other hand, these same leaders are being told to be more sensitive to public demands and to the wishes of lower-echelon workers. They are also told to institute a range of procedural devices that will slow down decisions and perhaps divert them from the "discipline of the market." At the same time, they are told to look to the private sector to learn how to manage government operations.

Contributing to the popular perception that governments are less effective than they were in the past is the fact that the policy problems they now face also appear less tractable than those of the past. Governments have already done the easy things and now are faced with a number of extremely difficult problems. For example, governments now must attempt to manage the economy in a more competitive and contentious environment. Yet most elected politicians realize that economic performance is one of the clearest predictors of their re-election, so they cannot escape from dealing with the economy, a task that is increasingly difficult in a world without frontiers.

In addition, the social problems that governments face now appear more difficult than those "solved" in the past. The welfare state programs of the past decades were reasonably simple programs, largely based on giving people money. This could be done through well-established methods such as social insurance or means-tested benefits, depending upon the type of social need addressed and the political values of the country in question. To be sure, these programs are now well-established, but governments now face some more formidable social policy tasks. These include coping with increasing social diversity and the need to manage social change peacefully. Add to those family breakdown, crime, drugs and persistent poverty. The list could be extended but the point would remain that there are few methods agreed upon for "solving" these problems and governments are left with the need to address the problems as best they can.

The new economic order is also leaving in its wake new challenges for government. The focus of new emerging activities is in urban areas which is forcing the hand of national governments to redefine their relations with cities. The competitive nature of the global economy may well set in motion a race to the bottom where nation-states compete to adopt weak laws to encourage firms to locate new activities in their jurisdictions. National governments may well need to consider "new" forms of citizenship as recent developments begin to erode the nation-state from below (e.g., minority nationalism) and from above (e.g., transnationalism).

Finally, even foreign policy is more difficult now than it was in the past. During the Cold War it was usually clear who the enemy was and what the general strategy should be. In a world with an increasing number of small conflicts, often based on internal cultural and ethnic differences, the approach of industrialized democracies is much less clear. September 11, 2001 has shown that the world has become a more dangerous place than even during the Cold War, but the dangers are more difficult to identify and classify. As well, the lessening of large-scale international tensions means that policy differences among former (and continuing) allies become easier to accept, and economic and other tensions are likely to become more important than military conflicts in international affairs.

If the policy problems of government taken individually are less tractable, then taken together the difficulties in governing are even greater. Policy areas have never been watertight compartments as they are sometimes portrayed, but the interactions across sectors appear to have increased significantly. Thus, governing effectively in one sector will depend to a greater degree upon decisions taken in other sectors. Policies such as welfare, education and the labour market interact to an ever greater degree and present more significant challenges of policy definition and management. The implications for Canadian federalism should be obvious.

The fundamental direction of change has been to make government function more like the private sector. The underlying assumption here is that if the public sector would only follow the lead of the private sector most problems of governance would be over. These reforms are all in pursuit of a model for governance that will be at once efficient, effective and democratic. Different political leaders will assign differential importance to each of those three criteria, and might impose some additional ones of their own, but almost all would see a better government as being the product of the reform process. However, as governments attempt to overhaul their operations, they are also expected to deal with powerful new political and economic forces that no longer respect political borders.

Indeed, in Canada, as elsewhere, the impact of the new economic order, the information revolution and the growing populist demand for greater public participation as a means of solving problems is being felt in virtually every sector and in every area of government activity. We know that profound change is redefining the relationship that Canadians have with one another, as well as how Canada's regions relate to one another economically and politically. We also know that old federal-provincial conflicts no longer resonate with Canadians. What is less clear is how new political and economic forces will shape the Canada of tomorrow and how governments and other policy actors can harness these forces to promote development.

It is against this backdrop that the Institute for Research on Public Policy and the Canadian Institute for Research on Regional Development decided to assemble an outstanding international team of scholars to review eight policy challenges as part of the overarching theme, *The Art of the State: Governance in a World Without Frontiers*. These authors delivered their papers in the presence of a number of leading Canadian analysts and policy practitioners drawn from academe, governments and the private sector at Château Montebello in October 2001. This led to a very fruitful interchange, so much so that for each of the sessions in addition to publishing the formal paper and the comments of a designated discussant, we also present a brief summary of the floor discussion.

We now turn to a brief overview of the eight selected themes.

A Preview

The new economic order

WITH GLOBALIZATION AND THE KNOWLEDGE/INFORMATION REVOLUTION SERVING to radically alter traditional policy conceptions of economic space and time it is only natural that *The Art of the State: Governance in a World Without Frontiers* should begin with an assessment of this new economic order (NEO). This task falls to Richard Harris and his paper "Old Growth and New Economy Cycles: Rethinking Canadian Economic Paradigms," which compares and contrasts the old and new economic paradigms in terms of their implications for the policy triad of growth/productivity, stabilization and distribution.

While the traditional drivers of growth and productivity—investment in machinery and equipment; education, training and human capital; and openness to trade and investment—remain critical, they cannot easily explain the mid-to-late 1990s relative burst in productivity in the United States. Enter the NEO which Harris views as "real and BIG" and "is being driven by the convergence of a number of *new* technologies in the computer and information technology (IT) sectors which are the basis of what [analysts] refer to as General Purpose Technologies (GPTs)." In more detail, Harris characterizes the interaction between the NEO and GPTs on the one hand, and the progression through the various phases of the business cycle on the other, in the following ways:

- As the old GPT matures, growth slows and productivity gains from the old technology become increasingly hard to obtain.
- The new GPT "arrives" in the form of a new set of generic technologies. At first, growth may slow even more, as experimentation and learning occurs with respect to the new GPT. Measured productivity growth slows down and inequality rises for technological reasons (skill-biased technological change) and because of the obsolescence effect on older industries and technologies.
- As the pace of adoption of both the new GPT and appropriate complementary investments rises, growth and productivity begin to pick up. Competition increases as the number of new entrants who are technologically enabled grows rapidly. Wage inequality continues to rise, but growth rates accelerate and show up in the form of lower prices, improved quality of new goods and services and higher profits.
- As diffusion of the new GPT through the economy begins to peak, advances in growth rates slow and consolidation begins to occur across a number of the new industries. Wage inequality falls due to (i) trickle-down effects and (ii) the factor supply response (more people choose to

be educated or skilled appropriately). Technological displacement in the old economy slows.

Harris argues that this version of the NEO can help explain the differences in the Canadian and US economic performance in the 1990s, in part because the US was further along in the GPT cycle. When one combines the NEO with increased north-south integration and with the increased importance of what are called global city regions, one of the implications Harris draws is that "whether Canada can sustain itself as a high-income economy within an integrated North America almost certainly comes down to how [our] cities will fare in relation to major US cities." Although global city regions do not receive much further attention in the various papers, we note that federal policy is rapidly moving in the direction of striking a closer relationship with these cities, in spite of what the provinces may say.

On the stabilization front, the NEO as outlined above obviously lends credence to the Schumpeterian process of "creative destruction" as a business-cycle theory. It also appears that the NEO has, via the Internet and especially business-to-business (B2B) linkages among other ways, ushered in some fundamental changes in labour markets such that the NAIRU (non-accelerating-inflation rate of unemployment) has fallen considerably which, in turn, means that sustainable non-inflationary growth may be much higher than heretofore was thought possible. Harris concludes his discussion of the stabilization implications of the NEO by suggesting that in terms of enhancing productivity, of successfully competing in NAFTA economic space and of ensuring a favourable proportion of North American investment, a common Canada-US or North American currency appears appropriate, although the politics on neither side of the border are as yet on side.

In terms of the income distribution, the disturbing news is that market incomes are polarizing, partly due to the education premium for highly educated workers. But when one controls for education, the data suggest that there has been a marked increase in measured within-group wage inequality. Arguably, the most promising explanation of the above two observations is the new economy hypothesis, and in particular the earlier description of the implications for wage inequality as the new GPTs diffuse through the economy. Harris concludes by recognizing that while there is some truth in the argument that governments of small economies are powerless in the face of intense globalization, there is also truth in the proposition that policy may be more important in the NEO because good policy will have higher returns and bad policy will lead to worse outcomes than was the case in the past.

In one of the two commentaries on the Harris paper, Pierre Fortin provides a needed perspective for all of the papers in this volume, namely that it may be all too easy to jump on the new economy bandwagon and proclaim the advent of a new societal paradigm. This he associates with Heraclitus, the Greek philosopher who was a believer in change for its own sake. Fortin prefers to take the side of fellow Greek philosopher Parmenides who was more interested in continuity. While Fortin readily admits that there has been an acceleration in US productivity, much of this can be viewed as a cyclical phenomenon. On the stabilization front, the drop in the NAIRU can, in part at least, be attributed to the fine tuning of Alan Greenspan. Finally, while market incomes may be polarizing, Fortin sees no reason to believe "that the old Canadian social compact made up of medicare, free or low-cost education, moderately high minimum wages, reasonable social security, and a progressive tax system cannot deal effectively with the particular challenges we are now facing."

Intriguingly, while Harris and Fortin may emphasize quite different perspectives on what the future may hold, they line up fairly closely in terms of what constitutes good policy now: remain open to free trade and investment and free movement of people; support investment in education, in machinery and equipment, and in research and development; strive for reduction in the public debt; and avoid overly-conservative monetary policy. While this is Fortin's list from his concluding paragraph, it parallels closely the policy preferences proffered by Richard Harris.

In his "Reflections on the New Economic Order," Don Drummond of the TD Bank Financial Group attempts to bridge the gap between Harris and Fortin. On the input side, Drummond is emphatic that the NEO is a BIG DEAL, in terms both of the diffusion of new technologies and knowledge workers, and in terms of the altered nature of North American economic geography. On the output side, however, Drummond is less certain that the NEO, as often interpreted, is determining. For example, many of the so-called "old-economy" sectors are rapidly adapting to the requisites of the NEO. This leads Drummond to follow both Harris and Fortin in emphasizing that we still need to pursue all the good policy initiatives that allowed us to excel under the previous paradigm. Nonetheless, globalization is forcing us to alter some of our old policy ways. On the taxation side, high marginal tax rates, for either personal or corporate taxation, are increasingly problematic. More generally, globalization is moving us in a direction of shifting reliance from taxing income to taxing consumption, including user fees.

The changing nature of power and democracy

There are numerous reports suggesting that citizens do not have confidence in national political and administrative institutions in the way they once did. Moreover, there is evidence that this is true in different political systems and in various parts of the world. That is, the drop in public confidence in national institutions is not only evident in Anglo-American democracies. As B. Guy Peters reports in his paper, "Democracy and Political Power in Contemporary Western Governments: Challenges and Reform," the problem is no less acute in countries such as Finland, Spain and Austria.

Our system of governance is being challenged on at least two fronts. Some insist that our democratic institutions, Parliament, cabinets and political parties can no longer do their jobs adequately. Others argue that the very concept of representative democracy itself may be dated in that it no longer enables the public to exert sufficient power over the policy-making process.

Peters reviews the calls for reform in our systems of governance and reports on recent developments. He explores the potential for direct democracy, its advantages and drawbacks. He also considers deliberative democracy and communitarism. Peters makes the point that these three approaches require "an active, informed and heavily involved citizenry." He adds, however, that new developments such as the Internet hold important possibilities for democracy, for citizen participation and for sharing information about key public policy issues.

Globalization, as many observers have noted, also holds important implications for democracy and the nation-state. Why, one may ask, should we worry about democratic governance at the national level if national governments are capable of controlling so little? However, Peters insists that the literature has overstated the case and that, while power may be moving up to supranational organizations and the international market and down to local government, it does not tell the whole story. He argues that the role of the nation-state may well have been strengthened in recent years and points to the European Union to make his case. Events surrounding September 11, 2001 would also suggest that nation-states will still have an important role to play in the future. He argues that the nation-state will remain the focus of our attention as we try to improve our system of governance, broadly defined.

Why, Peters asks, has our system of governance fallen into such disrepute? He argues that public expectations have been raised to such levels that no government could possibly meet them. Political campaigns are invariably filled with promises that are difficult or impossible to deliver.

Peters looks at the role of political parties, Parliament and the executive in planning efforts to reform representative democracy. He sees problems with all of them. For example, he insists that political parties have become part of the problem rather than part of the solution. They tend to obfuscate issues, protect incompetence and can hardly go beyond partisan considerations once in office. Moreover, parties are seen as "corrupted" if only because of the need to raise money to fight election campaigns. Peters also explores alternatives to conventional democracy. He writes that while direct democracy holds promise, it is not without problems. For direct democracy to work well, the public must be sufficiently informed and interested to make the right choice on complex issues. He also reports that voter turnout on referenda is lower than for elections to office. This would suggest that the general public may well be less interested in pursuing opportunities to shape public policy than it is generally assumed by political scientists and political observers. Peters also considers deliberative democracy and points to deliberative elections and deliberative polling to guide better policy choices. But, again, he argues that such mechanisms may not attract "citizens in droves."

Peters suggests that we should explore more fully citizen participation on the output side. That is, governments should look at ways to involve the public in the management of public programs that affect them. In fact, many citizens have more contact with tax collectors, the police, social workers and school teachers than with their elected representatives. Recent developments suggest that there are increasing opportunities for citizens to be directly involved in the management of public programs. Committees of parents are more and more involved in managing schools, advisory groups of one kind or another are being established to oversee program delivery and the development of such instruments as a "citizen's charter" are just a few examples of efforts to make government programs more responsive to the public.

André Blais acknowledges in his comments on Peters' paper that "everywhere citizens have become more distrustful of politicians and politics." However, he argues that we should blame people, not politicians, for the drop in public confidence. He makes this provocative claim by insisting that political institutions have not become less democratic, that governments and politicians are not systematically worse than they were 30 or 40 years ago, and that citizens do not have a narrower range of options to choose from than before. He points out that the emergence of the Reform/Alliance and the Bloc Québécois alone means that voters have a wider range of options than before. Blais argues that direct democracy holds considerable promise and that we should pursue it. He dismisses standard objections to direct democracy. Indeed, he maintains that the threat of direct democracy alone will make representative democracy work better.

Why, he asks, is cynicism on the rise? He points to education and secularization as factors. Education, he maintains, makes people more critically oriented. Religious people, he adds, tend to have greater respect for authority and to be less cynical. Whatever the reason for the current state of affairs, Blais applauds the instrument of direct democracy because it holds the promise of alleviating public discontent with our system of governance.

Managing interdependence in a federal state

In his paper, "Managing Interdependence in a Federal Political System," Ronald Watts provides a detailed record of the state of knowledge in the governance of federations. He looks at developments in many federal systems but pays close attention to the evolution of Canadian federalism, looking at these developments against the backdrop of globalization, the knowledge and information revolution and the increasingly horizontal nature of the public policy process. He seeks to identify lessons learned that could apply to Canada.

Watts reports that a form of intergovernmental cooperative arrangements was established virtually from the day federal systems were born and, in this, Canada is no exception. But it was only later, with the arrival of Keynesian economics and the rise of the welfare state, that cooperative federalism appeared in full force. Governments were forced to define new arrangements as they became more active in more policy fields and as the constitutional division of powers lost some of its application and new financial requirements began to surface.

He describes how the world is becoming more and more interconnected and that new orders of government continue to be established everywhere. European federations (e.g., Germany) are adjusting to life as members of the broader European Union. In Canada, a new order of government may well emerge to accommodate self-governing arrangements for the First Nations. In addition, global and regional trade and economic arrangements have also been implemented in recent years. Large metropolitan areas are also making their presence felt beyond their national borders, as well as their provincial or regional ones.

Watts also comments on recent trends to make federal systems accommodate emerging political and economic circumstances. Some federations have embraced asymmetry, others have turned to hybrid political structures, and still others have sought to combine features of "confederation and federation to define the most appropriate public policy instrument."

What does this mean for Canada? Watts maintains that there is no single ideal model of federalism that applies everywhere. He does, however, argue that new developments in governance in the federations provide an impressive list of options that Canada could draw from and further that many of them could be applied without formal constitutional amendments. Still, throughout his paper Watts warns that many developments and instruments in managing interdependence better can also add to the democratic deficit.

One thing is clear. However, interdependence in federations today involves more than two orders of government. It involves establishing new relationships with local governments, including the municipal governments of large urban areas and with international agencies. This is necessary because of the requirements of the global economy and the information society. This, in turn, means that virtually every policy issue flows into every order of government whether local, national or international.

Our system of government is not geared to deal with this development. Our political institutions still assume a vertical accountability of governments to Parliament and to their electorates for specific areas of responsibility. The question that we now need to address is: How can we ensure that governments remain accountable for policies and programs that they do not fully control or for which they do not have full responsibility? Whatever reform measures we may wish to introduce, Watts maintains that they should be "flexible" and "adaptable."

He concludes with the observation that emerging global and regional circumstances are forcing the hand of governments everywhere to introduce measures to promote collaboration with other orders of government. He insists that other federations have developed more and better intergovernmental collaboration mechanisms than has Canada. He argues that Canada must now search for new techniques to "consciously improve" intergovernmental collaboration. The search should be guided by the following values: provincial autonomy, political stability, democratic transparency, accountability and participation, equity, efficiency and innovative flexibility.

In his discussant's comments, Robert Young addresses one of the key observations made by Ron Watts, namely that because Canada is largely an arm's-length federalism rather than an interlocking federalism it is "less well-equipped to manage the contemporary challenges of interdependence than most other federations." In the Canadian context, Young associates arm's-length federalism with vertical and horizontal competition and interlocking federalism with intergovernmental collaborative mechanisms. Should Canada search for new collaborative techniques (as Watts argues) or can the process and dynamics of intergovernmental competition be counted on to address jurisdictional policy interdependencies?

Horizontal competition, or competition between provincial governments goes hand in hand with greater decentralization and with rising provincial autonomy. Its well-heralded virtues lie in the areas of responsiveness, innovation and accountability, among others. Yet Young also notes that it may have negative consequences: a failure to reap potential economies of scale; a tendency for very small units to generate negative externalities; the possibility of destructive competition (competing away tax bases or gutting pollution regulations); and a diminished capacity to ensure minimum national standards.

Young then explores the comparison between competition and collaboration in the context of relying on vertical or federal-provincial interactions in terms of addressing interdependencies. Defining vertical competition as including competition by both levels of government in providing goods and services, Young notes that this is frequently seen as leading to wasteful duplication and overlap. He offers some evidence to indicate these concerns are less serious than we have been led to believe and then proposes for further research that federal-provincial collaboration may well need a dose of vertical competition: "This might be especially appropriate where provincial governments have demonstrated neglect or inertia, and when emerging problems that demand federal government attention have inescapable links into areas of provincial authority (such as issues involving municipalities)." Young is fully aware that this would amount to the resurfacing of the issues surrounding the spending power.

Corporate governance

Given that capital is increasingly mobile in the new economic order, should it not follow that enterprises will actively pursue jurisdictions where the corporate governance regimes are more to their liking (where corporate governance embodies the framework of laws, regulations institutions and reporting requirements that condition the way in which corporations are managed)? In turn, should the loss of employment, investment and tax revenues associated with corporate exodus not trigger a "race to the bottom" in which states will compete to adopt weak laws to curry corporate patronage? In the face of this dysfunctional behaviour, should not the preferred solution be a monopoly/supranational regulator? Assessing this scenario constitutes the core of the paper by Ronald Daniels and Benjamin Alarie, "State Regulatory Competition and the Threat to Corporate Governance." They end up being highly sceptical of both the "race-to-the-bottom" hypothesis and of the capacity of supranational monopoly regulators to address any supposed deficiencies of national regulators.

Daniels and Alarie begin their analysis by noting that the competitive-regulatory-product model, under the assumptions of democratic accountability and the absence of externalities, is likely to be more innovative and responsive and also more likely to ensure that "all stakeholders whose interests are bound to the corporation are better served ... than if there were only a single monopoly supplier of rules." Moreover, corporations are not likely to be as "footloose" in response to alternative corporate governance regimes as they are often perceived. For example, corporate governance regulations are only one part of the regulatory and contractual arrangements influencing corporate behaviour; there will surely be significant sunk costs and relocation costs that will attend jurisdiction shopping; there is no certainty that currently appealing alternative regulatory climes will remain so, and so on. In tandem, these and other factors suggest that "corporations will not be nearly as feckless as some commentaries have proposed in relocating jurisdictions in response to marginal regulatory changes."

While this enhances the case for national corporate governance regimes, Daniels and Alarie devote most of the remainder of their paper to outlining alternative approaches to further ensure that states are not induced to "under-supply" optimal corporate regulatory product. One obvious option here is to effect "hands-tying agreements" among states that have as their objective either to seek to limit the scope for competing down standards in selected areas or to stiffen states' resolve against bending the rules in favour of corporations. Second, trade and economic sanctions constitute the primary way in which nation-states attempt unilaterally to impose their desires on rogue states for more humane labour practices, for fairer tax policy and for reasonable environmental protection, etc. A third route is the promotion of voluntary codes of conduct and self-regulation. For example, Daniels and Alarie note that the OECD *Guidelines for Multinational Enterprises* have provisions in areas of disclosure and transparency, industrial relations, competition norms, tax compliance, product safety and quality, the environment and the like. Along similar lines, the UN's *Global Compact* asks multinational enterprises to voluntarily endorse nine principles relating to human rights, labour rights and the environment, and many companies have done so. A final avenue, facilitated by the Internet, is the emergence of a new type of corporate lobby group: "a grassroots techno-savvy network of social advocates working together to point out the costs and negative effects associated with corporate irresponsibility the world over."

Thus, there exist a variety of mechanisms both for reining in the power of corporations in terms of their ability to demand lax corporate governance and for ensuring that government incentives to supply such corporate regulations are reduced. Indeed, the complex interplay among shareholders, management, stakeholders and governments in the context of national corporate governance regimes leads Daniels and Alarie to the implicit, if not explicit, conclusion that the regulatory race often tends to be to the optimal and not to the bottom.

Donald McFetridge's paper is not so much a comment on Daniels and Alarie as it is a different perspective on the relationship between globalization and corporate governance. Among recent developments in corporate governance that McFetridge elaborates are the tendencies for Canadian multinationals to come under increasing pressure to adhere to US securities regulations, to be subject to class actions launched by US investors, and to bend or otherwise respond to activist US institutional investors as well as to US and European corporate responsibility advocates. McFetridge also notes that while institutional investors are increasing in importance in both Canada and the US, those in the US are far more aggressive in monitoring aspects of corporate management (e.g., executive compensation) and more willing to seek seats on boards of directors of public companies than are Canadian institutional investors. Presumably, convergence to the US norm will occur here as well.

McFetridge then addresses the shareholder versus stakeholder tug-of-war in terms of approaches to corporate management. Under the former, the *raison d'être* of management is to maximize shareholder wealth. The alternative and, in some areas, increasingly popular stakeholder approach would have management sacrifice profitability to a variety of other objectives and in some variants would also include stakeholders' interests in corporate decision-making. McFetridge's view is that shareholder interests should be primary, since there are ample avenues for both influence and redress open to stakeholders.

In the final section of his comments, McFetridge follows Daniels and Alarie in addressing the "race to the bottom." His bottom line is that there is no such race:

> Capital is mobile and has been so for many years. This has not implied that corporations flit from country to country in search of greater concessions from potential host governments. To the extent that it does occur, interjurisdictional competition provides a welcome break on rent-seeking by domestic interest groups and bureaucrats. The redistributive consequences of this competition are, in all likelihood, largely domestic.

Also supporting his claim that there may be no race to the bottom are McFetridge's related summary observations, namely that the tax revenues of national governments have not declined as a proportion of GDP, and that there still exist many high tax jurisdictions that have high quality public services and a stable business environment.

New forms of public service

We have seen over the past 20 years, particularly in Anglo-American democracies, wave after wave of government reform measures. Politicians, from Margaret Thatcher onward, who set out to fix government started from the premise that bureaucracy was the problem. It is revealing to note that political institutions have remained largely intact. The Canadian and British Parliaments, the American

Congress and the American presidency have not been downsized and the relationships between parliaments and the executives in British parliamentary systems or between the president and Congress have not been overhauled. But things have been different for government bureaucracies and career officials: they have witnessed privatization, contracting-out, downsizing, new management practices and the list goes on.

Chris Pollitt, in "New Forms of Public Service: Issues in Contemporary Organizational Design," explores various forms of public service and their link to the legitimacy of the liberal democratic state. He presents a long list of things we expect from government programs and services: that they be accessible, high quality, flexible, reliable, integrated, efficient, transparent, accountable, equitable, participatory, and so on. The point is that citizens have high expectations of government and it explains why governments everywhere have been reorganizing government departments and agencies and experimenting with new ways of delivering services. They have tried various delivery models—some have been integrated into government departments, while others have been established at arm's length from the government. New organizational forms, however, have not meant smaller government. Indeed, in many cases expenditures have remained steady and the total number of staff has hardly been altered.

Pollitt maintains that we have in recent years witnessed a "positive orgy of experimentation with reforms" and that we are now in a position to choose from an extensive menu of reform measures. He also reports that when it comes to new forms of public services, we are truly living in a world without frontiers; the flow of ideas about appropriate organizational forms is strong between states and through international organizations and there are also important developments in international benchmarking to assess the performance of government departments and their programs. In addition, much of the IT infrastructure in Britain has been provided by US firms. Thus, it is not only international boundaries that are being crossed but also within states the traditional barriers between the public sector, the business community and voluntary associations are also breaking down.

Pollitt sees a strong link between forms of organizations and services and the legitimacy of government and the nation-state. He argues that decisions in governmental organizations are essentially political, not managerial. He concludes with suggestions on how we should determine which activities and services should remain in a government department and which ones should be contracted out or put at arm's length. Notwithstanding this advice, Pollitt insists that designing public service organizations is a very complex task and that there is no set answer available to policy-makers. He warns against solutions cast in "simple proverbs" such as "steer, don't row." He maintains that it is not possible to have one form that will consistently outperform all others. By way of explanation, he notes that an organizational form that maximizes speed and efficiency may not score well in terms of equity and participation.

Rather than search for one superior model that can accommodate all circumstances, Pollitt suggests that we should proceed in three phases. First, look to the more important criteria for a given situation: what is more important, efficiency or clear accountability? efficiency or participation? Second, determine the more important functions or service characteristics to be pursued. For example, to what extent does the function attract intense and continuing interest from politicians? Third, consider the broad cultural context into which the service needs to operate. He writes about the deep-rooted difference between what he labels public-interest states such as the United Kingdom and the United States and the juridical thinking that permeates administrative life in France and Germany.

Ralph Heintzman, in "The Dialectics of Organizational Design" agrees with Pollitt's view that a link exists between government services and the legitimacy of the state. That is, service delivery is not just about service, it is about democracy and strengthening confidence in public institutions. He adds that we need to focus on redesigning services within the state and on transferring functions outside government and their implications for public institutions. But he stresses that we should never lose sight of the fact that public service requires a high level of trust and a strong public ethic. By way of making his point, Heintzman quotes an earlier Pollitt article, "I do not want an entrepreneur looking after my state pension (or my aged grandparent) but neither do I want a cautious bureaucrat driving the fire engine or giving pump-priming grants to investors."

Heintzman underlines the importance of organizational culture. He writes about two cultures found in government departments: one is the culture of "managing up," which looks to the policy process, to ministers and senior career officials and the other is "managing down," to front-line staff, program delivery and citizens and clients. Past reform measures, he maintains, have not paid sufficient attention to this factor, nor to how one can bridge the two cultures. It may well explain why the most urgent new frontier of organizational design, according to Heintzman, is within traditional departments where service delivery functions may be suffering for lack of adequate organizational space.

Heintzman, a senior practitioner with the Government of Canada, acknowledges that Canada has not been as aggressive as have some other countries in reforming its public sector. He argues, however, that by being behind in public service reform, Canada has actually ended up ahead. He explains that Canada has been able to avoid some of the excesses of public sector reform and can now look to lessons learned from other jurisdictions.

Tom Kent draws on his extensive practical experience to offer important insights on the machinery of government. Kent begins with the statement "You can't settle on an appropriate form of organization until what is intended is clear: policy first, then structure." Hence, the "Policy First," title of his commentary.

Reorganization, he insists, is often the product of desperation. Kent acknowledges that a great deal has been said and written in recent years about the fading of public confidence in government. But, he argues, there is another side to this argument—the government's declining confidence in itself. Kent revisits three organizations with which he had a strong association to demonstrate this. He was directly involved in organizing two new federal government departments: Manpower and Immigration (M&I) and Regional Economic Expansion (DREE). The government, he insists, had a clear idea what it wanted to accomplish when it established M&I, but was uncertain in the case of DREE. The third organization was a wartime agency designed to decode enemy messages which was highly successful because it had a clear purpose, support from the highest political level and the necessary resources to get the job done. He concludes, like Pollitt, that political and administrative circumstances are by nature diverse and warns that what fits one set of policy and circumstances is not always a model for others.

New forms of citizenship

Globalization and the related development of supranational institutions (e.g., NAFTA and the EU) on the one hand and the internationalization of individual rights on the other have spawned a burgeoning literature on new ways to think about sovereignty, democracy and citizenship. Defining "old" citizenship as the (current) status quo resulting from the co-evolution of liberal democracy and the nation-state, Will Kymlicka, in "New Forms of Citizenship" asks whether either the globalization-related trend toward subnational political communities (minority nationalism) or supranational political communities (transnationalism) are undermining this traditional view. His answer is "no." "The "old" model of citizenship remains the touchstone from which new forms of citizenship may well depart but will eventually return.

Kymlicka begins his analysis with an evolution-cum-definition of the so-called "old" model of citizenship: "it is the culmination of two long-term processes: (i) a process of nation-building, in which national languages, cultures, loyalties, and institutions were diffused socially downwards from the elites to the working-class and geographically outwards to peripheral regions; and (ii) a process of liberalization and democratization, in which disadvantaged groups fought to gain non-discriminatory access to the civil, political and social rights of citizenship." The key issue for Kymlicka then becomes whether in a world without frontiers the linkage between universalistic and individualistic liberal democracy is likely to remain consistent with the particularistic and collectivistic aspect of nationhood. His insightful answer to this potential contradiction is that western states have tended to eliminate any such tension between the two, not by abandoning the centrality of nationhood but, rather, by liberalizing and democratizing the conception of nationhood, that is, by "thinning" nationalism as reflected, for example, in the shift from "white Australia" to multicultural Australia. Thus, "the fact that the boundaries of our nation are permeable to goods and ideas and people, and that our national cultures are now multicultural and multi-ethnic, does not change the fact that the nation remains the bearer of sovereignty, the central object of loyalty, and the basis of collective solidarity." Indeed, the argument for the link between liberal democracy and the nation-state runs even deeper: the "liberal democratic values of social justice, deliberative democracy and individual autonomy ... are best achieved in a nation state, that is, in a state that has diffused a common identity, culture and language amongst its citizens."

With this as backdrop, Kymlicka then focuses on those key aspects of the "new" forms of citizenship which are presumed to challenge the nation-state as the locus of citizenship. As already noted, these challenges come from eroding the nation-state from below (minority nationalism) and/or from above (transnationalism). While sub-state national movements along Québécois, Catalan or Flemish lines may well represent a serious challenge to the *integrity* of their respective nation-states, Kymlicka argues that they do not represent a challenge to the prevailing model of citizenship. This is so because both national and subnational models of citizenship "endorse the idea that citizenship is exercised within territorially bounded political communities which are simultaneously national in scope, liberal in values and open to the world culturally and economically." Indeed, minority nationalism becomes viable in a world without frontiers *precisely because* it can buy into the prevailing liberal-democratic model of citizenship.

In contrast, transnationalism/globalization represents a much more serious challenge to a territorially-bound conception of citizenship. While Kymlicka identifies five different forms of transnationalism—immigrant transnationalism, transnational advocacy networks, international legal authority, transnational legislative/parliamentary bodies and intergovernmental regulatory authorities—only the last of these, he claims, poses a real challenge to the liberal-national model and then only because it confederalizes the nation-state model.

Immigrant transnationalism does not challenge territorially-bounded national communities since immigrants are literally "dual nationals," not post-nationals, and are "as committed as anyone else to the view that politics should remain organized through bounded national political communities, both in their new home and their country of origin." Neither are *transnational advocacy networks* an example of people exercising political agency in forums beyond those of the nation-state. Rather, "[they] are an attempt to influence how nations exercise their sovereignty not an attempt to offer an alternative post-national or non-territorial forum for political decision-making."

The remaining three possibilities for the emergence of transnational citizenship all involve forms of supranational authority. The first of these—*international legal authority* or international law, especially human rights law—far from challenging the liberal/national model can be seen as exporting and universalizing it. Or, as Kymlicka notes, "there is nothing in international human rights laws which conflicts in any way with the liberal/national view of how political authority should be organized and exercised."

However, transnational or supranational organizations do offer organizational models with the potential for engaging citizens. *Transnational legislative/parliamentary bodies*, the fourth of Kymlicka's five alternatives, represents the most obvious possibility. While Kymlicka views a democratic transnational parliament at a global level as being currently off the radar screen, he admits that this remains a possibility at the regional (NAFTA, EU) level. However, his view is that this idea of cosmopolitan citizenship is met with "hostility in North America and indifference in Europe." In particular, the reason why Kymlicka feels that the EU Parliament will not become an agent for transnational citizenship is that there is no true *community of fate* at the EU level: "no pan-European media, no pan-European political parties, and no pan-European language, let alone intangible issues of common loyalties or solidarities."

How, then, might we remove the democratic deficits associated with the profusion of transnational organizations? Enter *intergovernmental regulatory authorities*, the last of Kymlicka's five alternative approaches to transnational citizenship, and the only one that he feels holds promise for addressing the democracy deficit. However, these international intergovernmental organizations are, from a citizen's vantage point, effectively processes of *indirect* democracy. They would be made accountable to citizens *through their respective national governments*. To enhance this accountability, one could imagine giving nation-states stronger vetoes over certain international intergovernmental organizations' decisions. And to ensure greater openness and transparency one could grant at least observer status to non-governmental organizations and international non-governmental organizations in the decision-making process. Kymlicka recognizes that this indirect form of democratic accountability through the national state is limited, but the alternative of seeking a more direct form of transnational democratic accountability may not be feasible. This is a bold claim since the evolution of the European Parliament will render all of this testable.

Thus, Kymlicka's conclusion is that the traditional conception of citizenship remains alive and well and any "new" forms of citizenship in a borderless world will have staying power only if they reinforce and work with (or work through) both the liberal democracy and sovereignty/ nationhood features of the "old" form of citizenship.

In her commentary, "The Frontiers of Citizenship: Reflections," Jane Jenson accepts much of the Kymlicka analysis as it relates to the likely supranational influences on the future evolution of citizenship. Her principal concern is that government policies under the guise of responding to globalization, and neoliberal ideologies more generally, are serving to create "internal borders of difference and inequality" across Canadian citizens. Her examples include: the shift from universality to targeting on the social policy front; the shift from horizontal equity to inequality as a key focus in terms of the parameters of the personal income taxation (refundable and income-tested tax credits); the primacy of children in the emerging social paradigm (to the potential detriment of families without children); and the association of full citizenship with having full-time and well-paying jobs (more obvious for health and social security coverage in the US, but also evident in the employment-related maternity benefits in Canada). Jenson argues that this has been a result of a "redesign of the architecture of welfare" or a re-assignment of responsibilities among governments, markets, families/individuals and the voluntary sector. This shifting of the "boundaries of citizenship" means that "less can be expected as a right of citizenship."

Subnational communities

Michael Keating's "The Territorial State: Functional Restructuring and Political Change" provides an historical context to the rise and transformation of the nation-state. He suggests that, regardless of the system of government in place, the centre in both unitary and federated states established similar relations with regions as the role of the state expanded. Whether in a federal state like Canada or in a unitary state like Britain, regional policies and programs were introduced which sought to steer development away from wealthy areas into needy ones under an apparent win-win scenario: wealthy areas would gain from relief of inflationary and development pressures, and needy areas would gain much needed new investments. Regional policies thus became part of a larger agenda: the rise of the welfare state.

But things are changing, and the forces of change are numerous and powerful, as regions seek to redefine their relations with the centre and with one another. The nation-state itself is now being challenged. As Keating argues, forces for change come from "above, below and alongside the state." He adds that in recent years the territorial state "has been treated as a phenomenon to be explained, rather than taken for granted." In addition, the economic rationale for transfer payments, if not for regional development policies, is increasingly being undermined in open economies.

Nation-states can no longer steer investments to certain regions and transfer payments are more difficult to maintain because they are no longer part of a "nationally-bound bargain" from which all regions believe they can draw benefits.

Wealthier regions, whether in Germany, Belgium, Spain or Canada, are complaining about the burden of supporting have-less regions. Cooperative federalism is being replaced by competitive federalism where regions seek to loosen ties with their nation-states and fellow regions. Competitive federalism also encourages governments to adopt "boutique policies" which are highly visible. They serve to establish a political presence in policy fields, but they often operate on the margins of a government's jurisdiction and may well represent a waste of resources.

The above comes at a time when a number of citizens are asking whether their political, national and regional institutions should be renegotiated. Indeed, the concept of sovereignty is no longer as straightforward as it once was since there are an increasing number of "sites of sovereign authority." As subnational regions become more autonomous vis-à-vis their parents, as it were, they will want to develop strategies to compete in the new global economy. This in turn will redefine the kind of relationship regions have with one another and with the outside world. Why then, wealthy regions will ask, should they continue to transfer resources to slow-growth areas only to see them use these resources to compete against them in the search for new investments. This is not to deny the fact, however, that some regions are in a much better position to compete in the new economic order, given their urban structure and access to financial and human resources.

Keating points to the rise of city regions as a major development in the global economy. Global cities are now the key sites for high value-added activities, headquarter services and modern living. They have also become the new form of "democratic impulse and reform and bases for political power."

Keating also writes about the democratic deficit as policy-making is increasingly moving away from nation-states only to "disappear" into regional and international trade agreements, intergovernmental arrangements and public-private partnership networkers. He maintains that we cannot turn back the clock and simply have the old nation-state institutional model provide for all democratic requirements. He calls for new approaches to accountability and a new capacity to formulate a democratic will. We may need to introduce a host of accountability mechanisms at various levels, including audit, legal control, special investigations and adversary politics. Similarly, deliberative democracy may need to take place at multiple levels. Keating writes that democratic will and identity "may be located at a very small scale, as in the small communes of many countries, which are too small to correspond to any functional system."

Jean-François Lisée builds on the "regional state" or "stateless nation-building" sections of Keating's paper to elaborate on Quebec's evolution toward a North American region state. He singles out two key features which prepared the way for Quebec to turn progressively toward focusing on the North American market. The first was Quebec's overwhelming support of the Canada-US Free Trade Agreement and the second was the province's converting its provincial sales tax into the export-import-neutral GST (and in the process collecting this combined federal-provincial value-added tax).

Lisée demonstrates that the resulting "harvest" from these and other policies/attitudes includes a dramatic shift in Quebec's trade from east-west (or interprovincial) to north-south (or international). And in the process, the composition of Quebec's exports have changed dramatically—raw material exports have been overtaken by aerospace production and telecommunications. Lisée interprets this export transformation, along with the impressive performance of Quebec in terms of 14 indicators of innovation, as evidence of a corresponding and fundamental transformation of the Quebec economy in the direction of a knowledge-based society.

International governance and Canada

In their paper, "Citizens, States and International Regimes," Pierre-Marc Johnson and Karel Mayrand conclude that it is only through building stronger democratic processes and pursuing a more balanced globalization agenda that global governance will begin extricating itself from the conceptual and physical barricades within which it is now imprisoned. Albeit implicit, this message is directed to those international players desirous of further World Trade Organization (WTO) rounds of globalization.

The two-stage analysis leading to this articulate call for renewing global governance begins with a careful assessment of the variety of ways that globalization has profoundly altered the three key players in the international governance game: citizens, states and international regimes. This is then followed by an analysis of the substantive, procedural and institutional requisites, among and between these players, if globalization is to work for people and not just for profits.

Toward this end, the authors focus initially on the rise of international civil society. In their view the proximate causes of this development are, on the "demand side," a declining confidence in the state and the related and growing awareness of the need for public participation in governance and, on the "supply side," the dramatic role of the Internet in creating the more than 20,000 new international citizen networks over the last decade. In tandem, these forces have eroded the former "permissive consensus" underpinning international governance and are leading the international system toward a "participatory consensus."

With powers passing upward and downward from central governments of nation-states and with the shift toward multi-centred and horizontal networks and away from traditional Weberian hierarchical lines of control, nation-states must now assert their control more and more in partnership with local authorities, civil society and the private sector and by utilizing innovative tools and strategies. In terms of the last of the three players—international regimes—the creation of the WTO, replete with a heightened degree of intrusion into domestic governance and a powerful dispute-resolution mechanism, exceeds anything possible let alone contemplated under the old General Agreement on Tariffs and Trade (GATT) regime. Parallel to this trade/economic regime are a series of other non-legally-binding regimes in fields of human rights, social development, environment, culture, etc. While some of these other regimes are extensive (there are more than 500 multinational environmental agreements) they remain no match for the power, scope and focus of the trade/economic regimes, which is, of course, part of the overall governance problem.

With this as backdrop Johnson and Mayrand then focus on the potential ways in which global governance might and ought to evolve. Not surprisingly in light of the above, the overriding challenge is two-fold. The first is the need for *integration*, namely ensuring that the regimes dealing with developmental and with non-trade issues develop coordination, coherence and a capacity to play on par with the WTO. The second is *participation*, namely developing democratic and procedural "space" in global governance so that the various regimes can accommodate international civil society into their decision-making and consensus-building processes. In terms of the first of these issues, while the authors recognize the inevitability of the eventual evolution of the environmental and trade regions into a coherent and balanced overarching governance structure, perhaps in the form of a world environmental organization (WEO) as a companion to the WTO, they also recognize that the prior challenge is to ensure internal coordination and capacity within the highly diversified, fragmented and complex environmental regime.

In terms of encouraging a participatory consensus, Johnson and Mayrand elaborate alternative approaches, such as allowing greater civil society participation in the WTO and encouraging international assemblies of national parliamentarians at the WTO and elsewhere. They conclude their paper with an appeal to Canada to don the mantle of leadership here, particularly since as a major trading country and a major natural-resource producer we ought to have a heightened interest in the future of global governance of the economic and environmental regimes alike.

While recognizing the Johnson/Mayrand paper as comprehensive, stimulating, constructive and focused on a key global dilemma, discussant Denis Stairs nonetheless feels that the underlying changes to global governance may not be as fundamental as the authors suggest. While the international players have indeed been evolving, and "the bottles may have new labels ... the wine itself is well and truly aged." For one thing states are still atop the hierarchy of actors: they have authority, the other players only have influence. And granted that civil society organizations (CSOs) are more numerous than heretofore, their predecessors (the campaign against slavery, for disarmament, etc.) were also "transnational." In terms of inter-regime linkages, Stairs echoes the Johnson/Mayrand suggestion for an environmental equivalent of the WTO and also shares the authors' concerns that expectations here should not be too high that the environmental club can soon get its act together.

Stairs is more or less on side with the "building participatory governance" section of Johnson/Mayrand, with one important proviso, namely that we recognize CSOs for what they really are. Although they have a right to an audience, one must remember that they are not elected. Rather they are self-appointed, and often are obsessively single-minded. In Stairs' words, "the more they are treated as if they are representatives of *demos* at large, moreover, the weaker becomes the position of those who are *really* supposed to represent *demos* at large—namely, the elected Members of Parliament." This leads Stairs, in his final comments, to support enthusiastically the Johnson/Mayrand recommendation to enhance the role of parliamentarians in global governance.

Policy panels: September 11, 2002 and common currency

The tragic events of September 11, 2001 occurred after the authors had submitted their papers but before the conference itself (October 11–13, 2001). In order to ensure that the floor discussions related to the various papers were not dominated by the implications of 9/11, we decided to hold a special evening roundtable to deal with the likely short- and longer term consequences. The resulting *A Roundtable on September 11* appeared in the November 2001 issue of *Policy Options Politiques* (pp. 37-46). Alternatively, it can be accessed from the IRPP website at www.irpp.org.

What we were not prepared for was that the floor discussion relating to the first session (The New Economic Order) appeared likely to become a debate on the pros and cons of a common currency for North America. We resolved this by holding a second roundtable, this one dedicated to the appropriate currency regime for Canada. The edited transcript of this currency roundtable appears in the Appendix.

Conclusion

ALL THAT REMAINS FOR US IS TO EXPRESS OUR SINCEREST THANKS TO OUR AUTHORS and discussants and to invite our readers to absorb, assess and, we trust, enjoy their reflections on *The Art of the State: Governance in a World Without Frontiers*.

The New Economic Order

Old Growth and New Economy Cycles: Rethinking Canadian Economic Paradigms

Introduction

THE PURPOSE OF THIS PAPER IS TO ANTICIPATE SOME OF THE CHALLENGES FACING THE Canadian economy arising from the emergence of the new economic order (NEO). Of necessity this is a far-reaching and speculative task, made dramatically more so in the wake of September 11, 2001. Much of the new economy literature that does exist relates to globalization, to integration, to the implications for sovereignty and the like. It is not obvious that I could add much to this literature. However, the prospects of an emerging global recession provides a different, yet fruitful, perspective for assessing the impact of the new economy, namely to ask how economic factors may alter the course of the next business cycle relative to the most recent cycles. It is important to recognize that it is extremely difficult at turning points in a business cycle to look forward with any degree of precision. It seems that each major economic cycle, which I characterize as beginning with a major recession, leads to new and large-scale structural change, which appears to be largely unanticipated by policy-makers and most professional economists. For example, the 1973 recession led to global inflation, a commodity boom, and the great productivity slowdown. The 1981–82 recession marked the transition to high interest rates, growing deficits, rising unemployment and the beginnings of what is now referred to as globalization. The 1990–92 recession led to fiscal retrenchment, a growing Canada-United States income gap, an unprecedented US economic boom driven by technology and stock markets, and the acceleration of the economic integration of Canada within North America. This is an economist's list. Other social scientists and policy-makers would have their own list of important structural shifts associated with each of these periods. Looking forward it seems clear that the 1993–2001 boom is over for now and we are entering the first new economy recession which may turn out to be much greater in scale than was first imagined. The only reliable forecast is that whatever is coming, the cycle will be different from the last.

While each of these economic cycles brings a change in the focus of economic policy, some problems are more enduring than others. The relative decline of Canadian living standards in the 1990s has become a central preoccupation of the Canadian economic debate, but other questions remain high on the list, including changes in the distribution of income, the "brain drain," currency depreciation, competition for global foreign direct investment (FDI), and the pressures of globalization on the Canadian welfare state. Attempting to provide an economic framework within which all of these issues can be conveniently explained and supported by relevant empirical evidence, replete with clear policy implications, would be highly desirable, but well beyond the scope of this or probably any other paper. Indeed, explaining the last cycle is still an unresolved matter at the same time that we are entering the next. Nevertheless, some of the fog is lifting, if only slowly.

Specifically, there is a fairly high degree of consensus at this juncture among what I would call the core mainstream of economists and policy-makers in terms of what characterizes good policy. This would incorporate both the central theoretical framework within which most economists operate, as well as the vast empirical literature of the last two decades on virtually the entire range of questions relating to growth, stabilization, efficiency and distribution. The consensus view can be summarized in the following set of principles:

- Markets are for most activities the most efficient, shock-proof and innovative mechanisms for resource allocation.
- Governments do best in the provision of pure public goods, social support and infrastructure. Taxation required to support these activities should be non-discriminatory, neutral and largely focused on consumption as opposed to other tax bases.
- Fiscal policy, other than through automatic stabilizers, should not be cyclically focused and deficit finance is a dangerous course of action except under the worst cyclical circumstances.
- Monetary policy should be preoccupied with inflation, not unemployment, and be run by a central bank which is independent of the legislative branches of government.

- Economic growth requires open markets and high levels of investment in physical, human and intellectual capital.
- International trade contributes to growth in incomes and productivity, and freer trade is relatively more important the smaller the economy.

In what follows, the discussion of future developments and their implications for governments and governance in the NEO is along the conventional Musgrave classification of the roles of government in the economy—growth, stabilization and distribution. In focusing on where we have been and where we may be headed, there are a number of themes or factors that are common to all these sections, including globalization, Canada-US integration, the new economy, knowledge-based growth, human capital and the changing roles of cities and regions within the national economy. In more detail, the section on growth begins with a discussion of the traditional (old economy) drivers of growth. Attention then shifts to the new economy, to the information technology (IT) revolution and the emergence of general purpose technologies (GPTs). Beyond visualizing growth from a new economy perspective, focus is also directed to the productivity issue, to the knowledge-based economy (KBE) and to the emergence of cities and regions as the key motors of growth.

The NEO as viewed from the stabilization perspective deals *inter alia* with rules versus discretion, with business-cycle synchronization, with fiscal policy and, finally, with the currency regimes, where the latter focuses on the NEO implications for the choice between fixed and flexible exchange rates.

The final substantive section addresses a range of issues relating to income-distribution implications of the new economy.

Growth: Productivity Drivers in the Old and New Economies

THE 1990S EMERGED AS THE DECADE THAT, AMONG OTHER THINGS, TRIGGERED A major debate among economists on the sources of economic growth. Broadly, the lines were drawn between those who focused on what might be called the "traditional determinants" of growth, including investment (capital formation), education and openness to international trade versus those who argued that the growth process is better explained by infrequent but major technological innovations which are bunched in time. The latter school of thought, which has become known more popularly by the term "new economy," gained considerable momentum and a great deal of academic support in the 1990s. Specifically, the belief that we are in the midst of a major global technological transition has permeated the business, academic and policy communities, most notably in the United States but also in most other countries. While the recent collapse in the NASDAQ has led to a substantial reduction in popular enthusiasm for this idea, it is nonetheless the case that in economic circles the evidence has been increasingly slanted in favour of these ideas. To put this in context, however, it is useful to start with a review of the more traditional determinants of growth.

Traditional growth determinants

Figure 1 presents gross domestic product (GDP) per hour worked, and GDP per worker in Canada relative to the US. The reader should be cautioned that both the US and Canada have recently revised some of these numbers, but the basic picture portrayed in figure 1 is the same. Canada's productivity is about 20 percent lower than that in the US and has been deteriorating in relative terms. The productivity performance of Canadian manufacturing held up reasonably well over the 1980–94 period, but then flattened out, whereas the US manufacturing productivity mushroomed (see figure 2).

The other major determinant of economic growth is the number of people employed in the population. Because this is subject to substantial cyclical variation, one usually focuses on the productivity statistics. Nevertheless, at certain times the employment growth record becomes of structural, as opposed to cyclical, significance. Canada, somewhat like Europe, has had a weaker employment growth record than has the United States, although in the last three years Canadian employment growth was above the US average (see figure 3). Debates among economists as to the reasons for this are part and parcel of the debate on growth determinants. One of the major limitations of research in this area has been its focus on national economies. There is a growing concern that this focus may be inappropriate, since regional growth rates often differ dramatically within the same national unit.

The outcome of the large international empirical literature on productivity growth has led to what I would call a mid-1990s mainstream consensus view

Relative Labour Productivity: Canada versus United States

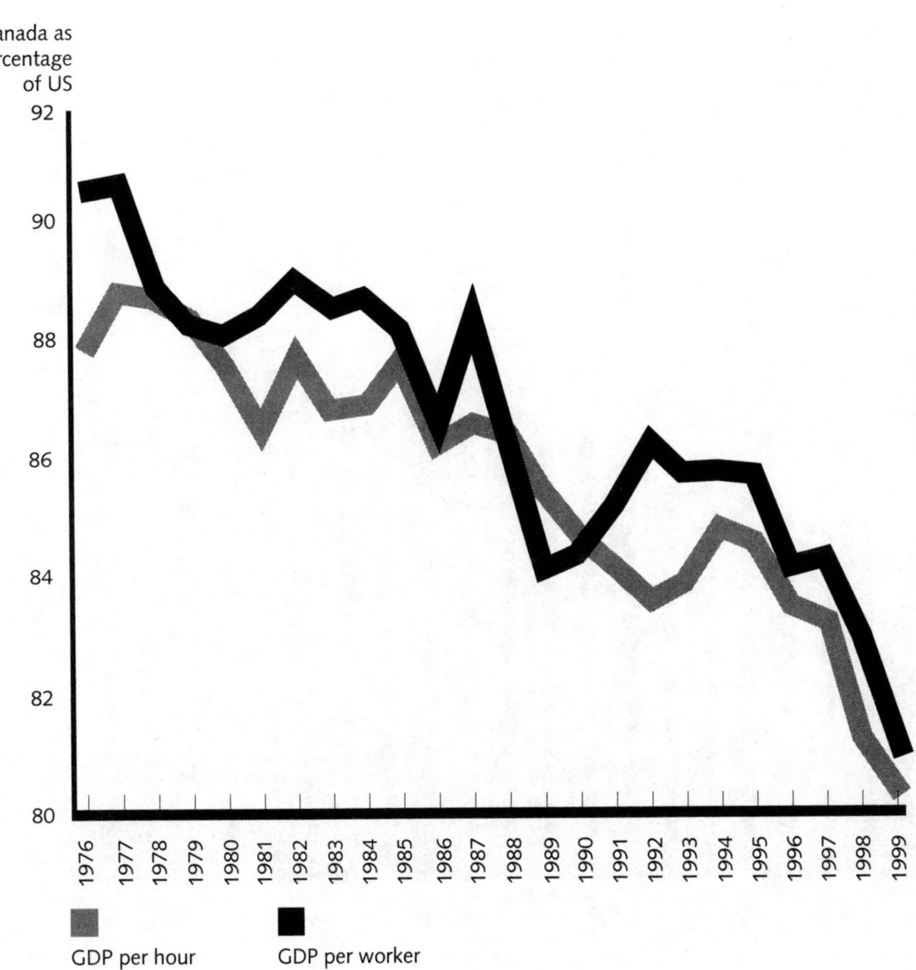

Notes: 1. Data for GDP per worker and GDP per hour for US recalculated from 1996$ into 1992$ with GDP price deflator ratio 1992/1996=0.917.

2. GDP per capita and GDP per hour for Canada recalculated into 1992 US $ with OECD bilateral 1992 PPP exchange rate estimate 1.23 CAD/$US.

Canada-US Labour Productivity Levels Manufacturing 1980–2000

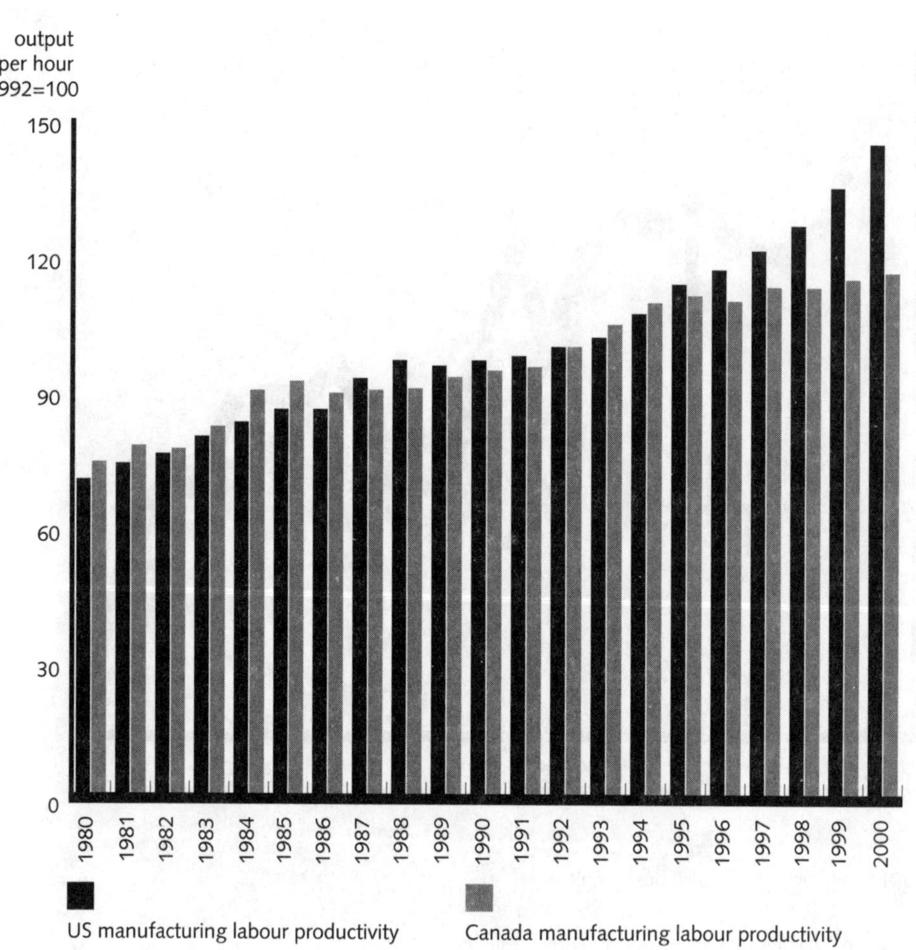

Canada-US Employment Growth

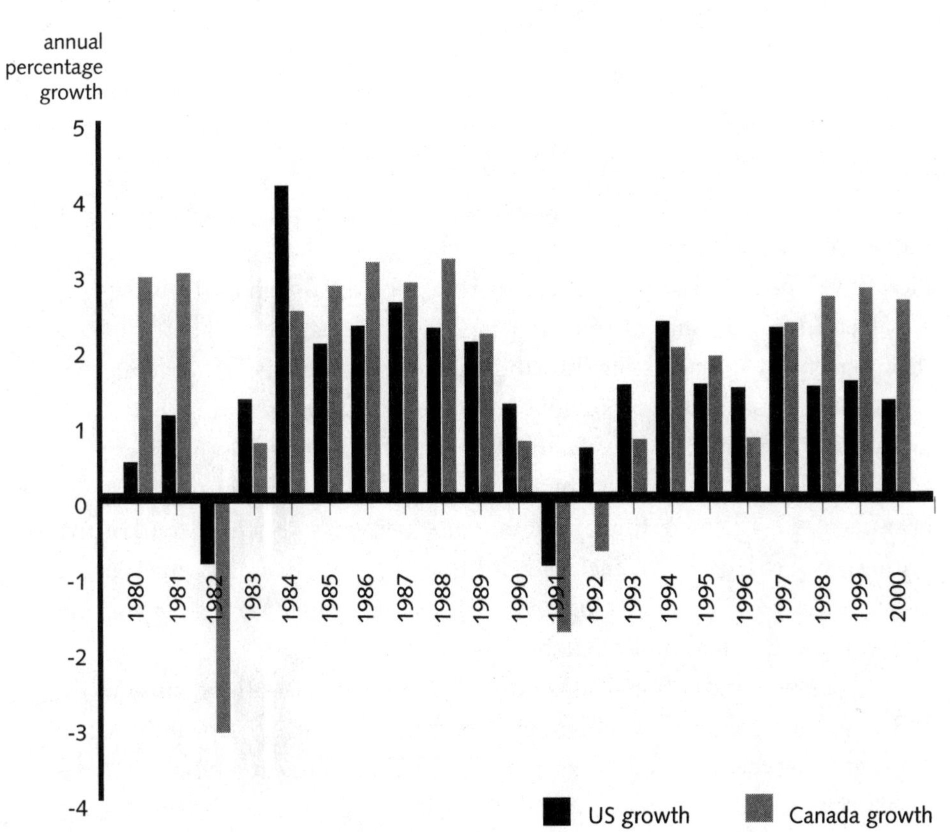

on the three main correlates or determinants of national productivity growth. They are, respectively, investment in machinery and equipment, human capital development and openness to trade and investment.

Investment in machinery and equipment (M&E). Countries with high rates of investment in M&E as a share of GDP have high growth rates on average. In making this observation, one has to control for obvious factors such as the initial level of income. This corrects for what is known as conditional convergence, or catch-up—other things being equal, a poor country can be expected to grow faster than a rich country. This caveat aside, the above strong correlation holds up over long historical periods and, based on more recent evidence, in both developed and developing countries. To be sure, it is subject to multiple interpretations. The conventional view is that M&E investment carries with it new technology and new ideas which diffuse slowly through the economy, ultimately contributing to further growth. De Long and Summers (1991) calculate that the social returns to M&E investment exceed private returns by a substantial margin. Estimates put social returns in the range of 16 to 18 percent while private returns are usually in the 6 percent range, suggesting substantial spillovers. Causality, however, remains a contentious issue. Some scholars point to the difficulty of showing that investment causes growth and some claim to find the opposite. Greenwood, Hercowitz and Krusell (1997), taking off from the observation that the real price of M&E investment has fallen steadily at the rate of 4 percent a year over the last two decades, point to such evidence as being strongly suggestive that much of the growth effects of recent technological change are transmitted through investment in new types of capital goods, notably computers.

Education, training and human capital. The "new" growth literature of the 1980s placed a good deal of importance on the role of human capital formation in the growth process, and these variables find considerable support in numerous growth and productivity studies in the 1990s. In Canada it is widely believed that our economic future is closely tied to human capital formation, as eloquently argued by Courchene (2001), for example. Human capital appears as an engine of growth in two ways.[1] First, it serves to facilitate knowledge spillovers, which raise the productivity of all factors of production. Expressed in more conventional language, being more skilled makes it more likely you will transmit what you know to others, who will then do the same and so on. Second, higher skills enter directly into the production of new technology (product and process innovation) and are necessary to facilitate the adoption of new technology. In other words, a computer without software is not very useful, nor is it of much use if the workers do not know how to run it. At the aggregate level, empirical work across a broad cross-section of countries, including developing countries, is fairly convincing that various proxies of human capital feature prominently in explaining the growth performance of national economies from 1970 to 1990. Early studies suggested extremely high social rates of return to investment and education and large spillover effects. Unfortunately, much of this work may not have a great deal of bearing on Canadian productivity performance, since the proxies used for human capital are sufficiently crude as to leave Canada indistinguishable from a number of other advanced countries.

More recent work is somewhat more qualified in its interpretation of human capital as an engine of growth, but it still remains significant. Griliches (1997) in reviewing the US evidence for the 1950s and 1960s concludes that the improvements in labour quality (measured by education attainment of the labour force) account for about 30 percent of the US *productivity residual*—that is, the growth in output that cannot be accounted for by growth in the *quantities* of capital and labour employed. In the 1950s and 1960s, this would correspond to an influence on the annual growth rate of aggregate output of around 0.5 percentage points; during the 1970s, the productivity slowdown, the impact of increased educational attainment on growth would have been lower, perhaps contributing to the growth rate by 0.2 or 0.3 percentage points. Murphy, Riddell and Romer (1999) note that Canada has had substantially faster growth in human capital than the United States in the 1980s as measured by educational outcomes in the two countries.

Yet the productivity performance of Canada was not as good as in the United States. Moreover, there is considerable evidence in the US that the social rate of return to education at higher levels has been falling, as, for example, argued by Acemoglu and Angrist (1999). If this evidence holds up it could precipitate an important debate on the rationale of public support for higher education and its growth dividend.

Openness to trade and investment. A substantial body of evidence points to the importance for productivity growth of openness to trade and investment.[2] This shows up in careful case studies and in a long list of panel studies on the postwar growth experience of a range of countries. While the correlation is strong between openness and productivity growth, there are a number of potential reasons for this link. Among the more important arguments suggesting why the link is so strong are the following:

- Low trade barriers facilitate better use of resources, based on traditional comparative advantage arguments.
- For small countries, openness allows the realization of scale economies which are necessary in modern manufacturing, and are not feasible if reliance is placed on the domestic market alone.
- International trade facilitates diffusion, learning and the transmission of ideas and technology from abroad. There is substantial evidence on the importance of such international spillovers in facilitating productivity growth.
- Similar effects are fostered through foreign direct investment. In addition to providing capital, inward FDI provides technology, skill upgrading and market access sometimes even in those industries where global concentration is high (e.g., commercial aircraft, where we sell parts). Outward FDI helps in generating market access (e.g., in the United States), and in securing durable links for Canadian firms with international networks (which provide high-wage jobs for Canadians) and in securing technology links in foreign countries.

These explanations for growth, while perhaps highly pertinent in selected cases are often country- and sample-period specific, and often interact with, or drive, the other variables such as investment, which have important implications for growth.

Parallel to these "traditional-determinants" evidence is a literature that suggests that long-term per capita growth rates are surprisingly stable. Long time-series evidence for the United States and the United Kingdom is generally supportive of this view. The most anomalous periods are the Great Depression with low growth and the 1950–72 period with high growth. If one views technological change as continuous and incremental, then the last 30 years have been about normal, and one would not expect the special features of the late 1990s to be indicative of these longer term trends.[3] But perhaps the traditional approach is being eclipsed by the new economy, to which I now turn.

The new economy, the IT revolution and GPTs

There is a burgeoning literature that views the recent growth experience of the Organisation for Economic Co-operation and Development (OECD) economies as being driven by the new economy hypothesis—the impact of major, economy-wide, technological changes attributable to innovations in information technology, computers and telecommunications, and the related shift to knowledge-based economic activity.[4] The macroeconomic evidence for this is in the form of accelerated productivity growth, initially in the US, but also now evident in Canada and some other countries. This recognition of the emergence of the new economy is now causing some economists to revise their views of the economic history of the latter part of the twentieth century. The new economy hypothesis figures prominently in Canadian policy discussion in a number of ways: (i) as part of the explanation for the Canada-US productivity and unemployment gaps; (ii) as an explanation for rising income inequality; and (iii) as an important background to industry and regional policy dealing with innovation, firm-level interventions, competition policy and trade policy.

I am of the view that there *is* a new economy, having moved from being agnostic on the subject to convinced that something BIG is going on. However, the economics profession remains deeply split on the issue, with at least three schools of thought:

> There is no new economy—long-run growth rates have remained the same and the late 1990's growth acceleration is largely cyclical in origin.[5]
>
> There is a modest new economy which appears in the productivity and inflation data and which is rooted in (i) the growth of industries producing IT capital and (ii) the adoption and investment in IT in a large number of sectors including most of the service industries. This pattern is very evident in the US, although less so in Canada and other OECD countries, suggesting international catch-up may be under way.[6]
>
> The new economy is real and global in scope. It represents a fundamental change in the sources of economic growth, in the nature of the business cycle, and in income distribution.

This third group incorporates a number of perspectives, but let me just focus on two of the most important. First, the new economy is being driven by the convergence of a number of *new technologies* in the computer and IT sectors which are the basis of what Lipsey, Bekar and Carlaw (1999) and others refer to as GPTs. Arguably, we are now about halfway through this cycle which will continue to evolve and mature, with the Internet proving to be to the new economy or information revolution what railroads were to the Industrial Revolution.

Second, the new economy at its most fundamental level represents the transformation of the growth and distribution mechanism in western economies from a shift to the production of physical goods and services to the production and distribution of knowledge. This transformation goes beyond computers and IT to encompass virtually all economic activities.

At this point, there is no easy method to resolve which of these views is correct. The current recession and end of the stock market bubble are, at one level, fully consistent with all three of the above schools of thought. However, the fact that the stock market bubble was heavily concentrated in technology firms, and that the current recession was initially triggered by a fall in investment in technology sectors is consistent with the theories grouped under the third of the schools, namely that the NEO is real and global in scope.

To re-iterate, my view is that there has been a fundamental change, although one should be careful not to buy into some of the more radical ideas put forward by new economy gurus. Among these more questionable ideas I would include such propositions as: (i) the business cycle is dead; (ii) inflation will be permanently replaced by deflation; and (iii) productivity growth rates will be permanently higher. This caveat aside, as a new economy believer I feel slightly more comfortable with the first (the technological interpretation) than with the second (the "knowledge" interpretation), but am willing to be proven wrong.

In terms of the relationship between the new economy and growth and productivity, the long lags that characterize major historical technological transitions suggest we are likely in the midst of a fairly extended period in which, other political developments held constant, the world economy will enjoy above normal, long-run growth rates. Long-run labour productivity growth has been in the range of 1 to 1.5 percent and the new economy might put us on a 20-year trajectory where the average rate could be in the 2 to 3 percent range. It is clear, however, that even if this is the case it does not mean that all is rosy. First, large-scale technological change creates a lot of losers—both by occupation, by industry and by region. Unfortunately, these creative destruction aspects are an important and necessary feature of growth. Hence, attempts to cushion adjustment or to preserve employment in old-economy sectors, whatever the merit of those policies for other reasons, will carry a larger cost in terms of foregone growth if potential productivity growth is 3 percent than if it is half that. In comparative international perspective, Canada has long relied on its resource industries to generate growth and employment. While comparative advantage dictates that Canada will continue to export natural resources, it is imperative that ever larger amounts of employment be shifted into the new-economy sectors. This is the natural market-driven outcome of a shift to a higher potential growth path, and should be a priority objective of Canadian policy.

The growth process will also be characterized by substantial consolidation in the more mature parts of the new economy. We are already seeing this happen in a dramatic way in the computer and IT sectors, as well as parts of the software industry. This type of pattern, which is typical with the middle phase of large-scale technological transitions, will undoubtedly continue with important consequences both for Canada's competition policy framework and its North America integration agenda. The layering of decline and advance across different sectors in the economy creates the possibility of strong swings in observed growth rates. There has even been some speculation that the pace of advances in computing and digitization are due to slow dramatically with limitations in the manufacture of new semiconductors. See Mann (2000), for example, on the end of Moore's law which predicts that processor speed will double every 18 months. This may be possible, but at the moment the pace of advance seems intact. Clearly a global slowdown in research and development spending will carry with it some slowdown in developing new technologies, but the diffusion of existing technology has a very long way to go, particularly the international diffusion of these technologies. For these reasons, the process is unlikely to be very even across time.

The GPT explanation for the new economy

The hypothesis that the last two decades is a period in which technological change of a particular form has both accelerated and constitutes a major shift from the past has come from a variety of theoretical and empirical perspectives. The analytical perspective that I would like to emphasize is that provided by the literature on general purpose technologies described in Lipsey, Bekar and Carlaw (1999) and Helpman (1999). A GPT is a set of generic and pervasive technologies that transform large sections and sectors of the economy. Most importantly, the appearance of a new GPT is accompanied by wide-spread complementary investments in physical and human capital, including learning by doing. Historical examples of GPT include the steam engine, electricity and the modern manufacturing-assembly-line method of production. Most of the visible evidence of the importance of a GPT is the degree and pervasiveness of the complementary investments that accompany its diffusion through the economy. Think of the number of people who had to learn how to use computers over the last decade. Economic growth is affected both positively and negatively by the process of investment and experimentation that accompany the maturation of the GPT.

We now realize that associated with the arrival of the new economy is the demise, in part at least, of the old. This leads to obsolescence of skills and industries, and possibly even countries or regions, all of which will likely be reflected in falling incomes, rising unemployment and painful structural adjustment, and which figure prominently in the modern Schumpeterian theories of endogenous growth. Economic and social policy have been responding to these pressures in predictable ways. The slow growth in the 1970s and 1980s led to increased spending on social support systems and rising debt and deficits. The 1990s led to the realization that the trends in debt accumulation were not sustainable and to major fiscal adjustments in all OECD countries, and dramatically so in Canada. These trends may or may not reverse depending upon how this technological transition works through the world economic system.

As emphasized by economic historians there is vast uncertainty as to the exact consequences of these technological transitions when you are in the middle of one. Part of this uncertainty is currently reflected in academic and policy debate on the causes of growth. The new economy hypothesis stresses that the causation is running from major technological innovations to growth, with a number of associated implications. Specifically, the dynamics of this process go through a sequence of stages, each stage overlapping the previous and each lasting for a number of years, perhaps even decades. The sequence of events goes something like the following.

> As the old GPT matures, growth slows as productivity gains from the old technology become increasingly hard to obtain.
>
> The new GPT "arrives" in the form of a new set of generic technologies. At first, growth slows even more as experimentation and learning occur with respect to the new GPT. Measured productivity growth slows down and inequality rises for technological reasons (skill-biased technological change) and because of the obsolescence effect on older industries and technologies.
>
> As the pace of adoption of both the new GPT and appropriate complementary investment rises, growth and productivity begin to pick up. Competition increases as the number of new entrants who are technologically enabled grows rapidly. Wage inequality continues to rise, but growth rates accelerate and show up in the form of lower prices, improved quality of new goods and services and higher profits.

> As diffusion of the GPT through the economy begins to peak, advances in growth rates slow and consolidation begins to occur across a number of the new industries. Wage inequality falls due to trickle-down effects and the factor-supply response (more people choose to be educated or skilled appropriately). Technological displacement in the old economy slows.

The hope is that we are already somewhere in the third stage. What is clear, however, is that the United States is undoubtedly further ahead of Canada in this transition.

The new economy: productivity evidence

The major piece of macroeconomic evidence supportive of the new economy has been the long US economic expansion with strong and accelerating productivity growth which began in durable manufacturing, but has now begun to spread to the entire business sector. The early productivity gains were almost entirely concentrated in the computer and electronic equipment sectors and the lack of evidence of accelerated productivity growth outside these sectors led to some scepticism as to how widespread gains they might be. They appear to be widespread indeed, with total economy-wide US labour productivity growth increasing dramatically by the end of the 1990s. See table 2, where the increases in US manufacturing productivity, if expressed in annual growth rate, would be in the 4 percent range at decade's end. While the most recent pace of growth is probably not sustainable, these data suggest that productivity growth in the US entered a new era of higher-trend growth rates. The dimensions of the new economy internationally are not yet clear, although the substantial globalization which has occurred over the past decade will probably lead to relatively rapid international diffusion by historical standards.

In contrast, Canada's productivity growth remained quite subdued in the early part of the decade and even as late as 1998, the new economy effect seemed to be in little evidence. More recently, however, the data are supportive of the view that the new economy is reaching Canada (figure 4). Labour productivity in the Canadian business sector grew at an annual pace of 2.1 percent from the third quarter of 1999 to the third quarter of 2000. While this evidence is only suggestive, it does point to similar trends in the United States.

Not surprisingly, perhaps, this evidence has generated some controversy in terms of the significance of information technology in fuelling the recent productivity advances (see, e.g., Bosworth and Triplett 2000). The major debate

Labour Productivity Growth Increased Steadily Since the End of 1998

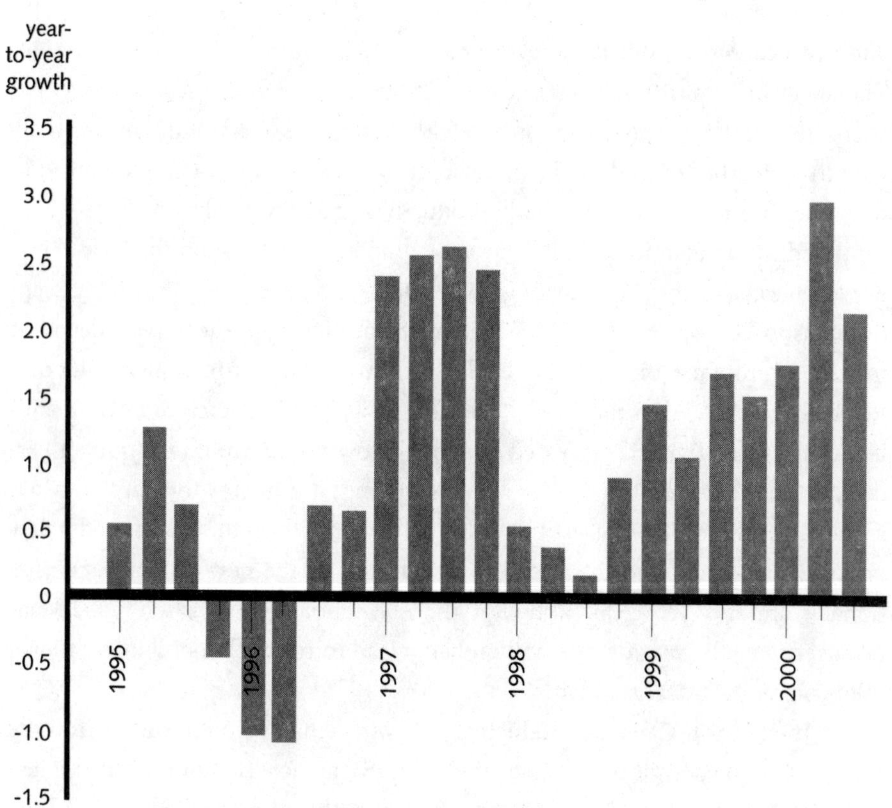

Note: Labour productivity is defined as real GDP per hour worked in the business sector.
Source: Statistics Canada website.

revolves around the fact that IT (principally as measured through its capital-deepening effects in a conventional total factor productivity [TFP] framework), can only seem to explain about one-third of the acceleration in productivity growth. The rest is attributable to growth in TFP—exogenous technical change. My own reaction to this evidence is that the basic economic model underlying TFP measurement is least likely to work when technological change is embedded in a GPT. As emphasized in the theoretical and historical work in the field, disentangling TFP growth from new capital goods is conceptually impossible.[7] The changes in labour productivity, which is what drives economic growth, is the only productivity measure in these circumstances that has an unambiguous interpretation. IT investments are undoubtedly part of the manifestation of the broader information and communication revolution, but they are only partly so. The dollar value of IT investment does not tell us anything about the way in which the distribution system is being transformed by these technological changes.

The knowledge-based economy and the new economy

That knowledge creation could prove to be the most important determinant of growth in living standards and new job creation in the next century has attracted an enormous degree of attention and support from business, government and academics in the 1990s. The knowledge-based (KBE) economy is a more elaborate set of explanations for the new economy than the GPT or technological explanation. For economists, it is admittedly easier to marshal evidence that supports the GPT technology view. Indeed, technological change has been the bread and butter approach of economic historians. The Industrial Revolution, railroads, electricity, the automobile, mass-production systems, etc. have all been extensively studied and fit within theories of economic growth as driven by the appearance, adoption, diffusion and improvement of these transforming innovations. It is interesting that the critics, like Gordon (2000), argue that the computer and Internet do not fit into the category of grand inventions.

The view that the new economy is "all about knowledge" is much harder to come to grips with. In Harris (2001*a*) I look at the arguments used by KBE advocates. While compelling in some dimensions, it is far from clear that the evidence supports the primacy of knowledge. Nonetheless, at the theoretical level, the KBE got a big boost from Paul Romer's interpretation of all productivity growth as being driven by knowledge creation. The claim is that ideas must precede inventions. While true at one level of abstraction, does it really mean that we can most usefully describe the current structural transition as one in which we are moving from the production and distribution of goods and services to an economy in which we substantially produce and distribute knowledge, either tacitly or as digitally codifiable objects? At this point I think these claims are exaggerated.

Cities, regions and agglomeration

Of central importance in assessing growth in the new economy is the role of agglomeration of economic activity across regions, and the interaction of these forces with firm-level strategies that lead to successful high-productivity/high-wage firms. The evidence on the growth consequences of spatial agglomeration of economic activity has become increasingly convincing. Most of this agglomeration is in cities, but it can also be defined at the regional level. As Courchene (1998) argues, this has impacted greatly on Canada, with Ontario, for example, much more a US midwest-centred economy than a Canadian regional economy. Greater continental integration in turn has raised the spectre of Canadian regions which may become largely peripheral to the North American core. Central to this process is the role of cities. From 1900 to 1950 in the US, the data reveal that in addition to growth in individual city size in every decade, the *number* of cities also increased. Overall, the urbanized population rose from 40 to 60 percent. At the same time, the large increase in average human capital, as evidenced by school completion rates, was also urban-based (Black and Henderson 1997). There is also very strong evidence that cities are where the bulk of productivity growth is occurring. Therefore, in explaining growth, regions may be less significant than the cities they contain.

Historically, economic integration has seemed to set off two sets of divergent trends. In the case of the completion of the US internal market there was substantial specialization across regions in terms of types of economic activity. Free movement of capital and labour led to the concentration of certain industries in certain regions. Economists in the neo-classical tradition argue that this will lead to a more efficient allocation of resources based on regional comparative advantage. With the completion of the North American Free Trade Agreement (NAFTA) and the European Union (EU) single market, a new set of policy concerns has emerged in terms of the consequences of regional agglomeration within each of these areas. In parallel with some new theory and evidence, the impact of mobility on regional concentration of industries, and more particularly on regional income differences, has received a great deal of attention. This literature, based on the early work of Krugman (1992) and generally referred to as the new economic geography, raises the question of whether greater freedom of location on the part of manufacturing and service firms will lead to a reallocation of activities across regions in response to the forces of spatial agglomeration. In the case of the EU there is freedom of labour movement as well as capital, while NAFTA essentially allows for the free movement of goods and capital. The evidence thus far is mixed, but certainly in the US the data point toward both general economies of agglomeration and industry-specific agglomeration or localization. The sources of agglomeration include general or industry-specific spillovers as in the case of technological clusters (Silicon valley), increasing returns to scale at the firm or industry level, factor-cost advantages, and unique site-specific natural endowments. There is growing consensus in the literature that there are strong economies of agglomeration in manufacturing. Agglomeration can be either at the city level or the regional level (Ellison and Glaeser 1997). In the Canada-US case, a natural question is whether greater economic integration will lead some activities, in particular the new economy sectors, to agglomerate primarily in the larger US urban areas, and how policy can affect this agglomeration. These concerns are evident not only in the case of Canada vis-à-vis the US, but also in the slower growth states of the US relative to the faster growing states on the east and west coasts.

Closely related to the regional agglomeration question are two issues upon which existing research is lacking. First, there is the possibility that the shift toward north-south and away from east-west trading patterns in Canada emphasized by Courchene (1998) will continue. E-commerce may be the technology that could easily exacerbate and accelerate these trends. If Canada also heavily specializes in a few industries, as predicted by the new economic geography theory, this is almost certain to occur. Second, and possibly more important, is the critical role that specialization within cities will have on trade and investment patterns. Cities are either economically specialized, usually into financial, business services or manufacturing, or they are highly diversified. Toronto would be viewed as diversified, for example, while Calgary would be viewed as specialized. Diversified cities tend to be larger than specialized cities, and diversity also tends to promote innovation. Feldman and Audretsch (1999) find, utilizing a data set involving US product innovations in 1982, that 96 percent of all innovations were made in the metropolitan areas accounting for only 30 percent of the US population.

For their part, specialized cities have some advantages—stronger localization economies within the sector of specialization and thus the ability to attract new plants or firms entering that type of activity. But they also have disadvantages—less innovation and greater exposure to risk as the specific sectors/technologies rise and fall. Canada is a small country with a large geography and with only four major metropolitan areas: Montreal, Toronto, Calgary and Vancouver. How much of non-resource Canadian trade is being generated from activity in these cities? In particular, how much of the newer high-growth activity is located in these cities? The answer is clearly a lot. The question as to whether Canada can sustain itself as a high-income economy within an integrated North America almost certainly comes down to how these cities will fare in relation to other major US cities. We need to know a great deal more about the sources of competitive advantage for cities and the relevant policy levers than we do now. The absence of policy-relevant research on this particular issue is striking.

Stabilization: Business Cycles, Inflation, Unemployment and the Currency Question

CANADA'S PAST MACRO PERFORMANCE IN TERMS OF OUTPUT GAPS AND INFLATION IS summarized in figures 5 and 6. From figure 6, which provides a comparison with the US, the evidence over the 1990s is one of a relatively poor performance on the output and better performance on the inflation front, with convergence on both counts by the end of the decade. This evidence has been grist for the debate on the wisdom of low-inflation strategies discussed below. More immediately, there is an active debate as to the cause of the current recession. One certainty is that this recession will probably change the modern new-Keynesian/monetarist/new classical views on the sources of business cycles. This is so because it is very difficult to pin this recession on either a major fiscal/monetary policy mistake or a large negative supply shock.[8] The notion that business cycles can be generated by Schumpeterian waves of investment in new industries and destruction in old industries looks a lot more credible at this point than would have been the consensus even a few years ago. Moreover, at least in the near term, the possibilities of future booms and busts in "dot coms" and high-tech industries, much as was the case with the railroads in the last century, cannot be discounted. New industries will be created and will fail with a surprising regularity as this GPT matures throughout the world economy. There is likely to be increased volatility in both national growth rates and in the international variability of these growth rates across national economies. It is also worth noting that these cyclical shifts may be impossible to forecast. After all, virtually no forecasting firm predicted the acceleration in US productivity growth in the mid-1990s. As Stiroh (2001) points out, prior to 1995 the average projection error of growth rates in the Blue Chip forecast survey was 0.1 percentage points, while after 1995 the average error was a staggering 1.7 percentage points. Given that the length of this last expansion was beyond any historical precedent there is much uncertainty as to whether past recessions provide evidence in terms of what is likely to happen next.

To the extent that there is a "new economy" business cycle, this raises a number of interesting issues, many of which relate to one's vision of globalization. First, globalization has tended to increase the synchronization of the cycles across countries. Second, the increased openness of the Canadian economy, and in particular Canada's reliance on the US market, raises the question as to whether in the next (current) recession Canadian output and employment will fall by more or less than that of the US. Third, political reactions to globalization may constrain policy-makers and increase the cost of any retreats from the existing levels of globalization. I now turn in more detail to some of these issues.

Rules versus discretion and speed limits

The central banking community is still split over the rules versus discretion debate. The importance of credibility in bringing down inflation was *the* debate in the 1980s and many central banks, the Bank of Canada included, maintained that credible rules should be a primary objective in the conduct and management of monetary policy. Nevertheless, in the view of many, Federal Reserve Chairman Alan Greenspan succeeded extraordinarily (at least in the boom) in the fine tuning of monetary policy. Not only did Greenspan lower inflation, he bought into

Canada Output Gaps and Inflation

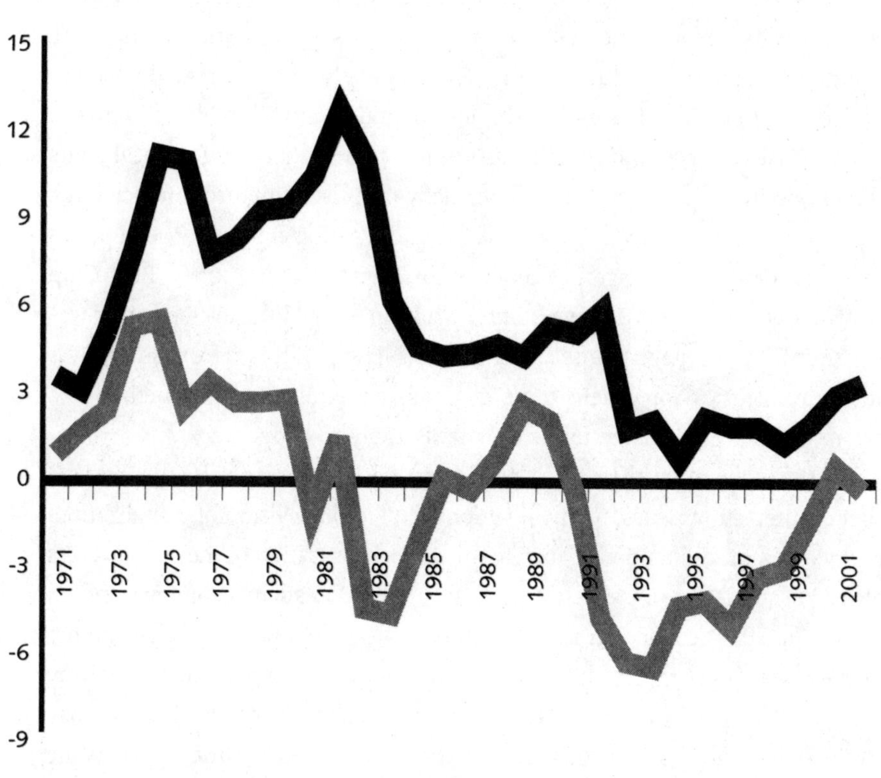

Note: The output gap is defined as actual GDP minus potential GDP, expressed as a percent of potential GDP. Hence, a negative value means that the economy is performing at less than potential.
Source: World Economic Outlook, IMF Washington, September 2002.

Canada-US Relative Macro Performance

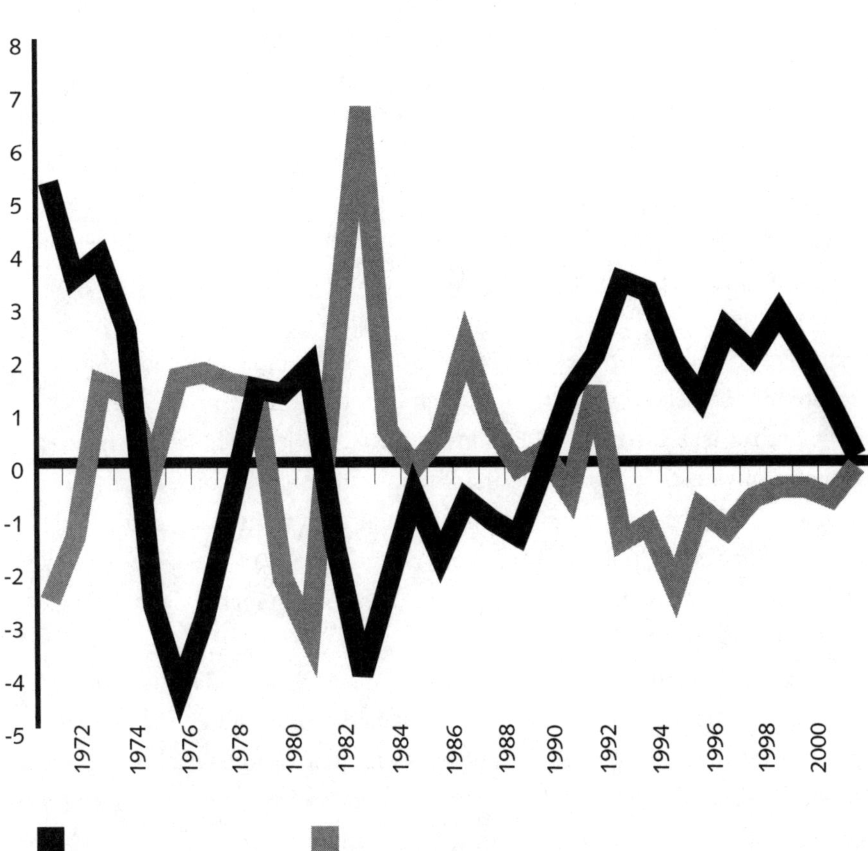

Note: When the US-Canada output gap is positive, the US is performing better than Canada and vice versa.

the new economy view which led to "raising the speed limits" on inflation-control-consistent growth targets. By explicitly not tightening in the face of unusually high growth rates in the mid- and late 1990s, he undoubtedly bolstered the belief in monetary fine tuning. However, it would be fair to say that he may have just been lucky in his timing; his successor may not be so fortunate.

In the 1990s, both unemployment and inflation fell substantially in the US, Canada and Europe. However, Canada's relatively poor macro record on *growth* (see figure 6 for a Canada-US comparison and figure 5 for the output gap as a percent of GDP) has led some economists such as Pierre Fortin (1999) to argue that monetary policy in Canada should have, in US fashion, pushed the envelope further with respect to growth. In the US there has been substantial discussion on the prospect that the natural rate of unemployment, the NAIRU, has fallen, perhaps due to the new economy. There is substantial divergence of opinion on this issue. Some economists argue that when one accounts for supply shifts, changes in import prices (energy, for example), and changes in inflation expectations, the observed shift in the unemployment-inflation data is entirely consistent with a stable structural Phillips curve. On the other hand, there is another point of view that argues that the Phillips curve has become largely useless as an analytical tool for economic analysis and policy. The lack of a professional consensus has left policy-makers with a wider range of plausible options in the inflation-unemployment trade-off, albeit with a much higher degree of risk attached to any particular choice.

If, as many supporters believe, the concept of a NAIRU is valid but the rate has fallen, then it must be due to some fundamental changes in the nature of labour markets. What might these be? Among the potential structural factors which may have contributed to a lower NAIRU would be reduced unionization, better job matching through innovations such as the Internet, more pay-for-performance incentive schemes, and increased fear of job loss to new technology and greater reliance on temporary help. However, many of these factors may turn out to be 1990s specific.

If the "speed limits" of growth have been raised, then that would suggest that the Bank of Canada should push the envelope further than it has in the past with the use of monetary policy as output growth accelerates. If the sustainable non-inflationary growth rate has gone from say 2–3 percent to 4–5 percent in most economies this would suggest that the traditional Taylor Rule approach to setting short-term interest rates should now embody a bias toward lower interest rates in the face of any given output gap.[9] However, the Bank of Canada has the unfortunate problem that any significant lowering of Canadian interest rates (relative to those in the US) has, in recent history at least, led to a fall in the Canadian dollar. A weaker currency has its own problems, as discussed below. Unless there is a dramatic change in market psychology there appears to be no way out of this particular strait-jacket. The fact is that Canada-US integration and the globalization of capital flows constrain the Bank of Canada from the pursuit of a vastly different policy than the US, as the North American economies weaken. The one potential bright spot here would be if the Canadian growth rate were to accelerate past the US rate as the recession ends. Should this happen, the Bank may be given an opportunity to translate "an increase in the Canadian speed limit" into a currency appreciation. However, one does not want to be overly optimistic about this possibility.

How labour market flexibility will evolve in response to the current recession will be closely watched. It is difficult, if not impossible, to divorce this problem from the aging population and the coming boom in demand for young workers. Market power of labour, particularly skilled labour, may overturn recent complacency with respect to wage inflation and lead in the next stage of the new economy to increased wage demands which are subsequently validated by price increases. The 1990s were characterized by intense product market competition which constrained price increases at the firm level. It is possible that competitive forces will prove less important in the next stage of the new economy as firms and technologies mature with the consolidation process. The Internet and e-commerce have been billed as the ultimate inflation killers by facilitating extreme price competition. Maybe. Until the shake-out in B2C and B2B e-commerce is complete, we will not know for sure.[10] If e-commerce largely becomes the domain of highly concentrated sellers with old economy names, then this may never happen. Rather the exact opposite can happen. Improved information can facilitate price collusion among sellers, which in turn allows them to pass on cost increases. If labour markets start to take advantage of this we may see a new era in which cost-push inflation comes back. Reduced speed limits and seat belts for central bankers might be the consequence, particularly if we have an episode of runaway inflation. Note that if this inflation occurs it will not be a commodity-based inflation and therefore will not have the usual commodity-boom implications for Canada that was observed in the 1970s.

However, the rising inflation scenario is largely discounted by most analysts, and indeed many think of deflation as an important permanent characteristic of the new economy. Could the US and thus Canada face a Japanese-like crisis of low growth and zero to permanent deflation in which monetary policy is largely ineffective? Consumer retrenchment and pessimism about the stock market might play out much as was the case in Japan, but the new economy and US-style capitalism make a Japanese-style recession highly improbable. The ability to politically tolerate business failures, the forces propelling, and the potential in, new innovation and the strength of the US banking system make the North American case fundamentally different than has been the case in Japan.

One feature of the next business cycle which *may* be different from some previous ones is the global adjustment to the US current account deficit, a deficit that has now persisted for almost two decades and has led the US to become the world's largest net debtor. The classical adjustment mechanism would be a rise in the US savings rate, a shift to the production of exportables and away from non-traded goods, and a depreciation of the US dollar and probably other US asset prices relative to the global average. However, this may not happen simply because the US continues to look like a good investment to the rest of the world relative to the alternatives. The good thing about a non-adjustment in the current account imbalances is that the North American business cycle will be shorter and Canadian exports to the US will recover faster than they would otherwise. The bad thing about US non-adjustment is that the US dollar will continue to be "overvalued" with the attendant consequences for Canada—more firesale FDI, more brain drain and lack of adjustment out of the old economy.

Globalization and synchronization

The last two recessions were worse in Canada than in the US. Is this likely to be a permanent feature of the Canadian economic landscape? We are all familiar with phenomenal rise in cross-border trade with the US, the increased export share of GDP (46 percent) and the falling share of interprovincial trade with the Courchene scenario of a regional reorientation of Canadian trade. The correlation of Canadian and US business cycles is certainly going to increase. The role of our resource regions as an offsetting damper to this correlation has been diminished and I predict this will continue. In any case, central Canada remains strongly tied to changes in US aggregate activity. For many small, open economies the export sector is both leading and more volatile than other forms of aggregate demand. Under this view of the macro adjustment process, a US-led recession ought to produce a worse recession in Canada. However, for two countries that are fully integrated, the business cycle should be fully synchronous across both countries. Where does Canada sit on the integration spectrum? We economists honestly do not know and given the change in the structure of the Canadian economy over the last decade we are in uncharted territory. You will find that most macroeconomic forecasts of the Canadian economy embody very pessimistic predictions, in large measure because these models are largely driven by shifts in aggregate demand and the historic role of exports to the US as a leading sector. What is wrong with such models is that they do not account for the complex *indirect* linkages between the two economies. It is no longer possible to simply assign industries and activities to an export-domestic classification. Much of what is done in Canada will now closely follow domestic US activity. The new economy has reduced both inventory cycles and increased the role of services in two-way trade. For these reasons our exports to the US may prove not to be as volatile as they have been in the past.

Fiscal policy

Currently we are seeing the beginnings of a debate as to where fiscal policy might be headed. The choice of tax cuts, debt retirement and expenditure increases will be pushed in a variety of ways by the new economy forces. First, for cyclical reasons the current recession will call on governments to live up to their traditional fiscal commitments through automatic stabilizers—unemployment insurance programs, welfare, etc. But there seems little about the new economy that is likely to revive the case for Keynesian fiscal activism based on aggregate employment objectives. There are, however, some potentially interesting aspects of the demands on fiscal policy that will be motivated by the "creative destruction" aspects of the cycle. Certain sectors are bound to be hit harder than others. Predicting which sectors will be most difficult given that destruction of the old economy is sometimes difficult to distinguish from consolidation in and of the new. But certainly the case where the recession will prove uneven in its impact both by region and by sector will be given added impetus with new economy arguments.

More importantly, however, will be the longer term debate on the burden of the debt and the aging population. There are two angles here. An aging population will require a number of policy adjustments, but clearly in the medium term reducing public sector debt would be a prudent course of action. The demands for debt repayment as a means of lowering debt-GDP ratios will be tempered to the extent the productivity growth data lends credence to the proposition that growth will be permanently higher and, therefore, "growing out of the debt" rather than paying it down becomes a viable option. Developments in both Japan and Italy, both of whom are facing an aging crisis in the near term, will have a major impact on our own public policy debate on these issues. The other is the extent to which new technology will facilitate an increase in labour supply on the part of older workers who would otherwise retire. We are just at the beginning of a potential revolution in the nature of work and employment which will have an impact in a number of ways on the labour force participation of older workers. To the extent that older workers respond by remaining in the labour force, the fears of fiscal non-sustainability of social security will be reduced.

The currency question

The "currency question" or the fate of the Canadian dollar has now been debated extensively among academics and appears repeatedly in the media. While Courchene and Harris (1999) have staked out a position on this, and therefore must be regarded as biased, this is an issue that will not go away. My own impression is that the question of political sovereignty still dominates the debate, relative to the economic pros and cons. It should be stressed that the currency question cuts across both the growth and stabilization agendas. Its assignment to this particular section is therefore somewhat arbitrary. Some of the more important arguments on both sides of the debate revolve around the issues of productivity, North American integration and depreciation-triggered bargain-basement prices for our assets.[11] We treat these in turn.

The productivity consequences of floating exchange rates. Exchange rate depreciation provides a cost disincentive to investing in productivity improvements. A 10 percent fall in the dollar also means a 10 percent rise in the price of US or US-priced capital equipment for productivity enhancements. In Harris (2000, 2001*c*) it is argued that Canada's attempt to shift away from a resource-based economy and toward one increasingly driven by human capital and technology was delayed by the significant 1990s currency depreciation (in comparison to what would have occurred under a fixed exchange rate), with very disturbing implications, including a slowdown in Canadian productivity relative to that in the US because we lag in adapting the GPT associated with the NEO.

North-south Canada-US economic integration. While common currencies and large volumes of trade go hand in hand, there are important questions as to how important the currency regime is for trade. At the aggregate level, Canada is integrated tradewise to the US to a greater degree than the average EU member is to the EU. Hence, on *economic integration* grounds, the argument for a common North American currency from Canada's vantage point is more compelling than that for the average EU member state. But is Canada-US trade already so large that a common currency would have little further effect? Rose (2000) estimates that common currencies more than *triple* the volume of trade, holding other factors constant. Frankel and Rose (2000) look at the impact on income growth of adopting common currencies for countries that trade a lot with one another. They get some interesting predictions for the two NAFTA partners of the United States. The estimated impact of adopting the (American) dollar should increase trade in Canada by 184 percent (as a percentage of GDP), and the GDP impact is predicted to be 81 percent. In comparison, if Canada decided to adopt the euro instead, the figures would be, respectively, 36 percent and 3 percent. However, Frankel and Rose are themselves suspicious of these large numbers and assert: "Indeed, for Canada and a number of other countries, the predicted effect is too large to be believable." But they nonetheless conclude: "a country boosts its income when it adopts the currency of natural trading partner, one that has high income, and preferably is geographically nearby as well" (Frankel and Rose 2000, 38). The behaviour of inter-European trade in the wake of the euro should provide an additional and perhaps more relevant test case of the likely impact of a Canada-US common currency on north-south economic integration.

Depreciations and fire sales. Canadian assets are regarded by Americans as "cheap" and the extensive purchase of Canadian assets (FDI, land, real estate, etc.) has been an important consequence of the depreciation. It is clear that, contrary to theories of monetary neutrality on real asset values, exchange-rate depreciations have reduced Canadian domestic asset prices *as measured in US dollars*. This can induce a host of wealth effects in the economy. One is referred to as "fire-sale FDI." Foreign firms can and do acquire Canadian firms (whose assets are priced in Canadian dollars) at bargain-basement prices when the currency depreciates. Beyond this, Canadian firms face higher acquisition costs in terms of entry to the US market.

There are a number of other arguments surrounding this debate that could be joined. Readers can find many of these in Courchene and Harris (1999). However, the above arguments are sufficient evidence to continue to adhere to my prediction that many smaller national currencies will disappear over the next decade and Canada will most likely ultimately follow them. One area in which there has been remarkably little research is the nature of the potential options for transition arrangements in the monetary regime in North America. Unfortunately, this part of the debate will not be fully joined until we engage the attention of the United States. From the Canadian research point of view it may be more important at this juncture to demonstrate to the US why a currency union may be a good idea from their own perspective than to concentrate on the Canadian cost-benefit calculations on optimal currency areas.

Income Distribution

There is a widespread perception that the income distribution is polarizing, and that economic integration between Canada and the US will lead to a situation in which the Canadian income distribution will converge to the more unequal US distribution.[12] This has obvious and significant consequences for the entire range of Canadian social and economic policy. It is my view that it is virtually impossible to separate the growth question from the distribution question. We need a coherent explanation of what is driving trends in both sets of statistics. It is instructive first, however, to assess the data that have been the principal driving force behind the policy dimension of this debate—the recent changes in measured income inequality.

Looking at aggregate income inequality of the working population, the changes have not been as dramatic as one might expect given the anecdotal evidence on this subject. As is well-known (and shown in table 1) inequality in total income (i.e., income from all sources, private and public) rose in the US and the UK from the mid-1970s through the mid-1980s—the Gini coefficients increased by 2.9 and 3.7 respectively, from column 3 of table 1. These trends were not as evident in other countries and they even slowed somewhat for the US and the UK over the mid-1980s to the mid-1990s. While the degree of inequality of aggregate income of the working population in Canada is higher than in Sweden (column 1 of table 1), there has been virtually no change in Canada's Gini coefficient from the mid-1970s to the mid-1990s.

However, with respect to *market* income (as distinct from the table 1 data that refer to market plus government income), the underlying trend in Canada has been similar to most other OECD countries. From the 1980s through to the mid-1990s there was a fairly significant shift in the distribution of market income toward the upper end of the distribution, despite the relatively mild changes in total inequality which measures incomes after taxes and transfers.[13]

The most interesting aspects of the developments in market incomes arises from studying the trends in *wage inequality*. This evidence points to three major trends which appear to be common across a number of OECD countries but, in particular, Canada, the United States, Germany and the United Kingdom.

First, there was a slowdown in average real wage growth through the mid-1990s, which corresponds to a slowdown in measured average labour productivity. The orders of magnitude here are considerable, particularly for low-skilled workers. In the US, workers in the tenth percentile of the wage distribution (i.e., low-skilled workers) saw their earnings fall in real terms to levels even below those of 1963.[14]

Second, there has been a substantial increase in the education premium for more highly educated workers. The college premium—the wages of college graduates relative to the wages of high school graduates—increased by over 25 percent between 1979 and 1995 in the US. Canada has had a smaller but qualitatively similar increase in the skill premia.

Third, overall earnings inequality also increased sharply. In 1971, a worker at the ninetieth percentile of the wage distribution earned 266 percent more than a worker at the tenth percentile. By 1995, this number had risen to 366 percent (Acemoglu 2000). A substantial part of this growth in inequality cannot be explained by education: rather, it is due to some unidentified factor. When one controls for education/experience as well as other variables there has been a remarkable increase in measured *within-group wage inequality*. Many studies attribute as much as 60 percent of the increase in wage inequality to *within group* inequality, that is, among persons that have apparently the same education and age.

The importance of these developments, and attempting to understand why they occurred, cannot be separated from one's views on the sources of growth, the role of social policy and education, and on where Canada might be headed as we

Levels and Changes in Inequality (working age population 1970s to 1990s)

	Levels		Absolute Changes Between Periods			
	Gini	P90/P10 Decile Ratio	Gini	P90/P10 Decile Ratio	Gini	P90/P10 Decile Ratio
	mid-90s	mid-90s	mid-70s to mid-80s	mid-80s to mid-90s	mid-70s to mid-80s	mid-80s to mid-90s
Canada	28.7	3.9	0.1	0.1	–0.1	0.0
Sweden	24.7	3.1	–0.6	2.3	0.0	0.2
United Kingdom	30.4	4.1	3.7	2.7	0.7	0.4
United States	33.3	5.3	2.9	0.6	1.0	–0.1

Source: Forster and Pellazari (2000).

enter the next economic cycle. In my view, the most promising and comprehensive joint explanation of all these trends is to be found in the new economy hypothesis.

We now realize that preceding the arrival of the new economy was the demise, in part at least, of the old economy. This led to obsolescence of skills and industries which, in the short term led to falling incomes, to rising unemployment and to painful structural adjustment. Economic policy and social policy have been responding to these pressures in predictable ways. The slow growth in the 1970s and 1980s led to an increase in spending on social support systems and to rising debt and deficits. The 1990s led to the realization that the ongoing trends in debt accumulation were not sustainable and, in response, led to major fiscal adjustment. The new economy hypothesis stresses a causal pattern running from technological change to both growth and inequality.[15] In tandem with the fact that social expenditure is income elastic (the Wagner hypothesis) this leads to a complex endogenous interaction among technological change, growth, inequality and social policy. For example, this theory can be used to provide a coherent story of the wage trends in Canada and the US. The productivity evidence suggests that the pace at which the new GPT is hitting Canada is somewhat behind that of the US, leading to less pressure from the demand side on the skill premia, but which should ultimately pick up. Recently Beaudry and Green (1999) have proposed an alternative explanation of the OECD wage inequality trends based on the arrival of a GPT characterized by a higher capital-labour intensity together with differences in the cost of capital across countries. While leading to slightly different implications, specifically with respect to the key role of investment, the general thrusts of their results are consistent with other GPT-based approaches to the new economy.

Explaining the slowdown in measured productivity at the same time that technological change accelerates has now been addressed in a theoretical literature that came out of the earlier work on GPTs and economic growth. These theories all have a similar mechanism which involves a new technology slowly displacing an old technology. The new technology requires large set-up costs in terms of learning-by-doing (LBD) and investment in complementary skills and equipment. All of this, together with the obsolescence of old technology, leads to a sustained period of slow to negative productivity growth. The slow growth in wages, particularly of the unskilled, is a reflection of these factors. In general, however, the long-run distributive impact of a GPT is theoretically ambiguous. It could in the long run lead to an increase in the relative wages of either the unskilled or the skilled, and it could raise or lower inequality.

Consistent with earlier-noted evidence, the general view of the current IT-driven GPT is that it both increases the returns to skills and leads to an increase in within-group wage inequality. There are a number of ways that the GPT can raise the returns to skills, but one of the simplest mechanisms is capital-skill complementarity, as first argued by Nelson and Phelps (1967). One major historical GPT which has been studied carefully by historians is electricity. Goldin and Katz (2001) provide strong evidence of technology-skill complementarity during the 1910s and 1920s due to the increased demand for skills coming from the introduction of electricity in manufacturing processes. This view is similar to that being advanced today with respect to ICT innovations. This current GPT is a type of technological change inherently biased toward the skilled, given that the skills required are complementary to the new capital goods. Collectively the new skill-capital mix tends to displace unskilled workers. And in the case of Europe, which has different labour market adjustment mechanisms, the GPT hypothesis has been used to explain the rise of unemployment.

Explaining increases in *within group* inequality is a major hurdle for any growth theory. One way it can be done is by appealing to the interaction between education and LBD on the new GPT. When the pace of technological progress embodied in new capital goods (computers) rises there is greater heterogeneity in outcomes such that those choosing to move into the new technology are in luck with higher *ex post* wages.[16] This within-group effect should dissipate over time as the new technology embodied in the GPT becomes pervasive in the economy and most workers learn how to use it. The lags involved, however, could potentially be very long. Older workers in particular are those most likely to be adversely affected, no matter what their skill level is for old economy technologies.

If the GPT view of wage inequality is correct, then there is the distinct possibility that market wage inequality will fall as the current GPT matures. There is some evidence in the US that this is now happening, given the recent wage increases in traditional low-skilled service sectors. The markets for human capital respond by increasing the supply of those skills that are particularly scarce—we have already started to observe this in the case of IT workers, for example. In addition, there are usually trickle-down effects across the skill spectrum. All of these factors contribute to reducing wage inequality.

The implications of this view for social policy are considerable. The new economy perspective provides a coherent explanation of both growth and inequality trends as endogenous reactions to a common cause—acceleration in the rate of technological change. The good news is that these effects are highly non-linear in time. As the new economy matures and diffuses productivity growth increases, one can only hope that high rates of economic growth will tend to "raise all boats" and that in the longer run income inequality will be reduced. A more pessimistic view is that offered by the "winner-take-all" metaphor in which labour markets reward only a very few with outrageous compensation, and the majority earn less. While some have identified the winner-take-all trend as part of the new economy, I fail to find the argument convincing. The major supporting evidence was the dramatic growth in the use of stock options during the tech-market boom—a trend which now seems to be evaporating. The Canadian brain-drain problem may be mitigated to some extent if winner-take-all compensation falls out of favour in the US. Nevertheless, Canada still lags in new economy sectors and innovation, and as we move into the next cycle it will be important not to lose the global race for attracting talent and for the firms that employ that talent. How we do this should be a high priority item on the economic agenda.

Conclusion

The paper has reviewed the possible forces working on the Canadian economy as the boom of the 1990s comes to an end and we move forward into the next economic cycle beginning with our first new economy recession. The basic hypothesis is that there will be some fundamental and unpredictable structural change that will occur as the new economy matures into its next phase. There is nothing inevitable about these changes but they do present some important opportunities to restructure and catch up. There is a very real chance that Canadian growth could catch up with the US and maybe even surpass it.

It is commonly argued that governments of small countries are powerless in this period of intense globalization. While there is one sense that this may be true, in another it is false. It is now the case that policy is more rather than less important in that good policies have higher returns and bad policies will lead to worse outcomes than was the case in the past. This is true not only of the policy responses to globalization but also how governments react to the opportunities that the next wave of economic growth will provide.

Notes

I am grateful to my discussant Don Drummond for comments and to Tom Courchene for editing. This paper was completed before the tragic events of September 11, 2001, the consequences of which may affect the ensuing perspective in any number of unpredictable ways. The usual disclaimer applies.

1 Temple (2000) provides an excellent overview of the evidence on the growth effects of human capital.

2 This section draws on Harris (1999).

3 The economic literature and the business press are virtually awash in alternative explanations as to what drives productivity growth. Prominent examples include innovation (both product and process), diffusion of technology (national and international), spatial agglomeration (Silicon Valley), external economies of scale at industry level, quality of management, public infrastructure (positive), income inequality (negative), taxes on capital (negative). However, evidence on these is generally mixed.

4 Evidence for and against the new economy is provided in CSLS (2000); Stiroh (2001); Bosworth and Triplett (2000); and Gordon (2000).

5 Robert Gordon is the most prominent and persistent advocate of this view. See Gordon (2000).

6 Jorgenson (2000) is representative of this set of views.

7 In most GPT theories, as the diffusion of the GPT accelerates and new complementary technologies are developed there is an acceleration in conventionally measured TFP growth. However, the cause of that acceleration lies with the adoption and diffusion of the GPT, which is not exogenous technological change.

8 September 11, 2001 can be viewed as a negative supply shock which will exacerbate the already evident global cyclical downturn of mid-2001.

9 The Taylor Rule, named after Stanford economist John Taylor, states that nominal short-term interest rates should be set equal to 1.5 times the rate of inflation plus 0.5 times the growth rate of real GDP.

10 Business-to-consumers (B2C) and business-to-business (B2B).

11 Some of this material is a summary of Courchene and Harris (1999), and Harris (2001*c*).

12 This section draws heavily on Harris (2001*b*).

13 Beach and Slotsve (1996) document these trends for Canada.

14 This is a summary of Acemoglu (2000) on the US wage evidence.

15 There is a literature that suggests that reduced income inequality increases the rate of economic growth. While there is some evidence that this has been true in the postwar developing economies there is very little evidence to support this hypothesis for OECD economies. See Harris (2001*b*) for a discussion.

16 Note that in this framework increased education or training—if it facilitates greater mobility across vintages of technologies—will tend to reduce wage inequality, thus offsetting the growth effect of the GPT on inequality.

References

Acemoglu, D. "Technical Change, Inequality and the Labor Market," NBER Working Paper no. 7800. Cambridge, MA: National Bureau of Economic Research, 2000.

Acemoglu, D. and J. Angrist. "How Large are the Social Returns to Education? Evidence from Compulsory Schooling Laws," NBER Working Paper no. 7444. Cambridge, MA: National Bureau of Economic Research, 1999.

Aghion, P. and P. Howitt. *Endogenous Growth Theory*. Cambridge, MA: MIT Press, 2000.

Beach, C.M. and G.A. Slotsve. *Are We Becoming Two Societies? Income Polarization and the Myth of the Declining Middle Class in Canada*. Social Policy Challenge no. 12. Toronto: C.D. Howe Institute, 1996.

Beaudry, P. and D. Green. "What is Driving US and Canadian Wages: Exogenous Technical Change or Endogenous Choice of Technique?" NBER Working Paper no. 6853. Cambridge, MA: National Bureau of Economic Research, 1999.

Black, D. and V. Henderson. "A Theory of Urban Growth." *Journal of Political Economy*, Vol. 107, no. 2 (1997): 252-284.

Bosworth, B.P. and J.E. Triplett. *What's New about the New Economy? IT, Economic Growth and Productivity*. Washington, DC: The Brookings Institution, 2000.

Centre for the Study of Living Standards (CSLS). "Trend Productivity and the New Economy." Unpublished paper. Ottawa: CSLS, 2000.

Courchene, T.J. *A State of Minds: Toward a Human Capital Future for Canadians.* Montreal: Institute for Research on Public Policy, 2001.

Courchene, T.J. and D.J. Savoie. "The Art of the State in a World without Frontiers." Unpublished paper. Montreal: IRPP, 2001.

Courchene, T.J. and R.G. Harris. *From Fixing to Monetary Union: Options for North American Currency Integration*. Commentary no. 127. Toronto: C.D. Howe Institute, 1999. Available from *http://www.cdhowe.org*

Courchene, T.J. with C. Telmer. *From Heartland to North American Region State: The Social, Fiscal and Federal Evolution of Ontario*. Toronto: Faculty of Management, University of Toronto, 1998.

DeLong, J.B. and L. Summers. "Equipment Investment and Economic Growth." *Quarterly Journal of Economics*, Vol. 106 (1991): 445-502.

Ellison, G. and E. Glaeser. "Geographic Concentration in U.S. Manufacturing Industries: A Dartboard Approach." *Journal of Political Economy*, Vol. 105, no. 5 (1997): 889-927.

Feldman, M.P. and D.B. Audretsch. "Innovation in Cities: Science-Based Diversity, Specialization and Localized Competition." *European Economic Review*, Vol. 43, no. 2 (1999): 409-429.

Förster, M.F. with M. Pellizzari. "Trends and Driving Factors in Income Distribution and Poverty in the OECD Area," Labour Market and Social Policy Occasional Paper no. 42. Paris: OECD, 2000.

Fortin, P. "The Canadian Standard of Living: Is There A Way Up?" C.D. Howe Benefactors Lecture, 1999. Available from *http://www.cdhowe.org*

Frankel, J.A. and A.K. Rose. "An Estimate of the Effect of Currency Unions on Trade and Growth," first draft, May 1, 2000. Available from *http://haas.berkeley.edu/~arose*

Goldin, C. and L.F. Katz. "The Legacy of U.S. Educational Leadership: Notes on Distribution and Economic Growth in the 20th Century." *American Economic Review, Papers and Proceedings*, May 2001.

Gordon, R.J. "Does the 'New Economy' Measure up to the Great Inventions of the Past?" *Journal of Economic Perspectives*, Vol. 14, no. 4 (2000): 49-74.

Greenwood, J., Z. Hercowtiz and P. Krusell. "Long-Run Implications of Investment-Specific Techological Change." *American Economic Review*, Vol. 87, no. 3 (1997): 342-362.

Griliches, Z. "Education, Human Capital, and Growth: A Personal Perspective." *Journal of Labor Economics*, Vol. 15, no. 1 (1997): S330-S344.

Gu, W. and M.S. Ho. "Comparison of Industrial Productivity Growth in Canada and the United States." *American Economic Review*, Vol. 90, no. 2 (2000): 172-175.

Harris, R.G. "The Determinants of Productivity Growth: Issues and Prospects," Industry Canada Discussion Paper no. 8, 1999. Available from *http://strategis.ic.gc.ca/SSG/ra01736e.html*

________ "The New economy and the Exchange Rate Regime." Paper presented at conference in Honour of Robert Mundell, May 2000. John Deutsch Institute for the Study of Economic Policy, Queen's University, Kingston. Available from *http://www.sfu.ca/~rharris*

________ "The New economy: Intellectual Origins and Theoretical Perspectives."

International Journal of Management Reviews (Spring 2001*a*).

________ "Social Policy and Productivity Growth: What are the Linkages?" Industry Canada Discussion Paper, 2001*b*. Available from *http://www.sfu.ca/~rharris*

________ "Is there a Case for Exchange Rate Induced Productivity Declines." In *Re-Visiting the Case for Flexible Exchange Rates*, ed. L. Schembri. Ottawa: Bank of Canada, 2001*c*.

Helpman, E., ed. *General Purpose Technologies.* Cambridge, MA: MIT Press, 1999.

Jorgenson, D. "Raising the Speed Limit: US Economic Growth in the Information Age." *Brookings Papers on Economic Activity*, Vol. 1 (2000): 125-211.

Krugman, P. *Geography and International Trade.* Cambridge, MA: MIT Press, 1992.

Lipsey, R.G., C. Bekar and K. Carlaw. "What Requires Explanation?" In *General Purpose Technologies*, ed. E. Helpman. Cambridge, MA: MIT Press, 1998.

Mann, C.L. "Electronic Commerce in Developing Countries: Issues for Domestic Policy and WTO Negotiations," Working Paper. Washington, DC: Institute for International Economics, March 2000.

Murphy, K.M., W.C. Riddell and P.M. Romer. "Wages, Skills and Technology in the United States and Canada." In *General Purpose Technologies*, ed. E. Helpman. Cambridge, MA: MIT Press, 1998.

Nelson, R. and E. Phelps. "Investment in Humans, Technological Diffusion and Economic Growth." *American Economic Association Papers and Proceedings*, Vol. 56 (1966): 69-75.

Organisation for Economic Co-operation and Development (OECD). *OECD Jobs Study: Evidence and Explanations.* Paris: OECD, 1994.

Rauch, J. "Productivity Gains from Geographic Concentration of Human Capital: Evidence from the Cities." *Journal of Urban Economics*, Vol. 34, no. 3 (1993): 380-400.

Rose, A. "One Money, One Market? The Effect of Common Currencies on International Trade." *Economic Policy*, Vol. 30 (April 2000): 4-46.

Schreyer, P. "The Contribution of Information and Communication Technology to Output Growth," Statistical Working Paper no. (99)4. Paris: OECD, 1999.

Stiroh, K.J. *New and Old Economics in the "New Economy."* New York: Federal Reserve Bank, 2001.

Temple, J. "Growth Effects of Education and Social Capital," Working Paper no. 263. Paris: OECD Economics Department, 2000.

Beware of Greeks Bearing Gifts: Old Growth and New Economy Recessions

BACK IN THE FIFTH CENTURY BC, THERE WAS A STARK CONFLICT BETWEEN TWO GREAT Greek philosophers: Parmenides who stressed continuity and Heraclitus who emphasized change. If the conflict was transposed to our current *neophiliac* times, Heraclitus would definitely be the most popular of the two. Discussions of the new economy based on information and communications technologies (ICTs) focus on the presumed immensity of the changes we are undergoing—something BIG, as Rick Harris says in his paper—generating an unending string of serious conferences on the supposed profound effects these will have on everything from bird migration to industrial policy to national sovereignty. International connectedness and globalization are already seen as near-complete. The benefits of technological progress are thought to be unlimited. Growth is viewed as proceeding at a rising exponential rate. The business cycle is dismissed. Some attention is also paid to income distribution, which is acknowledged to be slightly distorted in the short run, but will soon be taken care of by the trickle-down effect. The most extreme of neophiliacs are almost ready to say good-bye to the law of gravity.

Let me take Parmenides' side, the side of continuity, for a change. I will start by admitting that there is something new going on. A year ago, the published numbers showed a significant acceleration of measured US labour productivity, that is non-farm business output per hour worked, from an annual growth rate of 1.5 percent in 1975–95 to 2.8 percent since the end of 1995. Faster productivity growth translates into faster-growing real per capita income and standards of living. This increase represents nothing less than a return to the hectic pace of growth seen in the 1950s and 1960s. However, there are several kinds of uncertainty related to this 21.8 percent figure.

First, that number has already been significantly revised to 2.4 percent since the beginning of the year, and it is unclear whether this is going to be the last downward revision. Second, there is a serious measurement issue. The faster growth rate of productivity is closely associated with the production and use of semiconductors, computers, software and telecommunications equipment. However, US statisticians are very "aggressive." They use what is called the "hedonic method" for splitting, say, the dollar value of computer equipment into price and quantity. If the street price of a given brand of computer increases by 5 percent in a given year, they may, for example, end up assuming, based on complex calculations on the changing characteristics of computers, that this is actually the result of an implicit decline of 30 percent in the true, quality-adjusted price and, consequently, of a 50 percent increase in the true embedded quantity of computers (since 0.7 times 1.5 equals 1.05). Naturally, this gives an enormous boost to the measured increase in the real volume of computers produced in the economy and, therefore, to the measured productivity growth of the computer-manufacturing sector. However, it is far from obvious to everyone that this statistical procedure gives a faithful account of the true value put by buyers on what they get.

Third, in the five years since the end of 1995, where an acceleration of productivity has been measured, the US economy was on a strong expansion path. As Robert Gordon has argued, part of the acceleration (not all of it) from 1.5 percent to 2.4 percent a year may have come from the cyclical orientation of the economy, not from a change in the true underlying productivity trend. Since we are in uncharted territory, there is much residual uncertainty as to the magnitude of this cyclical component. Fourth, assuming trend productivity has indeed accelerated to some extent, we do not know how long that increase in the growth rate will last.

To Rick's insistence that the future is vastly uncertain, I would therefore add that the present and the recent past are very uncertain too. My best guess is that US productivity has accelerated modestly so far, but less than official measurement says it has, and very much less than the lyrical enthusiasm of the neophiliacs would have us believe. Coming to Canada, just as Rick, I see some productivity catch-up having taken place since 1997, but with so few years of data available the long-term trend is still impossible to extract from published numbers.

The stock market has now given its verdict on the new economy. Although there have been important technological advances leading to a more global economy and wonderful new products, there also has been somewhat of a cheese soufflé in the unbelievably large price-to-earnings ratios that the herd had been sustaining until April 2000. Exaggerated market values have at long last been put back in their place. People who bought companies for $4 billion are now reselling them for $200 million, or 5 percent of the initial price. Parmenides would observe that we have already experienced such changes in the past: with electricity, the telephone, the combustion engine, industrial chemistry, housing sanitation and refrigeration or television. I am not sure the computer stands that tall among these old inventions that completely transformed the lives of our grandparents. *Peu de nouveau sous le soleil.*

What are the consequences of the new economy for the short-run stabilization of the business cycle? I do not think they are very important either. It is true that the kind of economic slowdown we began to see in the middle of last year is very different from the 1958–61, 1981–83 and 1990–92 recessions. Contrary to the current slowdown, which is still rather shallow, those were deep and protracted recessions that were deliberately engineered to reduce and eliminate inflation. Since inflation has now abated, we are back to the kind of speculative excesses that were common in pre-1940 expansions: runaway stock markets and speculative installation of new capital equipment too much ahead of demand. (October 1987 was a preview.) But, meanwhile, we have learned how to end slowdowns and recessions: by not allowing mass bankruptcies in the financial sector and by quickly reducing interest rates. There is not one recession in North America in the last five decades that did not end when the Federal Reserve and the Bank of Canada decided it would—after perhaps a one-year lag. Rick alludes to Alan Greenspan being lucky. In a sense he has been. Food and energy prices, the strong US dollar and whatever productivity acceleration we have seen have helped keep inflation in check. But, basically, Greenspan just knows his trade very well. He watches inflation and its various leading indicators, and he manages aggregate demand prudently, exactly as Keynes would have recommended. Fine tuning has returned by the back door, and it is doing very well thank you. Again, *plus ça change, plus c'est pareil.*

Nor is there any connection between the new economy and the current synchronization of the business cycle in North America, Europe and Japan. That synchronization is purely fortuitous. North America is undergoing a temporary dip while it is digesting its growth-related speculative excesses. Europe has been stagnating for basically two decades, and Japan has been trapped for a decade in a vicious circle of recession and deflation. In both cases, the situation can be tracked to a conservative monetary management interacting with labour and capital market institutions and demographics that have nothing in common with the North American situation. As for Canada, its current slowdown is even shallower than that of the United States. Thanks to our previous monetary strategy and to our fiscal nightmare, our recovery began with a four-year lag behind the US recovery in the 1990s. Canada was in a sense lucky not to have time to fall into speculative excesses to the same extent as the United States.

As for income distribution and poverty, the most comprehensive comparison between Canada and the United States we have was done three years ago by Michael Wolfson and Brian Murphy of Statistics Canada. Combined with other evidence, their study (which they updated recently in the August 2000 issue of the *Canadian Economic Observer*) suggests four reasons why the situation has not deteriorated as much in Canada as in the United States, our school enrolment rates have been higher, our minimum wages have now been frozen for an entire decade, our union sector has held up well and, despite the recent restrictions to welfare and Employment Insurance, our tax and social policies have done a better job of protecting the median- and low-income population. There is no question that the particular characteristics of any given episode of technological change can have consequences for income distribution and poverty, as the rise in within-group inequality may suggest. But so far, in the world of the brave new economy, there is no reason yet to believe that the old Canadian social compact made up of medicare, free or low-cost education, moderately-high minimum wages, reasonable income security, and a progressive tax system cannot deal effectively with the particular challenges we are now facing.

My view of what good economic policy should be has not been changed one bit by the advent of the new economy: remain open to free trade and investment and free movement of people; support investment in education, machinery and equipment and research and development; accelerate the reduction in the public debt; and avoid conservative monetary policy. I think this is in perfect tune with Rick's own preferred policy package (even his idea of fixing the Canadian-dollar exchange rate would actually mean Canada would adopt the much less conservative US monetary policy!), but again I do not see any necessary connection with the new economy rhetoric. Someone has to say it loud and clear: Parmenides still has much going for him. Down with Heraclitus.

Reflections on the New Economic Order

The main issue is whether the new economic order, as Rick Harris puts in bold, capital letters, is a Big Deal, or something important but not fundamentally different. The answer is very important. If it is something fundamentally different, then we should be confident of an extended period of very robust growth. Whether your objective function is lowering poverty, supporting postsecondary education, or as Pierre Fortin flags, the need to further reduce the public debt burden, realization will be that much easier with strong output growth. Other changes flow from Harris' position that it is a big deal. He predicts the demise of some of the so-called "old industries" to be replaced by specialization on some of the new types of industries. Business cycles should be less prominent, in part from a dampened influence of inventory swings.

To form a view on whether the new economic order is a big deal I look at both the input and output side of the economy.

On the input side, there is no doubt this is a big deal. As my role is to be an industry practitioner, let me illustrate with some examples from my business, the financial services sector. Harris broke the inputs into machinery and equipment, knowledge and openness to trade. On the investment side, the five major banks together spent $3.15 billion on technology last year. That is not simply a Y2K phenomenon, that range of yearly expenditures has been going on for several years. It is no longer a question of people using automatic banking machines, 90 percent do that, 50 percent of our customers now use telephone and Internet banking services. Of the 40,000 employees in my company, at least 4,000 work almost exclusively on information technology.

As for the knowledge-based economy, of the 20,000 people who have joined the TD Bank Financial Group since 1997, only 11 percent do not have at least a college degree, 49 percent have at a minimum a BA or higher degree. On the openness to world trade, six years ago, only one-sixth of the banking-sector industry revenues came from outside Canada's borders. Last year, one-third came from outside Canada: a doubling of the importance of external revenues in only five years.

As for the output side, I would say that the changes are important, but not yet overwhelming. There is solid evidence that in recent years the US economy has moved to a higher productivity growth plane. The case for Canada doing the same is shakier. Harris and Johnson both point to some indications in 1999 and 2000 that Canada was getting on to that higher productivity plane, but I am sceptical, as that coincides with a period of very rapid growth. I do not think we have a long enough sample period to distinguish between cyclical and structural productivity gains.

It is interesting to look again at the financial services industry to see how the input changes are related to productivity. Did the $3.1 billion of technology lower costs and raise efficiency. It is not clear that it did. Coinciding with every cost reduction as people move to Internet and ABMs, customers increase the number of banking transactions that they perform. The two almost exactly offset each other. Now if we measured that properly, it could be argued that welfare has gone up. But I am not sure that knowing your bank balance every two minutes is really such a wonderful thing!

The evidence of a dampened inventory cycle is on very weak ground. In 1991, I calculate that the excess between actual and desired inventories was equivalent to 1.1 percent of the gross domestic product (GDP). I get a similar figure for early 2001, so the starting point seems like a fairly typical inventory cycle. The difference may be that rather than eliminating the business cycle, the inventory swing this time around will collapse its duration. In other words, just-in-time inventories may mean that businesses shed excess inventories much more aggressively in the past. The business cycle may then be shorter in duration, but if anything the amplitude may be more severe.

Another part of the lore of the new economic order is that policy authorities, particularly on the monetary side, have learned so much that even if a hint of a cycle makes it through after all the other changes involved in the big deal, then it can be extinguished through the new-found policy skills. Well the evidence on this front is shaky as well. The current downturn is not just caused from the collapse in business investment and the bursting of the stock market bubble. All of the typical signs of an overheated economy preceded the downturn. Americans bought a car for every member of their family and the Federal Reserve Board accommodated this consumption. I would argue that the monetary tightening came too late and it was too tepid.

Looking ahead, my advice is to hope that we are at the beginning of a big deal and we should do everything we can to push things in this direction. But we should not count on any of it coming automatically. We still need to pursue all the good policy initiatives that were in vogue before the new economic order.

From a sectoral perspective, one of the troubling aspects of talk of modern economic dialogue is to divide the economy neatly into the old economy and the new economy. Which category does the financial services industry fall into? It is one of the oldest industries. It does not produce information and communications technology. But it is a huge user of these products and services. Consider natural resources. Some of the biggest productivity gains have come in the mining industry. When Suncor started in 1980, they needed US$24 a barrel to break even on oil sands production. Now they need US$14–16 a barrel. And I am not even deflating that in constant dollar terms. Harris is absolutely right that we should not coddle, protect and subsidize industries that need to change. But we should also not underestimate the ability of many of the sectors in Canada to adapt to the new economic order.

One factor for the future that has not received enough attention in this discussion is demographics. Again consider the financial services industry. There is one more decade for the baby boomers to prepare themselves for retirement. Our business has traditionally made its money on interest rate differentials between loans and deposits. But that sort of business is not going to grow as rapidly as we shift more to the net saver generation. The successful bank in ten years time will be the one that convinces Canadians to pay a fee for assistance with wealth management.

Demographics also influence the public policy scene. In the mid-1990s, the federal government proposed a reform to Old Age Security in order to contain costs under an aging population. The government backed down and nothing has replaced the proposal. That just means that we had better ensure that our debt burden gets driven down low enough so that the resources can be allocated to seniors without heavier taxation or depriving other priorities. It also means we must do everything feasible to raise productivity growth.

Tax policy has also not received enough attention in this discussion of the modern economy. In the context of globalization, Canada's heavy reliance on certain taxes will surely wane. The worst tax from a growth perspective is the capital tax. We only have a few sources of growth and capital expansion is one of them. In Canada we are unique in directly and heavily taxing this source of growth. Beyond the capital tax, I think we will see corporate income taxes gradually arbitraged away around the world. We typically compare our corporate tax rates to those in the US. But we should realize that the US is heading toward being one of the highest corporate tax regimes in the world. That will not last forever. And particularly on the mobile capital front, the US is not our only relevant competitor.

Heavier reliance on personal income taxes will not make up for what we lose on the corporate tax side. We already have one of the heaviest reliances on personal income taxation in the world. The incentives to work, save and invest are being hurt by our high marginal rates in particular. And while most talk about these rates for the highest income earners, they are at their worst for families with incomes of between $20,000 and $40,000. For these families, marginal rates, after taking into account the loss of social benefits as income rises, can easily exceed 60 percent.

In future we are going to have to reduce our reliance on taxation from income, savings and capital. The tax base will have to shift more to consumption. That could be relying more on the existing goods and services tax and perhaps having more user fees, or some type of flat tax that integrates the personal and business sides.

In Canada we tend to get fixated on the federal level on tax issues. But the most interesting developments in coming years may well be from the provinces; in particular, tax competition among provincial jurisdictions. Hopefully, we will see more harmonization of tax bases. Otherwise there is a real risk of beggar-thy-neighbour policies. The competition should be on rates.

The aftermath of September 11, 2001 will hurt productivity. Productive private sector resources will be reallocated to military and security uses. There will be more time spent waiting for airplanes and at borders. The border, at the moment, is one of the most important issues facing the Canadian economy. The US is determined to put a secure perimeter around itself. If we are not inside the tent, Canada is dead economically. Thoughts immediately go to the potential threat to trade flows if the border is not relatively open. But the more significant cost over time may well be to foreign investment. What international operation would ever dream of locating, or staying, in Canada if free and easy access to the US market was not assured. A satisfactory border arrangement with the US must be established almost immediately to ensure the future prosperity of this country.

In conclusion, I am hopeful, but also sceptical that the new economic order is a Big Deal. Hope should never be an excuse to down tools on any of the other good policy pursuits that we have.

Discussion

GIVEN THAT THE MONTEBELLO CONFERENCE WAS HELD SCARCELY A MONTH AFTER the September 11, 2001 terrorist attacks, we anticipated that most floor discussion would, irrespective of the session, begin with questions relating to the implications of 9/11. In anticipation of this, we scheduled a special evening session to focus specifically on the likely ramifications of 9/11 for the range of governance issues addressed at the conference. An edited version of this discussion appeared in the November 2001 issue of *Policy Options Politiques* (and available at www.irpp.org). What we did not anticipate was the interest that was triggered by Richard Harris's suggestion that a common currency for North America might well be the appropriate exchange rate regime for the new economic order (NEO). Our solution was to schedule a special exchange-rate session involving panel members (Harris, Fortin, Drummond and Courchene) and former Bank of Canada governor and IRPP board member Gordon G. Thiessen. The edited version of this special session appeared in the *Financial Post* and is reproduced here in the Appendix.

Rick Harris began his responses to the various issues raised from the floor by reiterating his agreement with Fortin and Drummond that even if the NEO is real, it need not change the basic view of what constitutes good economic policy. But Harris then offers a note of caution: luck and chance can play a role. Consider New Zealand. This county followed almost every mainstream policy prescription that was offered, only to now find itself in an economic mess. Canada on the other hand was lucky—the combination of the US Smoot-Hawley tariff in the early 1930s and the British response with Imperial Preferences set the stage for a huge burst in foreign direct investment (FDI) which set the stage for the transfer of technology to southern Ontario, which in turn led to the build-up of the auto industry in Ontario and Quebec. One of the implications of the NEO is that we may be in the throes of another process of industrial relocations. The US midwest feels that they are being left out as economic growth has moved to the two coasts. And there is no guarantee that Canada will not lose the auto industry. Thus, while enacting good policy is necessary, it may not be sufficient to succeed in the NEO.

Harris also emphasized that while much of the current and future debate about the NEO will be assessed in terms of its implications for productivity, the measurement problem here is huge. In the banking sector, for example, the US has recorded negative productivity growth for two decades. Indeed, measured productivity for the entire services sectors is often negative. Yet we know that there have been important productivity-enhancing developments in many, if not most, of the services sectors. In short, the measurement framework/methodology emanating from the Keynesian tradition of national income accounting and central planning is seriously out of date and it requires an investment of resources in developing an appropriate productivity methodology for the NEO.

In response to a question on foreign direct investment Fortin noted that there has been a fundamental shift in the nature of FDI in Canada. In the previous era, FDI flowed into Canada in order to "jump the tariff wall" so as to exploit the Canadian market. In this era of lower or zero tariffs, however, FDI flows into Canada in order to serve the North American and world markets from a Canadian industrial base and location. The policies needed to encourage inward FDI must similarly undergo a fundamental shift.

Don Drummond closed the session by noting that one implication of 9/11 has already been to hasten the recognition that many of the information technology and other workers in banks (and other companies) need not work in downtown Toronto, the most expensive real estate in all of Canada. However, when they move away from the downtown core to other areas, these workers will likely face a transportation problem. Our transportation system is designed to get people downtown, not to get them to non-core workplaces. As a result, relocation of the workforce may mean a sharp increase, at least in the short term, in the number of persons forced to rely on private transportation. This is yet another of the myriad of adjustments that will be occasioned by the NEO.

The Changing Nature of Power and Democracy

Democracy and Political Power in Contemporary Western Governments: Challenges and Reforms

Introduction

There is little doubt that contemporary democratic government is challenged from a number of directions. At their most fundamental level these challenges and complaints are of two sorts. One set of challenges arises from the perceived failure of democratic institutions, especially the structures and processes of representative democracy—legislatures, political parties, cabinets and the like—to do their jobs adequately. The argument is that the process meant to translate public wishes into effective policy has become slow, deadlocked and to some extent subverted. The other set of concerns about representative democracy is more fundamental. These considerations are that the very concept and practice of representative democracy make it inadequate as a means of permitting the public to exert power over policy, and that they therefore must be modified in a fundamental manner if democracy is to perform as the public expects it to. These two sets of issues are obviously connected, but they should be considered separately in order to clarify both the problems and the possible remedies.

Evidence about the perceived failures of representative democracy, while accepting the basic premise of this form of government, comes from a number of sources. There are numerous reports, based both on survey evidence and anecdotes, that citizens do not have confidence in government in the way in which they once did. This drop in public confidence is certainly apparent in the United States, but it is now appearing in countries such as Canada, Denmark and Sweden which have a clearer history of effective and humane government (see table 1) (Dogan 1999; Norris 1999).[1] Not only do citizens express less confidence in their governments than in the past, they also appear less willing to vote or to

Declining Confidence in Government

	1980–1981 (%)	1990–1991 (%)
Austria	62	48
Belgium	50	43
Britain	64	60
Canada	61	46
Denmark	63	66
Finland	72	53
France	57	56
Germany	55	53
Ireland	66	61
Italy	44	41
Japan	46	41
Netherlands	54	54
Norway	75	66
Spain	53	45
Sweden	61	54
United States	63	56

Source: Dalton (1999).

participate in politics through other conventional mechanisms. Of all the forms of political participation in democracies, membership in and identification with political parties (other than in protest parties) appears to be especially devalued by changes in public attitudes and behaviour toward government (see table 2) (Schmitt and Holmberg 1996). Dalton and Wattenberg (2000) suggest that we now have "politics without partisans."

In some ways the total level of political activity in contemporary societies may not be diminished as much as might be thought, given the level of discussion on "talk radio," or the often intense activity of single-issue interest groups. What has changed is that this political activity is not directed so much at winning elections and governing as in the past. Indeed, a good deal of contemporary activity appears to be directed toward preventing effective governance and questioning the legitimacy of government. The disconnection between the political elite and the increasingly apolitical, or even anti-political, electorate appears to present a serious problem for democracy as we have known it.

Not only is the familiar representative form of democratic governance challenged at the level of mass politics, it is also challenged at the institutional level. Some institutions of government themselves, perhaps most notably legislatures, continue to find decision-making increasingly difficult and appear to have become incapable of exercising autonomous powers vis-à-vis the political executive. Paradoxically, the strength within legislative bodies of the same political parties that appear to be so weakened at the mass level has become a major source of the problem in enforcing traditional accountability. Party members now appear to "always vote at their party's call," at least in Westminster democracies, so that the possibilities of seriously calling a government to account for action or inaction is limited. Further, legislatures often have lacked the will and resources to institutionalize mechanisms such as articulated committee structures that would enable them to be more effective at oversight.

The more fundamental complaint about contemporary democracies is that the institutions and elected representatives have become so remote from the public that no real popular choice of policy can be made. Citizens say in surveys that they do not believe that elected politicians do what their constituents want, but rather pursue their own career interests (see the paper by André Blais in this volume).[2] The sharp disjuncture, which is argued to exist between the political elite and the ordinary citizens, is conceptualized as preventing democracy from being

Declining Party Membership (party members as a percentage of electorate)

	End of 1960s (%)	End of 1980s (%)	End of 1990s (%)
Austria	26	22	18
Finland	19	13	10
Belgium	8	9	7
Norway	16	14	7
Italy	13	10	4
Netherlands	9	3	3
Germany	3	4	3
United Kingdom	3	4	3

"genuine," and as being the source of popular discontent with representative democracy (Barber 1984). For advocates of this perspective no amount of tinkering would be sufficient to deal with the problems of representative democracy; what would be required is a more sweeping set of changes, or at a minimum an augmentation of the existing forms of representation and decision-making with more direct public involvement.

The demands for more fundamental changes in the institutional apparatus of democracy have provoked a number of responses. Some have involved tinkering with the institutions of decision-making. Again, more than a little paradoxically, many of these responses to the failure of representative democracy depend upon a much more active public and the involvement of ordinary citizens in making policy decisions about complex issues. Devices such as direct democracy, deliberative democracy and communitarianism—relying on active, informed and heavily involved citizenry—are now cited frequently as appropriate responses to the problems of democracy. These would create a "strong democracy" and replace representative democracy with (in the minds of their adherents at least) more meaningful, effective and above all democratic means of making collective decisions. These mechanisms depend, however, upon the same citizens who presently cannot be bothered to place an X on a ballot, especially if it is rainy or cold on election day.

The proposals for more basic changes to enhance democracy also involve changes in the electoral system. The argument (implicit or explicit) being advanced is that it is not so much discontent and distrust of politicians that keep people away from the polls and from politics, but rather the process of elections themselves. The solution offered most often for this aspect of the problem now is some form of "e-democracy" permitting people to vote in the comfort of their own homes. This mechanism might be extended to integrate some aspects of direct and deliberative democracy; the vision of some advocates of electronic democracy is that citizens might be engaged in successive referenda on virtually the whole gamut of policy issues (Barney 2000; Kamarck and Nye 2002). These voting mechanisms would provide government not only instantaneous feedback on its actions, but also direct policy guidance from the public.

The proposals for Internet democracy raise obvious possibilities about voter fraud, but also raise more fundamental questions about the meaning of democracy. In marked contrast to deliberative models of democracy, and to much of the contemporary social capital literature (Putnam 2000; Boix and Posner

1998), the implicit assumption of the work on e-democracy is that minimal involvement by individuals in politics is acceptable (and perhaps even laudable). All that citizenry must do is to motivate their computer "mouse" on election day and democracy will be saved. There is also some elements of a "Field of Dreams" scenario operating here; the assumption is that if there are greater opportunities for participation that appear to be directly related to policy choice then the public will invest time and energy in politics in a way they have not been willing to do with representative institutions. Using those representative institutions appears to involve numerous steps between voting and the choice of policies (Rose 1974) and citizens feel that voting really does not matter. The other optimistic element of this literature is the assumption, again often implicit, that if citizens can be coaxed into participating in a minimal manner they may become willing to become more deeply involved in public life.

Real or perceived institutional failures in representative democracy have also prompted a rather different type of response. This response has been to minimize the political and to rely more on "non-majoritarian institutions" (Majone 1996) to perform the tasks that citizens had generally considered to be the responsibility of elected governments. The classic example of using a non-majoritarian institution is the role of the Federal Reserve Board in economic policy in the United States, or the Bundesbank in Germany. Because of their expertise, past successes and the very fact that they are not tainted by partisan politics, these institutions are often more effective in governing than are legislatures or political executives. Further, these institutions are able to govern consistently without the "stop-go" that has characterized economic policy and other areas affected by swings of the partisan pendulum. The courts in the United States, and apparently increasingly also in Canada, can play that role, although its politicized involvement in the 2000 election debacle has cast more than a small shadow over the US Supreme Court (Dershowitz 2001; Posner 2001). This response reminds us of something that has often been forgotten in the debate about declining confidence in institutions—legitimacy is a product of effectiveness, just as it is a product of the procedures by which the political elites are selected.

Both these levels of complaints about contemporary democracies should be set in the contest of a seeming erosion of power at the level of the nation-state and the movement of power upward to supranational organizations and the international market, downward to subnational governments, and outward to private and quasi-public organizations. Why should we worry about any shortcomings of democratic governance at the national level when it appears to be capable of controlling so little? The argument to be made here is that the loss of state power is exaggerated in much of the literature (see, e.g., Strange 1996, 1998), and especially if citizens want to be able to exert any democratic control over many crucial economic and social forces we had best find a way to make the nation-state perform as well as possible (Hirst 2000; Pierre and Peters 2000).

The apparent increased strength of international and supranational organizations may actually have strengthened the state. For example, in the European Union, the budgetary convergence criteria in the Maastricht Treaty strengthened the hand of governments in Italy and Belgium, *inter alia*, against domestic forces that had always been able to produce budget deficits. Also, organizations such as the World Trade Organization are composed of representatives of national governments, so that government becomes crucial for defining the way in which the international market will work. The supranational agreements, whether regional or global, become the functional equivalents of non-majoritarian institutions at the national level, and provide a means of making difficult policy choices while limiting the domination of institutions such as markets.

I will cast this discussion of contemporary democracy and its challenges in terms of the need for governance, and especially democratic governance, in societies such as those with which we are most familiar (Peters and Savoie 1994, 2000). Governing is in the first instance about steering the economy and society and about providing a means for collective goal-setting and goal attainment. This paper is primarily about the process of choosing goals for society in some democratic manner, although the process of deciding on goals and putting them into effect cannot readily be divorced. In order to be effective in implementing its policies, perhaps the most important resource a government can have is legitimacy. If the government is accepted as a legitimate and trusted source of regulation then administering the society is relatively easy for a sitting government. If, on the other hand, the government is distrusted then governing becomes difficult and expensive.

Developing democratic mechanisms that involve citizens in goal-setting and giving them more of an immediate stake in the outcomes of the process of governing, is potentially the start of a virtuous spiral of enhanced legitimacy and effectiveness. Governments have been involved in attempting to initiate such an upward spiral, including major efforts for "citizen engagement" in Canada and in "empowerment" in a number of other countries (Handler 1996; Hoff 1993). Those efforts do not appear to have been very successful in altering the mood of the public, while cynicism and discontent appear to continue to be the dominant public sentiments. It is easy to blame this discontent on the media, but that facile sloughing off of responsibility does not address more basic questions about governing and the nature of contemporary democracy.

The Roots of the Problem

Joseph Nye has asked in print why people do not trust government (Nye 1997). It would be easy to dismiss the apparent loss of trust and involvement of citizens as simply a passing fancy, or as a rather costless means of protest against what may be rather minor problems in government. Also, many people in government have dismissed the loss of confidence as a media-inspired phenomenon, rather than a true reflection of public opinion. It has now become so much a part of popular culture, at least in the United States, to assume that government is ineffective and inefficient that respondents to a survey would not want to be thought so naive as to answer that government was doing at least an adequate job. Those facile dismissals of the apparent loss of confidence may be comforting, but they may also understate the real problems in government that have generated the popular discontent.

Although popular discontent with government and politicians is real, governments have not done as badly in serving the public as their critics have argued. The Brookings Institution's list (2001) of the 50 major accomplishments of government in the United States during the past 50 years is indeed a formidable list of programs and activities that have made the lives of the average citizen better. Other countries could develop their own lists which might focus more on the social, rather than the technological or military, program but in all cases governments as institutions have delivered on many of the promises that politicians have made. The events of September 11, 2001 indicate that in times of crisis governments can respond with reasonable efficiency, even if their ineffectiveness may have contributed to the initial crisis. Further, there is some evidence that the public is now beginning to see that government can at times be the solution, not the cause of problems.

Before going into the list of apparent causes of the problems of contemporary democratic systems, we should first note some apparent inconsistency on the part of citizens. Often citizens will report in interviews that government as a whole is incompetent and that bureaucrats are insensitive lay abouts. Frequently, these are some of the more positive features that are reported. On the other hand, when the same citizens are asked about specific programs, especially the ones of which they are beneficiaries, they generally report that these government programs do a fine job in delivering those public services (see Bodiguel and Rouban 1991; DOXA 1996). For example, public education is often considered by respondents to polls to be failing its students when discussed in general, but the schools that the children of respondents attend are often given high marks.[3]

Now, why do members of the general public appear to dislike government so much? One answer is that public expectations have been raised to such a level that failure is almost inevitable. Political campaigns are filled with promises that may be difficult if not impossible to fulfil. Some, if not most, promises are sufficiently vague that the politician can claim later to have been on target, but the public will see that there are still long waiting times for care in the health service, rivers are not clean or there is still more unacceptable crime on the streets. Further, the success of governments in macroeconomic management for much of the postwar era created the sense that any decent government could indeed manage the economy to produce continued economic growth and low unemployment.[4] The sustained boom of the Clinton years in the United States reinforced the popular perception that governments could create economic successes if they wanted it hard enough. With that background, the economic slowdown—beginning even before September 11, 2001—has come as a shock to many in the public, especially younger workers who have no memory of a bear market or unemployment.

Perhaps the most basic expectation, or hope, that citizens have about their elected politicians is that they will be honest, and at least as interested in public service as in personal gain. That expectation has not been fulfilled in any number of cases in almost every country, while newspapers continue to be filled with stories of financial and sexual scandals involving political leaders. We do not need to recount all the scandals, real or contrived, that have beset governments over the past several years. We do know, however, that scandals do matter to the public. Indeed, in some ways it is remarkable that faith in government has remained as high as it has in countries with successive internal embarrassments.

Governments have also been their own enemies in more than the scandals that have been exposed to the public. The numerous administrative reforms of the past several decades have had many positive consequences for the capacity of the system to govern, but they have had less positive consequences as well (Pollitt and Bouckaert 2000). For example, the tendency toward "agentification," or the creation of a large number of quasi-autonomous public organizations[5] may have enhanced efficiency of service provision for each individual organization, but it has made coordination and political accountability of their actions that much more difficult (Peters 2001, ch. 6). Government has sought to regain control over these structures through a variety of means, including the increasing politicization of the public service, and implementation of performance management systems and other procedures for control (see Light 1996; Peters and Pierre, forthcoming).

Likewise, the increasing use of the private sector, or public-private partnerships, to deliver services may have had some of the same negative consequences for government as the shift toward increased use of agencies. The reform of the state in many political systems has substituted private sector control over major industries for public sector control, and with that governments often find themselves at the mercy of individuals and organizations that generally do not place the public interest at the centre of their value system.[6] Failures of the private firms and agencies that replaced British Rail to pay adequate attention to public safety have been among the more egregious examples of this problem. However, it does appear to be rather common after privatization and deregulation. As well, airport security in the United States has been provided by private firms paying their workers the minimum wage. It has become clear that this may reduce the apparent role of the state but it may not produce the best services to the public.

Reforming Representative Democracy

We now turn to the specific problems in representative democracy and the ways in which the structures of representation, largely political parties, and the structures of decision-making, primarily parliaments, appear related to problems of governing in contemporary democracies. This topic could constitute a paper, or a book, all by itself, but this discussion will be an attempt to point to some of the principal issues in a representative system, and the ways in which they interact in the process of governance.

Political parties and democratic governance

Parliaments have been the centrepieces of democracy for several centuries in some countries, and a properly constituted and independent legislature is now a *sine qua non* for any functioning democracy.[7] As well as passing legislation, one of the principal functions of these organizations has been to enforce accountability over the political executive and over the public bureaucracy. The prevailing constitutional doctrine for parliamentary systems is that the executive is accountable to parliament and through parliament to the people (see Day and Klein 1987). For presidential systems the chain of accountability is more complex, but the legislature plays an important role in accountability even in those systems.

Going hand in hand with the idea of a legislature in most democratic systems has been the idea of political parties as another essential element of a properly functioning democracy. Political parties conventionally have been considered crucial for organizing the legislature, recruiting political elites, and channelling public participation in ways that will create effective governance for society. For a good portion of the history of democratic government political parties fulfilled these functions rather well, and the public identified with them, and thought of themselves as adherents to one or the other; even if those citizens might be only minimally involved in politics, they knew their party allegiance.

For much of the population now, however, political parties have become part of the problem with democratic governance, rather than part of the solution. Rather than contributing to effective governance, political parties are now often considered to be obfuscating issues, protecting incompetence, and failing to think beyond partisan advantage while in office. To some extent the parties have only themselves to blame, given the numerous instances in which political parties have rallied around party leaders who have obviously erred politically or personally, and the numerous times that parties have been seen to abuse the office in just the way they criticized the previous incumbents. In most democratic countries confidence in political parties has declined even more than has confidence in the formal institutions of government; it is clear that parties are not doing what the public might want them to do.

Parliamentary regimes. Political parties have a special role in parliamentary political systems, given that they are the means through which the legislature is organized and the executive is selected. Although legislatures in most democratic political systems predated the formation of political parties as we have come to know them, parties and party discipline now ensure that an executive can be selected with minimal transaction costs within parliament, and that there will be substantial stability in the executive that is selected.

The minimization of transaction costs is especially evident in Anglo-American political systems, or as Lijphart called them, majoritatian political systems (Lijphart 1984). The "first-past-the-post" electoral system in these political structures ensures that an absolute parliamentary majority is almost always produced in elections. Therefore, a government from a single party (or at worst one with a minor partner) will be produced. Even party systems as fragmented as presently in Canada, and now to some extent in the United Kingdom, are able to deliver those majorities on a regular basis. In the Westminster model this strong, responsible majority government historically has been considered a virtue, permitting the government to truly govern while in office and to offer rather clear choices to the electorate at the subsequent election. The political accountability may be retrospective, but it is accountability nonetheless.

The problem with contemporary democracies, again especially in the majoritarian democracies, may be that the parties have been perhaps too successful in creating majorities and in putting their stamp on government once elected. The success of majority parties poses several problems for the conduct of democracy. The first difficulty is that there is little check on the capacity of the majority to rule, and hence little constraint on their capacity to adopt the decisions they want. This lack of formal limitations means that the only real constraints on a government's decision-making is its own political judgement, and its common sense. In addition, some of the norms that guided the conduct of parliamentary responsibility for parties have been weakened, so that governments, which at one time might have been expected to resign, continue in office without sanctions.

Finally, political parties have come to be seen as corrupted by the need to raise money. Even parties of the political left are now closely linked to monied interests—perhaps the most notable, the Labour Party in Britain—so that the democratic ideal that the average citizen can exert real influence over politics and policy appears even more naive to average citizens. It seems to many, if not most, that political parties are in the pockets of the wealthy and/or those of strong special interests.

A digression on American presidentialism. The large majority of democratic systems in the industrialized world are parliamentary, and that form of democracy does have its own important issues and problems. The experiences of the American presidential system over the past decade or so may, however, illuminate some of the issues of governance with which we are concerned in this paper. The conventional, and largely accurate, description of the constitutional system in the United States is that it was designed with the explicit intention of making action by the public sector difficult. The ability of one branch of government, or at times even one subcommittee of one house of Congress, to stymie action would seem to make governance unlikely, if not impossible.

One of the standard remedies for the structural impediments to governance existing within American democracy has been to develop responsible political parties (Ranney and Kendall 1956). Part of the problem, it has been argued, is that the United States does not have political parties like those found in Canada or the United Kingdom. The US has been for much of the postwar period a four-party system, with the Democratic and Republican parties espousing rather different values in different parts of the country.[8] Likewise, once elected, Senators and Congressmen have acted more as individual entrepreneurs than as members of organized and coherent political parties (Fenno 1978; Mayhew 1974). The argument advanced in favour of developing a more coherent party system was that if voters were confronted with such parties they could then more easily choose policies and could then hold the parties accountable for their actions once elected.

There were some scholars and practitioners who questioned the need for European-style political parties in the United States. If, for example, we begin with David Mayhew's rather famous research on divided government in the United States we can see that having all three major law-making institutions—the president and both houses of Congress—coming from the same political party does not make a great deal of difference to the capacity of the system to legislate.[9] Major pieces of legislation were adopted during divided and undivided governments. Further, the individualized nature of congressional careers may lead those individuals to provide greater service to their constituents than would be true for more party-focused legislators. If legislators have to please their electors more than the leaders of the party they will behave rather differently than in more partisan-controlled systems.

The good news for the advocates of responsible political parties is that the United States appears now to have such entities, at least on the Republican side of the aisle. The Republican Party now votes together in Congress at about the same rate as European political parties vote together in their parliaments, and although the Democratic Party remains more internally divided, its party unity scores have also risen substantially. Further, there is now somewhat greater partisan agreement between the president and the congressional party, again more clearly on the Republican side than on the Democratic, with President George W. Bush being able to count on support from almost all of his party almost all of the time.[10] Thus, the capacity of a president to lead his party in Congress will be enhanced and an implicit check on government, which has operated for decades, has now been weakened if not completely eliminated.

The bad news is that this change in the meaning of political parties within American democracy appears to have made governing harder rather than easier, except in the rare case in which all three institutions are controlled by the same party: only 16 of the 51 years since 1950. Once parties have come to mean something, then compromise and bargaining become more difficult and governing becomes harder. This is all the more true since there is no way short of impeachment to remove a sitting president, unlike the vote of no-confidence in parliamentary regimes. With the growth of more meaningful parties, the capacity of policy entrepreneurs, most notably the president, to broker deals on policy is minimized. Presidents such as the quintessential broker Lyndon Johnson, or even Richard Nixon, could develop policy coalitions that spanned party lines and moved government ahead. Even a rather skillful politician such as William Jefferson Clinton found building those coalitions difficult, even before his presidency was wounded by the Lewinsky affair.

The brokerage style of politics in American democracy has not been without its costs. There have been numerous claims of politicians selling their political "souls" for a new dam or interstate highway, or trading away their votes on issues of marginal relevance to their constituency for benefits. The "pork barrel" and "log-rolling" are certainly real considerations that present ethical as well as practical questions about the conduct of representative democracy. That having been said, however, they did make a political system designed to not work particularly well function. Many of the same people who complained about logrolling now complain about deadlock and gridlock and sclerosis of the system operating (or not) in Washington presently.

Raising the problems of American democracy points again to the issue of money in politics. This issue is most pronounced in the United States but has posed problems in a number of democracies. For example, the disgrace of Helmut Kohl in Germany centred on the necessity of raising funds for campaigns, as have scandals about fundraising in many other industrialized democracies. The corruption in question was not for personal gain, it was simply for the purpose of keeping their parties competitive in political systems fuelled by money. Interestingly, many of these scandals arose in countries with public financing of parties and limitations on campaign expenditures.

Alternatives to Conventional Democracy

If conventional mechanisms of representative democracy are not performing up to expectations are there alternatives that could provide more acceptable governance for their societies. As noted already, the perceived failures of representative democracies have resulted in a number of proposals for basic changes in the associated institutions and even more sweeping revisions of the way in which democracy is practised. At the simplest level, should Canada or other Westminster systems adopt proportional representation in order to provide citizens with genuine choices in parliamentary elections? And should the United States abolish the electoral college in favour of a direct popular vote for president? These are hardly new questions and they may be able to provide some improvements in the way in which government is regarded by the public.

I have chosen not to discuss the tinkering elements of change in electoral systems, preferring to focus on the more fundamental options being advocated by some reformers. This is not to denigrate the potential impact of the more marginal changes. If indeed one-party governments do raise problems of accountability then changing electoral systems may well be a major change. I do believe, however, that the presence and seeming popularity of several proposed reforms that go more to the heart of the representative nature of these political systems requires that they be treated more fully. If these advocates of the more extreme reforms are correct then no amount of internal reform will make sufficient changes to alter the prevailing negative attitude of the public.

Direct democracy

One of the most popular alternatives to representative democracy is direct democracy—the use of initiatives and referenda that permit the public to vote directly on policy options.[11] The underlying concept of direct democracy is extremely appealing. It would permit citizens to say directly what they think about policies and prevent some of the seemingly endless machinations found in legislative bodies. This form of democracy is already used extensively in Switzerland (Kobach 1993), by state and local government in the United States, and increasingly in Europe for issues concerning European Union (EU) membership or the expansion of powers of the EU (Gallagher and Uleri 1996). In Canada the referendum has also been used to address a major constitutional issue in Quebec, as well as being discussed as a more general option for assisting government in resolving difficult and fundamental issues, as it was with conscription in the past.

Appealing as this idea is, direct democracy has a number of problems for coping with the complexities of modern democratic governance. The most fundamental is that it assumes that the public is sufficiently informed and sufficiently interested to make the right choices on difficult policy issues. The public may become engaged concerning highly emotional issues that are being considered in a referendum, such as legalizing marijuana or extending rights to the gay and lesbian communities, but it may be more difficult to involve the public in the complex and difficult questions that governments must face (Linder 1994).

In addition, the referendum and initiative assume that difficult issues can be reduced to simple dichotomous choices, the format for most referenda. Even if that hurdle is overcome, minor differences in wording appear to make huge differences in the outcomes of referenda, so that the framers of the question may be as important as the wishes of the public in making a decision on the issue. Finally, the available evidence is that turnout for referenda is lower than for elections to office, even when the votes are held on the same day (for examples, see Blais 2000, 40-42). We, as political analysts, may think that the public is avidly concerned with the opportunity to make a difference on policy; the problem is that the public appears not to be nearly as interested.

The low turnouts to vote point to a final question about referenda and whether they are really the populist instrument for democracy that they appear at first glance to be (for Canada, see Mendelsohn and Parkin 2001). If the principal objections to referenda are to be met then the public will have to be informed about the issues. Making that information available to the public requires substantial amounts of money, and that will favour one side of a debate over the others. There are, of course, opportunities for public funding and public information programs for disseminating the necessary information in a fair and impartial manner, but without severe limits on spending and the use of media, the better financed side of a referendum campaign will have a pronounced advantage. This is, of course, true of American politics in which funding is so important, but also appears to be true in other settings in which referenda have been used (Bowler and Donovan 1998).

Deliberative democracy

The idea of deliberative democracy elaborates on the general reform idea of permitting the public to make their own decisions, rather than depending upon elected representatives to make those policy choices. Rather than just voting on a proposition put to them by the legislature, deliberative democracy requires more active and extended participation, with decisions not made so much by a simple vote as by a consensus-building process. The idea of deliberative democracy in many ways resembles the classic New England town hall meeting, or annual cantonal meetings in parts of Switzerland, where citizens come together to discuss the issues and arrive at their decisions. All citizens are permitted to take part and the issues are to some extent framed as well as resolved through the process of discussion.

Political theorists have developed the concept of deliberative democracy with a number of criteria to ascertain the extent to which any particular process is fair, inclusive and truly deliberative (Bohman and Rehg 1997; Hunold 1998). For example, students of deliberative models argue that the agenda for deliberation, and the definition of the issues should not be predetermined. As well, there should be opportunities for continual involvement in the process, rather than just one-time events such as public hearings (Fearon 1998). Further, unlike public hearings the deliberative processes are meant to be decisive, rather than advisory, so that the participation is argued to be "authentic" rather than merely a rationale for decisions that would be made anyway. Finally, expertise is not privileged in these deliberations so that all participants are able to advance their ideas and have an equal opportunity to influence the proceedings.

The concept of deliberative democracy has deep roots in western cultures, and this Athenian ideal is extremely appealing to many citizens and to many analysts. That having been said, this style of democracy is almost certainly impossible to attain outside small communities. The communitarian philosophy (Etzioni 1993) that has become popular in the United States, and to some extent other industrialized democracies, argues that most public policy issues can and should be resolved at the lowest level possible in a society, and that making decisions at this level would make more collective deliberation possible.[12] Deliberative democracy may be a wonderful way to manage the neighbourhood, or perhaps even a small city, but the prospects of running Canada or the United States in such a manner are, at best, remote.

That said, there may be means of approximating the type of involvement required for deliberative democracy. One strategy that has been advocated is to have "deliberative elections." This technique involves first allowing a panel of citizens to deliberate on an issue and make assessments of the argument, followed by a referendum informed by the judgements of the panel (Gastil 2000). The idea is that the public should be consulted on policy and be involved more in policy than it is in most representative democracies. If we cannot all come together to talk, then at least the polling that is used to guide political choices can involve a better informed public (Fishkin 1991). The notion of deliberative polling is that rather than phoning a citizen at dinner time and asking a series of questions, the results of surveys might be more meaningful if those citizens were given more information on the issues, and perhaps even had the opportunity to discuss the issues among themselves and with experts. If polls are to be a guide for politicians and bureaucrats when they are making policy, as appears inevitable, then it would help if the opinions expressed were grounded on more substantial knowledge and reflection. Even this device may require a greater investment of time and energy than the average citizen appears willing to make on any but the most exceptional cases. Other countries may have citizens who are more willing to participate than does the United States, but even in those more participatory systems highly deliberative mechanisms for policy-making may not attract citizens in the numbers that we would like to believe they might.

Participation on the output side

Democracy is usually discussed in terms of political parties, elections, interest groups and all the other events occurring on the input side of the political system. To the extent that the formal institutions of government are assumed to be related to democracy, it is parliament (see above) that is the focus of greatest attention. Those events and institutions are certainly important elements of democracy, but changes in the nature of governing mean that other forms of participation have become important in defining the way in which citizens relate to their governments (see Peters 2001, ch. 3). Democracy on the output side of government—direct citizen engagement in making and implementing policy—is now becoming as important for many citizens as is the act of voting, and it presents another important alternative to the conventional forms of representative democracy.

The explicit recognition that government and citizens interact more on the output side than on the input side is in many ways long overdue. The average citizen has many more contacts with government in the persona of the tax collector, the policeman, the social worker, the school teacher and a host of other service providers than he or she does with their elected representatives. These interactions with "bureaucrats" may not correspond to the usual descriptions of citizen participation in the public sector, but these public encounters may be important in shaping citizens' attitudes about the public sector (Goodsell 1981; Hasenfeld, Rafferty and Zald 1987). As noted above, however, the relatively positive accounts by citizens of their interactions with public officials often do not produce more generally positive perceptions of government as a whole. Still, except in the rare cases of abuse such as those occasionally committed by police, the individual appears to have few complaints about treatment. Further, many of the reforms undertaken during the past several years have been directed at ensuring that citizens are treated better and in a more considerate and efficient manner by public bureaucrats.[13]

The opportunities for citizens to be directly involved in the management of public programs that affect them are increasing. Perhaps the most commonly arising opportunity is in education, where increasing numbers of schools are being managed by committees of parents and teachers, albeit within the guidelines established by some public authority (Vander Weele 1994). This form of management for schools is common in Scandinavia and is being used in the

United States, Britain and a number of other countries. Parents tend to have some claims on government for policy-making by virtue of their role in society (as parents and taxpayers), but government has also developed opportunities for clients of public programs directed primarily at the less advantaged. These citizens who might not have been thought to have the political entitlements of the middle class are also being encouraged to take part directly in the governance of their programs. For example, housing programs in Denmark and Sweden permit residents a greater role in the management of their projects (Sorenson 1997), and some more limited versions of client management have also been instituted in the United States.

As important as democracy on the implementation side of the public sector is for providing additional opportunities for public participation and citizen engagement, there are also significant political and normative problems arising from this development. Perhaps the most important problem is the paradox that this instrument for enhancing democracy may, in fact, enhance the control of the more powerful elements in society, rather than equalizing power. Simple voting procedures provide a mechanism of one person, one vote, one value, while most forms of co-management of facilities by clients and professionals involve participation in meetings, working on committees and similar activities. In that type of democratic participation people with higher education and middle-class verbal and organizational skills are more likely to be effective than are the less well-educated and less affluent.[14] As noted, this same pitfall also applies to attempts at creating "deliberative democracy" in a range of political settings, where a political arrangement, which is presumed to be open to all, may actually advantage some groups over others. What Schattschneider wrote some years ago about pluralist versions of representative democracy may be all the more true of deliberative democracy: "in the pluralist heaven the heavenly choir sings with a strong upper-class accent" (1960, 35). And, paradoxically, this methodology of democracy was intended to make access more equal for the average citizen.

This apparent predicament with enhanced elitism does not have so much relevance when the programs that are being managed by their clients are more homogenous socially. In the case of public housing co-management in the United States mentioned earlier, all the individuals involved were from working-class or "under-class" backgrounds. Therefore, the management of these facilities was more representative of the clientele and also gave opportunities for effective participation to people who might otherwise be excluded. The danger with this type of program, as demonstrated with programs of "maximum feasible participation" in other urban and poverty programs is that the working-class citizens who become most effective at participation and management become "povertycrats" and are absorbed into the bureaucracy itself (see Moynihan 1969). They as individuals become much better off, but the communities from which they spring have been deprived of much of its indigenous leadership.

Democracy is a powerful *shibboleth* to employ when advocating a policy, but an emphasis on the output-oriented aspects of public participation also raises some dangers of excessive democracy. That is, governments must be responsible as well as responsive. They need to follow the rule of law as well as respond to the wishes of their clients. The street-level bureaucracy literature has pointed out that administrators who must interact frequently with clients often adopt the perspectives of those clients, provide more benefits to the clients, and thus may undermine the nominal policies of the organizations in which they are employed (Keiser 1999). This may please the citizens who are the direct clients of the organizations but it is unlikely to please citizens whose taxes are financing the programs.

Another example of the potential problems with democracy focused on the output side of government can be found in the United States. The Internal Revenue Service has been attacked repeatedly as being insensitive to the demands of taxpayers and as being abusive (US General Accounting Office 1996). The response to congressional hearings and other complaints against the employees of the agency has been lower levels of enforcement, especially against more affluent and powerful taxpayers who are likely to contest enforcement actions and to have strong links to political leaders. Any concern about lower levels of enforcement should not be taken as a defence of the abuse of power and discretion by bureaucracies, but rather it is a defence of some balance between the use of fear of detection and enforcement to gain legal compliance and responsiveness to citizens who do not want to comply with tax laws that cost them a great deal of money.[15]

Summary

There are a number of alternatives to responsible representative democracy as it has come to be practised in the industrialized democracies. These proposed alternatives involve more than simple reform of the institutions and favour forms of democracy that would be more direct and presumably more populist (Kazin 1998). The common base of at least three of these proposed alternatives is that the public can do at least as well as the politicians in making policy, and can certainly do better in representing their own views on policy than can the elected officials. As we have attempted to point out above, the conclusions drawn by the advocates of change are based on some unchallenged assumptions that may well be false. The public may not be as capable of making those decisions in the informed manner required, and these populist mechanisms may not, in fact, be as effective in representing the range of views of the public as a whole as are the familiar and often maligned institutions of representation.

The concerns expressed above about direct democracy are not intended to denigrate unnecessarily the average public, but rather to point to the problems of policy-making in contemporary democracies. Many industrialized democracies may now be in the situation of "post-industrial politics" that Samuel Huntington worried about some years ago (Huntington 1974). Developed democracies now have populations that are better educated than ever before, and they have information technologies that enable the public to access information with speed and efficiency that was impossible even a few years ago (Snellen 2000). The problem is that the issues that governments face, and the decisions that must be made, may have increased in complexity even more rapidly. The decisions that governments must make often involve detailed scientific and technical training, and may exceed the capacity of even a generally well-educated public to process effectively. Even the best educated citizen who is not an expert in a field may have difficulty with some contemporary policy issues, and may not be willing to invest the time and energy in becoming as fully informed as he or she might need to be.

This availability of information in the context of difficult policy choices is the classic situation that produces alienation—the presence of ends in the absence of means to achieve those ends. It may be little surprising, therefore, that there is popular discontent with government. This discontent may be all the more evident given that the character of much of the information being supplied is that it is condensed and placed into 45-second news clips. Government by sound-bite may be convenient and keep ratings high, but it is far from a desirable way to impart information on complex policies to the citizens. This should not be taken to place the entire burden of the problems of democracy on the shoulders of the media, but on the other hand, they are not without culpability either.

Although it is fashionable to blame the broadcast media for problems in democracy, in some ways the alternatives are worse. Of course, total ignorance of public affairs is worse than even limited knowledge, but "narrow-casting" may be worse than broadcasting. That is, if the public begins to receive the majority of its political information from specialized sources, most notably sites on the Internet, then we will all be working with highly differentiated, and often highly biased, sources of information (Sunstein 2001). While the news media are far from perfect, at least their sources are to some extent confirmed and there is some attempt at objectivity. There is no intermediation or verification on the Internet so there are always sources to agree with our biases or to provide the most titillating suppositions.

What Is to Be Done?

To this point the paper has been much more concerned with presenting problems than in offering solutions. We are still confronted by the seeming requirement of offering ideas about how to reform contemporary democratic systems.[16] The first point is that although I have been critical of many of the proposed more fundamental alternatives to representative democracy, these should be seen as friendly criticisms. That is, anyone interested in democratic government cannot help but applaud the drive to make government more participatory and to allow greater public deliberation on important policy issues. The difficulty is in finding ways of making what are very promising ideas work in practice, and also work in ways that do not produce outcomes exactly the opposite of those intended by their proponents.

We should not be too quick, however, to dismiss the possibilities for more direct involvement of the public in making policy. The procedural solutions discussed all have their difficulties and all beg the question of whether they are really more democratic than the representative institutions they are meant to replace or perhaps complement. The alternatives to conventional democracy all appear appropriate for small communities, rather than for large complex nation-states. Even for those small communities, for some issues and for some situations these mechanisms of direct democracy may not be able to involve a public that often seems disinterested at best.

At the level of institutional change, parliament in the familiar Westminster model appears to be at the heart of the questions about how to make government perform better. The Westminster model should impel voters, political parties and politicians toward doing some important things. Those pressures are to make parties responsible for their actions (at least by voting together and defending their stances) and enable the electoral system to produce majority governments. This should produce strong government. The paradoxical outcome is that it may produce governments that are too strong and consider compromise a sign of weakness. That tendency toward strong and uncompromising parties, combined with the presidentialization of the office of prime minister (Foley 1996; Peters 1997), drives governments in an almost authoritarian direction, permitting little internal discussion of policy and reducing parliaments to the rubber stamps that have been feared by commentators for decades.[17] Thus, restoring a popular sense of effective democracy may mean reducing some of the features that have been considered to be positive in governments. Paradoxically, strength may be weakness when attempting to govern a population that may be able to see the virtues of moderation and finding true middle ground.

Political parties also must be a major focus of any attempts to restore a greater sense of effective democracy. Political parties are one of the central features of political democracy but can also be an impediment to making those political systems effective in providing democratic governance. Parties are a mechanism for transmitting the wishes of the public to government, but because of the demands of the politicians for control, and for perpetuation of their stay in office, the parties now have a difficult time in doing other than defending their positions in parliament. As noted, American political scientists have long argued on behalf of a more responsible party system such as that found in Europe and in Canada, but the fragmented and individualistic nature of our parties may have some virtues in enforcing accountability on government. In that model, individual party members have strong incentives to defect and oppose the leadership of the party if there is some potential electoral advantage. Further, the parties do not have sufficient sanctions to punish those defectors.[18]

Notes

1 For Denmark, see Denmark. Ministry of Finance (1998); for Sweden, see Holmberg and Weibull (1998).

2 For example, 63 percent of Americans who said they had lost confidence in government argued that part of the reason was that "politicians were pursuing their own agenda" (Council on Excellence in Government 1997).

3 In the United States these differences can be seen in the annual *Phi Delta Kappan* grading of public education. Citizens often rate public education in general as meriting a "D+," while they grade their own public schools as meriting at least a "C." This is lower than most people would like, but there is a difference.

4 Economic performance continues to be a major explanatory factor for popular evaluations of government. See Lewis-Beck (1988) and Nannestad and Palgram (2000). As the 2000 campaign in the United States pointed out, however, good economic performance is not sufficient to produce electoral victory.

5 Special operating agencies (SOAs) in the Canadian context are versions of this type of organization.

6 In fairness, market organizations are meant to pursue profit rather than the public interest as their primary value.

7 Even countries that are not in any meaningful way democratic tend to have legislative bodies that serve to legitimate the actions of the government and to give the appearance of democracy to the international community.

8 Specifically, there were northern and southern Democrats and eastern and western Republicans who differed markedly on many policy issues.

9 Mayhew's interpretation and his methodology have been challenged in a number of places. See Mayhew (1991).

10 There are exceptions, perhaps notably on issues such as stem-cell research, where he lost the support of some religious conservatives, as well as on the issue of the tax cut.

11 In a referendum the public votes on an issue sent to them by the legislature. In an initiative the public is able (by petition) to have an issue considered by popular vote, bypassing the legislature entirely.

12 This idea is similar to that of subsidiarity that has been used to guide development of the European Union.

13 For example, the various versions of the Citizens' Charter are designed to provide individuals with a better sense of their rights involving treatment from public employees. Also, the market-oriented reforms that stress the role of the citizen as customer tend to place a greater emphasis on quality in service provision.

14 I observed one interesting case making this point. Danish schools have for some time been managed in this participatory manner, and while spending a term in Aarhus the big issue at the (almost mandatory) departmental lunch was whether the local school committees would ban serving pork, because of the increased number of Muslim students. This was a major issue in a country with more pigs than people.

15 For better or for worse, much of the literature on tax evasion points to the importance of fear of detection as a major motivator in voluntary compliance.

16 We should remember, however, that even Hercules was only required to clean the stables, not refill them.

17 Bracher's (1964) comment on the evolution of parliamentary government remains applicable today. See also Von Mettenheim (1997).

18 A good example would be Senator Liebermann who strongly criticized President Clinton over the Lewinsky affair, but was the Democratic Party's candidate for vice-president at the next election.

References

Barber, B. *Strong Democracy.* Berkeley: University of California Press, 1984.

Barney, D. *Prometheus Wired.* Chicago: University of Chicago Press, 2000.

Blais, A. *To Vote or Not to Vote: The Merits and Limits of Rational Choice Theory*. Pittsburgh: University of Pittsburgh Press, 2000.

Bodiguel, J.-L. and L. Rouban. *Le fonctionnaire detrôné?* Paris: Presses de la Fondation Nationale des Sciences Politiques, 1991.

Bohman, J. and W. Rehg. *Deliberative Democracy*. Cambridge, MA: MIT Press, 1997.

Boix, C. and D. Posner. "Social Capital: Explaining its Origin and Effects on Government Performance." *British Journal of Political Science*, Vol. 28 (1998): 686-693.

Bowler, S. and T. Donovan. *Demanding Choices: Opinion and Voting in Direct Democracy*. Ann Arbor, MI: University of Michigan Press, 1998.

Bracher, K.D. "Problems of Parliamentary Democracy in Europe." In *A New Europe?* ed. S. Grabaurd. Boston: Beacon Press, 1964.

The Brookings Institution. *Government's Greatest Achievements of the Past Half Century*. Washington, DC: Brookings Forum, December 20, 2000.

Budge, I. *The New Challenge of Direct Democracy*. Cambridge, MA: The Polity Press, 1996.

Council on Excellence in Government. 1997. *Findings of Research Project About Attitudes Toward Government*. Available from http://www.excel-gov.org/publication/poll97/hart.htm

Dalton, R. "Political Support in Advanced Industrial Democracies." In *Critical Citizens*, ed. P. Norris. Oxford: Oxford University Press, 1999.

Dalton. R. and B. Wattenberg. *Politics without Partisans*. Oxford: Oxford University Press, 2000.

Day, P. and R. Klein. *Accountabilities*. London: Tavistock, 1987.

Denmark. Ministry of Finance. *Borgerne og den offentlige sector.* Copenhagen: Finansministeriet, 1998.

Dershowitz, A.M. *Supreme Injustice: How the High Court Hijacked Election 2000*. New York: Oxford University Press, 2001.

Dogan, M. "Déficit de confiance dans les démocraties avancées." *Revue internationale de politique comparée*, Vol. 6 (1999): 510-547.

DOXA. *Alcuni Aspetti dell'Opinione Pubblica*. Milano: DOXA, March 3, 1996.

Etzioni, A. *The Spirit of Community*. New York: Crown Publishers, 1993.

Fearon, J.D. "Deliberation as Discussion." In *Deliberative Democracy*, ed. J. Elster. Cambridge: Cambridge University Press, 1998.

Fenno, R.F. *Home Style: House Members in their Districts*. Boston: Little, Brown, 1978.

Fishkin, J.S. *Democracy and Deliberation: New Directions for Democratic Reform*. New Haven: Yale University Press, 1991.

Foley, M. *Rise of the British Presidency*. Manchester: Manchester University Press, 1993.

Gallagher, M. and P. V. Uleri. *The Referendum Experience in Europe*. Basingstoke: Macmillan, 1996.

Gastil, J. *By Popular Demand: Revitalizing Representative Democracy through Deliberate Elections*. Berkeley: University of California Press, 2000.

Goodsell, C.T. *The Public Encounter: Where States and Citizens Meet*. Bloomington, IN: Indiana University Press, 1981.

Handler, J. *Down from Bureaucracy: The Ambiguity of Privatization and Empowerment*. Princeton, NJ: Princeton University Press, 1996.

Hasenfeld, Y., J.A. Rafferty and M.N. Zald. "The Welfare State, Citizenship and Bureaucratic Encounters." *Annual Review of Sociology*, Vol. 13 (1987): 387-415.

Hirst, P.Q. "Globalization and Governance: The Search for Democracy." Presented at the Triannual Conference of the International Political Science Association, Quebec City, 2000.

Hoff, J. "Medbergskap, brugerrolle og makt." In *Medbergsmakt*, ed. J. Andersen. København: Sistema, 1993.

Holmberg, S. and L. Weibull. *Opinions Samhallshället*. Gothenberg: SOM Institut, University of Gothenberg, 1998.

Hunold, C. "Public Deliberation and Democracy: Low-Level Radioactive Waste Disposal Facility Siting in Germany, Canada and the United States." PhD Dissertation, Department of Political Science, University of Pittsburgh, 1998.

Huntington, S.P. "Post-Industrial Politics: How Benign Will It Be?" *Comparative Politics*, Vol. 6 (1974): 163-192.

Kamarck, C. and J.S. Nye. *Governance.com*. Washington, DC: The Brookings Institution, 2002.

Kazin, M. *The Populist Persuasion: An American History*, rev. ed. Ithaca, NY: Cornell University Press, 1998.

Keiser, L.R. "State Bureaucratic Discretion and the Administration of Social Welfare Programs: The Case of Social Security Disability." *Journal of Public Administration Research and Theory*, Vol. 9 (1999): 87-106.

Kobach, K.W. *The Referendum: Direct Democracy in Switzerland.* Aldershot: Ashgate, 1993.

Lewis-Beck, M.S. *Economics and Elections: The Major Western Democracies.* Ann Arbor: University of Michigan Press, 1988.

Light, P.C. *Thickening Government.* Washington, DC: The Brookings Institution, 1996.

Lijphart, A. *Democracies: Patterns of Majoritarian and Consensus Governments*. New Haven: Yale University Press, 1984.

Linder, W. *Swiss Democracy*. New York: St. Martin's, 1994.

Majone, G. *Temporal Consistency and Policy Credibility: Why Democracies Need Non-Majoritarian Elements.* Florence: Robert Schuman Centre, European University Institute, 1996.

Mayhew, D.R. *Congress: The Electoral Connection*. New Haven: Yale University Press, 1974.

________ *Divided We Govern: Party Control, Lawmaking and Investigations, 1946–1990*. New Haven: Yale University Press, 1991.

Mendelsohn, M. and A. Parkin. "Introducing Direct Democracy in Canada." *Choices*, Vol. 7, no. 5 (2001): 3-35.

Moynihan, D.P. *Maximum Feasible Misunderstanding: Community Action in the War on Poverty*. New York: Free Press, 1969.

Nannestad, P. and M. Paldam. "Into Pandora's Box of Economic Evaluations: A Study of Danish Macro VP-Function." *Electoral Studies*, Vol. 19 (2000): 123-140.

Norris, P. *Critical Citizens: Global Support for Democratic Government*. Oxford: Oxford University Press, 1999.

Nye, J.S. *Why People Don't Trust Government.* Cambridge, MA: Harvard University Press, 1997.

Peters, B.G. "Presidentialism in Parliamentary Systems." In *Presidential Institutions and Democratic Politics*, ed. K. Von Mettenheim. Baltimore: Johns Hopkins University Press, 1997.

________ *The Future of Governing*, 2d. ed. Lawrence, KS: University Press of Kansas, 2001.

Peters, B.G. and D.J. Savoie. *Governance in a Changing Environment.* Montreal and Kingston: McGill-Queen's University Press, 1994.

________ *Governance in the 21st Century*. Montreal and Kingston: McGill-Queen's University Press, 2000.

Peters, B.G. and J. Pierre. *Politicization of the Civil Service: Myth or Reality, and Does it Matter?* forthcoming.

Pierre, J. and B.G. Peters. *Governance, the State and Public Policy*. Basingstoke: Palgrave, 2000.

Pollitt, C. and G. Bouckaert. *Public Management Reform*. Oxford: Oxford University Press, 2000.

Posner, R.A. *Breaking the Deadlock: The 2000 Election, the Constitution, and the Courts.* Princeton, NJ: Princeton University Press, 2001.

Putnam, R.D. *Making Democracy Work*. Princeton, NJ: Princeton University Press, 1993.

________ *Bowling Alone: The Collapse and Revival of American Community*. New York: Simon & Schuster, 2000.

Ranney, A. and W. Kendall. *Democracy and the American Party System*. New York: Harcourt Brace, 1956.

Rose, R. *The Problem of Party Government*. London: Macmillan, 1974.

Schattschneider, E.E. *The Semisovereign People*. New York: Holt, Rinehart and Winston, 1960.

Schmitt, H. and S. Holmberg. "Political Parties in Decline?" In *Citizens and the State*, ed. H.-D. Klingemann and D. Fuchs. Oxford: Oxford University Press, 1996.

Snellen, I. "Governance in an Information Society." In *Governance in the 21st Century*, ed. B.G. Peters and D.J. Savoie. Montreal and Kingston: McGill-Queen's University Press, 2000.

Sorenson, E. "Democracy and Empowerment." *Public Administration*, Vol. 75 (1997): 553-567.

Strange, S. *The Retreat of the State*. Cambridge: Cambridge University Press, 1996.

________ *Mad Money: When Markets Outgrow Governments*. Ann Arbor: University of Michigan Press, 1996.

Sunstein, C. *Republic.com*. Princeton, NJ: Princeton University Press, 2001.

United States. General Accounting Office. "Tax Administration: IRS is Improving its Controls for Ensuring that Taxpayers are Treated Properly." GAO/GGD-96-176. Washington, DC: USGAO, August 30, 1996.

Vander Weele, M. *Reclaiming Our Schools: The Battle Over Chicago School Reform*. Chicago: Loyola University Press, 1994.

Von Mettenheim, K. *Presidential Institutions and Democratic Politics*. Baltimore: Johns Hopkins University Press, 1997.

Democracy and Political Power in Contemporary Democracies: Some Reflections

THE STARTING POINT OF GUY PETERS' PAPER IS THE DROP OF PUBLIC CONFIDENCE THAT has taken place in many democracies. This is a most appropriate starting point. The rise of public cynicism is well supported by empirical evidence and seems to hold in most established democracies.[1] There may be disagreement about its exact meaning, its sources and consequences, but there is very little doubt that almost everywhere citizens have become more distrustful of politicians and politics.

The first question that comes to mind is whether people have become more cynical because democratic performance has declined. I would argue that this is *not* the case. There are good reasons to assume that governments and politicians are *not* systematically worse now than they were 30 or 40 years ago. There is no reason to believe, for instance, that politicians are more dishonest than they were in the 1960s or 1970s. The overall level of corruption has either remained stable or might even have diminished. To take another indicator, there is no evidence either that citizens have a narrower range of options to choose from than before. Differences between the parties have *not* eroded over time (see, in particular, Klingemann, Hofferbert and Budge 1994; Blais, Blake and Dion 1997). A recent study even indicates "a strengthening of the left-right partisan divide over total government spending" (Imbeau, Pétry and Lamari 2001, 24). In Canada, the emergence of two new parties—the Reform/Alliance and the Bloc Québécois—means that voters have a wider range of options than before.

Finally, political institutions have *not* become less "democratic" or responsive to the concerns of citizens. For instance, referenda remain relatively infrequent in most countries but they are more frequent than they used to be. In the same vein, most countries have kept the same electoral system and those that have changed have tended to adopt the "mixed" variety (Massicotte and Blais 1999).

This suggests that it is citizens themselves, not governments or parties, who have changed. People have become less and less willing to accept the shortcomings of representative democracy. Which shortcomings? Hibbing and Theiss-Morse (1995) have argued persuasively that most people do not appreciate that politics is in good part the art of finding a compromise between a plurality of competing and conflicting views about what should be done on a given issue. They note:

> People do not wish to see uncertainty, conflicting options, long debate, competing interests, confusion, bargaining, and compromised, imperfect solutions. They want government to do its job quietly and efficiently, sans conflict and sans fuss. In short, we submit, they often seek a patently unrealistic form of democracy … Like public opinion in so many other areas, the public wants it both ways. Not only do they want lower taxes and more services, they also want democracy and no mess (1995, 147-148).

My point, therefore, is that we should blame people, not politicians, for the drop of public confidence. I have no doubt that many politicians will privately agree with my diagnostics.[2]

This does not explain, however, why public confidence has been going down. It appears unlikely, in particular, that in the "golden days" people were more appreciative of the necessity and complexities of compromise. Why, then, is cynicism on the rise?

The first two factors to consider are education and secularization. The role of education is complex. On the one hand, the better educated tend to be less cynical than the less educated, probably because they are more informed and understand the necessity of compromise. On the other hand, education has another, contradictory effect, which is to make people more critically oriented. If I am right, the most distrustful citizens would be those who are very well-educated and do not follow politics at all. In short, even if, at the individual level, the better educated are more confident, at the aggregate level, public discontent may well flourish in societies with high levels of education.

The impact of secularization is more straightforward. More religious people tend to have greater respect for authority and that tends to make them less cynical in general.[3] The decline of religiosity is thus a logical source of the drop in public confidence. In that sense, I concur with my colleague Neil Nevitte: the declining confidence in government institutions is part of a larger paradigm, the decline of deference.

Nevitte (1996) indicates, however, that the decline in confidence in political institutions is sharper than that in non-political institutions. Why it is so remains to be explained. The usual suspect here is the media. The argument is that the media have become more and more negative in their coverage of politics (Patterson 1993) and that they have contributed to the decline in political confidence. Pippa Norris has tested the hypothesis at the individual level and she found, on the contrary, that "the attentive public exposed to the most news consistently displayed the most positive orientation towards the political system" (2000, 250). It could be that the impact of the media is, like that of education, a complex one. It is possible, for instance, that those who follow the news closely become less cynical (because they learn about the difficulty of compromise) but that those who do not follow closely become more distrustful.

It may be appropriate to add a caveat at this point. We know that cynicism is both widespread and rising. We do not really know, however, how deep or shallow that cynicism is. Public distrust may be less deep than we are inclined to assume. Consider some of the findings of the survey we did for the Lortie Commission. We found that a majority of Canadians believe that politicians do not care about the problems of ordinary citizens and are willing to lie to get re-elected. But the respondents were more nuanced when we forced them to think in comparative terms. A majority said that politicians are, on the whole, about as honest as the average citizen and that there is as much corruption in business as in government (Blais and Gidengil 1992).

It could be that it is in part because public discontent is not that deep that its consequences on political life are still relatively modest. From that perspective, I am struck by the fact that few politicians voluntarily depart from political office and that many are still attracted to the job. Either all these people are completely naïve or they sense that despite all the grumbling there is still some genuine respect for politics and politicians.

One possible reaction to these observations is that there is no reason to be too concerned with the drop in public confidence. The "problem" comes from the people who do not understand the complexity of politics and their discontent remains relatively shallow. This is *not* my position. The compelling evidence of widespread discontent should induce us to think through how to improve democratic performance.

Guy Peters is right on the mark when he notes that "the more fundamental complaint about contemporary democracies is that the institutions and elected representatives have become so remote from the public that no real popular choice of policy can be made." I would argue (with a qualifier to follow) that representatives are not more remote than they used to be. But representatives could be closer to their constituents, and we should try to make that connection as strong as possible.

The most obvious alternative to "conventional" democracy is direct democracy and this is where, appropriately so, Guy Peters starts. I was a little disappointed by that section of the paper. Peters does outline the potential problems of direct democracy, and his description is quite accurate. The paper fails to ascertain, however, how "serious" these problems really are. In my view, they are not as serious as they appear to be.

The standard objection to direct democracy is that the public may not be sufficiently informed to make the right choices on complex policy issues. In my view, the objection is only superficially valid. It is true that most voters are not well-informed and that many do not make the right choices in a referendum. In fact, this is one of the main conclusions of our analysis of the vote in the 1992 referendum on the Charlottetown Accord (Johnston, Blais, Gidengil and Nevitte 1996).

But so what? What we know about voter behaviour suggests that most of the time more voters get it right than wrong. It is possible for the electorate in any referendum to come to a decision that is not in the best interests of the majority. But the risk of a "wrong decision" is higher, it seems to me, if we leave the decision to the elected representatives. There is the risk that the representatives will not care about their constituents and there is also the risk that, even if they do care, they misread the public mood.

There is an additional, and in my view crucial, argument in favour of having some form of direct democracy. Governments behave differently when they know that those who are dissatisfied may be able to force a referendum on a particular issue. Governments pay more attention to public opinion when such a threat exists. The threat of direct democracy makes representative democracy work better, it strengthens the connection between the representatives and their constituents.

Referenda are also criticized for reducing difficult issues to simplistic dichotomous choices. It is true that at the end of the day a referendum is typically about saying "yes" or "no" to a given proposal. But that is true only at the end of the day. Usually, people or governments put forward proposals that they think have some chance of being approved and the final proposal is itself the outcome of long discussions and compromises. Furthermore, in the case of the abrogative initiative *à la italienne*, if the law is rejected by the electorate, new amendments can be considered and introduced by the legislature.

Another argument against referenda is that the better financed side may have an undue advantage. This is true. But the same applies to elections. I do not see why the bias should be more serious in a referendum than in an election. The regulation of contributions and spending in referenda is absolutely crucial, but so is it in elections.

Referenda are no panacea and there is no guarantee that they always produce the outcome that is in the interest of the majority of the electorate. But they keep politicians on their toes and they can prevent politicians from adopting policies that are strongly opposed by the population. Referenda should be used sparingly and they should be construed as safeguards for the enhancement of representative democracy. This is why the abrogative initiative, utilized in Italy, is particularly interesting. Through such initiatives, voters are allowed to veto a given legislation, but they are not able to impose one. The final decision about what to do is left with the representatives.

Another alternative to conventional democracy is participation on the output side. I find Peters' analysis of the merits and limits of that approach both lucid and compelling. This is a most interesting venue for enhancing citizen engagement, but co-management may well increase the power of those with verbal and organizational skills. In the end, the control of the more powerful elements of society may be enhanced. This is why, while we should encourage citizen involvement in making and implementing policy, the simple one person/one vote principle that underlies direct democracy is even more appealing.

Let me end this discussion by raising another issue that is not mentioned by Peters, and that may be an important source of the democratic malaise: the size of the political community. In a penetrating analysis, Oliver shows that civic engagement is much lower in larger cities. Oliver demonstrates that it is size per se that matters and not the rural or urban setting: "people in smaller rural places and in smaller suburban places are equally more likely to participate relative to people in large cities" (2000, 367). The reason is that as city size grows, people are less socially connected with their neighbours and less interested in local politics.

The size of political communities has increased over time and this may be yet another "cause" of declining public confidence. It is so much easier and tempting to believe that all politicians are corrupt and insensitive when we do not count any of them as friend or relative. From that perspective, the recent trend toward creating huge mega cities is cause for concern.

In short, we have strong evidence that public confidence has declined in many democracies but we should not infer that democratic performance itself has declined. The source of the problem is that people have become less willing to accept the messiness that necessarily characterizes representative democracy. This should be no excuse for not trying to improve the functioning of democracy. It seems to me that allowing some form of direct democracy may contribute to (slightly) alleviating public discontent.

Notes

1 In addition to the sources cited by Peters, see for Canada, Nevitte (1996, ch. 3) and Blais and Gidengil (1992, ch. 3).

2 All those who want to be re-elected cannot afford to publicly agree.

3 This relationship is surprisingly neglected in Nevitte (1996) and Norris (1999).

References

Berger, E. and S. Hug. "Legislative Response to Direct Legislation." In *Referendum Democracy: Citizens, Elites, and Deliberation in Referendum Campaigns*, ed. M. Mendelsohn and A. Parkin. London: Palgrave, forthcoming.

Blais, A., D. Blake and S. Dion. *Governments, Parties, and Public Sector Employees: Canada, United States, Britain, and France*. Pittsburgh, PA: University of Pittsburgh Press, 1997.

Blais, A. and E. Gidengil. *Representative Democracy: The Views of Canadians*. Ottawa: Royal Commission on Electoral Reform and Party Financing, 1992.

Hibbing, J. R. and E. Theiss-Morse. *Congress as Public Enemy*. Cambridge: Cambridge University Press, 1995.

Imbeau, L.M., F. Pétry and M. Lamari. "Left-Right Party Ideology and Government Policies: A Meta-Analysis." *European Journal of Political Research*, Vol. 40 (2001): 1-29.

Johnston, R., A. Blais, E. Gidengil and N. Nevitte. *The Challenge of Direct Democracy: The 1992 Canadian Referendum*. Montreal and Kingston: McGill-Queen's University Press, 1996.

Klingemann, H.-D., R.I. Hofferbert and I. Budge. *Parties, Policies, and Democracy*. Boulder: Westview Press, 1994.

Massicotte, L. and A. Blais. "Mixed Electoral Systems: A Conceptual and Empirical Survey." *Electoral Studies*, Vol. 18 (1999): 341-366.

Nevitte, N. *The Decline of Deference: Canadian Value Change in Cross-National Perspective*. Peterborough: Broadview Press, 1996.

Norris, P. *A Virtuous Circle: Political Communications in Postindustrial Societies*. Cambridge: Cambridge University Press, 2000.

Oliver, J.E. "City Size and Civic Involvement in Metropolitan America." *American Political Science Review*, Vol. 94 (2000): 361-373.

Patterson, T.E. *Out of Order*. New York: Knopff, 1993.

Discussion

THE FLOOR DISCUSSION TOOK UP THE ISSUE OF THE APPARENT GROWING LACK OF confidence in government. Participants, however, sought to clarify the issue further and to pinpoint where the lack of confidence was being felt the most. One argued that the loss of confidence was mostly with political elites: elected representatives, ministers and political parties. The argument was made that if one looks at the civil service, particularly front-line workers, one does not detect a loss of confidence and that Canadians appear to be happy with the level and quality of public service. Another pointed out that to get at the root cause of the problems, we need to separate out which sectors need fixing. There are considerable and obvious differences between school administration, for example, and monetary policy. In brief, not every aspect of government is hurting and one probably should concentrate only on fixing things that need fixing: political institutions.

Another participant argued that legislatures, in particular, need fixing if only because they have lost the capacity to hold the executive accountable. He did not, however, hold much hope that we would soon see reform measures. He noted that the countries that have reformed their legislatures are either those who were defeated in war (e.g., Germany) or experienced a revolution (e.g., Russia). However, the decline in the relative influence of the legislature has resulted in the increase in the power of the executive. This being the case, the executive has little interest in reforming political institutions because it would invariably attenuate its power.

A number of observers suggested that the adversarial nature of politics is making citizens uncomfortable. Question Period in the Canadian Parliament, one participant insisted, is not about sorting out the best policy, but rather it is a "stylized, ritualistic, cock fight that is a complete and utter waste of time." Perhaps, another participant suggested, the problem is that parliamentarians simply lack the resources to do a proper job and to hold the government to account for its decisions. The lack of resources to do a proper job and the lack of credibility in society may well mean that we are no longer able to attract quality people to run for political office. Another participant went to the heart of the issue by noting that "I would not want to be perceived to be a member of a class that is deemed to be corrupt and insensitive." Still, she added, there is no firm evidence to suggest that political parties are not able to attract strong candidates. In addition, few politicians seem to depart voluntarily.

The merit of e-democracy was debated with participants arguing both sides of the issue. Some argued that e-democracy holds a great deal of promise in involving more citizens in the democratic process. Governments will have no choice but to take into account "hits" on the Internet in shaping public policy. Others, however, insisted that the Internet and e-democracy are not without important constraints. We may only be using the Internet to tap messages to each other without engaging in any kind of discourse and to throw anything on a chat line without going through an editing or vetting process. We all tend to read the things that reinforce our own opinions and nowhere is this easier than on the Internet. The point here is that e-democracy may exacerbate the differences that already exist among us rather than serve to pull us together into a more democratic community.

Managing Interdependence in a Federal State

Managing Interdependence in a Federal Political System

Introduction

AS EMPHASIZED THROUGHOUT THIS VOLUME, GLOBALIZATION AND THE KNOWLedge/information revolution are dramatically changing relations both between and within countries (see also Courchene 2001). The world is becoming more and more interconnected. This is apparent whether we are considering integrated production facilities, environmental concerns, global warming, the Internet, AIDS, illicit drugs, foot-and-mouth disease in animals, pop music, or as driven home by the events of September 11, 2001, security against terrorism. Thus, within federations, this increasing interconnectedness relating to significant public policy issues has accentuated the degree of interdependence between governments and consequently, the measure of intergovernmental collaboration required.[1]

This paper, therefore, sets out to explore the increasing intergovernmental interdependence within contemporary federations generally and the implications for managing intergovernmental interdependence within the Canadian federation. The paper consists of three parts: the first outlines some conceptual issues, the second and major part reviews the degree and varied character of interdependence within contemporary federations generally, and the third attempts to draw out some implications for managing interdependence in the Canadian federation.

Interdependence in Federal Systems: Some Conceptual Issues

Dual versus interdependent federalism

THE TRADITIONAL CONCEPTUAL MYTHOLOGY HAS BEEN THAT THE CLASSICAL CONCEPT of federation was that of "dual federalism": one involving dual sovereignties—general and regional—existing side by side, each separate and virtually independent in its own sphere (Wheare 1963, 10, 14). From this view propounded by authors focusing primarily on the legal aspects of federal systems, such as A.V. Dicey, the Judicial Committee of the Privy Council in its judgements on Canadian cases and K.C. Wheare, a number of implications have generally been taken to follow (Dicey 1959, xxxii, 138-180; Cairns 1971; Wheare 1963). There must be an explicit constitutional demarcation of powers and functions between the general and regional governments; both orders of government must each be limited to their own sphere of action and must each be independent within their own spheres; the division of authority must be specified in the constitution so that neither order derives its authority from the other; and there must be an independent judiciary to interpret the supreme constitution and to act as guardian of the constitutional division of powers.

According to the traditional account, in the classical federations of the United States (1789), Switzerland (1848), Canada (1867) and Australia (1901), developments first in the 1930s and then following World War II led to the replacement of "dual federalism" by "cooperative federalism" (Clark 1938*a*, *b*; Benson 1941; Birch 1955, 304-306; Corry 1958). In these federations, the extension of nation-wide commercial enterprise, the development within each federation of an interdependent economy, and the growth of national sentiment, resulted, particularly under the pressures of the Great Depression and of war, in extensive intergovernmental cooperation and at least partial dependence of the governments of the federated units upon the federal governments. This trend to interdependence was described by J.A.Corry in 1958 in the following terms:

> It has arisen because several separate governments share a divided responsibility for regulating a single economic and social structure. It is most unlikely that any constitution could be devised which would enable each to perform its specific functions adequately without impinging on the others. So their activities

> are inevitably mingled and co-operative arrangements must be worked out. In the result, formal powers are not co-terminus with operating responsibilities; the two penetrate one another in many places and ways. Under the heat and pressure generated by social and economic change in the twentieth century, the distinct strata of the older federalism have begun to melt and flow into one another (Corry 1958, 121-122).

Thus, it became clear that the notion of "dual federalism," of separate general and regional governments acting, with only minor exceptions, in distinct watertight compartments each independent of the other, was outmoded. Interdependence and a variety of intergovernmental relations between the two orders of government in federations became the characteristic feature of federations (see, e.g., Wright 1982).

By the end of the twentieth century, interdependence in federations was increasingly coming to be seen as applying, furthermore, not just to the two orders of government within federations, but to their international relationships and the operation of local governments under the pressures of what Thomas Courchene has called "glocalization" (Courchene 1955).

The first writers to emphasize the interdependence of general and regional governments within federations and the need, therefore, for intergovernmental cooperation, usually considered this a mid-twentieth-century transformation, representing a radical departure from the traditional dualistic conception of federations during the nineteenth century. This misinterpretation arose from focusing upon the original legal structures rather than the actual political and administrative interactions between governments during the nineteenth century. Studies by such authors as M.J.C. Vile, Daniel Elazar and Morton Grodzins have suggested, however, that from the beginning, the traditional conception of federation as requiring a sharp demarcation of responsibilities between two independent sets of sovereignties had in the United States never worked in practice. In fact, in the nineteenth century, as in the twentieth century, administrative cooperation and political interdependence between federal and state governments was a dominant characteristic of the United States as a federal system, despite formal legal pronouncements to the contrary (Vile 1961, ch. x; Elazar 1962, ch. 1; Grodzins 1966). The fact that most federations, unlike Canada, have included in their constitutions extensive areas of concurrent jurisdiction, also pointed to their recognition from the outset of large areas of interdependence. Even in the case of Canada, Garth Stevenson, in his comprehensive account of federal-provincial relations in Canada during the period from Confederation to the formation of Wilfrid Laurier's government in 1896, has pointed out the extent of intergovernmental interdependence and interaction right from the beginning of the Canadian federation (Stevenson 1993, 301-320, also 177-207, 230-252). Particularly notable was the extensive federal-provincial cooperation in immigration and agriculture, two closely related areas of great political importance in the early years of the Canadian federation and both constitutionally areas of concurrent jurisdiction. Indeed, the first federal-provincial conferences were devoted to this subject: no less than six federal-provincial conferences were held between 1868 and 1874. During this period, too, the first shared-cost program was initiated in 1872 in support of immigration. These origins of cooperative intergovernmental relations were subsequently lost sight of due to the focus of scholars upon the legal pronouncements of the Judicial Committee of the Privy Council and its dualistic emphasis, but the fact remains that from the beginning the Canadian federation was characterized by intergovernmental interdependence.

The intensified "cooperative federalism" of the 1930s and post-World War II, apparent in all the classical federations, therefore, did not represent a radical modification to the essential nature of federations, but rather a sharp accentuation of the characteristics already implicit in the operation of all federal systems as forms of partnership. Three factors contributed to this intensification of interdependence within federations in the twentieth century. One was the general trend to increased activity of governments at all levels. This meant that typically in all federations the increased activities of both orders of government led to greater areas of overlap and interpenetration and hence the need to manage this intensified interdependence in order to minimize intergovernmental competition, friction and conflict. A second was the development of new policy areas not envisaged at the time their constitutions were drafted a century or more ago. Examples have been such fields as the environment and energy where complementary action by different orders of government proved necessary.[2] Third, in the area of financial arrangements within federations, interdependence was sharpened by the different considerations for allocation of taxing powers and expenditure responsibilities to different orders of government. These almost invariably created vertical and horizontal imbalances requiring intergovernmental transfers and processes and institutions for periodic adjustment of financial relations among governments (Watts 2000). Now, as federations move into the twenty-first century, the interdependence inherent in all federal systems is being further extended and complicated by its widened scope embracing even more both the international and local spheres.

Objectives and instruments for managing interdependence

Given, then, the inevitability of intergovernmental interdependence in federal systems, consideration needs to be given to the objectives and instruments for managing this interdependence. A primary consideration in organizing intergovernmental relations is to balance on the one hand the objectives and values of coordination with the value, on the other hand, of enabling autonomous provincial (state) or local action. The former aims at achieving common objectives and reducing unnecessary overlaps in jurisdiction. The latter aims at permitting policy innovation and differentiated responses to different economic, social, cultural and historical conditions in the federated units.

A particularly important objective is to ensure that a coordinated structure of intergovernmental relations does not undermine the democratic accountability of each order of government to its own electorate. One effect of the knowledge-based economy and information society has been to broadly extend the interrelation of different policy issues with each other. This means increased horizontal overlaps in virtually every policy area with both levels of government having a role to play (Courchene 2001, 267). But this horizontal interdependence conflicts with the vertical institutional provisions for governmental and democratic accountability. The institutions of democratic parliamentary government assure a vertical accountability of governments to their electorates directly for each of their specific areas of responsibility. Consequently, where interdependence makes necessary a wider range of shared programs, questions inevitably arise about how governmental accountability to the electorates for these is to be assured. An important objective in organizing intergovernmental relations, therefore, is to develop processes for ensuring adequate channels of accountability for the management of such programs. Otherwise, the political costs in the form of the public perception of democratic deficits may in the end outweigh the benefits of intergovernmental collaboration.

Another important objective is to avoid complexity and rigidity and to ensure as far as possible flexibility and adaptability. In considering objectives for intergovernmental relations, experience has shown that attempting to "eliminate" intergovernmental competition or conflict is not a realistic goal anywhere; a more realistic objective is to "manage" competition and conflict through processes encouraging cooperation. In this respect, institutions and processes for intergovernmental relations in contemporary federations serve two important functions: first, conflict avoidance and resolution and second, a means of adapting to changing circumstances without having to resort to formal constitutional amendments.[3] Consequently, the management of interdependence within federations has taken three general forms. One has been through the development of procedures and processes facilitating legislative, executive and financial relations between the different governments within a federation. Another has been through institutional arrangements for the representation of regional viewpoints or governments in the decision-making processes of the federal government itself, what in the 1980s came to be described in Canada as "intrastate federalism" (Smiley and Watts 1985). A third has been through reliance on the courts using judicial review to resolve disputes and interpret the constitution in changing circumstances.

Intergovernmental relations within federations have two important dimensions. There are vertical relations between governments of different orders: federal government and federated units (provinces), federated units (provinces) and local, and federal government and local. Increasingly such vertical relationships may also involve supra-federation organizations or other national governments. In the Canadian context, another developing level in multi-tiered governance relates to the self-governing arrangements for the First Nations as another order of government. The horizontal dimension relates to different governments within the same sphere, such as interprovincial or inter-local relations. Typically, in all areas of multi-sphere governance, both kinds of intergovernmental relations have been important. Within each of these, intergovernmental relations may involve all the governmental units within a federation, regional groupings of governments, or be bilateral (for example, a federal government and one province, or two provinces).

All complex, multi-level constitutional systems, including federations, have had to develop a variety of tools or forms of interaction between governments to coordinate the exercise of powers distributed among the various decision-making entities (Poirier 2001, 7; Painter 1998; Galligan *et al.* 1991; Wright 1982). Effective policy delivery frequently requires intergovernmental collaboration or coordination both in areas of concurrent jurisdiction or where legally exclusive jurisdictions are closely related.

Intergovernmental interaction occurs in a variety of ways: independent policy-making, consultation, coordination, joint decision-making, conflict resolution and formal agreements. Independent policy-making occurs where in matters affecting other governments, a government takes action without consulting other governments or considering their interests and those other governments are forced to adjust independently. Consultation represents a process whereby governments recognize that their actions affect other governments and therefore exchange views and information before acting, but ultimately the action of each government remains independent. Coordination occurs where governments not only consult but attempt to develop mutually acceptable common policies and objectives, which they then each apply and develop within their own jurisdictions. Joint decision-making requires the individual governments to work together, committing themselves to particular courses of action and standards of conduct. Shared-cost programs and matching legislation are examples of implementing joint decision-making. Conflict resolution is achieved by intergovernmental negotiation culminating in an agreement resolving the issue, by applying agreed-upon special conflict-resolution procedures, or by appeal to courts to adjudicate the despite. In most multi-order regimes each of these various types of intergovernmental interaction may be found, although the extent or predominance of each type of intergovernmental relationship has varied from federation to federation.

In terms of making intergovernmental relations effective, there are two important aspects: one is the establishment of *intergovernmental* structures and processes facilitating consultation, coordination, joint decision-making and conflict resolution among governments; the other is the development within each government of *intragovernmental* structures and processes enabling each government to coordinate its own relations with other governments so as to participate effectively in its interaction with other governments. As the extent and complexity of the former have increased, it has become imperative for greater effectiveness of the latter. Indeed ineffectiveness of the latter may seriously impede the former

With regard to the former, three important types of intergovernmental interaction, all of them important, can contribute to cooperation through consultation, coordination or joint action. The first of these is day-to-day informal contacts between ministers, officials or legislators in different governments. These contacts may be by letter, by telephone, or face-to-face, directed at exchanging views and information, sustaining relationships and implementing programs. Frequent informal communications can contribute to the development of the mutual trust and respect necessary for effective collaboration.

A second important channel is the establishment of both formal and informal councils, committees and conferences held frequently enough to enable representatives of the different governments—ministers, officials or legislators—to share information, discuss common problems, contemplate coordinated or even joint action and where appropriate establish joint bodies or agencies. In most multi-order polities such formal councils, committees, conferences and agencies are numerous.

A third mechanism for intergovernmental cooperation is the establishment of formal or informal intergovernmental agreements (Poirier 2001, 7-8). In their most formal manifestation they may take the form of legally binding treaties or "concordats" of which there are examples in Switzerland, Belgium, Spain and the United States, and following devolution the United Kingdom (Poirier 2001, 9-18). More often, however, they take the form of non-binding agreements, especially in Canada, Australia and Germany. These may relate to agreed processes for collaboration, agreed administrative arrangements or programs, or to the delegation from one government to another of executive and administrative responsibilities in a particular sector. As Johanne Poirier has noted, these agreements may fulfil one or more of five functions: substantive policy coordination, procedural cooperation, para-constitutional engineering, regulation by contract and quasi-legislation (Poirier 2001).

Interdependence in Contemporary Federations

The changing character of interdependence in federations

Toward the end of the twentieth century, as the old-style nation-state has increasingly struggled to maintain a place for itself in a world where the historic attributes of national sovereignty are being eroded by transnational and subnational political forces and economic pressures, there has resulted a seeming paradox of simultaneous global integration and regional fragmentation (Kincaid

1995; Laforest and Brown 1994). In such a context, more and more people have come to see some form of federalism, combining shared government for specified common purposes with autonomous action for purposes related to maintaining their regional distinctiveness, as providing the closest institutional approximation to the complex multinational reality of the contemporary world (Watts 1999*a*, 4; Kincaid 1995, 30; Elazar 1995; Courchene 2001, 259). Furthermore, in this context, both older and newer federations have had to come to terms with the changing scope and character of interdependence among governments.

As a consequence there have been significant developments, including a number of innovations, in the application of the federal idea in the contemporary world. Among these have been: the trend to multi-level forms of federal organization involving supra-federation organizations of a broadly confederal character and also formal recognition of the importance of local governments; extended, intensified and often formalized intergovernmental relations (although the degree of interdependence has varied from interlocking to arm's-length collaboration with differing impacts upon policy outcomes); the institutionalization of intrastate federalism; increased state (provincial) involvement in foreign relations; an increasing number of federal systems recognizing asymmetry among their federated units; and the development of hybrids combining elements of federal and unitary institutions and of federal and confederal institutions.

Multi-tiered interdependence

A notable feature in the contemporary world is the number of federations within wider federal organizations (Watts 1999*a*, 69-70). Worldwide and regional economic arrangements have become essential to the peace and prosperity of the world and in practice, states or federations have been unable to remain outside these intensifying economic networks which have acquired an increasingly confederal dimension (Elazar 1995). Thus, for example, Germany, Belgium and Austria as federations, and Spain, virtually a federation in all but name, are members of the broader European Union (EU), itself a hybrid which is predominantly confederal in character but has some of the characteristics of a federation. This has had implications for the internal relationships within its member states, which are themselves federations. Among the issues that have arisen has been the role of the federated units within each of these federations in negotiations with the institutions of the wider European Union. Federated units within the member federations have established offices at the European Union capital in Brussels and have obtained direct representation not only in the Committee of Regions but in other councils of the European Union. This has introduced a new dimension into their internal interdependence and an element of complexity into intergovernmental relations in these federations. The impact upon the internal intergovernmental balance within each federation of the transfer of certain powers to Brussels has also become a contentious issue, most notably in Germany where it led to an important case before the German Constitutional Court.[4] Indeed, Germany has been a pioneer both in terms of ensuring participation of the Länder in decisions within Germany concerning its relations with the EU, and in securing institutionalized participation of the Länder within the institutions of the EU itself. It should also be noted that a factor in the resistance within Switzerland to joining the EU has been concern about the possible impact upon the character of the Swiss federation. Other illustrations of federations in wider supra-federal organizations are the membership of Canada, the United States and Mexico, all three themselves federations, within the North American Free Trade Area (NAFTA), Malaysia in the Association of Southeast Asian Nations (ASEAN), India and Pakistan in the South Asian Association for Regional Co-operation (SAARC), and St. Kitts-Nevis within the Caribbean Common Market (CARICOM). In each of these cases membership in the wider organization, especially where that has taken on a confederal character, has had implications for the internal relations and balance within the member federations. Thus, increasingly in the contemporary world federal interdependencies have taken on a multi-tiered character creating a more complicated context for the operation of individual federations participating in these wider organizations.

The multi-tiered character of contemporary federal systems has also been extended by the increased attention given to the role of local governments. Traditionally, federations were viewed as two-tier systems with the determination of the scope and powers of local government left to the state or provincial governments. Within such a context, the importance and autonomy of the tier of local government has in practice varied enormously, being perhaps most prominent in Switzerland and the United States and least in Australia. In some federations intergovernmental relations (including financial transfers) directly between federal and local governments have been considerable, whereas in others, including Canada, such relations have been funnelled through the provinces or states as intermediaries. But recently in a number of federations, the importance of local governments as a distinct tier within the federation has received greater emphasis. Consequently, the new constitutions of South Africa (1996) and of Switzerland (1999) formally recognize the position and powers of local governments. Indeed, the South African constitution in article 40 (1) declares that "In the Republic, government is constituted as national, provincial and local spheres of government which are distinctive, interdependent and interrelated," and chapter 3 lays out the principles of cooperative government and intergovernmental relations applying to the three spheres of government.[5] Some older federations, notably Germany and India also now recognize formally in their constitutions the position and powers of local governments.[6] One particular aspect of the growing importance of local governments within federations has been the recognition that globalization has brought large metropolitan cities to the fore as dynamic motors of the information economy (see, e.g., Courchene 2001, 31-34, 276-284). This development has important implications for their relative role in the operation of federal systems. A significant illustration of the importance of both the supra-federal and local government dimensions in managing interdependence within federations is the Council of Australian Governments (COAG) established in 1992 to improve intergovernmental collaboration on economic development policies. COAG not only includes representation for the Australian Local Government Association, but for some of the ministerial councils that it oversees, including representatives of New Zealand and of the Australian Local Government Association (COAG 2001). It would appear that Pennock's advocacy of the effectiveness of multi-tiered governance is increasingly coming to be recognized in practice (Pennock 1959).

Intergovernmental relations

Given the inevitable interdependence between the orders of government in a federation in which neither order of government is subordinate or derives its powers from the other but rather from the constitution and acts directly in relation to its own electorate, intergovernmental relations have been an essential feature in the effective operation of all federations. An examination of contemporary federations makes it clear that extensive intergovernmental relations are a pervasive feature of federations, although the form they have taken has varied. Indeed, one might conclude, as Alen and Ergec writing about the Belgian federation do, that a distribution of jurisdiction ensuring federated units autonomy, the formal participation of representatives of the federated units in the institutions of federal government, and intergovernmental relations and cooperation constitute the *three* fundamental requirements for an effective federation (Alen and Ergec 1998, 29-30). Most federations have used extensively all three forms of intergovernmental interaction referred to in the first section of this paper: informal contacts, formal and informal councils and committees, and formal and informal intergovernmental agreements. Thus, as most students of federalism have accepted as common place since Carl Friedrich first made the point in 1968, focus upon process, rather than simply state structures, is essential to understanding federal systems, in view of the interdependence inherent in them (Friedrich 1968; also Bastien 1981, 48).

There have been significant variations, however, in the extent and character of these intergovernmental relationships. First, in some federations at least some of the procedures and processes governing intergovernmental relations have been formally set out in the constitution, while in others these have been left to be established pragmatically. Germany, Switzerland, South Africa and India provide examples of the former. In the case of Germany, the Bundesrat, which operates as a federal second chamber composed of delegates from the Land executives, has, through its committees, provided numerous channels for intergovernmental negotiations. Thus, apart from serving as a legislative chamber, the Bundesrat has become the focal point for a complex web of intergovernmental deliberations and agreements. At the same time it should be noted that in addition to the Bundesrat and its committees there has been added a vast network of ministerial and official councils and committees going well beyond what is specified in the constitution. The new Swiss constitution (1999) not only contains a section (articles 44-49) specifying the principles for collaboration between the federal and cantonal governments, but at many points in the distribution powers identifies areas in which federal-cantonal collaboration will be required.[7] The South African constitution (1996) devotes a chapter to the principles of cooperative government and intergovernmental relations (articles 40 and 41), and in addition has many references elsewhere to specific intergovernmental relations. The Indian constitution (1950) made provision for an Inter-State Council (article 263) and for periodic finance commissions, but in addition, India has established a large number of extra-constitutional bodies and processes affecting intergovernmental relations, including the Planning Commission, a National Development Council, Zonal Councils, the

National Integration Council, the Central Council of Health, the River Boards, the Inter-State Transportation Commission and a number of other intergovernmental councils of varying effectiveness. While most of the extensive intergovernmental institutions and processes in Australia have been established extra-constitutionally, the Loan Council, an intergovernmental body with its own voting rule that makes binding decisions on the level of public borrowing by both orders of government, was established by a formal constitutional amendment in 1927. In some federations, the constitution makes no provision for formal intergovernmental bodies or processes, but does set out the procedures or limits for formal intergovernmental agreements or concordats, examples being the United States and Belgium. In the latter case the need for these was imposed by the process of incremental devolution of powers creating the need for some continuity of service, particularly in relation to welfare services (Poirier 2001, 10-11).

In a number of federations the constitution contains few or no formal provisions governing intergovernmental relations, but nevertheless intergovernmental interdependence has given rise to a wide range of intergovernmental institutions and processes to facilitate collaboration. In such instances the development has been largely of a pragmatic and ad hoc nature, as in the United States and Canada. On the other hand, Australia has been something of a pioneer in formalizing and coordinating these extra-constitutional intergovernmental relations, as illustrated by the role played by the Premier's Conference, the Commonwealth Grants Commission and more recently the Council of Australian Governments established in 1992 and the efforts of the latter in 2001 to rationalize the ministerial councils under its oversight (COAG 2001).

The impact of parliamentary and non-parliamentary institutions upon intergovernmental relations

A major variable affecting both the character of relations between governments within federations and the internal coordination within each government of its relations with other governments, has been whether the governments in a federation have been organized on the principle of the separation of powers, as in the presidential/congressional institutions of the United States and the Latin American federations and in the Swiss collegial form of executive, or have involved the fusion of legislative and executive powers in the responsible parliamentary Cabinet systems as in Canada, Australia, Germany, India, Belgium and

Spain. Where there are parliamentary executives, because of their dominance in their legislatures, there has been a common tendency for these executive bodies in turn to dominate intergovernmental relations, creating a situation often described in these federations as "executive federalism" (Watts 1989, 8-9). Australia, Germany, India, Spain and Belgium have provided typical examples. In these federations there has also been a common tendency for matters relating to intergovernmental relations to be placed within each participating government under the coordination or control of a special staff agency or with specialists exclusively concerned with intergovernmental affairs (Watts 1989, 10-11). This has contrasted with the dispersed pattern within non-parliamentary federations. Intergovernmental relations in the United States and Switzerland, for example, have been expressed through a variety of uncoordinated vertical and diagonal relationships between the many dispersed distinct centres of political decision-making within each level of government. Furthermore, the national legislatures in these federations, where typically party discipline has been relatively weak and the second chambers relatively stronger, have played a more prominent role in resolving intergovernmental issues through establishing a variety of programs supported by grants-in-aid or subventions that are administered by state or cantonal officials. The resulting dispersed administrative and political interlacing and interpenetrating of governmental activities led Morton Grodzins to employ the image of "marble cake" federalism to describe the United States in contrast with the characteristically "layer cake" character of federalism in parliamentary federations (Grodzins 1966).

The impact upon intergovernmental relations of the form of the constitutional distribution of jurisdiction

Another variable affecting the character of interdependence and hence the scope and nature of intergovernmental relations is the form of the constitutional distributions of jurisdiction. By contrast with those federations where the legislative and executive jurisdiction of each government largely correspond, as in the United States, Canada (except the administration of criminal law) and Australia, some federal constitutions, particularly European ones such as Switzerland, Germany and Austria, prescribe large areas where the administration of federal law is constitutionally assigned to the governments of the constituent units. In these federations the extent of interdependence is magnified. This has required even closer intergovernmental collaboration in these areas of split legislative-administrative jurisdiction. Also, where the constitution establishes extensive areas of concurrent jurisdiction, as in the United States, Australia, Germany, India and Malaysia, even where there is federal paramountcy there have tended to be more areas of interdependency. A noteworthy form of concurrent jurisdiction is in Germany where the constitution ascribes authority to the federal government for "framework legislation" in certain fields but specifically leaves legislative responsibility in these fields in the hands of the Länder. Nevertheless, even those federations such as Canada and Belgium, where the constitutions have emphasized the exclusive jurisdiction of each order of government, have found that in practice overlapping responsibilities are unavoidable and intergovernmental collaboration is necessary (Alen and Ergec 1998, 29-30).

In addition to establishing areas of concurrent jurisdiction there have been a number of devices used in the constitutional distribution of authority within federations to enable governments to handle interdependence. These include, in many cases, specific arrangements permitting bilateral transfers of powers. In some, Canada being a notable example, provisions for provinces or states to "opt out" of programs have provided added flexibility. An important instrument in many federations has been the provision of a federal spending power in expenditure areas beyond those specifically assigned by the constitution to the federal government, although the extent to which state or provincial consent for the use of this power is required has varied (Watts 1999*b*). Another device for facilitating what Richard Zuker has referred to as the need for "reciprocal federalism" (i.e., complementary state [provincial] and federation action) as a response to unavoidable interdependence has been the use of formal intergovernmental agreements (Zuker 1995). There have been variations in the extent to which formal intergovernmental agreements have been employed and the degree to which they are binding (Poirier 2001, 7-18). Intergovernmental agreements have played a key role in the functioning of most federations, although there is variation in the degree to which these are binding. Many such agreements in Spain, Belgium, Switzerland and the United States are binding, whereas in Canada, Australia and Germany most are not. The degree to which they are binding or not has had some effect on the degree of intergovernmental trust. In either form, however, most agreements have played similar functions. A major purpose of such agreements has been to achieve substantive policy coordination in areas of overlap and to provide redistributive financing schemes.

Some agreements provide general operating principles and others define responsibilities for very specific projects. Some establish interjurisdictional agencies. Their general purpose has been "to rationalize the exercise of distinct but related competencies, avoid duplication and coordinate policy initiatives" (Poirier 2001, 10). Agreements have also been used to outline procedural mechanisms for cooperation. Examples would be the establishment of COAG in Australia, and in the case of Canada, the Canadian Interprovincial Agreement on Internal Trade and the Social Union Framework Agreement (SUFA). Agreements have also been used to adapt the distribution of jurisdiction among governments without formally amending the constitution, to regulate contractually governments of the federated units to provide certain services in return for federal provision of resources, and to provide "soft law" norms for the activities of civil servants at both levels (Poirier 2001, 12-18). A notably successful Canadian example has been the use of agreements to harmonize the collection of personal income taxes (Courchene 2001, 261-262).

The range from interlocking to arm's-length intergovernmental relations

Broadly speaking, intergovernmental relations in federations may be classified as falling within a range between two distinct patterns. On the one hand, there are "interlocking relations" and on the other "arm's-length relations" (Wachendorfer-Schmidt 2000, 6-9, 247-248; Kincaid 1991). The former, typified by Germany and Austria, involve a high degree of joint decision-making. The latter, typified by the United States, may involve a considerable amount of cooperation, but emphasizes the autonomous decision-making of the constituent governments. In between these extremes are systems that might be described as having "collaborative relations" involving a more voluntary form of cooperation than in the former and higher degree of intergovernmental collaboration than in the latter. Switzerland and Australia provide differing examples.

Each of these different models of intergovernmental interdependence has its strengths and weaknesses. The interlocking model, as exemplified by Germany has ensured a high level of intergovernmental collaboration in virtually every field. But it has been criticized by Scharpf because the requirement of joint decisions in so many areas has reduced the autonomy and freedom of action of governments at both levels. This has stultified governmental decision-making, leading to inflexibility and underperformance (Scharpf 1988). Wachendorfer-Schmidt, on the other hand, has argued that in fact these problems in practice have been largely overcome and that

German interlocking federalism has been more flexible than it has been credited with being by its critics (2000, 8-9, 81-111, 247). Nevertheless, it is noteworthy that there have recently been strong calls for disentanglement to loosen up the interlocking character of German intergovernmental relations (see Bertelsmann Commission on Governance and Constitutional Policy 2000).

Arm's-length intergovernmental relations have the benefit of retaining the autonomy and freedom of action of governments at both levels, thereby ensuring opportunities for innovation and flexibility, and the benefits of governments competing to provide citizens with better service (Kincaid 1991; Breton 1985). This intergovernmental competition may be either vertical, that is, federal versus states (provinces), or horizontal, that is, among states (provinces). In the case of the latter the competing governments are appealing to different electorates and so the competition is mainly in terms of comparative performance or the laboratory effect of demonstrating how alternative or innovative policies may benefit citizens. In the case of the former, however, the appeal is to the same electorate, but among governments serving these citizens in different or overlapping policy areas for which they are responsible. As a result of this effort to show that they are serving the same citizens better than the other level of government, not infrequently the competition deteriorates into a turf war over which government should be responsible for policy or financing in a particular field of shared jurisdiction, or which should be blamed for problems. Thus, "competitive federalism" to excess may lead to intergovernmental conflict and acrimony, and undermine the spirit of trust necessary for cooperation between governments. Significantly, Switzerland and Australia provide two different examples of "collaborative relations" between the extremes of interlocking and arm's-length relations. Klaus Armingeon, for instance, has argued that the Swiss federation has been a success story because it avoids the tight coupling found in Germany, but has also avoided the interjurisdictional competition of the United States by developing a collaborative solidarity among the constituent governments (Armingeon 2000). In the case of Australia, Martin Painter's analysis of intergovernmental relations points to a highly developed intergovernmental collaboration, but because these processes are embedded in a constitutionally arm's-length structure, collaboration has avoided the rigidities and deficiencies associated with the German example (Painter 2000). What these various examples indicate is that different patterns of intergovernmental relations are significant in generating different policy outcomes.

managing interdependence in a federal state

Intrastate federalism

The label "intrastate federalism" adapted from Karl Lowenstein by Donald Smiley became fashionable in Canada in the 1980s (Lowenstein 1965, 405; Smiley and Watts 1985). Although that label is little used outside Canada, the principle that interdependence between the orders of government in a federation requires adequate formal representation of the governments, or at least the concerns and interests, of the federated units within the institutions of the federal government has been widely recognized. Indeed, Preston King (1982) has even suggested that this, not the division of jurisdiction, is the defining characteristic of federations. A more balanced interpretation would be to say that two of the essential aspects in the constitutional design of effective federations have been the constitutional distribution of jurisdiction between coordinate orders of government (i.e., neither order being constitutionally subordinate) and the "participation" (the term favoured over intrastate federalism in the European literature on federalism) of representatives of the federated units as such within the federal government institutions.

Intrastate federalism is deliberately defined broadly here. It refers to the adequate formal representation of the federated units within the institutions of the federal government. In one form it may be expressed in a federal second chamber or council, as exemplified by the German Bundesrat, in which the governments of the federated units are themselves directly represented. The German experience suggests that where the governments of the federated units have participated in setting federal policy, they are more likely to be cooperative in its implementation. At the same time, this may result in reduced freedom of action for the participating governments. Alternative forms of intrastate federalism aim at representing within the federal institutions the different regional concerns of the provincial legislatures or the provincial citizens, rather than of governments. Among such examples are the indirectly or directly elected federal second chambers found in a considerable number of federations. Thus, the notion of intrastate federalism, broadly conceived, raises the issue of which interests are to be represented within the federal institutions, and which are likely to sensitize federal policy-making most effectively to particular regional concerns.

The most highly developed example of intrastate federalism is Germany, where the Bundesrat, the federal second chamber composed of instructed delegates of the Land governments, has an absolute veto on federal legislation affecting the Länder (in practice about 60 percent of all federal legislation because so much federal law is administered by the Länder) and a suspensive veto on all other federal legislation. While decisions in the Bundesrat are shaped by party alliances, the variety of coalition governments in the different Länder has meant that particular Land viewpoints have had a strong impact upon the development of federal policies. Indeed, it could be said of the German federation that *intrastate* federalism has largely prevailed over *interstate* federalism, and this has contributed to the interlocking character of the relations between governments within the German federation.

While in no other federation has intrastate federalism prevailed over interstate federalism to the degree that it has in Germany, intrastate federalism has been an important element in the design and operation of most federations (Smiley and Watts 1985, ch. 4; Watts 1999, 83-95). In the United States, the Connecticut Compromise at the Philadelphia Convention, which established a bicameral Congress with an indirectly elected Senate with equal representation of the states, played a key part in the agreement to convert the American confederation into a federation. While the Senate later became a directly elected body and over time more national in its outlook on issues, it still continues to be an important body for expressing state interests in Congress. Contemporary federations with federal second chambers indirectly elected by the state legislatures include Austria and India. Those with directly elected senates include Australia and Switzerland. Some have a mixture of methods of selection. Most require some weighting of representation favouring the smaller federated units (e.g., Germany, India, Austria and Malaysia) and a few go so far as to provide equality of state representation (e.g., United States and Australia). One significant feature is that in non-parliamentary federations the federal second chambers, ostensibly representing the interests of the federated units, have had equal or even additional special powers by comparison with the popularly elected legislative chamber. In parliamentary federations, on the other hand, with the exception of the unique German Bundesrat, the federal second chambers have been relatively weaker because their Cabinets have been responsible to the popularly elected legislative house.

A further point to note is that in addition to federal second chambers, the desirability of intrastate federalism and regional balance in composition has also been a major factor in the composition of the federal executives, the federal public services and federal agencies. Indeed, the Swiss constitution of 1999 (article 175) goes so far as to include in the constitution a provision that there shall be no more than one member from the same canton in the seven-person Federal Council (i.e., federal executive).

The conduct of foreign relations

A marked feature of recent development in federations has been the much increased involvement of the governments of the federated units in the area of foreign relations. Traditionally, foreign relations and treaty-making were regarded in federations largely as an area of exclusive federal government responsibility. But growing international interdependence in the economic, environmental and cultural areas has meant that foreign relations have more and more impinged on matters within the responsibilities of the federated units. As already noted above, this has occurred where federations have become members of supra-federal organizations. But in addition, the interests of federated units in their own economic development and environmental situations generally along with the intensification of cross-border relations with neighbouring states have contributed to this trend. Among the older federations, such as the United States and Australia, states and even major cities have established many missions abroad. In the Australian case, furthermore, as already noted above, some of the Commonwealth-state interministerial councils have included participation by New Zealand representatives. Furthermore, in the newer federal constitutions such as that of Belgium (1993) and Switzerland (1999) specific provisions have been included setting out the role, including a treaty-making power, for federated units to operate in the realm of international affairs (in areas under their jurisdiction) in consultation with the federal government, and to participate in the processes of foreign policy-making by the federal government.[8] It would appear that involvement of the federated units both in the establishment of federal foreign policy and through their own international relationships is increasingly the norm in federations rather than an exception.

Asymmetry

Another contemporary trend has been an increasing acceptance of asymmetry in the relationship of member units to federations or to supranational organizations as a means of facilitating the management of interdependence with federated units that have different intensities in their insistence upon autonomy (Agranoff 1999; see also Watts 1999*a*, 63-68). One example is the asymmetry among the autonomous communities of Spain. Others are the relationships of the different federated units within Belgium, India and Malaysia, and the extra-constitutional policies relating to the eastern Länder in Germany. Perhaps the most complex current example of asymmetry in practice is displayed by the majority of the 89 subjects of the Russian federation which, despite the formal symmetry prescribed by the Russian constitution, have negotiated with the federal government special treaties relating to their powers. Other significant examples have been the European Union, which has taken significant steps toward becoming a union of "variable speeds" and "variable geometry," and the pattern of asymmetrical devolution within the United Kingdom.

The fact that in Spain, Russia and Canada pressures for asymmetry have induced counter-pressures for symmetry suggests that there may be limits to asymmetry beyond which, in extreme form, asymmetry may become dysfunctional. Nevertheless, in a number of federations, of supranational confederations, and of devolution within unions, it appears that a considerable degree of constitutional asymmetry has provided an effective way of managing interdependence among constituent units with major differences among them.

Hybrid political systems

Another recent trend arising from efforts to manage interdependence has been the development of hybrid political structures combining characteristics of different kinds of political systems (Watts 1999*a*, 9). These have occurred because statesmen are often more interested in pragmatic solutions than in theoretical purity. One group of examples is provided by constitutions that are predominantly federal in their legal framework and operation but have some overriding federal government powers more typical of a unitary system. Examples include India, Malaysia and South Africa. These are sometimes described as "quasi-federal," as was the original Canadian constitution of 1867 with its provisions for reservation and disallowance of provincial laws and the public works power. Another form of hybrid is provided by Germany which, while predominantly a federation, has a confederal element in the Bundesrat, the federal chamber composed of instructed delegates of the Land governments.

Yet a third form is provided by the post-Maastricht European Union. This combines in an interesting way features of a confederation and of a federation. Among the confederal features are the intergovernmental character of the Council of Ministers, the distribution of commissioners among the constituent nation-states and the role of the latter in nominating commissioners, the almost total reliance upon the constituent national governments for the implementation and administration of EU law, and the derivation of EU citizenship from citizenship in a member state. Among the elements more typical of a federation, on the other hand, are the role of the Commission in proposing legislation, the use of qualified majorities rather than unanimity for many categories of legislative decision-making by the Council of Ministers, the role of the Council's secretariat in developing more cohesive policy consideration than is typical of most international or traditional confederal intergovernmental bodies, the expanding co-decision role of the European Parliament with a veto power now over something like half of the EU's legislation, the supremacy of Union law over the law of the member states, and the role of the Court of Justice whose decisions are binding on all member states (Lodge 1993; Nugent 1991, 382-408). The net effect is that, while member states, in the interests of managing their interdependence, have "pooled" their sovereignty and have accepted increasing limitations on their power of independent decision-making (to a degree considerably greater than in some federations), the common legislative and executive institutions still lack the characteristics of a federation in which the federal institutions clearly have their own direct electoral and fiscal base. Not surprisingly, the resulting technocratic emphasis and "democratic deficit" have undermined public consent and support for the European Union. This provides a warning to federations which, in the effort to manage interdependence, may develop the processes of intergovernmental relations to the point where they undermine the democratic transparency, accountability and legitimacy of the processes in the eyes of their electorates.

Implications for Managing Interdependence in Canada

The thrust of this paper has been to focus upon the management of interdependence in a variety of contemporary federal systems in terms of the lessons that they may provide for the Canadian federation. It is clear that the beginning of the twenty-first century is a time of great fluidity in the theory and practice of federal political systems. As they are responding to the challenges of a widening interdependence at all levels there is a growing diversity of processes, mechanisms and innovations that they have been employing to respond. There is no single ideal model of the federal idea applicable everywhere.

There have been many variations in the application of the federal principle to the management of interdependence. Examples are variations among federations in the number and size of their constituent units, in the form and scope of the distribution of legislative and executive powers and financial resources, in the degree of centralization or non-centralization and degree of economic integration, in the character and composition of their federal government institutions, in the processes and mechanisms for facilitating intergovernmental relations, in the structure and role of their courts, and in the emphasis upon individual and collective rights. Ultimately, federalism is a pragmatic, prudential technique, whose effectiveness may well depend upon whether the particular form is adapted to the particular conditions and circumstances of the society in question. Furthermore, effectiveness may even depend upon the development of innovations in the application of the federal idea. Nevertheless, federal experience elsewhere does provide an impressive range of examples and options upon which Canadians may draw in addressing the challenges being faced by all contemporary federations (Watts 1999*a*, 1-2, 120-121; Saunders 1995). Moreover, many of the lessons from these examples can be applied without comprehensive formal constitutional amendment, through pragmatic political adaptation (Watts 1999*a*, 122-123).

As noted in the introduction, there has been considerable interdependence within the Canadian federation from the beginning and this was much accentuated in the latter part of the twentieth century. Furthermore, in the past decade the almost total dominance of north-south trading patterns has not only increased the interdependence between Canada and the United States but has further reinforced the need for interrelated federal and provincial policies. Nevertheless, in comparative terms, on the spectrum of federations ranging from interlocking intergovernmental relations to arm's-length relations, Canada comes close to the extreme of arm's-length relations. To some extent the constitutional structure has contributed to this. The constitutional distribution of legislative and executive jurisdiction emphasizes the exclusive jurisdiction of each order of government and provides fewer areas of concurrent jurisdiction than almost any other federation. Furthermore, while the unavoidable interdependence between orders of government was recognized in 1867 by the inclusion of some unilateral quasi-federal imperial powers assigned to the federal government, most of these, by convention, have now fallen into disuse. Moreover, among contemporary federations the constitutional provisions in Canada for intrastate federalism are particularly weak, given the lack of legitimacy of the appointed Senate, the increasing dominance of the Prime Minister's Office in relation to the Cabinet and Parliament, and the rigidity of party discipline within the governing parties, not to mention an electoral system that has undermined the ability of federal governments to be representative of the federation as a whole. In addition, there have been frequent appeals, especially from the larger and wealthier provinces, for less interdependence and for "disentanglement" to enable them to carry out their responsibilities with more independence, although even they have generally come to recognize that there are limits to the possibility of such independence (Courchene 2001, 256-260, 266-268). Thus, in comparative terms Canada has been less well-equipped to manage the contemporary challenges of interdependence than most other federations.

Nevertheless, it must be recognized that in practice a considerable degree of interdependence has evolved within the Canadian federation. David Cameron and Richard Simeon have analyzed recent trends in Canadian intergovernmental relations evolving through several phases. There was the cooperative federalism of the 1950s and 1960s focused on the construction of the Canadian welfare state. Then there was the competitive federalism of the 1970s and 1980s arising from the impact of Quebec nationalism, western regionalism and Trudeau's new National Policy upon constitutional negotiations. This was followed by the accentuation of competitive federalism in the 1990s as a result of the unilateral federal cutbacks in transfers to the provinces in order to reduce the federal deficit. Recently, there has been the emergence of collaborative federalism characterized by the principle of co-determination of broad national policies (Cameron and Simeon 2001). They point out that many of the issues unsuccessfully dealt with in the constitutional debates over the Meech Lake Accord and the Charlottetown Agreement have re-emerged in the intergovernmental arena: the economic union, the social union, "who does what" in terms of jurisdiction and the spending power. But now, instead of being expressed in the uncompromising language of constitutional clauses, they are being expressed as intergovernmental "accords," "declarations" and "framework agreements." They cite the examples of: the Agreement on Internal Trade (AIT), 1994; the Calgary Declaration, 1996 and the Social Union Framework Agreement (SUFA), 1999. Not only have these been the result of provincial initiatives and interprovincial negotiations, but although negotiated behind closed doors in processes with very low public profile, they have included considerable emphasis in the latter cases upon accountability, transparency, the necessity of securing the ongoing input and feedback from citizens and other interested parties (Ibid.).

Collaborative federalism would appear to provide a response to the challenges of interdependence that recognizes a fundamentally federal relationship: collaboration between the orders of government as partners, neither subordinate to nor dominated by the other. On the part of most of the provinces, the pressure for collaborative federalism has represented an acknowledgement of the reality of interdependence in a range of policy areas. At the same time it shows a desire to see that interdependence is managed on the basis of partnership or equality. This contrasts with the earlier periods of cooperative federalism based on federal government unilateralism. Collaborative federalism is viewed now as more appropriate when provincial governments are fiscally more autonomous and command greater policy expertise than they did four decades ago (Lazar 2000, 34). It also appeals to the notion that the essence of the federal idea is that neither order of government should be subordinate to the other (Watts 1999*a*, 6-7). In this respect it represents a middle way between the extremes of interlocking relations and arm's-length competitive relations between governments within the federation. It is too early to judge yet whether collaborative federalism is merely rhetoric or reality and whether it will in the longer term take root in Canada (Lazar 2000, 34). There is still a tendency for federal government ministers and officials to regard themselves as "senior partners," and there are concerns that with the return of federal surpluses the federal government may revert to the unilateral initiation of programs. A noticeable feature of the Chrétien regime has been the avoidance as much as possible of First Ministers' Conferences (FMCs). This contrasts with the recent revival in Australia of COAG as a body overseeing and rationalizing interministerial councils and meetings noted earlier in this paper. Ironically, the resulting decline in the frequency and significance of FMCs in Canada has given a new prominence to the role and impact of the provincial premiers acting together at the Annual Premiers' Conference. Intergovernmental meetings at the level of ministers and deputy ministers have declined from the Mulroney years when they reached peaks of 130 in 1985–86 and 127 in 1992–93, and never dropped below 82 per year; nevertheless their frequency remains significant at 70 in 1997–98 and 98 in 1998 (Cameron and Simeon 2001; CICS 1998). In 1997–98, 60 percent of these meetings involved federal, provincial and territorial governments and 40 percent provinces and territories without the federal government. Most commonly, the subjects considered have been social policy, the environment, health, economic policy and education: all policy areas of major public concern.

A number of other recent trends in Canadian intergovernmental relations are worth noting. First, despite the concerns raised during the debates over the Meech Lake Accord about recognition of Quebec's distinct status, collaborative federalism as it has evolved in the 1990s has in practice recognized and increased the degree of *de facto* asymmetry within the federation. Quebec's representatives, although participating in the meetings, have dissociated themselves from many of the resulting agreements on the grounds that fields like education, welfare and health are areas of exclusive provincial jurisdiction. This development simply recognizes what a number of other polities have learned: that a degree of asymmetry may assist in managing interdependence.

Second, there has been some recognition of the interdependence of provincial responsibilities with issues of international relations, as illustrated by the federal government consultations with the provincial governments during the negotiations of the Canada-US Free Trade Agreement and of NAFTA, by the Team Canada trade missions abroad, and by the participation of Quebec and New Brunswick in *La Francophonie*. Nevertheless, by comparison with such examples as Switzerland and Belgium or even Germany, participation of the provinces in decisions on foreign policy and the development of direct relations between the provinces and foreign countries is far less developed in Canada.

Third, the importance of local governments and particularly international cities as interdependent elements in the federation as a whole rather than just subordinate provincial institutions, has by contrast to some other federations received little encouragement since the provinces have jealously guarded local government as an area of their exclusive responsibility.

Fourth, as Cameron and Simeon note, the developing collaborative relations have "no constitutional or legislative base, no established schedule of meetings, little backup by bureaucrats linked to the success of the process rather than to individual governments, no formal decision-rules, and no capacity for authoritative decision-making" (Cameron and Simeon 2001). Consequently, the prospects for continued collaborative intergovernmental relations depend heavily upon whether the first ministers find them advantageous. This renders the system highly fragile and leaves a return to arm's-length competitive relations as a very possible default situation.

Fifth, the challenge of reconciling the predominance of ministers and officials in these processes of intergovernmental relations with the democratic expectations of citizens for full transparency, accountability to the voters and public consultation has not yet been fully met. Although there has been much greater consciousness of the need for accountability and transparency in the conduct of intergovernmental relations and for ensuring ongoing public input and feedback, as exemplified by the Calgary Declaration and SUFA, in actual practice much more remains to be done if the impression of a democratic deficit in such matters is to be avoided.

Sixth, the events of September 11, 2001 will almost certainly have some impact, at least in the short and medium term. They will heighten the relative importance of the federal government in the eyes of citizens. At the same time, some of the security arrangements that will need to be developed, particularly in cooperation with the United States, are likely to relate significantly to areas that fall within provincial jurisdiction and, therefore, require increased collaboration between the federal and provincial governments.

Conclusions

INTERGOVERNMENTAL INTERDEPENDENCE HAS ALWAYS BEEN AN ESSENTIAL CHARACTERistic of the operation of federal systems, but its importance has been accentuated by contemporary global and regional considerations. While contemporary federations in response have ranged somewhere along the spectrum between interlocking intergovernmental relations and arm's-length relations, most have developed intergovernmental collaboration to a much higher degree than Canada. Federations elsewhere, therefore, illustrate possible improvements which Canadians would do well to consider carefully. At the same time, it is important to keep in mind, of course, that there are no universal solutions since account needs to be taken of the particular social, economic and constitutional context of each federation. Furthermore, sight must not be lost of the advantages of multiple channels of decision-making within federations over single hierarchical processes of decision-making (Landau 1973).

Intergovernmental interaction has been an important feature of the Canadian federation from the beginning, and shows signs currently of developing a genuinely collaborative character. But that trend is a fragile one. In the context of the current global and information revolution, and the increasingly closer relations with the United States, it is imperative that the processes for intergovernmental collaboration within Canada be consciously improved. In evaluating potential techniques and processes for responding to the pressures for greater interdependence, among the important values that will need to be borne in mind are the objectives of shared goals, provincial autonomy, political stability, democratic transparency, accountability and participation, equity, efficiency and innovative flexibility. In institutionalizing these values and finding a balance among them, difficult choices and value trade-offs will be unavoidable (Kincaid 1991, 44). But they must be addressed, for the future effectiveness of the Canadian federation in a changing world is at stake.

Notes

1 Harvey Lazar, "Trends in Canadian Federation." Unpublished paper, September 3, 2001. I am particularly grateful to Harvey Lazar for helpful comments on a number of points in my paper.

2 More recent federations have in fact distributed responsibility for different aspects of these fields to different orders of government, but these have often required cooperative action.

3 For a dissenting view favouring intergovernmental competition rather than collaboration, see Albert Breton (1985, pp. 485-526. See also the subsection in paper on "Intergovernmental Relations."

4 On this, see especially the articles by Hrbek, Leonardy, Bulmer and Jeffery in Jeffery (1999).

5 In addition, chapter 7 (articles 151-64) lays out the status, functions and powers of local governments.

6 In the case of India, by the 73rd and 74th Amendments, 1993.

7 See, for instance, articles 58(3), 60(2&3), 63(2), 66, 67, 69(2&3), 70, 72, 73, 74, 75, 76, 78, 80(3), 85, 86, 88, 89, 94, 95, 97, 100, 111, 112, 115, 116, 123, 124, 126-135.

8 *Constitution of Belgium* (1993), articles 127(1:3), 128(1), 131(1:4-5) and Annexes (Les Relations Internationales-Les Accords de Cooperation); *Constitution of Switzerland* (1999), articles 54(3), 55 and 56. On Belgium, see Alen and Ergac (1998, pp. 22-26).

References

Agranoff, R., ed. *Accommodating Diversity: Asymmetry in Federal States*. Baden-Baden: Nomos Verlagsgesellschaft, 1999.

Alen, A. and R. Ergec. *La Belgique fédérale après la quatrième réforme de l'État de 1993*, 2d ed. Brussels: Ministère des Affaires étrangères, F/98/1, 1998.

Armingeon, K. "Swiss Federalism in Comparative Perspective." In *Federalism and Political Performance*, ed. Ute Wachendorfer-Schmidt. London: New York Routledge, 2000.

Bastien, R. *Federalism and Decentralization: Where Do We Stand?* Ottawa: Supply and Services Canada, 1981.

Benson, G.C. *The New Centralization*. New York: Farrar and Rinehart Inc., 1941, esp. chs. 4, 6, 10, 11.

Bertelsmann Commission on Governance and Constitutional Policy. *Disentanglement 2005: Ten Reform Proposals for Better Governance in the German Federal System*. Gutersloh: Bertelsmann Foundation Publishers, 2000.

Birch, A.H. *Federalism, Finance and Social Legislation in Canada, Australia and the United States*. Oxford: Clarendon Press, 1955.

Breton, A. "Supplementary Statement." In Royal Commission on the Economic Union and Development Prospects for Canada, *Report*, Vol. 3. Ottawa: Supply and Services Canada, 1985.

Cairns, A.C. "The Judicial Committee and Its Critics." *Canadian Journal of Political Science*, Vol. 4 (1971): 301-345.

Cameron, D. and R. Simeon. "Federalism and Intergovernmental Relations in Canada at the Millennium." *Publius: The Journal of Federalism* (forthcoming in 2002).

Clark, J.P. *The Rise of a New Federalism*. New York: Columbia University Press, 1938*a*.

________ "A Symposium on Co-operative Federalism." *Iowa Law Review*, Vol. 23 (1938*b*): 455-616,

Corry, J.A. "Constitutional Trends and Federalism." In *Evolving Canadian Federalism*, ed. A.R.M. Lowe et al. Durham, NC: Duke University Press, 1958.

Council of Australian Governments (COAG). *COAG: Reform of Ministerial Councils*. June 8, 2001.

Courchene, T.J. "Glocalization: The Regional/International Interface." *Canadian Journal of Regional Science*, Vol. 18, no. 1 (Spring 1955): 1-20.

________ *A State of Minds: Toward a Human Capital Future for Canadians*. Montreal: Institute for Research on Public Policy, 2001.

Dicey, A.V. *Introduction to the Study of the Law of the Constitution*, 10th ed. London: Macmillan, 1959.

Elazar, D.J. *The American Partnership*. Chicago: University of Chicago Press, 1962.

________ "From Statism to Federalism: A Paradigm Shift." *Publius: The Journal of Federalism*, Vol. 25, no. 1 (Winter 1995): 5-18.

Friedrich, C. *Trends of Federalism in Theory and Practice*. New York: Praeger, 1968.

Galligan, B. et al., ed. *Intergovernmental Relations and Public Policy*. Sydney: Allen & Unwin, 1991.

Grodzins, M. *The American System*. Chicago: Rand McNally, 1966.

Jeffery, C., ed. *Recasting German Federalism: The Legacies of Unification*. London and New York: Pinter, 1999.

Kincaid, J. "The Competitive Challenge to Cooperative Federalism: A Theory of Federal Democracy." In *Competition among States and Local Governments: Efficiency and Equity in American Federalism*, ed. D.A. Kenyon and J. Kincaid. Washington, DC: Urban Institute, 1991.

________ "Values and Tradeoffs in Federalism." *Publius: The Journal of Federalism*, Vol. 25, no. 2 (Spring 1995): 29-30.

King, P. *Federalism and Federation*. Baltimore: Johns Hopkins University Press, 1982.

Laforest, G. and D. Brown, ed. *Integration and Fragmentation: The Paradox of the Late Twentieth Century*. Kingston: Institute of Intergovernmental Relations, Queen's University, 1994.

Landau, M. "Federalism, Redundancy and System Reliability." *Publius: The Journal of Federalism*, Vol. 3, no. 2 (1973): 173-195.

Lazar, H., ed. *Canada: The State of the Federation, 1999/2000: Toward a New Mission Statement for Canadian Fiscal Federalism*. Montreal and Kingston: McGill-Queen's University Press, 2000.

Lodge, J., ed. *The European Community and the Challenge of the Future*, 2d ed. London: Pinter, 1993.

Lowenstein, K. *Political Power and the Governmental Process*. Chicago: University of Chicago Press, 1965.

Nugent, N. *The Government and Politics of the European Community*, 2d ed. Basingstoke: Macmillan Education Ltd., 1991.

Painter, M. *Collaborative Federalism: Economic Reform in Australia in the 1990's*. Cambridge-NY-Melbourne: Cambridge University Press, 1998.

________ "When Adversaries Collaborate: Conditional Co-operation in Australia's Arm's Length Polity." In *Federalism and Political Performance*, ed. Ute Wachendorfer-Schmidt. London: New York, 2000.

Pennock, J.R. "Federal and Unitary Government: Disharmony and Reliability." *Behavioural Science*, Vol. 4, no. 2 (1959): 147-157.

Poirier, J., *The Functions of Intergovernmental Agreement: Post Devolution Concordats in a Comparative Perspective*. London: The Constitution Unit, School of Policy, University College, London, 2001.

Saunders, C. "Constitutional Arrangements of Federal Systems." *Publius: The Journal of Federalism*, Vol. 25, no. 2 (Spring 1995): 78-79.

Scharpf, F. "The Joint-Decision Trap: Lessons from German Federalism and European Integration." *Public Administration* 66 (Autumn 1988): 238-278.

Smiley, D.V. and R.L. Watts. *Intrastate Federalism in Canada*. Toronto: University of Toronto Press, 1985.

Stevenson, G. *Ex Uno Plures: Federal-Provincial Relations, 1867-1896*. Montreal and Kingston: McGill-Queen's University Press, 1993.

Vile, M.J.C. *The Structure of American Federalism*. London: Oxford University Press, 1961.

Wachendorfer-Schmidt, U., ed. *Federalism and Political Performance*. London and New York: Routledge, 2000.

Watts, R.L. *Executive Federalism: A Comparative Analysis*. Kingston: Institute of Intergovernmental Relations, Queen's University, 1989.

________ *Comparing Federal Systems*, 2d ed. Montreal and Kingston: McGill-Queen's University Press, 1999*a*.

________ *The Spending Power in Federal Systems: A Comparative Study*. Kingston: Institute of Intergovernmental Relations, Queen's University, 1999*b*.

________ "Federal Financial Arrangements: A Comparative Perspective." In *Canada: The State of the Federation, 1999/2000: Toward a New Mission Statement for Canadian Fiscal Federalism*, ed. H. Lazar. Montreal and Kingston: McGill-Queen's University Press, 2000.

Wheare, K.C. *Federal Government*, 4th ed. London: Oxford University Press, 1963.

Wright, D. *Understanding Intergovernmental Relations*, 2d ed. Monterey, CA: Brooks/Cole, 1982.

Zuker, R. "Reciprocal Federalism: Beyond the Spending Power." Ottawa: The Caledon Institute, unpublished paper, May 1995.

Managing Interdependence in a Federal Political System: Comments

Introduction

THIS IS A TYPICAL RONALD WATTS PAPER—COMPREHENSIVE, SCHOLARLY, UP-TO-DATE, thoughtful, descriptive rather than prescriptive, subtle and optimistic. According to the conference outline, he was asked "to identify ways for the two senior orders of government to cooperate and to make decisions as the new economic order takes root." Professor Watts did not spend much time setting the paper in the new economic context; instead he argues that interdependence has always characterized federal systems and that now increasing interconnectedness "has accentuated the degree of interdependence between governments and consequently, the measure of intergovernmental collaboration required." This is an important chain of logic to which I will return.

The bulk of the paper concerns the instruments, mechanisms and processes that have been deployed to manage interdependence in federations; that is, to promote intergovernmental cooperation. Here the range is encyclopedic, as Watts builds on his remarkable corpus of work, one that marks him as the world's leading scholar in comparative federalism. Indeed, it is possible to think of Ron Watts as a jeweller of federalism. His emporium is set modestly in Kingston, Ontario (though the proprietor is always willing to travel, with a suitcase of wares). Arranged throughout the crowded store are the myriad jewels; that is, the constitutional, structural and procedural variants of the federal world. Professor Watts accumulates them and keeps them on display. Herein enter the novices and the clients (troubled, normally) to find a range of *bijouterie* spectacularly wider than their limited ken—the flamboyant Bundesrat, the unassuming but finely crafted articles 44-49 of the 1999 Swiss constitution, the lustrous Council of Australian governments and many, many proverbial gems—that constitutions may mix federal and confederal elements, that intergovernmental agreements need not be binding, that there are many forms of asymmetry, and so on. In the midst of the vast inventory stands the congenial proprietor, always ready with suggestions for remedying disharmony and always insistent that while federations elsewhere "illustrate possible improvements" it is essential to remember "that there are no universal solutions since account needs to be taken of the particular social, economic and constitutional context of each federation." I have had the opportunity to observe Professor Watts serving some of his customers, always sensitive to their needs, helpful and continually forward looking. Apart from his practical activities, it is a major intellectual accomplishment that he manages to get all the new designs in stock despite rapid changes of the sort that he documents in this paper, and to arrange them comprehensively and sensibly. The emporium continues to flourish.

The Dynamics of Competition within Federal Systems

MY SUBSTANTIVE COMMENTS CONCERN INTERGOVERNMENTAL COLLABORATION AND the dynamics of competition within federal systems. These fit into Watts' account of the continuum between "interlocking" relations and "arm's-length" relations (with "collaborative" relationships lying between these two extremes). Here it is important to remember the contention above that interdependence requires more collaboration, and also to note Watts' statement that because Canada is very much an arm's-length system it "has been less well-equipped to manage the contemporary challenges of interdependence than most other federations." Overall, this conclusion may be correct, but I would be remiss in my duty as commentator if I did not lay out an alternative account and suggest competing conclusions. My emphasis is less on the structures of contemporary federalism in Canada and more on the dynamics, and my focus is not so much on collaboration as on competition between governments.

In a brief survey of recent federal-provincial relations in the field of environmental policy, Mark Winfield (2001) delivers a stinging attack on collaborative federalism. He argues that in earlier periods of activism in this field, both orders of government were involved, and there existed an "upward competition," especially in setting environmental standards. By the 1990s, however, there was pressure for more collaborative arrangements, which resulted in the 1998 Canada-wide Accord on Environmental Harmonization and three sub-agreements on standards, inspections and environmental assessment. According to Winfield, the Accord's provisions for "one-window" program delivery by the government best situated to provide it—generally the provincial governments—led to weaker federal legislation, decreased environmental protection as the provincial governments chopped spending and reformed regulations and new collaborative standards that were disappointingly weak. As Winfield notes, much depends on public opinion, and not much time has passed since the Accord was signed. As well, the environment may be a special case (Oates and Schwab 1988). But it seems that collaboration may be a mask for decentralization. More importantly, Ottawa may have to maintain a regulatory presence in the field to ensure minimum national standards; otherwise, destructive competition between the provinces can lead to much weaker environmental control and even the emergence of pollution havens.

This raises the first dynamic of intergovernmental relations: horizontal competition. Increased competition between provincial governments accompanies greater decentralization and rising provincial autonomy, trends that arguably are accelerating with globalization and the information revolution. Horizontal competition has been analyzed a great deal. Its virtues lie in promoting responsiveness (because citizens will exit if their wishes are not met), accountability (because competing jurisdictions provide a yardstick for performance evaluation) and innovation (because governments have an incentive to produce new or cheaper baskets of goods and services). But it can also have negative consequences. Decentralized service provision in some policy fields can mean that economies of scale are not realized, so costs are greater than they need be. As well, smaller units may produce externalities that negatively affect their neighbours, and they may have no incentive to realize potential positive externalities. Finally, a lack of coordination can produce destructive competition, as when jurisdictions compete away tax bases or gut anti-pollution regulations in order to be attractive to industry.

If horizontal competition is virtuous for the most part, however, then it might be preferable to collaboration, or at least to the vertical (federal-provincial) collaboration that is central to Watts' paper. This is a crucial issue upon which analysts are sharply divided. One position is that federal systems need an umpire to monitor interprovincial competition, with national standards where required and with a central government prepared to level the competitive playing field (through providing equalization payments, for example) (Breton 1996). Along these lines, Antonia Maioni has applied to the health field some elementary regime theory borrowed from international relations and shows that interprovincial agreements are unlikely to be adequate substitutes for federal enforcement (Maioni 1999). Others, however, have strongly argued that interprovincial accords can work, as long as there is information available so that governments can be held accountable to electorates (Courchene 1996). As well, it can be worth sacrificing some uniformity for the benefits of more experimentation.

This is also a highly political debate. It marks an important cleavage between the Canadian Alliance Party and the federal Liberals. And it divides the Liberals themselves, with a majority fearing that moves toward decentralization generally will allow provinces to race to the bottom, and that these developments will threaten Canada itself because national programs and the social safety net in particular are critical to Canadians' sense of national identity. In this view, Ottawa must maintain a strong presence in fields like health and the environment in order to keep the visibility and legitimacy of the central government (and to reinforce the loyalty of Quebecers to Canada as well). This issue is also divisive regionally, because apprehension about the consequences of decentralization is much greater in Ontario and the Maritimes than in Quebec and most of the west.

Unfortunately, we have very little systematic empirical research on these questions. Research will never resolve such a broad and contested set of issues, of course, but it could structure and inform the debate in the future. And we have a very good laboratory for such work. In the wake of the Charlottetown Accord's failure and the near-victory by the "yes" side in the 1995 Quebec referendum, the Government of Canada moved to withdraw from several policy fields and in others to substantially decentralize power (or to collaborate more closely with the provinces). Apart from environmental protection, these include employment training, mining, forestry and much of tourism. A well-integrated set of studies of these fields could reveal much about horizontal competition between the provinces and in particular about the trade-offs between flexibility, innovation and accountability on the one hand and poor coordination and destructive competition on the other.

This brings us to the other, related axis of competition: vertical competition between provincial governments and the federal government. Compared to horizontal, interprovincial competition, this is less well-understood theoretically. But it is generally taken to mean not that the central authority monitors and regulates relationships between provincial governments but rather that it competes with them directly in supplying goods and services. As federal-provincial disputes about the *Canada Health Act* demonstrate, the distinction blurs in reality.[1] But vertical competition is often seen as destructive when it produces wasteful overlap and duplication through two orders of government providing similar services, and when it leads to "turf wars" or corrosive exercises in blame avoidance. In Watts' phrasing, an excess of competitive federalism "may lead to intergovernmental conflict and acrimony, and undermine the spirit of trust necessary for cooperation between governments." If collaboration is required to handle the interdependence caused by increased interconnectedness, then vertical competition may well be generally destructive. And overlap and duplication can represent the sort of waste that cannot be tolerated in a competitive world.

There has not been much research devoted to overlap and duplication in the Canadian federation. But a recent survey showed that the problem is less serious than many suspect, at least as governments downsized during the 1990s, and that the effects of overlap vary according to the policy field in question and the kind of policy instruments involved (Lindquist 1999; Meekison 1999). Moreover, there is a general case to be made for the safety of redundant systems, at least in some sectors. Finally, an even stronger argument for vertical competition is that it protects against monopoly power, its concomitant inefficiency and its potential for abuse, by providing citizens with alternative policies and paths for participation, short of the costly option of exit. As Professor Watts states in his essay, "sight must not be lost of the advantages of multiple channels of decision-making within federations over single hierarchical processes of decision-making."

This can be pressed into an argument for vertical competition more generally in Canada. It may well be that the new economic order requires more decentralization and interprovincial competition, and less collaboration between the provinces and Ottawa. On the other hand, intervention by the central government may be necessary to avoid destructive horizontal competition in some policy fields, and there clearly is some public demand for the central government to take new initiatives. After all, the increase in interconnectedness remarked by

Professor Watts is perceived differently by the different orders of government, a function of different electorates, bureaucracies and jurisdictional responsibilities. So a case can be made that the Canadian government should enter new policy fields, even if this impinges on provincial jurisdiction and programs. It should perhaps compete more with the provincial governments, establishing and institutionalizing new programs and crystallizing public expectations (Young 1997). This might be especially appropriate where provincial governments have demonstrated neglect or inertia, and where emerging problems that demand federal government attention have inescapable links into areas of provincial authority (such as issues involving municipalities). Of course, the spending power is the major instrument for such vertical competition. This is bound to create conflict with the provinces, but perhaps conflict on some fronts is as healthy for the system as is collaboration in other areas.

Conclusion

TO CONCLUDE, I WILL SIMPLY RECAPITULATE SOME POINTS. IN CANADA, "COLLABORATION" may sometimes mask decentralization. When this occurs, the resulting horizontal competition can be destructive; however, in the current context of Canadian federalism we may need more of the benefits of such competition, especially policy innovation and clearer governmental accountability. More research is needed on this issue. As well, federal-provincial collaboration may need a dose of vertical competition. This could increase citizens' choice and sharpen our responsiveness to external change, at the cost of some increase in conflict in the system. Again, we need more study and thought about when collaboration and competition best occur. In so doing, it will be essential to contemplate the many structures and processes laid out by Watts—all those jewels of federalism past and present—in order to assess which might channel intergovernmental relations most constructively.

Notes

1 "Central governments must monitor both vertical and horizontal competition, that is, the competition among themselves and the other governments of the system and that among junior governments. In monitoring vertical competition, central governments are both judges and juries" (Breton 1996, p. 248).

References

Breton, A. *Competitive Governments: An Economic Theory of Politics and Public Finance.* New York: Cambridge University Press, 1996.

Courchene, T.J. *ACCESS: A Convention on the Canadian Economic and Social Systems.* Working Paper prepared for the Ministry of Intergovernmental Affairs, Government of Ontario, Toronto, 1996.

Lindquist, E.A. "Efficiency, Reliability, or Innovation? Managing Overlap and Interdependence in Canada's Federal System of Governance." In *Stretching the Federation*, ed. Robert Young. Kingston: Institute of Intergovernmental Relations, 1999.

Maioni, A. "Decentralization in Health Policy: Comments on the ACCESS Proposals." In *Stretching the Federation*, ed. Robert Young. Kingston: Institute of Intergovernmental Relations, 1999.

Meekison, J.P. "Comments." In *Stretching the Federation*, ed. Robert Young. Kingston: Institute of Intergovernmental Relations, 1999.

Oates, W.E. and R.M. Schwab. "Economic Competition among Jurisdictions: Efficiency Enhancing or Distortion Inducing?" *Journal of Public Economics*, Vol. 35 (1988): 333-354.

Winfield, M.S. "Environmental Policy and Federalism." In *Canadian Federalism: Performance, Effectiveness, and Legitimacy*, ed. H. Bakvis and G. Skogstad. Don Mills: Oxford University Press, 2001.

Young, R. "Defending Decentralization." *Policy Options*, Vol. 18, no. 2 (1997): 42-44.

________, ed. *Stretching the Federation: The Art of the State in Canada.* Kingston: Institute of Intergovernmental Relations, 1999.

Discussion

THE FLOOR DISCUSSION CENTRED MOSTLY ON CANADIAN FEDERALISM. ELIZABETH Beale, head of the Atlantic Provinces Economic Council, who was asked to bring a practitioner's perspective to the session, identified several concerns with collaborative federalism among the smaller provinces. She pointed out that the federal government can exacerbate regional differences by establishing new federal-provincial collaborative mechanisms, because smaller cash-starved provinces cannot participate fully in the new arrangements. She also made the point that interdependence and collaborative arrangements are forcing the hand of smaller provinces with limited resources to establish or beef up analytical and administrative capacities to consult with senior orders of government and outside groups.

A number of participants sought to explore ways to bring practical meaning to the phrase "the west wants in." As one participant observed, the phrase has one inescapable solution, "if the west wants in then it must be the case that the centre wants to keep the west out." Another argued that the reality of Canada's political culture is rooted in regional conflicts, grievances and animosity. Added to this is the nature of Canadian federalism which, in recent years, has tilted toward a more competitive nature. Given the above, how could one reform Canada's institutions to accommodate these tensions?

A number of participants argued that things may not be as bad as they appear. They reported that a great deal of collaborative work takes place between officials in a variety of federal-provincial committees where the great majority of intergovernmental decisions are actually made. One participant pointed to a number of instances where strong cooperation was evident in dealing with specific issues, ranging from the Y2K problem to the aftermath of September 11, 2001.

The difficulty often is at the political level which, by definition, is much more visible to the general public.

Others insisted, however, that the problem was not so simple. Canada has, for the past ten years, been essentially a one-party state dominated by the Ontario caucus. One option was for westerners to vote Liberal. Another option is to adopt some form of proportional representation so that the 25 percent of western Canadians who voted Liberal in the last general election would have greater representation on the government side.

Still others maintained that "centralist elements" in the Canadian federation remain strong. One participant argued that the federal government has been busy of late trying to develop a new form of federalism, one that seeks to bypass the provinces to establish direct relations with municipalities, the private sector, and individuals. One asked how a world without borders could accommodate Canada's political culture. The culture is based on regional conflict, regional grievance and regional animosity. Our federal system, he added, could best be described as a form of competitive federalism based on competition and conflict between the two senior orders of government. This begs the question: How can such a culture be made to work to encourage cooperation or co-decision-making to promote a more competitive national economy?

In his wrap-up comments, Watts observed that when one compares the Canadian federation to other federations, we see that we have fewer institutional channels for intrastate federalism than virtually any other contemporary federation. He noted that for a variety of reasons Canada seems to be "fearful" of proportional representation but that all European federations rely upon proportional representation and expect their federal governments to be coalitions representing a spectrum of views within the federation. He concluded with the suggestion that proportional representation *might be* an improvement on how our system operates. Watts cautioned those who would look to Europe for solutions for Canada. He maintains that the European Union is not a pure confederal form. Rather, it is a unique hybrid housing both confederal and federal features.

Corporate Governance

State Regulatory Competition and the Threat to Corporate Governance

Introduction

THE SUBJECT OF THIS PAPER IS THE IMPACT OF THE NEW GLOBALIZED ORDER ON THE integrity of corporate governance. Corporate governance is the system of laws, markets and institutions that seeks to control and discipline corporate activity in the service of the public interest. Over the last several years, many critics have bemoaned the growing integration of various economic markets across national boundaries because it is seen to lessen the capacity of states to regulate corporate behaviour. Essentially, the claim is that in a setting of reduced barriers to factor and product mobility, corporations are rendered much more effective in their capacity to extract regulatory concessions from host governments, and these concessions have the effect of lowering social welfare. The argument is that in a setting of high international corporate mobility, footloose corporations will relocate their operations to whichever jurisdiction offers the most congenial (meaning least stringent) regulation.

In the face of certain corporate migration in response to more stringent regulation, states will have no choice but to refrain from adopting socially optimal regulation. This is because states fear the loss of benefits associated with corporate activity: namely, employment, investment and tax revenue. The effect is an international "race to the bottom" in which states are rendered helpless in countering the effect of heightened corporate mobility.

Equally clear is the obvious prescription: an enhanced role for multinational or supranational state regulators in constraining the scope for welfare-reducing regulatory arbitrage. This is necessary to counter the efforts of corporate migration, and to ensure the integrity of the corporate regulatory regime.

Despite the frequency of these claims in favour of eviscerated state capacity to regulate corporate behaviour, we are sceptical of the case in favour of wholesale adoption of new supranational institutions or multilateral agreements that seek to ensure corporate fidelity to the public interest. We do not argue that there is no prospect for welfare-reducing state competition emanating from increased economic integration nor that initiatives designed to control destructive state competition in the regulation of corporate behaviour are perverse. Rather, we seek to develop a more nuanced analysis of corporate mobility in an increasingly globalized world that recognizes the benefits of state competition in certain circumstances, as well as the challenges that policy-makers face in devising principled constraints on corporate behaviour through multinational agreements.

We embark on this task in several distinct stages. First, we set out the case that has been developed against unfettered state competition in the production and enforcement of corporate regulation. Then we evaluate these concerns by considering the capacity of stakeholders to protect themselves through a variety of contractual and non-contractual mechanisms. We also assess how footloose corporations really are in changing jurisdictions in response to more lenient regulation. Against this backdrop, we discuss the scope for competitive states to ensure the production of socially valuable regulation and then identify those cases in which state competition is unlikely to produce outcomes that compromise social welfare. Here, we will identify those cases where state competition will be inimical to social welfare either because of interstate externalities or shortcomings in the political institutions of the regulating state. Having recognized that state competition in the provision of corporate regulation is not always conducive to the maximization of social welfare, we then discuss different instruments to correct this problem. Interestingly, we find that the problems that lead to a destructive race to the bottom in interstate corporate regulation are manifest in the context of efforts to develop multilateral agreements that restrict the scope for destructive competition.

The Role of State Competition in the Production of Corporate Regulation: Normative and Positive Perspectives

Normative perspectives

Does intense interjurisdictional competition for corporate patronage necessarily mean a loss of social welfare? For many critics of globalization, the answer to this question is in the affirmative. As described earlier, interjurisdictional competition invariably forces states to adopt weak laws that secure corporate patronage (and resultant benefits), but which nevertheless impose targeted losses on sundry stakeholder groups. In the absence of the threat of credible exit, states would refrain from adopting suboptimal laws, and corporations would have no choice but to comply. The state's powers would be restored and global welfare would increase.

Nevertheless, in sharp contrast to this analysis, proponents of competitive governments have long argued for the value of state competition (typically at the subnational level because this literature was developed in the context of the theory of federalism) in promoting responsive and innovative government. This analysis recognizes that although the state has extensive and coercive powers, its accountability to the citizenry in relation to how it exercises those powers is subject to endemic accountability problems. Politicians, for instance, worry more about re-election and short-term "credit taking" than the long-term welfare of society. Risk-averse bureaucrats worry more about their job security and scope of authority than the quality of policy and regulatory products for which they are responsible. Compounding problems is the fact that it is difficult for the public to ascertain individual responsibility for government decision-making.

Forcing governments to compete with one another to secure citizen patronage ensures that governments produce and enforce laws that are responsive to citizen preferences. Under the Tiebout model of competitive government (Tiebout 1956), highly mobile citizens will opt to reside in the jurisdiction offering the regulatory product that most closely satisfies their individual preferences. So long as states differentiate their regulatory programs and these programs do not entail externalities, the resulting equilibrium will be superior to that available in a setting of monopoly government where citizens lack credible exit options, thereby hobbling their voice.[1] Not only does this model promise more innovative and responsive government, but more specialized government as well. Governments, like firms in private product markets, will be forced to specialize so as to differentiate their product offerings from competitor states. In this way, all stakeholders whose interests are bound to the corporation are better served in a competitive marketplace for regulatory products than if there were only a single monopoly supplier of rules (or, alternatively, a producer cartel offering the same basic regulatory bundle).

In the case of national governments "competing" to attract corporate patronage, in the form of jobs, investment and tax revenue, the question is whether there is any *a priori* reason to expect that the conditions for optimal state competition will not obtain. In the received economic model of the corporation, the corporation stands as a "nexus of contracting relationships." In this model, parties only enter into explicit or implicit contractual relations with the corporations if it is in their rational economic interest to do so. Further, parties will have reasonable *ex ante* opportunities to secure appropriate protections from the corporation that safeguards their interests. So, for instance, employees will not agree to make significant firm-specific investments unless the corporation provides credible assurances that their up-front investments in the corporation, in the form of firm-specific human capital investment, will be protected through higher compensation or through long-term contractual commitments (security of tenure bonded by generous severance payments). The same is true for other stakeholder groups who enjoy opportunities for value-enhancing bargaining.

So long as parties have cost-effective opportunities for informed bargaining, the prospect of interjurisdictional corporate mobility should not be problematic. Corporations will not opt for the "consumption" of a new regulatory bundle, obtained through interstate migration, that will breach either explicit or implicit undertakings to existing stakeholders, in the current jurisdiction, or that will diminish their ability to attract new stakeholders (in the destination jurisdiction). Doing so would have the certain effect of imposing costs on the corporation emanating from deflated stakeholder expectations. Alienated shareholders, for instance, can discipline corporate management by working to remove them from office by invoking the corporation's normal governance processes. Further, they can sell their shares in the corporation, thereby lowering the value of stock-based managerial compensation.[2] Employees can commence legal actions against the corporation based on breach of contract, and can impose losses on the reputations of the firm's managers that will hobble them in their future negotiations with other stakeholder groups. The same is true for other stakeholder groups like suppliers and creditors. Indeed, as exemplified by the recent Enron scandal in the US, not only are corporations and their direct principals subject to discipline in the event of failed expectations, but so too are their professional advisers (lawyers and accountants) whose reputations are intimately linked to the corporation's conduct.

In light of the scope that stakeholders enjoy in being able to secure effective *ex ante* or *ex post* constraints on welfare-reducing corporate relocations by corporate managers, what is the case against reliance on the competitive framework for ensuring socially optimal corporate regulation?

The first concern relates to externalities. To the extent that certain stakeholder groups are unable to bargain effectively with the corporation because of a variety of information, coordination and bargaining difficulties, then the scope for the corporation to "jurisdiction shop" in a way that inflicts targeted costs on these groups is increased. The classic example is dispersed downstream or downwind residents who are injured by effluent discharged by an upstream or upwind polluter. Collective action problems and information asymmetries prevent the residents from bargaining directly with the corporation, thereby justifying the role of the state in imposing protections that fully informed parties negotiating in a transactions cost-free world would have adopted on their own. If the regulatory regime imposed by governments does not adopt these environmental protections owing, for instance, to the fear that affected corporations will be relocated to competitor jurisdictions, then concentrated losses will be visited on identifiable stakeholder groups.

Whether or not certain stakeholder groups will suffer losses from state competition in the production of regulation turns on a number of different factors: first, the quality of information that stakeholders receive respecting new or impending regulations; second, stakeholder expertise in understanding and responding to the risks to their interests created by the corporation; third, the scope for coordination among similarly situated stakeholders; and fourth, the opportunities for meaningful citizen voice in the political processes used to vet prospective legislative or regulatory changes. In respect of this last point, where stakeholders adversely affected by corporate behaviour are afforded transparent opportunities to participate in public rule-making, then there is less opportunity for corporate interest groups to steam-roll dissent in the regulation-making process.

In the context of international jurisdiction shopping, concern over externalities is most acute when prospective jurisdictions lack basic democratic institutions that would normally permit certain adversely affected interests the opportunity to temper the rules deemed desirable by corporate managers (presumably, but not always, related to the advancement of shareholder wealth). What is of concern here is *not* that states will in some cases decide to adopt rules that entail costs for certain corporate stakeholder groups that are more than offset by the benefits realized by other corporate stakeholder groups. After all, this is the essence of law-making in liberal democratic countries, where legislation is often the by-product of complex negotiation processes in which different interests are weighed and balanced in the pursuit of improved social welfare. Indeed, assuming basic human rights have been respected and that the process of regulation-making is procedurally robust, the argument is that states have the right to adopt regulatory outcomes that differ from outcomes adopted in other—often more advanced—countries, and which reflect their own unique preference functions. Rather, the more pressing concern relates to those states that systematically deprive certain corporate stakeholder groups (e.g., employees) of the opportunity to have their interests accounted for in the policy development process in favour of other stakeholder groups (e.g., shareholders). These concerns are exacerbated by the specter of non-transparent bribes and other side-payments to public officials that will further skew the regulatory process against less powerful stakeholder interests.

Although the task of determining whether a state's institutional framework passes democratic muster is a difficult one, it is not insuperable.[3] What is required is not the widespread adoption of a standard template of legislation or rule-making that duplicates the institutions and processes extant in one particular state, but rather regard to whether affected interests have opportunities to participate meaningfully in the deliberative processes surrounding regulation-making. These "bare conditions of democracy" have previously been invoked to inform the accession of certain countries to such international agreements as the General Agreement on Tariffs and Trade (GATT). There is no reason to expect that similar standards could not be established in this area. A similar approach is appropriate in relation to human rights standards. Again, the enterprise is not one of forcing countries to adopt the precise tapestry of human rights protections found in the one national context, but rather to ensure that the basic conditions of humanity and dignity are respected by prospective regulators.[4]

While attention to the character of domestic political institutions and human rights regimes is responsive to concerns over the impact of prospective laws on the welfare of certain domestic interest groups whose welfare might be affected by competitive regulation, it is deficient in addressing the impact of state competition on interests who are outside the regulating jurisdiction. Returning to the environmental example discussed earlier, the concern would arise when the stakeholders who are principally affected by prospective regulation, say, downstream/downwind residents, are located outside the regulating jurisdiction, and they have only limited (and costly) opportunities to participate in a fulsome manner in the regulation-making process.[5] No doubt, these problems are exacerbated by the relatively weak voice they would have in any domestic regulation-making process. In the absence of full rights to public participation, such as the ability to vote in public elections, foreign interest groups will not have the same public salience as domestic interest groups. One possible response to this problem is for adversely affected foreign interests to forge coalitions with domestic interest groups. However, issue-specific alliances are often highly fragile, and, from the perspective of the foreign citizen, unreliable. This discussion suggests that the concern over externalities is most compelling in the context of foreign citizens who are adversely affected by prospective regulation, and casts doubt over the efficacy of state competition's capacity to produce socially desirable outcomes in these contexts.

One final externalities-related problem is that of paternalism, namely what kind of importance should we accord to the *indirect* impact on the preferences of foreign citizens from seeing citizens in another country being harmed by the regulations of that country. Take, for example, the decision of country A to adopt laws that adversely impact workers in country A by restricting collective bargaining rights. Quite apart from the impact on domestic citizens of that country, citizens in country B observing these rules and knowing their impact on the welfare of least-advantaged members of country A may suffer consequent reductions in welfare. From a global welfare perspective, domestic regulators *should* take account of these reductions in the welfare of foreign citizens, but as discussed above, in the absence of institutionalized opportunities for participation by these citizens, are unlikely to do so.

A further complicating factor with intervention based on paternalism is the problem of revealed preferences, namely that citizens will be prone to exaggerating the impact on their welfare of foreign regulations because it is not costly to do so. This gives rise to concerns that citizens will express disaffection with foreign regulation in order to achieve protectionist goals. Concern over the open-ended (and malleable) character of paternalism-based claims translates into a need to find ways of disciplining these claims. One option is to treat paternalism claims seriously only when they are accompanied by demonstrable evidence of disregard for the core tenets of individual autonomy and dignity. Further, to the extent that domestic policy-makers can demonstrate that affected interests were afforded meaningful opportunities for participation in the regulation-making process, the force of foreign complaints will be dulled commensurately.

Positive perspectives

Given the scope for corporations to relocate their activities to jurisdictions offering more lenient stakeholder regulation than that which currently obtains, how interested are corporations in exploiting these opportunities? The first difficulty in answering this question is to acknowledge that although managers *ought* to pursue shareholder wealth maximization as an overarching goal, it is not clear that they actually do so. Endemic agency costs—namely the costs to shareholders of supervising and disciplining corporate managers—mean that managers enjoy some scope to favour their own interests at the expense of the shareholders. In the context of corporate strategic decisions regarding the location for corporate economic activity, the presence of agency costs lowers the commitment of managers to undertake search, negotiation and, if necessary, relocation activities that serve shareholder interests. Managerial reluctance to do so is heightened by the personal costs sustained by managers if relocation means that they will have to uproot their homes and families by moving to another, less-familiar jurisdiction.[6] Predictably, the personal costs of relocation can be attenuated if senior managers are able to move discrete portions of the corporation's activities to a foreign jurisdiction without having to themselves suffer relocation (and its attendant costs).

However, let us assume that corporate managers are wholly devoted to shareholder interests and are, therefore, committed to continuous review of the location of the corporation's economic activities and to strategic relocation where necessary to realize cost-savings.[7] The question is how footloose corporations will be in response to perceived regulatory differences between the current and the prospective jurisdiction. In discussing this issue, it is important to recognize that any decision to move corporate activities to another jurisdiction faces non-trivial costs.[8] The corporation may have location-specific investments — namely plant and equipment, — the value of which may not be easily be recouped if relocation means transferring existing activities to a more congenial regulatory regime.[9] Of course, the same may be true of firm- and location-specific investments in human capital. Some employees or suppliers having highly specific investments in their relationship with the corporation may decline to relocate, again implying the loss of sunk investments. Alternatively, they may only agree to migrate if the corporation continues to respect, at least insofar as their situation is concerned, existing and perhaps more stringent levels of regulation than that offered by the destination jurisdiction. Indeed, even the relationship, and familiarity, that managers have with existing regulators and regulation is characterized by sunk investments that cannot be recovered in the event of migration.

Even if corporations could recover part of this sunk investment, they still face significant uncertainties in contemplating relocation to another jurisdiction. Can corporations be confident that the regulatory standards offered by prospective jurisdictions will be maintained into the future? This question is of considerable concern to corporations because once they relocate their activities and make sunk investments in the destination jurisdiction, they are vulnerable to "bait and switch" strategies by the destination state. Given the status of regulatory product as consisting of several different elements (namely law, the institutions enforcing the law and the level of enforcement), corporations need to worry about non-trivial adverse changes in regulations that can be effected through relatively informal means (say, for instance, more vigorous enforcement).

Another important dimension of the relocation calculus facing corporations is the tied goods character of a prospective destination's regulatory product. Because corporations cannot consume only certain aspects of the destination jurisdiction's regulatory system and ignore others, managers must worry about the interplay of all of the destination jurisdiction's law and regulations on the profitability of corporate activity. Despite the fact that a prospective jurisdiction's environmental laws, for instance, may be attractive, its labour standards may be much higher than the corporation's current jurisdiction, thereby offsetting the benefits of migration associated with the environmental regulatory regime. Further complicating matters is the fact that regulatory obligations cannot be separated from input factors markets. It is one thing for a state to offer a comprehensive and highly attractive regulatory matrix. It is another for it to combine this structure with an attractive business climate that ensures corporate access to a highly skilled and reliable set of employees and suppliers. Indeed, even beyond the content of specific regulations and the state of a country's factor markets, corporations will be interested in the more general features of a country's political, social and economic climate.

In tandem, these factors suggest that corporations will not be nearly as feckless as some commentators have proposed in relocating jurisdictions in response to marginal regulatory changes. Migrating corporations face certain and non-trivial costs and uncertain benefits from relocation. This does not, however, imply that corporations will never be prepared to relocate in response to perceived regulatory differences, only that the calculus is a complex one, and this reduces the threat value of defection to more congenial regimes.

The complexities of the demand-side for regulation are mirrored by complexities extant on the supply-side. In the highly stylized model of the hyperglobalists, states (through their elected politicians and appointed bureaucrats) seek to retain corporate patronage, and the jobs, investment, and tax revenue that follow in train, through the provision of a more congenial regulatory product. Constraints imposed by ideas, institutions, or competing domestic interests are given short shrift, or dismissed altogether. Simply put, states will do whatever it takes to retain corporate activity, even if this requires abandonment of core democratic values or alienation of salient interest groups.

Of course, this account is highly implausible. Democratic states are accountable to a number of different constituencies. Although politicians and bureaucrats may yearn for the benefits of corporate activity, they will not agree to paying any price to achieve this goal, particularly when it compromises the realization of other goals and values. A government, for instance, that systematically favours foreign corporate interests at the expense of certain stakeholder groups, even if they lack a powerful political voice, may jeopardize its overall standing with the citizens. The magnitude and timing of that discipline depends on a number of different factors: the salience of the interest groups affected (both positively and negatively) by proposed regulation, the concentration of political power, the role of the media, and the country's political traditions and values. This more nuanced depiction of state behaviour means that ideas and institutions are equally important parts of a country's production process, and will affect the commitment of state actors to providing regulations that seek to attract corporate patronage.

Instrument Choice

IN LIGHT OF THE SCOPE FOR STATES TO SUPPLY SUBOPTIMAL LEVELS OF REGULATORY product in certain circumstances (most particularly, as described above, when states have deficient democratic institutional arrangements and/or support industrial activity that generates targeted transborder externalities), we now direct attention to the various ways in which the propensity of states to supply this regulatory product can be constrained.

Regulatory cooperation via multilateral agreements

To the extent that unfettered state competition is regarded as inimical to social welfare, one obvious option is to effect hands-tying agreements among competing states that seek to limit the scope for competition. Strong movements toward regulatory cooperation (if not outright harmonization) can be currently witnessed in several international institutional contexts, perhaps most obviously in the context of the international trade regime with the steady diminution and elimination of barriers to trade that the GATT/World Trade Organization (WTO) has engendered since its introduction in 1947.[10]

Despite the positive effects that harmonization of international standards using multilateral agreements may engender in some contexts, such as the international trade context, it is not always the best way to ensure that the lack of power felt by nation-states in the presence of large corporations is contained. There are generally two main problems associated with the use of multilateral agreements or conventions for solving what amount to international collective action problems and the race-to-the-bottom. The first of these problems is that states fully retain their sovereignty in the context of multilateral agreements and can decide whether or not they want to adopt a convention or sign onto a multilateral agreement. If corporations exert pressure at this stage of the process (either latently or explicitly), it is understandably much the same situation as if the country on its own were solely adopting the policies because there will almost always be states that are not parties to the agreement, thereby enjoying an accretion in competitive advantage and becoming more attractive to economically driven corporations seeking to minimize costs and maximize profits. The second problem with multilateral agreements as a solution to the problem of countervailing corporate power relates to the reality that being a signatory to a multilateral agreement is not the same as guaranteeing full future compliance. If the stakes are high enough, many states will carve out pockets of exceptions by which they can both accommodate the wishes or needs of corporations and yet, sometimes plausibly, sometimes facetiously argue that they are abiding by the spirit of their international commitments.

One advantage of multilateral instruments as a means of checking corporate power is that multilateral agreements may serve as a credible way for governments to stand their ground against the pressure by corporations for a "better deal." By being able to state that they are bound by international commitments not to legislate, regulate or enforce their laws in a compromised manner (e.g., in a manner prejudicial to environmental protection interests, labour standards or fair tax policies) and to point to the executed instruments that establish those obligations, countries may be able to alleviate much of the pressure they feel to bend the rules in favour of corporations.

Unilateral nation-state actions

Trade and economic sanctions constitute the primary way in which nation-states attempt to unilaterally impose their desires for more humane labour practices on the rest of world, to promote fair tax policy competition, and to endorse reasonable protective environmental standards. However, the effectiveness of these types of sanctions is largely dependent upon the size and importance of the economy or economies imposing sanctions. For instance, American-led sanctions against South Africa for human rights abuses associated with the country's apartheid policies are widely reported to have been of considerable importance in promoting democracy and an abandonment of apartheid, even though the United States was only one of a large number of nations that had imposed economic sanctions on the country. According to Peter Fitzgerald, "The South African sanctions remain the preeminent example, cited by proponents of state and local sanctions, of the value of selective purchasing law and similar measures that essentially force businesses to decide who is the more important customer—the targeted company or the state and local government in the United States" (2001, 7-8).

In addition, trade sanctions imposed against Burma by the US federal government also proved to be effective, at least to a limited extent, by causing some large American-based corporations, such as Apple Computer, Phillips Electronics, PepsiCo and Texaco to abandon their Burmese operations (Fitzgerald 2001, 11). Anecdotal evidence is certainly interesting, but it is not especially compelling. A comprehensive study conducted by Hufbauer, Schott and Elliott examined 115 instances of economic sanctions imposed over a period of approximately 40 years. The authors found that in the case studies examined, a success rate of 34 percent was achieved through the use of economic sanctions—a success that is not extraordinarily high, but certainly significant (Trebilcock and Howse 1999, 450).

One of the main uses of trade and economic sanctions surround the use of the threat of withdrawal of a generalized system of preferences (GSP) to developing countries by the US and the European Committee. The threat of the removal of these benefits has reportedly worked well in persuading small rogue nations of the benefits to be had through cooperation. For example, Trebilcock and Howse refer to changes in labour law in Malaysia, Chile and the Dominican Republic that were at least partly engendered by these types of threats (Howse 1999, 449).

The findings of Hufbauer, Schott and Elliott and recent anecdotal experiences with American-led sanctions against Iraq and other states suggest that the unilateral imposition of trade and economic sanctions on rogue states is probably of moderate usefulness. On the one hand, the evidence suggests that trade and economic sanctions can be a powerful tool in causing unjust regimes to collapse (as with apartheid). On the other hand, evidence also seems to suggest that trade and economic sanctions can sometimes backfire on sanctions-imposing states. For example, Thomas Henriksen has observed that

> unintended consequences often flow from sanctions; instead of political shipwreck, they have motivated people to improvise and develop economic self-sufficiency. One classic illustration of this process is the former Rhodesia (now Zimbabwe). When first Britain and then the United Nations placed sanctions on the breakaway Rhodesian government, the landlocked African state found itself almost friendless in the world community. During the decade from 1965 to 1975, Rhodesia transformed its economy from a near-total dependence on imported manufactured goods in exchange for raw materials to a high degree of self-sufficiency. Only oil production and industrial machinery eluded Rhodesian enterprise. Moreover, Rhodesia's economy initially increased its productivity (1999).

One thing can be said for certain regarding trade and economic sanctions: the greater the number of economies participating in the sanctions and the greater the importance of the participating countries' economies to the rogue state, the greater the impacts will be felt and the greater the *prima facie* potential for the success of the sanctions. However, there is always the possibility that sanctions will be felt deeply, but the response, as in Rhodesia, will be stronger nationalism and self-reliance.

Promotion of the adoption of voluntary codes of conduct and self-regulation

Corporations can also be encouraged to respect the rights of workers and environmental standards through voluntary codes of conduct, although it is unclear to what extent such self-regulation is or has been successful in the past. Among the leaders in promoting corporate self-regulation have been the member countries of the Organisation for Economic Co-operation and Development (OECD). In 1976 the OECD first announced the *OECD Guidelines for Multinational Enterprises*. Since then, the OECD has revamped the *Guidelines* three times, most recently in June 2000. The most recent version of the *Guidelines* is intended to "ensure that the operations of enterprises are in harmony with government policies; strengthen the basis of mutual confidence between enterprises and the societies in which they operate; improve the foreign investment climate; and enhance the contribution of multinational enterprises (MNEs) to sustainable development" (Canada 2001). More specifically, the *Guidelines* provide recommendations in these specific corporate operational areas:

- *Disclosure*: covers the public dissemination by MNEs of reliable and relevant information on their activities.
- *Employment and industrial relations*: covers, *inter alia*, the issues of non-discrimination, forced labour, child labour and freedom of association and collective bargaining.
- *Environment*: covers issues such things as MNEs' environmental management systems and contingency planning.
- *Combatting bribery*: aims to eliminate bribery of foreign public officials.
- *Consumer interest*: seeks to ensure that MNEs respect consumer rights, including regarding the quality and safety of products.
- *Science and technology*: recognizes that MNEs can play an important role in improving local knowledge without compromising their intellectual property rights.
- *Competition*: promotes respect for competition rules and avoidance of anti-competitive behaviour.
- *Taxation*: addresses MNE compliance with tax laws and regulations (Canada 2001).

Since the *Guidelines* have been reviewed several times and have benefited from considerable input from interested parties, including member and non-member governments, non-governmental organizations and corporations, they represent a current and comprehensive set of operational recommendations for corporations. This wealth of information and guidance has not been squandered by corporations. According to the OECD, nearly all *Fortune 500* companies have voluntarily adopted firm-wide codes of conduct—many of which have likely drawn heavily from the *Guidelines*. In addition, the OECD reports that over 60 percent of the top 500 firms in the UK have adopted similar codes of conduct (OECD 2000, 8).

Despite the widespread adoption of these codes of conduct by corporations, however, there remains the question of how effective they are at deterring corporations from engaging in ethically suspect behaviour. Unenforced codes of conduct are unlikely to govern behaviour any more than unenforced laws do. Whether corporations monitor their far-flung operations sufficiently to ensure robust (or even marginal) compliance with their codes of conduct is not entirely clear. Given the costs associated with monitoring for violations of the codes of conduct and the gains potentially to be had in operating income from violating codes of conduct, it would not be surprising if compliance with corporate codes of conduct was less than perfect. Given the relatively benign outcome of the posited "race-to-the-bottom" with respect to labour rights and environmental protections, however, it is very likely that these voluntary codes of conduct have imposed at least some positive measure of discipline on corporations.

Social responsibility movement and its impact on the governance of corporations

The rise of the Internet, and the enhanced communication and coordination of private party activities that it allows, has given rise to a new type of corporate lobby group—a grassroots, techno-savvy network of social activists working together to point out the costs and negative effects associated with corporate irresponsibility the world over. One recent example of the new social activism that the Internet has facilitated is the Burmese example referred to earlier. Although sanctions imposed by the US federal government had much to do with some of the large corporations presently in Burma abandoning their operations there, much of the motivation behind the US government's decision to impose those sanctions in the first place was a direct result of strong public pressure to act to denounce the actions of the Burmese authoritarian military government.

Another way in which the social responsibility movement has impacted upon corporations is through "ethical investing" initiatives. One of the leading organizations dedicated to promoting socially responsible investing is a Canadian organization called the "Social Investment Organization" (OECD 2000, 63). According to them,

> socially responsible investing (sometimes known as ethical investing) is the application of peoples' values to their investments. It includes all the financial decision-making processes that are a part of a prudent investment management approach, but it also includes the selection and management of investments based on peoples' ethical, moral, social or environmental concerns (Social Investment 2000).

The socially responsible investment movement not only decreases the demand for shares of firms that are engaged in the traditional "sin" businesses of alcohol or tobacco, but also for companies that have been alleged to abuse labour rights, harm the environment, engage in military contracts, or engage in otherwise undesirable corporate behaviour. Correspondingly, the socially responsible investment movement increases the demand for shares of companies that positively and proactively seek to promote ethical ends such as finding ways to limit environmental damage through recycling of waste. As a consequence of the reduced demand engendered for misbehaving companies' shares resulting from the socially responsible investment movement, even corporations that pay attention only to the share price will receive negative feedback from their unethical deeds.

The extent to which this share-price suppression will occur, however, is highly debatable, and may only represent a very small (a fraction of a percent) discount over what the stock would otherwise trade at. This is the case because investors who are morally neutral will always have an incentive to buy stocks that are underpriced according to expected future cash flows. To the extent that there are enough of these investors in the market to keep the market efficient, the discount engendered by socially responsible investors will approach nil.

Since morally neutral investors will probably bid up the share price of companies who fall out of favour with ethical or socially responsible investors and because social activists' main impacts are on lobbying their own governments to either take multilateral or unilateral action against so-called "rogue states," the primary role of social responsibility movements appears to be in the movement's ability to influence domestic governments. To the extent, however, that social activists can impose considerable market costs on corporations, which is usually restricted to high-profile consumer goods producers such as PepsiCo, social activists can play an important role independently of their influence on the state.

Conclusion

WHILE IN A COMPLETELY COMPARTMENTALIZED INTERNATIONAL GEOPOLITICAL SYStEM the threat that corporations will continue to erode the power of nation-states and hold societies hostage through their "outlaw" status is considerable, it is not necessarily a *fait accompli* in light of our expanding and developing supranational legal mechanisms for reining in rogue states and impairing the ability of corporations to exercise power adversely. There are several strong mechanisms for constraining the power of corporations in terms of their ability to capture governments to cater to their desires for low taxes, low labour standards and low environmental regulatory overhead. For instance, nation-states are increasingly engaging in multilateral agreements to help promote a united front against corporations willing to take advantage of collective action problems and the implicit gains from defection they involve. This is not a solution for every problem, however, because of the difficulties associated with trying to force other countries to assume obligations under the agreements as well as the issues related to the enforcement of these agreements. Multilateral solutions work best in conjunction with the other mechanisms described above. Unilateral action is somewhat problematic because it gives extraordinary power to large economies such as those of the US and the EU to effect change, whereas most other nations are virtually hamstrung to achieve any sort of momentum for change by imposing sanctions. Voluntary codes of conduct have limited ability to constrain the actions of corporations because it is unclear exactly how such codes of conduct can be policed or enforced. Indeed, this may explain their perverse appeal for some socially irresponsible large corporations—they can stem the tide of public discontent arising from their behaviour in both developed and developing countries by pointing to their voluntary codes of conduct, while turning a blind eye to the actual practice of their operations in far-flung parts of the globe. Finally, the social responsibility movement appears to be a promising source of constraint on corporations, although the extent to which this is possible has yet to be conclusively demonstrated. More research is needed in this area.

Thus it appears that corporations, although constrained to some extent by the considerable costs associated with moving core activities wantonly from jurisdiction to jurisdiction, still do have some mobility and some power to bend nation-states to their will. To the extent that their threats to leave or relocate from developed countries are not credible, the abuse of their power can be mitigated. To the extent that their threats are credible, which they often are in the context of production and manufacturing, their power to influence and capture governments is real. This is especially the case because most corporation manufacturing and production takes place in developing countries which have the most to gain from the presence of corporations, but strangely also perhaps the most to lose. In any event, the multilateral agreements and other international movements working together to contain the adverse effects associated with corporate power and collective action problems represent one of the most promising and potentially effective ways yet devised of dealing with the negative effects of globalization.

Notes

1 The terminology is from Hirschman's famous book, *Exit, Voice and Loyalty* (1970).

2 Shareholders can also rely on a host of other market and legal mechanisms such as shareholder suits (breach of duty of care and loyalty) and hostile takeovers to deal with corporate relocations which reduce shareholder wealth.

3 For a very thoughtful discussion of this issue, see Leebron (1996, p. 72). Leebron expresses scepticism over the capacity of external observers to determine whether a state has sound democratic processes in place that provide confidence in outcomes that are generated.

4 This suggestion is taken from Trebilcock and Howse (1999).

5 We should further assume that these problems are not reciprocal, that is, that neighbouring states do not generate equivalent and offsetting externalities upon each other.

6 Managers, like all citizens, derive benefits from their communal affiliations. This is true for their families as well. A decision to relocate jeopardizes sunk investment in community affiliations and reduces managerial welfare.

7 In considering how a corporation will react to the possibility of lower effective regulation that is achieved through jurisdictional relocation, it is important to bear in mind that corporations will often strategically overstate the costs of complying with existing or higher standards of regulation in an effort to secure immediate reductions in the regulatory burden from the regulating state. But when those efforts fail, they demonstrate remarkable agility in accommodating themselves quickly and at low cost to the disputed standard. More than that, many regulations that corporations publicly posture against at the time of initial introduction later turn out to be value-enhancing from the perspective of the corporation. There is now a significant body of data demonstrating that the adoption of *higher* levels of social and labour regulation by states are consistent with (rather than inimical to) enhanced factor productivity. An insistence, for example, on shorter work hours for labour or more stringent occupational health and safety standards may improve employee performance, and be revenue-neutral, or perhaps even revenue-enhancing to the corporation.

8 The costs are in addition to the personal costs borne by the corporation's managers, which were discussed above.

9 Further, if relocation motivated by reduced regulatory burdens is seen by stakeholders to unfairly exploit certain stakeholder groups by, for instance, managers opportunistically breaching quasi-contractual commitments made by the corporation, then relocation to a less stringent regime could impose significant reputational costs on the corporation and its managers that will necessarily increase the future cost of contracting to them.

10 Regional multilateral agreements have played a key role in harmonizing international legal and regulatory regimes, most prominently in the EU and under the North American Free Trade Agreement (NAFTA). The motivation behind and effects of the operation of each of these multilateral regimes—the GATT/WTO, the EU and NAFTA—are highly controversial. The reason often given for this prevalent discontent with economically driven multilateral regimes is that many observers fear that entering into binding multilateral trading agreements with other nations will erode the legitimate democratic power of the nation-state, and lead to a loss of sovereignty, lower labour standards and poor environmental protection. More specifically, the fear is that countries will lose the ability to address the degradation of the environment, poor labour rights protections and other compelling social issues in a flexible way, and that this will be replaced with international multilateral commitments that are functions of gov-

ernmental fiat thoroughly pervaded and influenced by corporate economic interests. Some suggest that multilaterally negotiated agreements made by elected government representatives are too removed from direct democratic influence and stakeholder lobbying and thus too subject to trade-offs and political log-rolling to be legitimate despite the fact that the majority of the government representatives participating in the negotiations are democratically elected. Fears of this type (admittedly among others) served to spark recent violent public protests, *inter alia*, in November 1999 in Seattle at the eighth ministerial conference of the WTO, in April 2001 at the Summit of the Americas in Quebec City, and in July 2001 at the G8 Summit in Genoa, Italy and seem to suggest widespread public perception that current multilateral agreements do not do enough to provide for the furtherance of labour rights and environmental protection. See Shaffer (2001).

References

Canada. "Canada's National Contact Point for the OECD Guidelines for Multinational Enterprises" (October 2001) digital document available online at http://www.dfait-maeci.gc.ca/tna-nac/ncp-pcn/about_guidelines-e.asp.

Fitzgerald, P. "Massachusetts, Burma, and the World Trade Organization: A Commentary on Blacklisting, Federalism, and Internet Advocacy in the Global Trading Era." *Cornell International Law Journal*, Vol. 34, no. 1 (2001): 7-8.

Henriksen, T.H. "Using Power and Diplomacy To Deal with Rogue States." *Hoover Essay in Public Policy* (February 1999) accessed October 1, 2001, digital document available online at http://www.hoover.stanford.edu/publications/epp/94/94a.html

Hirschmann, A.O. *Exit, Voice and Loyalty: Responses to Decline in Firms, Organizations and States*. Cambridge, MA: Harvard University Press, 1970.

Hufbauer, G.C. and J.J. Schott with K.A. Elliott. *Economic Sanctions in Support of Foreign Policy Goals*. Washington, DC: Institute for International Economics, 1983.

Leebron, D.W. "Lying Down with Procrustes: An Analysis of Harmonization Claims." In *Fair Trade and Harmonization: Prerequisites for Free Trade?*, ed. J. Bhagwati and R.E. Hudex. Vol. 1: *Economic Analysis*. Cambridge, MA: MIT Press.

OECD. *An Update of the 1996 Study "Trade Employment and Labour Standards: A Study of Core Workers' Rights and International Trade."* Paris: OECD, 2000.

Shaffer, G. "The World Trade Organization Under Challenge: Democracy and the Law and Politics of the WTO's Treatment of Trade and Environment Matters." *Harvard Environmental Law Review*, Vol. 25, no. 1 (2001).

Social Investment. "Introduction" (October 2001) digital document available online at http://www.socialinvestment.ca.

Tiebout, C.M. "A Pure Theory of Public Expenditures." *Journal of Political Economy*, Vol. 64, no. 4 (1956): 416-424.

Trebilcock, M. and R. Howse, *The Regulation of International Trade*, 2d ed. New York: Routledge, 1999.

Corporate Governance: Comments

Introduction

THE WORD GOVERNANCE IS WIDELY USED, INDEED, OVERUSED. IT IS APPLIED IN A VARIety of contexts, but in general, a governance structure is simply a set of rules. Corporate governance is the framework of laws, regulatory institutions and reporting requirements that conditions the way corporations are managed.

Corporate governance has traditionally been concerned primarily with the responsibility of corporate management to shareholders. This issue was brought to the public or at least professional attention almost 70 years ago in the book, *The Modern Corporation and Private Property* by Adolf Berle and Gardiner Means. Berle and Means observed that since those who managed large corporations owned only a tiny portion, if any, of the shares, they would not necessarily have any interest in maximizing the profits of the corporation. They gave examples of cases in which even significant minority shareholders (such as John D. Rockefeller Jr. in Standard Oil) were unable to unseat what they regarded as unsatisfactory incumbent managements.

Berle and Means focused attention on a fundamental dilemma. Widespread ownership of corporate stock reduces risk and this reduces the cost of capital. It is also difficult, however, for shareholders of widely held companies to ensure that the corporation in which they own shares is managed in their interest and this increases the cost of capital.

Corporate governance systems differ from country to country. While each system has its strengths and weaknesses, all are conditioned on national institutions and economic characteristics. Nevertheless, there has been some convergence. Access to US capital markets requires adherence to US governance regulations and adoption of US governance practices. Management of European companies may have become more responsive to shareholder concerns, for example, as more European companies are listed on US stock exchanges. Similarly, foreign companies (including Canadian companies) listed on US stock exchanges have become subject to more aggressive shareholder oversight in the form of class-action lawsuits.

The nature of corporate governance has also been changed by exogenous factors. Institutional investors, both foreign and domestic, hold an increasing portion of the shares of public companies and have been playing an increasing and sometimes controversial role in managerial oversight. Institutional investors may be better informed both because they are larger and more specialized and possibly because they represent the employees of the very companies in which they are investing. US institutional investors tend to be more aggressive and Canadian companies may be subject to increasing pressure from this quarter in the future.

The term corporate governance now connotes much more than a concern with shareholders' rights. Indeed, for those concerned with corporate responsibility, the problem is that there is excessive concern with shareholders' rights. According to those holding the corporate responsibility view, management should forego profits to support the causes they espouse. The corporate responsibility movement is international in scope but tends to reflect US and European concerns. The pressure it exerts is on industries, individuals and communities as much as on corporations.[1]

In his paper, Ron Daniels addresses the issue of the footloose corporation. He asks whether the ability of corporations to seek out the most favourable jurisdictions in which to locate will reduce the discretion of national governments and result in a "race to the bottom" in which governments are forced to abandon cherished social programs. He suggests that intergovernmental competition may constrain domestic rent-seeking and result in greater governmental efficiency rather than eliminating programs with broad appeal. While this may mean smaller government, it need not imply a race to the bottom.

My comments are in three areas. First, I discuss traditional corporate governance concerns and how globalization has affected them. Second, I examine the evolution of governance institutions in the marketplace and how this has varied internationally. Third, I comment on Daniels' views on the effect of corporate mobility on the policy discretion of the nation-state.

My general view is that corporate locational mobility is an old phenomenon which, over a period of 40 years, has resulted in barely a hint of a reduction in the political discretion of national governments. Indeed, corporate mobility itself is seldom the issue. The political tension is frequently between contending interest groups, some of them foreign, with corporations, while not disinterested, being minor participants.

Conventional Corporate Governance Issues

TRADITIONAL CORPORATE GOVERNANCE CONCERNS HAVE INVOLVED DISCLOSURE, directorial oversight, shareholders' rights and, ultimately, the efficient functioning of equities markets. Measures to decrease information asymmetrics (increase corporate disclosure) and to enhance the ability of shareholders to monitor and discipline management continue to be discussed in Canada. The Dey Report (1994) and the interim report of the Joint Committee on Corporate Governance (2001) have been concerned principally with disclosure requirements and the responsibilities, liabilities and remuneration of corporate directors. The Senate (Kirby) Committee (1996) report examined both these issues and the role of institutional investors in corporate governance.[2]

There is still considerable disagreement as to whether inquiries into corporate governance practices should be educational or prescriptive. The argument for a prescriptive approach is that the failure of one public company to disclose relevant information raises doubts in the minds of potential shareholders of all companies and this increases their cost of capital. Thus, disclosure has a public good element. The other side of the argument is that potential shareholders can separate companies seeking to raise capital on the basis of their respective governance structures as well as their economic potential. As a consequence, suspicions of potential shareholders that they will be taken advantage of by insiders are built into the price they are willing to pay for shares and are thus effectively internalized. Insider-trading rules have always been controversial (Lemieux 2001). Regulation of the flow of information to the market is problematic. The events of September 11, 2001 have reminded us that opportunities for "outsider trading" may be just as great as the opportunities for insider trading.

The most recent discussion of corporate governance issues comes from the Joint Committee on Corporate Governance which was established by the Toronto Stock Exchange, the Canadian Venture Exchange and the Canadian Institute of Chartered Accountants. It has commissioned discussion papers on corporate disclosure, auditing and what responsibilities directors should have. Its March 2001 interim report has made a number of recommendations in this regard (Moldoveanu and Martin 2001; Joint Committee 2001). The Joint Committee notes in its interim report that similar proposals are being discussed in Britain and the United States.

Both the Joint Committee's interim report and the response to it recognize the international constraints and influences on corporate governance in Canada. The Joint Committee observes that Canadian companies listed on stock exchanges in other countries will have to abide by securities legislation in those countries. Among the companies subject to this requirement would be the 145 Canadian companies listed on the NASDAQ as of 1998.[3] The Joint Committee also recommends that Canadian companies raising funds on US capital markets be allowed to file financial statements in Canada that conform with US generally accepted accounting principles (GAAP) rather than Canadian GAAP. Comments on the interim report have noted that, in some cases, it recommends practices (a non-executive board chair) that deviate from current US practices and this may discourage companies from listing their shares in Canada.

In addition to conforming to securities legislation, Canadian companies listed on either the NASDAQ or on other US exchanges are subject to the general mode of corporate governance in the US. This includes shareholder class-action lawsuits. Class-action lawsuits have been launched against Nortel, for example, in connection with the decline in the price of its share in the autumn of 2000.[4]

Institutional investors

One of the most important changes in the nature of corporate governance has been the increased importance of institutional investors. According to the Kirby Committee Report (1996):

> Pension and mutual funds now own nearly one-half of the shares in Canadian publicly traded corporations; institutional holdings were just over 10 percent as recently as 1988, and 20 years ago, they were less than one percent.[5]

Paul Halpern notes that institutional investors account for 60 percent of the shares in the thousand largest US companies and 80 percent of the shares of listed British companies. Institutional investors, holding larger blocks of shares than individuals, may have a greater economic incentive to monitor managerial performance. Halpern observes that institutional investors, particularly public sector pension funds are becoming increasingly active both through the proxy process and through informal discussions with corporate managements. He attributes this increased activism to "the increasing holdings of financial institutions, especially index funds, the potential significant cost of unwinding equity positions, and the adoption of firm and state anti-takeover provisions that lead to entrenched behaviour." He predicts that pension and mutual funds will invest increasingly in both domestic and foreign equities and these equity holdings "will place them in a good position to generate the same pressure on management and boards in international companies as is currently being done in some domestic markets" (Halpern 1999). This is likely to give rise to increasing pressure on managements of Canadian public companies from foreign institutional investors.

US public sector pension plans (such as CalPERS) have been highly aggressive and confrontational, especially with respect to matters of executive compensation.[6] Canadian institutional investors have apparently been less confrontational. This is confirmed by some Canadian public companies who testified before the Kirby Committee that their US institutional investors tend to be more aggressive than their Canadian institutional investors.

Canadian institutional investors maintained in submissions to the Kirby Committee that they have been active in protecting the interests of all stockholders of the firms in which they have an interest, although there are apparently instances in which they have not been. Canadian institutional investors are most likely to meet privately with management to voice their concerns. Moreover, they are reluctant to seek seats on boards of directors of public companies because of potential conflicts of interest (e.g., they may also have investments in competing firms).

A continuing concern regarding institutional investors, particularly public sector institutions, is that they may be pursuing industrial policy or other interests antithetical to those of their fellow shareholders. Allegations of this nature continue to be made regarding the Caisse de depot (Fraser 2001). The Caisse rejects these allegations.

International convergence of governance institutions?

There have been some recent developments in the positive analysis of corporate governance. This should hardly be surprising since one of the features of market institutions is that they are evolutionary and adaptive. If natural selection prevails, the better institutions survive. For example, 15 years ago industrial policy analysts were convinced of the virtues of bank-centred financial systems. These systems, which were most highly developed in Japan and Germany, were characterized by large cross-holdings of equity between banks, other financial companies and industrial companies. They insulated management from the threat of takeover and were said to be characterized by a better flow of information, greater recognition of external effects and more patient investors than the equities-market-centred systems in the United States and Britain. Less is heard these days both about the virtues of bank-centred systems and about the vices of equities-market-centred systems.

Halpern (1999) revisits this issue and concludes that the bank-based managerial oversight serves the interests of debt-holders rather than equity-holders and leads to both managerial entrenchment and inflexibility. Although he anticipates that European and Japanese companies listed on US stock exchanges will become more shareholder-oriented, Halpern does not see a convergence of the two systems. He also suggests that the relevant institutional distinction is not between bank and market-centred governance but between contestable and non-contestable corporate control.

Concentrated ownership

In terms of corporate governance systems, Halpern (1999) also observes that a further important distinction between systems dominated by closely-held companies and those dominated by widely-held companies without a controlling shareholder. Widely-held companies are the exception in Canada and those that do not have legislated ceilings on individual shareholdings are even less common. Halpern cites evidence to the effect that in most advanced countries "the Berle and Means 'company' is not widespread, the separation of cash flows and voting rights is pervasive, occurring more frequently through a pyramid structure than dual class shares, and banks do not control many companies" (1999).

Closely-held companies raise governance issues of a different kind than widely-held companies. Specifically, closely-held companies raise a governance issue if there remains an "outside" minority shareholder interest. In this case there is an incentive for the "inside" controlling interest to divert the flow of profits away from the outsiders and toward themselves. This incentive is greater the greater the divergence between the distributions of cash-flow rights and voting rights respectively. Of course, if potential outside shareholders anticipate their outside minority status, they will discount the value they place on these shares accordingly. It is for this reason that non-voting shares typically sell at a discount.

There is some evidence that founder-controlled companies tend to be managed in the interests of the founder rather than the shareholders as a group. Morck, Srangeland and Yeung (1998) find that heir-controlled Canadian firms show low industry-adjusted financial performance relative to other firms the same ages and sizes. They argue that concentrated, inherited corporate control impedes growth, and they dub this "the Canadian disease." It is perhaps more accurate to call it *a* Canadian disease, since there are many "Canadian diseases" and some of them are highly debilitating if not fatal.

It is important to understand that, from a shareholder-wealth-maximization perspective, concentrated ownership does not present a problem when the cash-flow rights of insiders are commensurate with their control rights. In this case, inept or self-indulgent insiders are largely hurting themselves. Even if cash-flow rights are more widely distributed than control rights, outsiders are still protected to the extent that they anticipated this problem when they bought in.

New Governance Institutions for the New Economy

PERHAPS THE MOST INTERESTING RECENT DEVELOPMENT IN CORPORATE GOVERNANCE has been the rise of the venture capitalist. Venture capitalists have played a crucial role in both the financing and the governance of knowledge-intensive start-ups. Indeed, it is interesting to speculate as to where the information-technology revolution would be without the development of venture capital governance. By bringing their own technological and industrial knowledge to the table, venture capitalists are able to mitigate the information asymmetry problem which is most severe in the case of knowledge-intensive firms with no track record. The venture capitalist bridges the period between start-up and the point at which the market at large can assess the firm's prospects:

> VCs [venture capitalists] are specialized monitors who offer investee firms valuable guidance once the investment has been made. VCs monitor and sometimes replace management, participate in strategic decisions, and offer informal advice on decisions of lesser importance. The ability to monitor is closely connected with the ability to resolve information asymmetries. It is only by virtue of a keen understanding of the enterprise and what is needed to achieve success that the VC can monitor effectively. In turn, monitoring not only addresses problems of moral hazard, but also reduces information asymmetry by resulting in enhanced information flow between the entrepreneur and the VC....
>
> Once the firm has an established product and has demonstrated profit potential, other sources of funding may become available. Management may have matured sufficiently that the marginal value of the VC's monitoring, advice, and participation in strategic decisions has greatly declined. Contacts between the firm and suppliers, marketing experts, lawyers and investment bankers may be in place and need little further massaging by the VC. At this point (aside from choosing the timing and means of exit), the VC's unique skill set is no longer particularly useful to the enterprise, and it is time for the VC to turn its investment into cash and move on to other ventures to which it can add value (Cumming and MacIntosh 2000).

The contribution of venture capital finance to innovation in the United States has been documented by Kortum and Lerner (1998). They find that venture-capital-financed research and development (R&D) is much more likely to produce patented innovations than R&D spending financed by other means. They find that between 1982 and 1992 venture-capital-financed R&D accounted for 3 percent of total corporate R&D spending, but produced 15 percent of industrial innovations. Venture-capital-backed companies in a given industry tend to patent more, their patents are more frequently cited and more frequently litigated. The authors argue that this is not simply a reflection of venture capital being attracted to the best opportunities.

There is widespread international recognition of the importance of venture capital in the knowledge economy. Of course, countries want their own domestic venture-capital industry.[7] For small countries such as Canada this may be difficult. The essence of venture capital is specialized knowledge. The requisite degree of specialization is probably not possible within the context of a small market. With an international venture-capital market, however, there is always the feat that returns from domestically generated technology will be realized abroad.[8]

Stakeholders versus Shareholders

There have been historically two views of appropriate objectives for corporate management. The first is that the objective of management should be to maximize profits or more appropriately, to maximize shareholder wealth. The virtues of profit maximization are well-known. A profit-maximizing firm operating in competitive markets uses resources efficiently. Profit, being the excess of the value created over the opportunity cost of resources used, is the ultimate measure of the contribution a corporation is making to society. Milton Friedman once suggested that the only social responsibility of business is to increase profits, only as long as it stays within the rules of the game, that is, engages in open and free competition without deception or fraud. This does not mean that management should behave in a miserly Dickensian fashion. It may be possible to do well by doing good. That is, it may well be profitable to be a "model" employer and corporate citizen. It has certainly been argued that "clean" production can be profitable as well as environmentally benign. All the shareholder wealth-maximization view requires that management not sacrifice long-run profitability in pursuit of its own objectives or what it thinks are society's objectives. It is for individual shareholders to decide how to distribute their wealth among charitable causes. It was Andrew Carnegie, not United States Steel, who funded the construction of public libraries across Canada and the United States.

Maximization of shareholder wealth does not mean that all other relevant interests are ignored. As Ron Daniels has pointed out, the corporation is a nexus of contracts. There are contracts with customers, employees, input suppliers and lenders. Contracts with each group have their own governance structures which specify rights and obligations and contain provisions for interpretation and enforcement. The historic concern of what is now called corporate governance is with the implicit contractual relationship between the corporation and the suppliers of equity capital, that is, shareholders. As residual claimants, the shareholders somehow have to ensure that there is a residual for them to claim.

Corporate social responsibility

The alternate and apparently the more popular view is that corporate management should be "socially responsible." That is, management should sacrifice profitability to a variety of other objectives. The ranking of these alternate objectives depends on the interest group involved. Advocates of corporate social responsibility make use of a number of different mechanisms to change corporate objectives. Broadly speaking, there are three types of tactics employed: (i) using the political process to further regulate business activity; (ii) product and factor market boycotts; and (iii) shareholder activism.

Advocates of corporate social responsibility would also alter both the managerial decision-making process and the structure of corporate governance. In their view, the corporate decision-making process should also include the views of all stakeholders with a stakeholder being anyone who wants to have a say.[9] The most vocal advocates of this point of view in recent years have been the non-governmental organizations (NGOs). There are numerous domestic, foreign and international codes of corporate responsibility to which Canadian companies are either trying or being pressured to adhere.

Shareholder activists use their voting power as shareholders to force management to support the causes they espouse.[10] Market boycotts are, of course, more effective in big markets. This has led and is likely to continue to lead to the imposition of the frequently self-interested views of interest groups from large markets on firms based in smaller countries such as Canada. Campaigns often led by foreign politicians and NGOs have attempted to force Canadian companies to change their activities. The most recent example is Talisman Resources, a Calgary-based company with a 25 percent interest in an oil project in the Sudan, a country with a 40-year history of civil war.

> Shortly after Talisman started work in Sudan, it became the target of an American-led divestment campaign, a campaign that branded Talisman investors as holders of "slave stock." Following criticism from the American Secretary of State, Canada's Minister of Foreign Affairs was pressured by interest groups to impose sanctions on Talisman. The news media picked up the story, concluded that oil revenues were funding the bitter civil war and left the public with a horrifying image.... the result was predictable and public reaction was both swift and furious. Talisman's critics grew in number, shareholders started to divest, the stock price fell and the company's efforts to communicate the benefits of its involvement in Sudan fell on deaf ears (Falkenberg 2000).

Footloose Corporations

In his paper, Ron Daniels investigates the consequences of corporate mobility for the policy discretion of national governments. He suggests that there are two views. One is that corporate jurisdiction-shopping will inexorably force governments, desperate for jobs, to reduce corporate taxes and labour and environmental standards in order to attract corporate investors. This is the race-to-the bottom view. The alternate view is that interjurisdictional competition will force governments to offer efficient tax and public services packages. This implies that there will be a range of offerings, from low taxes and low public services to high taxes and high public services available in various jurisdictions. It does not imply a race to the bottom. Daniels takes the latter view, concluding that corporate mobility need not result in an undersupply of public services except in cases where there are interjurisdictional externalities.

The Tiebout (1956) model

Daniels' view that interjurisdictional competition may result in a range of tax and public services packages from which locationally mobile corporations may choose is inspired by the Tiebout model. Tiebout hypothesized that when individuals can choose among competing jurisdictions, they migrate to the jurisdiction offering the best deal, that is, the best public services for the lowest taxes. Among the assumptions necessary for the Tiebout model to work effectively are: costless mobility of individuals among jurisdictions; no interjurisdictional externalities; and communities that compete to provide public goods financed by head taxes or benefits taxes.

The Tiebout model implies an equilibrium in which everyone lives in the jurisdiction that provides the level of public goods they prefer. Competition among jurisdictions ensures that each jurisdiction provides its chosen level of public services efficiently. This is all to the good if it constrains interest group and bureaucratic rent-seeking and there are no interjurisdictional externalities. There is no race for the bottom in which taxes and public services are eliminated.

The limitations of the Tiebout model are well-known in public economics. The model relates to the provision of public goods financed by a head tax. It does not produce an equilibrium when individuals have different levels of wealth and are taxed according to their ability to pay. In essence, it does not deal with the redistributive activity. While the Tiebout model does not imply an equilibrium with no public goods and no taxes, it can be taken to imply an equilibrium with no redistributive activity. Wealthy people may well wish to consume very high levels of public goods but they will prefer not to pay more for them than the less wealthy. The same holds true for corporations. Corporations may opt for higher tax, higher public service jurisdictions, but they will presumably opt for the lowest tax bill for a given level of public service. It is the loss of redistributive power rather than an inability to provide public goods with which anti-globalists are concerned.

The consequences of taxing mobile capital to finance public expenditures are not addressed in the Tiebout model. A number of papers have shown that there is a tendency toward under-provision of local public services when they are financed by taxes on mobile capital (Mieszkowski and Zodrow 1989). If capital has become more mobile internationally, the revenues to be derived from taxing it might decline in relative terms and this could have an impact on public finances.

We can say that Tiebout's analysis does not rule out the under-provision of public services to the extent that they are financed by taxes on mobile capital, human or otherwise. Whether there has, in fact, been a race to the bottom then becomes an empirical question.

Jurisdiction-shopping and the race to the bottom

There has been concern about corporate "jurisdiction-shopping" for almost 40 years. Concerns about so-called "stateless corporations" go back almost as far.[11] Empirical studies of offshore sourcing and entry and exit behaviour going back to the early 1970s were summarized by McFetridge (1989). The extensive evidence available at that time did not support the idea of "capital on wheels," that is, of multinationals flitting from country to country in an unceasing attempt to extract ever lower tax rates, labour standards and environmental standards from host governments. Other studies found no multinational enterprise that qualifies as being truly stateless. Indeed, Halpern (1999) cites evidence that a surprising number of large firms in advanced industrial countries remain family-controlled.

John Baldwin (1997) studied the entry and exit behaviour of multinationals more recently. He reports that in Canada over the period 1970–79, the incidence of both Greenfield entry and closedown exit is much lower in industries dominated by foreign-owned firms than in industries dominated by domestic firms. Baldwin also finds that the incidence of changes in control of ongoing establishments is greater in industries dominated by foreign firms. This he attributes to the continuing opportunities for synergies offered by the type of intangible assets which characterize markets in which multinational enterprises (MNEs) are prevalent.

Altshuler, Grubert and Newlon (1998) have investigated the responsiveness of the international allocation of US foreign investment in manufacturing industries to differences in host country business tax rates. They find that, other things being equal, the stock of real capital (property, plant and equipment) held by manufacturing affiliates of US companies in a given country is greater, the lower that country's effective average tax rate in manufacturing. The response elasticity in 1992 is 2.7 implying that a 10 percent decrease in a country's average effective tax rate (given the tax rates of all other countries) would result in a 27 percent increase in the stock of real capital held by US manufacturing affiliates in that country. The response rate in 1984 was 1.5. The implication is that the location of foreign manufacturing activity by US firms became more sensitive to tax factors over the period 1984–92.

The evidence is that multinationals do not shift facilities from country to country in pursuit of concessions from host governments. This does not mean that there is no tendency for production of tradeable goods to expand over time in the most economically attractive locations and contract in the least attractive locations (as noted above). Taxation, labour standards and environmental standards may all influence the attractiveness of a particular location. But labour and environmental standards can cut both ways. Similarly, high tax jurisdictions may also have high quality public services and a stable business environment. Tiebout reasoning is useful here. It is the overall cost-benefit package delivered by a jurisdiction that counts. Even high-cost jurisdictions may continue to be attractive if there are significant agglomeration economies.

Capital mobility is not a new phenomenon. There has been plenty of time for a race to the bottom to manifest itself. Yet there is little evidence that a race to the bottom has even begun. The proportion of gross domestic product (GDP) collected in taxes in most countries of the Organisation for Economic Co-operation and Development (OECD) has increased, if anything, and some of the most open OECD countries have some of the highest percentage tax takes.[12] Some argue that the share of corporate taxes in total tax revenue is declining and that this is evidence of an incipient race to the bottom. In response, it can be argued that corporate income taxes always accounted for a small share of total tax revenue and that a reduction in corporate income taxes does not mean that corporate profits are not being taxed. They continue to be taxed as dividends and capital gains income in the hands of shareholders. Corporations operating in Canada are also taxed in other ways. User fees have become more prevalent as have consumption taxes. The incidence of these taxes may be in part on corporations and ultimately their foreign shareholders.

What may be new in all of this is human capital mobility. Government efforts to tax human capital may be increasingly frustrated by the brain drain. This has implications not only for the size of the government sector and the amount of redistributive activity but also for the terms of access to government-provided services such as education.

Globalization or domestic political economy?

The race to the bottom proponents see this issue as a struggle between multinationals and host governments. It is important to understand that conflicts between "jobs" and "the environment" can and often do involve contending domestic interest groups and that the transfer of wealth involved is often largely domestic. MNEs, while not disinterested, are not the principal beneficiaries of these transfers. Jobs have a value only if the workers involved are being paid wages in excess of their opportunity cost. In essence, the use of tax concessions by governments to "buy" jobs involves transfers from taxpayers-at-large to the workers involved. They could make these wage concessions themselves were it not for unions, minimum wages and the obvious willingness of politicians to coerce others into doing it for them.

Low corporate tax rates are not necessarily the result of corporate or capital mobility. Canada offers Canadian-controlled small businesses some of the most generous tax treatment in the world (Canada 1997). This cannot be the result of fears that these businesses will migrate elsewhere. It is more likely the result of domestic political considerations. At the same time, however, Canada has maintained preferential tax rates for manufacturing and processing firms for 35 years, presumably on the grounds that their products had to compete on world markets.

Conclusions

AMONG THE INTRIGUING RECENT DEVELOPMENTS IN CORPORATE GOVERNANCE ARE the rise of institutional shareholders, the emergence of the international corporate responsibility movement, and the emergence of new economy governance structures centred on venture capitalists. Moreover, multinational corporations based in small countries such as Canada will come under increasing pressure to adhere to US securities regulations, to defend themselves against class-action suits launched by US investors and to respond to activist US institutional investors as well as to US and European corporate responsibility advocates.

Capital is mobile and has been so for many years. This has not implied that corporations flit from country to country in search of greater concessions from potential host governments. To the extent that it does occur, interjurisdictional competition provides a welcome break on rent-seeking by domestic interest groups and bureaucrats. The redistributive consequences of this competition are, in all likelihood, largely domestic.

The tax revenue of national governments has not declined as a proportion of GDP. Corporate tax takes may be declining but this does not mean that income from capital is not taxed. It continues to be taxed in the hands of shareholders although opportunities for evading taxation may have been increasing prior to September 11, 2001. Human capital may also be increasingly mobile and this could serve to curb the redistributive bent of individual national governments more than corporate mobility has done so far.

Notes

1 For example, "We the undersigned will not purchase Canadian timber, meat, oil, pharmaceuticals, alcohol, tobacco, paper or travel in Canada until:
- the clubbing of baby seals stops or any other form of seal killing
- the hunting of Canadian grizzly bears is outlawed everywhere, not just in British Columbia
- the mass slaughter of elk and deer diagnosed with Mad Elk and Mad Deer Disease stops
- the Calgary Stampede, which causes the brutal pulling apart of calves by cowboys on horses and many other cruelties, stops." At http://petitiononline.com/seal/petition.html

2 The Standing Senate Committee on Banking, Trade and Commerce, *Corporate Governance*, Chairman, Michael Kirby, August 1996. Available from http://www.parl.gc.ca/english/senate/com-e/bank-e/cgo-tc-e.htm

3 Available from http://www.nasdaqnews.com/about/99factbook.pdf

4 On February 27, 2001, a Philadelphia law firm commenced a class-action lawsuit in United States District Court against Nortel Networks Corporation on behalf of those who purchased Nortel Networks Corporation securities during the period from November 1, 2000 through February 15, 2001. The plaintiffs allege that the defendant Nortel issued materially false and misleading information that misrepresented its financial condition and prospects and violated the *Securities Exchange Act* of 1934. As a result of this misrepresentation, the prices of Nortel securities were artificially inflated. The lawsuit seeks to recover losses suffered by individual and institutional investors who purchased Nortel's securities at artificially inflated prices. "Spector, Roseman & Kodroff, P.C. Files Class Action Suit Against Nortel Networks Corporation Alleging Securities Fraud." Available from http://www.spectoranddroseman.com/nortel.html

5 Kirby Committee Report. Available from http://www.parl.gc.ca/36/1/parlbus/commbus/senate/com-e/bank-e/rep-e/rep16part3-e.htm#INSTITUTIONAL%20INVESTOR%20ACTIVISM

6 "Kayla Gillan: Calpers' Grand Inquisitor: Meet the new scourge of underperforming companies." Available from http://www.businessweek.com/1997/08/b3515105.htm

7 See, for example, "Australia Announces Major Initiative to Attract Foreign Venture Capital." Available from http://www.utoronto.ca/onris/Australian%20%20VC%20reform.htm

8 See *A Canadian Innovation Agenda for the Twenty-first Century*, Fifth Report of the Standing Committee on Industry, Science and Technology, June 2001.

9 Canadian Business for Social Responsibility recognizes six main stakeholder groups: communities, employees, customers, suppliers, shareholders and the environment. It is also suggested that Aboriginal peoples be recognized as a stakeholder group. See Mees (2001).

10 The California Public Employee Retirement System (CalPERS) is supporting shareholder proposals calling on Exxon Mobil to consider environmental and social factors in setting executive compensation levels, as well as a proposal calling on the company to develop a policy to promote renewable energy. See "Nation's Largest Pension Fund Votes Against Exxon Mobil Management on Renewable, Environmental Resolutions for 2001." Available from http://www.campaignexxonmobil.org/ news/PR.Calpers.shtml

11 The most frequently cited popular treatment of the "stateless" firm can be found in Reich (1991).

12 Available from http://www.economist.com/displayStory.cfm?Story_id=796053

References

Altshuler, R., H. Grubert and T.S. Newlon. "Has U.S. Investment Abroad Become more

Sensitive to Tax Rates?" NBER Working Paper no. 6383. Cambridge, MA: National Bureau of Economic Research, 1998.

Baldwin, J. *The Dynamics of Industrial Competititon*. Cambridge: Cambridge University Press, 1995.

Cumming, D.J. and J.G. MacIntosh. "Venture Capital Investment Duration in Canada and the United States," 2000. Available from http://www.mgmt.utoronto.ca/cmi/papers/paper5-1.htm

Department of Finance. *The Report of the Technical Committee on Business Taxation*. Ottawa: Supply and Services Canada, 1997.

Falkenberg, L. "Learning the Ropes: Winning in the International Arena Takes Strong Performances on a Triple Bottom Line." *Oilweek*, October 2, 2000. Available from http://www.talisman-energy.com/responsibility/oilweek1.html

Fraser, M. "Rogers is Proud, But He's No Match for the Caisse." *The Financial Post*, March 28, 2000.

Halpern, P. "Systemic Perspectives on Corporate Governance Systems." Presented at the Conference and Symposium on Corporate Governance and Globalization, Toronto, 1999. Available from http://www.mgmt.utoronto.ca/cmi/papers/paper1-4.htm

Joint Committee on Corporate Governance. "Beyond Compliance: Building a Governance Culture." Interim Report. Available from http://www.cica.ca/cica/cicawebsite.nsf/public/JCCG/$file/March16E_InterimReport.pdf

Kortum, S. and J. Lerner. "Does Venture Spur Innovation?" NBER Working Paper no. W6846. Cambridge, MA: National Bureau of Economic Research, 1998.

Lemieux, P. "Regulatory Bullies." *The Financial Post*, July 28, 2001, C-11.

McFetridge, D. *Trade Liberalization and the Multinationals*. Ottawa: Economic Council of Canada, 1989.

Mees, A. "The Role of Governments in Promoting Corporate Citizenship." June 11-12, 2001. Available from http://www.multinationalguidelines.org/oecd/Documents/mees.htm

Mieszkowski, P. and G. Zodrow. "Taxation and the Tiebout Model: The Differential Effects of Head Taxes, Taxes on Land Rents and Property Taxes." *Journal of Economic Literature,* 27 (September 1989): 1098-1146.

Moldoveanu, M. and R. Martin. "Agency Theory and the Design of Effective Governance Mechanisms." Toronto: Rottman School of Management, University of Toronto, 2001. Available from http://www.cica.ca/cica/cicawebsite.nsf/public/JCCG_backgrdpapers/$file/AgencyTheory_Eng

Morck, R.K., D.A. Stangeland and B. Yeung. "Inherited Wealth, Corporate Control and Economic Growth: The Canadian Disease." NBER Working Paper no. W6814. Cambridge, MA: National Bureau of Economic Research, 1998.

Reich, R. *The Work of Nations: Preparing Ourselves for 21st Century Capitalism*. New York: Knopf, 1991.

Tiebout, C. "A Pure Theory of Local Expenditures." *Journal of Political Economy*, Vol. 64, no. 4 (1956): 416-424.

Toronto Stock Exchange Committee on Corporate Governance in Canada. *Where Were the Directors?: Guidelines for Improved Corporate Governance in Canada*. (Dey Report), December 1994.

Discussion

In his role as the designated practitioner for the session, Lawson Hunter, former head of the competition bureau and currently with Stikeman Elliot, offered some reflections on the impact of globalization on the two principal legal systems as they relate to corporate governance. One is the common law system, developed in Britain, which holds sway over the Commonwealth and the United States. The other, and really the dominant legal system, is civil law which can be traced back to Roman law. The common law system is adversarial, fact-oriented and informed by precedent, whereas the civil law system tends to be far more discretionary and more administrative. Hunter went on to note that in the anti-trust area, for example, practitioners on this side of the Atlantic were frustrated with the way the European Union initially began enforcing its anti-trust laws and it seemed so discretionary, so opaque and so uncontestable from a common-law vantage point. Although the possibility existed that the civil law approach would become more dominant, the opposite has tended to occur. Hunter recalled that in the context of Petro Canada buying Petro Fina, the Europeans had no idea of what insider trading was. Moreover, in the same time frame, there was no such thing as a meaningful market for corporate control in Europe. In both these areas, convergence has been to the common law mode.

More generally, and continuing with the example of anti-trust laws, Hunter noted that there are more than 80 countries that are in the game and this "globalization" is happening on the corporate law side as well.

The formal floor discussion focused initially on the so-called race to the bottom. One participant noted that while we may not have a race to the bottom, it now seems harder to "raise the bar" in terms of *increasing* environmental standards, or at least it seems hard for Canada to even consider environmental standards that are more strict than those in the United States. The questioner then added that perhaps we should at least be grateful to have some progressive American states that can help raise the standards for North America. While Ron Daniels acknowledged that it can be difficult to raise standards, he noted that one can find cases where, without central coordination, there has been a kind of upward competition. This has certainly occurred in terms of higher disclosure standards (even before the Enron debacle). We have also seen the emergence of a market for corporate control in Japan and Germany, a move dictated not by the US but by stakeholder interests. And shareholders are expressing interest in raising the productivity of their workforce through compliance with standards beyond those specified by the state. Daniels suggested that the statement in his paper that there is a race to the optimal should have been amended to note that the optimal could also be upward. He also agreed with the questioner that competitive concerns can prevent Canada from adopting environmental standards that it might otherwise prefer and that the role of demonstration affects arising from California and other progressive states are important for standard-setting in both Canada and the US. Another participant added that, post-NAFTA, the investment that has gone to Mexico has been subject to much higher environmental standards than Mexico itself requires.

Several participants suggested that where there really is a race to the bottom is in terms of corporate taxation. New greenfield investments both within and between countries are much more sensitive to tax rates than hitherto has been the case. Indeed, when was the last time a country raised its corporate income tax rate? Actually, all developed countries (except the US) have decreased their corporate taxes in the 1990s. In response to this general line of questioning, four general points were made. First, the fall in corporate tax rates is part of a broader trend that sees taxation shifting from mobile factors to more immobile factors. Second, there is also an efficiency rationale for decreasing corporate taxes, although this is not independent of capital mobility. Specifically, figures produced by Finance Canada indicate that the real output loss from raising an additional dollar from corporate taxation is in the order of 150 cents, whereas the real output loss from a dollar of sales taxes is under 20 cents, with personal income taxes and payroll taxes somewhere in the middle. While these costs are, as already noted, presumably related to the mobility of the respective tax bases, it is nonetheless the case that there is also an efficiency rationale for reducing corporate taxes. The third and related response from participants is that there also is a jurisdictional issue at the heart of the tax issue. Canada made a mistake in devolving inheritance taxes to the provinces who, in quick order, competed them away. The externalities are such that these taxes should have remained at the national level. Finally, many economists who support a reduction in Canada's corporate tax rates would at the same time favour a *global* corporate tax since, increasingly, this is the appropriate jurisdiction for taxing mobile capital.

Might it not be useful for Canada to abandon independent regulation in selected areas and simply rely on other countries' systems? Lawson Hunter (who served in the capacity as the designated practitioner for the session) responded by noting that a supranational regulator in the North American context essentially means a US regulator since the Americans are not about to cede jurisdiction in these areas. While relying on the US may make sense in some areas, in other aspects of corporate governance the Americans are into an era of triple damage actions within the context of an entrepreneurial legal culture, so that one obvious concern would be that we would be buying into US-style remedies if we relied on their regulatory framework. Donald McFetridge responded by referring to the area of food and drug regulation. On the surface, it appears that the national agencies seem to be competing by generating speedier decisions, by using alternative tests, and so on. But his view is that this national competition may well be evolving in the direction of some kind of specialization where Canada could rely on the regulatory decisions of others with respect to certain classes of drugs and could take a more active role for other classes of drugs. McFetridge also felt that there was room for piggybacking on the US in other areas. For example, the Task Force on Corporate Governance recommended that if a Canadian prospectus meets certain US standards it should be accepted throughout Canada.

Gordon Thiessen made the case that in some areas, financial regulation for example, international cooperation has worked quite well. Once the international community agrees (and documents) that a problem exists, the degree of international cooperation can be impressive. The most recent case was the concern over the state of financial regulation in Asian countries after the Asian financial crisis. This led to the successful movement to establish international standards for domestic financial regulation.

The panellists were rather unanimous in downplaying the linking of corporate social responsibility with corporate governance. The argument that corporations should be acting in the public interest runs against the underlying rationale for corporations. There may be a correlation between the way the corporations choose to act and the public interest, but that will be because they think it is in their interest too. To try to impose on a corporation a responsibility to act in the public interest would be a mistake.

New Forms of Public Services

New Forms of Public Service: Issues in Contemporary Organizational Design

Introduction

THIS PAPER IS FOCUSED UPON THE ISSUE OF CHOOSING ORGANIZATIONAL FORMS FOR public services. Given the existence of a public service—an office that issues licences, a school that teaches children, an inspectorate that measures pollution—what kind of form should it take? Should it be part of a ministry, or at arm's-length, or contracted-out or privatized, or something else again? Should it be closely tied in to the demanding requirements of parliamentary accountability, or given certain freedoms? Should its activities be tightly specified in an annual contract, or should it be steered through some looser, longer term arrangement that allows for greater discretion and managerial autonomy?

In the face of some of the other issues examined between these covers, globalization, the nature of political identity and so on, such a question of organizational choice may appear to be relatively mundane. Yet it is an issue on which politicians and civil servants in many western states have spent much time and energy over the last couple of decades. It is one where mistakes can hamper the work of vital public services, or obstruct the desires of parliamentarians and citizens for transparency and accountability. Selecting a "wrong," or inappropriate, organizational form can lead to ineffectiveness, frustration or loss of trust. Furthermore, the choice of organizational form, while undeniably a practical issue, is also directly connected to some of the wider and grander themes that animate the other papers in this collection. Can organizations be created which unite federal and provincial levels of activity in a "joined-up" manner? How can the transparency and accountability of seemingly closed international or transnational organizations such as the World Trade Organization (WTO) or the European Commission be enhanced? Under what conditions might the members of legislatures be persuaded to take a rest from party political point-scoring and cultivate a more sustained interest in the actual week-by-week performance of major public services? Is there a link between public services and the legitimacy of the liberal democratic state? These are some of the issues that connect this paper's concern with designing organizations to the foci of the other contributions in this collection.

The Vision: What Kind of Public Services Do We Need?

I WILL BEGIN AT THE END, WITH THE ANSWER TO THE QUESTION: "WHAT KIND OF PUBlic services do we need?" Then we can work back toward some design considerations.

Superficially, at least, it does not seem a very difficult question to answer. Of course, we want public services to be *effective*, to do what they are created to do: pay benefits, give appropriate clinical care, issue licences, or whatever. But we want a lot else besides. An international chorus sings of many other requirements: from government statements of one kind or another—from many Organisation for Economic Co-operation and Development (OECD) countries—we listen to an infectious melody (e.g., Prime Minister and Minister for the Cabinet Office 1999; Gore 1997; Ministère de la Fonction Publique 1994; OECD 1996; Finland. Ministry of Finance 2001). The tune goes as follows: public services should be:

- high quality, and systematically committed to continuous improvement;
- accessible (and not just to the young, mobile and technologically sophisticated);
- fast to respond to legitimate citizen demands and needs;
- flexible when faced with the varying needs of individual citizens;
- reliable: continuously available, without interruption or over-frequent changes of procedure that will confuse many citizens;

- integrated, so that citizens do not have to trail from one office to another in order to get their problems solved;
- efficient, so that tax dollars are not wasted;
- transparent, so that the public can see what is being provided, how and at what cost;
- accountable, so that elected representatives and their oversight bodies, such as audit offices, can readily fix responsibility for success and failure;
- equitable, so that citizens in similar situations receive equal treatment;
- participatory, so that citizen-users and other stakeholders are able to have a say, not only in the delivery of existing services but also in the design of new services; and
- open to complaints and grievances, so that service-users feel they have simple, fair and rapid means of redress when things do go wrong.

Of course, this is a wonderful list. One cannot be opposed to its individual elements, all 12 of which are virtuous and politically correct. However, contemplation of this impressive assemblage of *desiderata* soon leads to some further observations and questions.

First, the list is noticeably longer than it would normally be for private sector commercial services. Especially the items in the second half of the list—transparency, accountability, equity, participation and so on—are not usually part of the manifesto at my garage or bank or travel agency or supermarket. One implication of this is that we are asking *more* of our public services than of their private counterparts, and, by extension, management in these contexts is therefore even more challenging and complex.

A second point is that this is a list drawn from the context of rich, stable Western European, North American and Australasian states. In some other parts of the world the list would begin with some other, rather fundamental requirements that we tend rather to take for granted, such as the rule of law, freedom from corruption and patronage, and so on (World Bank 2000). Thankfully, in the Canadian context, we do not need to worry so much about these things, although, having said that, it would be wise to remain vigilant so as to ensure that other changes we make do not allow corruption or illegalities to reinfect any part of our administration.

A third thought is that such a long list of varying requirements is highly likely to contain, if not actual contradictions, then at least some tensions and trade-offs (Pollitt and Bouckaert 2000, ch. 7). For example, high levels of participation may sometimes slow decision-making and reduce the speed of response. Or a drive for efficiency may result in standardization and a reduced capacity to respond flexibly to the varying needs of individual citizens. A strong concern for equity may, likewise, have some inhibiting effect on an organization's willingness to craft individual solutions for different clients. Adaptability to the diverse needs of different cultural and ethnic groups may load costly burdens onto the taxpayer. Reliability and continuity—highly prized, for example, by many elderly citizens—may be in tension with the desire to innovate and take advantage of the latest information technology, and so on.

A fourth observation is that quite a few of these demands are relatively new. Ideas about continuous quality improvement, about integration and "joining-up," about responsiveness to a socially and ethnically diverse population and about the participation of that population have each developed rapidly over the last decade or two. These developments reflect the broader shifts in society, economy and technology that frame this set of papers and the conference that gave birth to them. They are features of public services where rapid learning is having to take place, and some mistakes, misunderstandings and downright errors are almost inevitable.

A final thought concerns the speed of change in organizational forms. During the past decade or two some countries have become accustomed to a rapid cycle of change for public services. Some social services departments in the United Kingdom have been reorganized four or five times in the last ten years (May and Brunsdon 1999, 235-236). The UK Next Steps agencies are subject to an in-depth review of their status and form at least once every five years. Both the British and the New Zealand national health services have undergone two or three major upheavals since 1990. It is worth asking whether this state of affairs, virtually continuous reorganization, is desirable. Yes, say some management theorists, change is both good and inevitable. Organizational stability should be regarded as a warning sign, an indicator that an organization has lost touch with its rapidly-changing environment. No, say some experienced public servants, who point to the typical (but usually unmeasured) costs of reorganization, in the shape of general uncertainty, an introverted staff focus on job security, loss of acquired knowledge and experience, discontinuities in service provision and confusion among clients (Pollitt 2000). No doubt there is some truth on both sides of this debate, but, to my mind, the evidence that incessant organizational change distracts staff attention from their main service-providing function is quite strong. If this is so, then it provides an additional argument for care to be taken in the choice of organizational form. Rushed or short-sighted reorganizations, those that perhaps focus on only one or two criteria and ignore the others, merely speed the arrival of the next reorganization and the next period of distraction and uncertainty.

Further comments could easily be added. However, enough has already been said to provide some background to our enquiry into *forms* of public service. It is already clear that the chosen forms will have to operate in a context of rapid change and unavoidable learning, that they will be judged against a long and diverse set of criteria, and that they will have to cope with multiple tensions and trade-offs.

Forms for Public Services: The Available Menu and Recent Trends

The menu of forms has expanded considerably during the past 20 years. To read some textbooks and speeches, one might be led to believe that until recently there was only one form on the list—*bureaucracy*. Bureaucracy, it seems, ruled the pre-1980s' earth like a dinosaur (Osborne and Gaebler 1992; Hughes 1998). It was cumbersome, slow-moving, inefficient and "one size fits all." Now, the story goes, we enjoy a multiplicity of forms: executive agencies, various types of free-standing public bodies, contracting-out to commercial firms, contracting-out to third sector, non-profit organizations, franchising, a variety of types of public-private partnerships (PPPs), networked service delivery arrangements and so on (see, e.g., Lane 2000; Pollitt et al. 2002; Walsh 1995).

Another storyline, often, but not necessarily, associated with the one above, is that of "rolling back the state" or "the end of big government" (respectively Margaret Thatcher's and Bill Clinton's phrases). In this particular narrative big government—overweight and over-costly—is the enemy, and must be defeated by a forced dieting regime consisting of privatization, contracting-out, greater use of the voluntary sector and downsizing. Again, therefore, new ways of organizing public services are crucial. It might be noted, however, that both the right-wing supporters of this program and its left-wing opponents tend to have a vested interest in exaggerating the extent of rolling back.

Unfortunately, these simple readings of history, from monochrome grey bureaucracy to the colourful, international variety and from big government to the lean state, just do not fit the facts. To begin with, there never was only one, centralized, hierarchical type of organization. The public sectors of Europe and North America have always contained a wide variety of species. Many important services were effectively run by professionals rather than bureaucrats, and in highly non-standardized, collegiate ways (Clarke and Newman 1997). Second, the international traffic in forms and ideas for public administration is as old as the modern state. This makes the past more interesting and, occasionally, may remind us that the problems we encounter with what we think of as "new forms" actually have many precedents (Hood 1976, 1998; Hood and Jackson 1991).

Third, while many states have undoubtedly announced dietary regimes, the extent of slimming (as with real dieting) has often been quite modest. If we take the two most commonly used indicators of state size—government spending as a percentage of gross domestic product (GDP) and the public sector workforce as a percentage of the total labour force—then we find a very mixed picture. As between 1985 and 1996 the OECD database shows the picture given in tables 1 and 2.

Thus, general government spending as a percentage of the GDP has come down significantly in some countries (New Zealand, United Kingdom), remained fairly level in others (France, Germany) and actually risen in yet others (Finland, Denmark). Over the same time period the share of the total labour force represented by public sector workers has fallen in most countries, but risen in Denmark, Finland, France and even New Zealand. This is hardly the dramatic, one-way, global movement that some of the small government enthusiasts would have us believe.

However, we must beware that, concealed beneath these huge aggregates, may lie many changes that are significant for organizational designers. Organizational forms may change while expenditure remains steady. Total staff numbers may not alter much, but within that total there can be (and has been in a number of countries) a major shift out from central government to local government and to quangos, and from full-time working to part-time working. Part-time workers in a decentralized quango may well not possess quite the same "public service spirit" as full-time workers in a ministry.

Changes in General Government Expenditure as a Percentage of GDP, 1985–1996

Country	1985	1996
Canada	45	43
Denmark	59	60
Finland	44	56
France	52	52
Germany	47	46
New Zealand	62	49
United Kingdom	44	41
United States	33	34

Source: OECD analytic databank.

Changes in Public Sector Workforce as a Percentage of Total Labour Force, 1985–1996

Country	1985	1996
Canada	21	19
Denmark	30	31
Finland	19	25
France	23	25
Germany	16	15
New Zealand	16	22
United Kingdom	22	14
United States	15	13

Source: OECD analytic databank.

One further line of argument that has been popular in government circles in a number of countries is that government needs to concentrate on its core tasks, and that all non-core activities should, in principle, be put out to other organizations: agencies, quangos, firms, voluntary associations, or whatever. Various principles (most often the economist's distinction between public and non-public goods) have been advanced to help with the task of identifying the core. However, this, too has its complications as a design principle. To begin with, the economic perspective clearly fails to include many of the criteria listed in the previous section of this paper (participation, transparency, accountability, etc.). Yet these non-economic criteria are evidently important to (some) politicians and (some) citizens alike. Also, both comparative and historical perspectives tend to show that almost any function one may care to think of has at some time and in some places been organized within the state and at others organized outside the state. Even armies and police forces have been private. In the UK a number of prisons have been contracted out to the private sector. Many countries have long enjoyed a mix of state, voluntary sector and commercial provision in education and health care. At the other pole, some surprising activities have been run by the state: the Carlisle brewery and pubs (in northwest England) being one of my favourite examples. In short, there seems to have been considerable historical volatility as to what constitutes the core.

Allowing for all these important qualifications, despite the mixed pattern of aggregate employment and expenditure statistics; despite acknowledging that the past also contained a variety of organizational forms and a very wobbly boundary between public and private sectors, it remains clear that the last 15 years have witnessed a positive orgy of experimentation with forms. We can now choose from an extensive menu, with some novel dishes. For example, confining ourselves for the moment to PPPs alone, just one major category of form, we can see significant differences between operations and maintenance contracts, design-build contracts, turnkey operations, wrap around additions, build-lease-operate arrangements, temporary privatization, lease-develop-operate contracts and build-transfer-operate contracts. As one moves through this list from beginning to end, the risk borne by the private sector partner tends to increase and the level of control which the public authority involved can exert tends to diminish. So the question becomes one of *how to make the most appropriate choice of form, in the light of the diverse criteria for success and failure referred to earlier.*

A World Without Frontiers?

THE CONTEMPORARY ORGANIZATIONAL FORMS REFERRED TO IN THE PRECEDING PARAgraphs may involve a good deal of frontier-crossing: between central, provincial and local government; between the public, market and third sectors, and indeed, between countries. Much of the information technology (IT) infrastructure of British central government is provided and maintained by US companies; large chunks of the English water-supply system are owned by French companies, the hard-pressed British National Health Service not only sends some patients to UK private hospitals owned by US health-care organizations, but is currently exploring the possibility of reducing waiting times for surgery by exporting patients to France and Germany (Dunleavy 1994; Elliot 2001).

It is not only in the operational delivery of public services that frontiers are becoming more permeable. Ideas about appropriate organizational forms are heavily traded both bilaterally between pairs of states and through international organizations such as the World Bank and the Public Management Service (PUMA) of the OECD (see Halligan 1996; Pollitt et al. 2001; Premfors 1998).

Furthermore, we are beginning to see the development of international benchmarking. For example, the UK Cabinet Office has conducted a benchmarking project that has compared UK Next Steps agencies with a variety of bodies, including some in other countries (Next Steps Team 1998). Such studies may cross several boundaries simultaneously, a public service organization in one country may be compared with a commercial or voluntary sector organization in another (needless to say, such comparisons are replete with methodological pitfalls). Less formally, many national public sector organizations now deal with international non-governmental organizations (INGOs). Influential and well-informed INGOs exist in fields such as the environment, human rights, public health and development aid. They can and do make international comparisons, for example, Greenpeace may criticize the environmental protection arrangements in country X on the grounds that they fall well short of those adopted by country Y. Even in the mainstream "domestic" public services such as health care and education, international comparisons are now frequently made, even in the mass media.

It is not only international boundaries that are being crossed. Within the nation-state, the frontiers between the public sector, the market sector (profit-oriented firms) and civil society (voluntary associations, sometimes referred to as the third sector) are becoming hazier by the week. In the Anglo-Saxon countries, but also the Nordics and elsewhere, PPPs and contracting-out have become more commonplace. Such arrangements can sometimes offer considerable advantages, including additional finance for public services from the private sector, risk-sharing, innovative management skills, superior local or technical knowledge and sheer enthusiasm. On the other hand, horizontal cooperation with the market and voluntary sectors may also bring problems—ambiguous allocations of responsibility, diminished political steering capacity, the "bureaucratization" of voluntary non-profit organizations, opportunism by commercial corporations and so on. Liberal use of comfort words such as "partnership" and "synergy" does not diminish the fact that public authorities are having to learn new skills fast, and that self-seeking and territorial behaviours are present in the market and voluntary sectors just as they are in the public sector. The short history of public-private partnering as a labelled, self-conscious craft contains both triumphs and disasters, and moments of competition and power-playing occur even in the best regulated PPPs (Ling 2000; Lowndes and Skelcher 1998; Newman 2001, ch. 6).

One should not exaggerate. Many frontiers still have high fences, metaphorically speaking. International benchmarking is still in its infancy. National and sectoral "path dependencies" are still highly visible (Pierson 2000). In many countries vast public services such as schools or social security continue to be financed, planned, delivered, regulated and staffed almost entirely by public servants. Yet inter-organizational, intersectoral and international borrowing and comparison does seem to be on the rise. The challenge, of course, is to become a sophisticated user of transboundary ideas, techniques and comparative information, not just a dupe who uncritically buys the latest fashion to come to town.

Choosing: Is There One Best Form?

One possibility is that there could be one form that consistently out-performed all the others. This seems inherently improbable. The list of criteria is just too long for one form to be the best on every count, in every circumstance. An organizational form that maximized speed and efficiency would be unlikely to score highest on equity and participation and so on. Empirically, this author knows of no studies that suggest that there is "one best way" for all public services: on the contrary, the literature is full of examples of forms that appear to work in one context but then fail or are quite transformed when transferred to another (e.g., Guyomarch 1999; Pollitt et al. 2001; Premfors 1998; Schiavo 2000; Stewart 1992). Therefore our analytic task is a more complicated one than just picking a winner. My argument will be that it is desirable to proceed in three stages. First, we need to look at each desired *criterion*—and then consider what we know about how well (or badly) different forms of organization measure up to that criterion. Second, we ought to take account of the *characteristics of a particular function or activity*, because these also influence choice of form. For example, it matters quite a lot how far the outputs from an organization are standardizable and observable (Wilson 1989). Third, we also need to consider the broader *cultural context* into which the service is supposed to fit—delivering health-care services or community care in Sweden may be significantly different from delivering these services in the US (compare Micheletti 2000 with Peterson 2000). Only when we have performed such an analysis will we be able to pick "horses for courses," organizational forms that stand some chance of meeting the specific priorities of a specific service delivered within a specific community.

Criteria, Again

THE FIRST PARAGRAPH OF THIS PAPER LISTED A DOZEN PLAUSIBLE CRITERIA FOR PUBLIC services. Whilst it is not practicable in one paper to analyze the interrelationships between all of them, there are some that have become particularly prominent over the past five years or so, and merit attention because of the problems they pose for designing public services in the twenty-first century. Three such issues will be discussed: (i) the tension between efficiency and accountability; (ii) the tension between efficiency and integration; and (iii) the tension between efficiency and participation.

Efficiency and accountability

One of the persistent, nagging criticisms of the new public management (NPM) has been that it tends to diminish the traditional form of public accountability through ministerial responsibility (e.g., the debate over the "primacy of politics" in the Netherlands, or the reform of national boards in Finland, or the criticisms of the lack of accountability of quangos and agencies in the UK, all in the mid-1990s). This undermining occurs, critics claim, in a variety of ways. One is by creating autonomous or semi-autonomous agencies, at arm's-length from ministries, and able to exercise large discretion in the way they tackle their tasks. Another is by contracting-out a wide range of services, which are then performed by commercial firms or non-profit organizations. A third is by the privatization of public utilities such as the railways or water supply. NPM enthusiasts deny the charge, claiming that well-designed agencies are if anything *more* accountable, because they work within frameworks of well-specified performance targets. Similarly, they argue that a good contract *increases* the possibility for accurate political steering, whilst simultaneously reaping the reward of enhanced efficiency (e.g., Lane 2000; Waldegrave 1994).

This debate will probably never be resolved by some conclusive piece of evidence, because the truth seems to be that both sides are right. What I mean by this is that there is no deterministic answer that can be read off from the organizational form alone. Usually, organizational structure is what 30 years ago Aaron Wildavsky called "an intermediate variable," though as the "new institutionalists" have reaffirmed, it can be an important one (Peters 1999). The creation of agencies and quangos can undermine ministerial responsibility and, equally, a well-designed performance contract can increase both "steerability" and transparency. The literature contains both kinds of case (e.g., Algemene Rekenkamer 1995; Chancellor of the Duchy of Lancaster 1997). In other words, everything depends on the details—on the skill of the designer and the willingness of the operators of that design to play by the spirit as well as the letter. This is a theme that will reappear at intervals throughout this paper.

One message that emerges strongly from the contemporary debate about public management reform and accountability is that the classic doctrine of ministerial responsibility, whilst still fundamental, is no longer enough by itself (it probably never was). The new world of agencies and quangos and PPPs demands new forms of accountability to supplement the old (Behn 2001). Even with the UK Next Steps program of agency creation, where Mrs. Thatcher insisted that constitutional doctrines of ministerial accountability stood unchanged, subtle but significant shifts have incrementally taken place (Gains 2002). Less debated, but perhaps even more important, the advent of electronic case management and expert systems has in many organizations radically shifted the locus of discretion from the "street level bureaucrat" to the systems analysts and software designers (United Kingdom. National Audit Office 1999; Bovens and Zouridis 2001). The arrival of such systems level bureaucracies poses new issues for accountability. For example:

> Parliament must have the opportunity to check and make adjustments to the digital translation of its policy frameworks and general rules.
>
> Citizens must be given the opportunity within the organization to draw attention to specific circumstances that do not fit within the existing algorithms or [lead] to patently unjust outcomes.
>
> Citizens, as well as interest organizations should be able to access the electronic forms, decision trees and checklists used by the organization to make decisions directly, via the internet (Bovens and Zouridis 2001).

In short, designing new forms of public service frequently entails designing new forms of accountability, not just organizations that will achieve ever higher efficiency and quality.

Efficiency and integration

According to NPM doctrines, one of the main routes to increased efficiency is through specialization. Steering should be separated from rowing, and the rowing left to specialist professionals (Osborne and Gaebler 1992). In a number of countries (especially Australia, New Zealand and the United Kingdom) activities have been carved out of ministries and allocated to specialized, single-purpose agencies or to other types of autonomous public bodies. Further, former in-house functions have been contracted-out, so that it is now common for both ministries and agencies to contract out not only catering and cleaning and garbage collection, but also training, computing, security, legal advice and even the provision of Christmas presents for staff.

Arguments persist over the extent to which this kind of task specialization has indeed realized efficiency gains (for an interesting piece on contracting-out in US local government, see Boyne 1998; for a more optimistic general treatment, see Lane 2000). But even where such gains do occur, the price may include a fragmentation of control and an increase in the difficulty governments have in coherently steering their policies and programs. Academics write of the "hollowing out" of government (e.g., Rhodes 1997), and even governments themselves worry that narrow, efficiency-oriented reforms have undermined integration (Prime Minister and Minister for the Cabinet Office 1999). Hence the recent fashion for joined-up or holistic government (Cabinet Office 2000; Kavanagh and Richards 2001; Newman 2001; Peters 1998). Thus one of the currently prominent design questions that manifests itself when the form of a public service is under consideration is "what other services does this service need to be integrated with, and what form of integration is most appropriate?" For example, at the moment, the UK government is making a major attempt to join up all those services that are heavily used by older people. There have already been attempts to join up the approach to school truants, involving schools, the police, local authority social services and the juvenile justice system. This kind of thinking can run directly contrary to the efficiency incentives faced by individual institutions or departments. In the UK, the schools, whose results were being closely measured by their students' examination results, increased their exclusion of students with behavioural difficulties (because they were a disruptive influence) but thereby drove up juvenile crime (DETR 2000). Inter-agency collaboration is also a major topic in the US and elsewhere (Bardach 1998; OECD 2001).

There can be little doubt that "joined-up-ness" appeals to citizens. One-stop shops/one-window/single-portal arrangements make immediate sense to most of those who use public services (United Kingdom. National Audit Office 1999; Lowndes, Pratchett and Stoker 2001). However, the problems they pose for organizational design are challenging. Joined-up delivery eventually demands joined-up policy-making (and vice versa), and joined-up policy-making may well require ministers themselves to behave in new ways, accepting corporate goals above purely departmental ones. Furthermore, it demands new skills from civil servants, and probably needs a shift in the criteria for recruitment and promotion (Cabinet Office 2000).

Efficiency and participation

Participation is definitely an unopposable virtue. Who would dare to argue for less of it? In the UK there seems to be a government drive for more and better participation about once every generation, we had one in the late 1960s and early 1970s, and now we are in the midst of another. Citizen participation is vital, we are told, not only in influencing the form in which a public service is received, but in the original choice of what type of service to have, and in the operating decisions of the managers of service delivery. The scope of participation, it seems, is ever widening. For any given service it may cover an ascending range:

- satisfaction with current outcomes,
- satisfaction with current outputs,
- satisfaction with current processes,
- inputs to medium-term service planning,
- inputs to the basic design of the service, and
- choice between different types of service that could be provided (Pollitt 1998).

Public administration is awash with client-satisfaction surveys, focus groups, user panels, citizen juries and interactive websites (Audit Commission 1999; Seargeant and Steele 1999). But what is the relationship of all this to efficiency?

On an immediate, practical level, higher participation may often seem the enemy of efficiency. Planning and decision-making are slowed down while the surveys, focus groups and public hearings take place. Managers are not infrequently deeply sceptical about what the added value of such processes is. They say that little new is learned, and that typical participatory devices such as public meetings lead mainly to the airing of uninformed and highly sectional interests by tiny and unrepresentative samples of the citizen population likely to be affected by the new service or project of development (e.g., Lowndes, Stoker and Pratchett 1998, 64).

Arguably, however, such cynicism is unjustified. Recent research indicates that there may be a wide potential willingness to participate, one that is not being tapped because the methods used have tended to be narrow and unimaginative (Lowndes, Pratchett and Stoker 2001). Perhaps individuals have to be invited, and even offered incentives to participate? Perhaps modern ICTs can be used to reach out to groups (including the young) who tend to shun the classic public meeting? Perhaps governments have to do more to explain and convince potential participating citizens that their efforts to take part will have some effect? The sophisticated defence of participation argues that doing it right is important, but doing the right thing is even more important, and knowing what is the right thing requires the participation (at least) of those who will be affected. So without adequate participation, professional managers may merely succeed in doing the wrong thing in the cheapest way.

Yet, at the same time, participation is not without its own risks: “Our findings underline the fact that ‘more participation’ is not the same as ‘more democracy'—participation initiatives may reinforce existing patterns of exclusion and disadvantage" (Lowndes, Pratchett and Stoker 2001, 453; see also Pollitt 1998). So participation is by no means a straightforward matter. It can warp the public voice toward the articulate, the self-confident, the organized, the busy-bodies or simply those who have more time on their hands. On the other hand, these dangers cannot be used as an excuse for dropping the idea altogether. The organizational designer is obliged to confront the issue of participation, and seeks to find the best possible mixture of techniques for eliciting views and encouraging debate. As Peters indicates in his paper in this volume, more "output participation" may make a significant contribution to program, even governmental, legitimacy.

Service Characteristics

IT IS ONE OF THE CURIOUS OMISSIONS OF NPM DOCTRINES THAT THEY GENERALLY show little sensitivity to differences between *functions*. Much of the prescriptive management literature seems to proceed on an unspoken, but rather unlikely, assumption: that all functions can be managed in roughly the same way. However, a deeper reading of the public administration literature reminds us that functions *do* matter. They have peculiarities which the organizational designer ignores at his or her peril. One important effect they have is to give some order to the long list of criteria set out at the beginning of this paper. They promote one or two particular criteria to the top of the list, making the others relatively less important. Thus, for example, it is vital that a fire brigade is accessible and is reliable; it is less important that it is participatory.

The importance of functional differences will be illustrated by reference to four different dimensions:

- Standardizability: the extent to which the outputs of a service can be standardized.
- Observability of outputs and outcomes: the extent to which outputs and outcomes can be seen and measured.
- Political salience: the extent to which the function is one that attracts intense and continuing interest from elected representatives.
- Consequentiality: the kinds of effect the service has on the lives of citizens; for example, is service failure a matter of inconvenience, or of life and death?

Standardizability

This is important because it influences, *inter alia*, efficiency, accountability and equity. It influences efficiency because the less the outputs of a service can be standardized, the more difficult it becomes to measure efficiency (in the technical sense of an input-output ratio). If an organization is issuing licences or paying standardized benefits, then its output can be straightforwardly monitored. Unit costs can be calculated. However, if it is a school, offering lessons, or a social services department offering a wide range of clients different types of advice, then the counting of outputs becomes more problematic. Standardizability also influences accountability, because reporting unstandardized activities takes longer and tends to assume a more discursive, less quantitative format. In a way it requires more of the accountee (receiver of the account). Standardizability influences equity because, when a service cannot be measured in standard units, it is harder to be sure that users in similar circumstances are receiving similar service. For all these reasons unstandardized services are harder to successfully contract out (Lane, generally an enthusiast for contractual forms of relationship in the public sector, acknowledges that human services pose particular problems, Lane 2000). The contracts are incomplete, because of the difficulties of defining outputs. The monitoring of performance is also more difficult. Trust becomes correspondingly more important, long-term relational types of contracting more appropriate, and transparency more elusive.

Observability of outputs and outcomes

Outputs and outcomes that are difficult to observe generate some of the same challenges as outputs that are not standardizable. Thus, a lack of observability makes contracts more difficult to frame, accountability more precarious and trust a more precious asset. However, lack of observability is not the same as lack of standardizability, the two characteristics are analytically separate. One can have a standardized health intervention (water fluoridization, vaccination) whose outcomes are not visible for a long time. Or one can have an unstandardizable intervention that is perfectly visible, such as a policeman dealing with a fight on the street or a teacher teaching a class while parent helpers are present in the classroom.

Outputs that are difficult to observe include advice and emotional support (as a teacher may offer to a student who lacks self-confidence, or a social worker may offer to a harassed working single parent). Yet these are the things those citizens in receipt of such services may look back on as having been the most crucial aspects of the service. Outcomes may be difficult to observe because they occur over a very long time, or because they are multiple caused, or both. A significant reduction in environmental pollution may take many years to achieve. The success of an educational program for young children from deprived backgrounds may not bear fruit for a decade, and then be hard to separate out from other influences. It may be a long time before the cumulative effect of planning controls becomes visible on the face of a crowded urban environment, and such controls will probably need to place reliability high on their agenda if they are to achieve their purpose. Low observability therefore points toward organizational forms that maximize the public service ethic, a spirit of professional commitment to clients, and good security of tenure. The application of a regime of tight, short-term performance indicators and/or contracts may in these circumstances generate perverse incentives, as staff lower hidden aspects of quality in order to pass the measurement test.

On the other hand, governments also perform many activities of a relatively standardized nature, and where outputs can be observed and measured in reasonably convincing ways. The issue of driving licences or passports, the registration of births, marriages and deaths, the payment of fixed benefits against standard criteria of eligibility, and a variety of testing and inspection tasks all fall into this category. In these cases, *ceteris paribus*, a variety of "at a distance" forms of organization may be both feasible and advantageous.

Political salience

Some functions tend to attract high levels of political attention, while others go on their quiet way, seldom hitting the headlines (Judge, Hogwood and McVicar 1997). Compare, for instance, the prison service with the meteorological office, or the health service with weights and measures. High political salience tends to mean a high need for transparency and accountability, a continuing readiness to satisfy various enquirers as to what has been done and why. When political salience was combined with private sector managers, with little experience of Whitehall, trouble followed for the UK prison service and Child Support Agency. When political salience was combined with a public sector manager, accustomed to the politician's insatiable desire to intervene, serious trouble was avoided (UK Benefits Agency, see Gains 2002).

So putting matters of high political salience at a great distance—at the other end of a commercial contract, or, in the case of British Rail, by privatizing and fragmenting it altogether, can easily lead to difficulties. Only if there is a party political truce—a lasting agreement that some function should deliberately be put beyond politics—is an arm's-length solution likely to be stable. The most common cases of this kind involve quasi-judicial functions, where a majority of politicians, and the general public, want party politics entirely removed from the decision-making process. The problem of achieving such a consensus may be greater in decentralized, federal states than in centralized, unitary states such as the UK, because there may be a larger number of independent political *fora* involved.

Consequentiality

Most of us can afford for the tax office to make a mistake, as long as their procedures are open to complaint and correction (our twelfth criterion). Most of us cannot afford for the emergency services—fire, ambulance, police—to make mistakes, at least not when they are dealing with life-threatening situations. Their actions are more immediately consequential. It is no coincidence that they tend to be the most trusted, most admired public services, and those that the public in many countries are least willing to see contracted-out to commercial operators. Every time there is a major accident or calamity, recent rail crashes in Britain, the horrific terrorist attacks in New York, this public perception is reconfirmed.

Less dramatically, one may consider the case of the Canadian Food Inspection Agency (CFIA). Whilst amalgamation of various food inspection activities within a single agency was apparently driven principally by an efficiency logic, the consequentiality of food safety meant that the positioning of the agency was also shaped by "the pervasive belief within the food safety policy community that the federal inspection and regulation functions ought to remain within the federal government domain" (Prince 2000, 219).

Therefore, high consequentiality tends to promote certain criteria to the top of the list of priorities. Effectiveness, of course, is paramount. Accessibility, speed of response and reliability are also crucial. Recent public concerns about the London ambulance service have not focused on its efficiency or transparency, or on the extent to which citizens have been able to participate in planning and decision-making. They have focused on how quickly the ambulances arrive, and whether one can always get through immediately on the telephone.

Cultural Context

A MASS OF LITERATURE TESTIFIES TO THE ENDURING SIGNIFICANCE OF CULTURAL DIFferences in public administration. Such differences include the contrast between centralized, majoritarian systems such as the UK and (until 1993) New Zealand, and more decentralized, multi-party consensual systems, such as usually prevail in the Nordic countries and the Netherlands. They also include the deep-rooted difference between "public interest" states, such as the UK and the US, and the kind of ingrainedly juridical thinking that pervades administrative life in France, Germany and most of the Mediterranean states (Pierre 1995; Pollitt and Bouckaert 2000). These differences can easily lead to misunderstandings: for example, both the UK and Germany have set up independent state telecommunications regulation bodies, which has led some commentators to write of convergence. The convergence, however, is limited, because decision-making *inside* the German agency follows the classic German juridical pattern, whereas inside UK OFTEL it does not (Böllhoff 2000).

What is the significance of such differences for the designer of the organizational forms of public services? One message would be that choosing an organizational form that represents a big leap away from the existing cultural tradition is highly risky. Culture cannot be just "switched off." "Path dependency" is a strong force, in the UK Next Steps program it soon became clear that traditional ministerial responsibility remained the dominant rule of the game, usually trumping managerial freedoms whenever the two came into conflict (Gains 2002). The radical reforms in New Zealand have been a focus for so much international attention partly because of their rarity, one of very few examples of a seeming "breakthrough" from an old to a new system. Yet careful analysis shows both that this breakthrough was the product of an unusual window of opportunity (of a kind not often available to reformers) and that, in the end, the brakes were applied and some edging back toward past practices began (Aberbach and Christensen 2001).

Path dependency is not a sin, but a recognition of previous investments of political capital, acquired administrative skills and trust (Pierson 2000). Occasionally reformers may be able to jump through a window of opportunity (and it is part of the skill of a reform leader to recognize one), but for the most part they would be well advised to "go with the grain." This means, *inter alia*, that attractive foreign imports may need considerable editing before they can be made minimally acceptable to the local cultural *status quo* (Pollitt et al. 2001; Sahlin-Andersson 2001).

Organizational Design: A Summary

BY NOW IT SHOULD BE ABUNDANTLY CLEAR THAT THOSE RESPONSIBLE FOR DESIGNING public service organizations face an exceedingly complex task. In the first paragraph of this paper a total of 12 desirable criteria were identified, plus basic effectiveness, and there could have been more! Then there is probably at least an equal number of basic organizational forms to choose among. But that was only the beginning of the design challenge. On a third dimension, we need to take into account particular service characteristics, such as the observability and standardizability of outputs (at least another four variables, possibly more). Fourth, there is also a need to consider the broader cultural context, to be very parsimonious we might restrict ourselves to just three rather broad cultural categories. All of this, if presented in the form of a matrix, would have more than 1,700 cells—well beyond the capacity of most of us to comprehend.

This kind of analysis highlights the insufficiency of simple proverbs such as "steer don't row," or "market test" or "quality is free." To my mind it also casts doubt on the formulaic prescriptions of rational choice theory. But such a perspective may seem rather depressing, how can we ever hope to master all these interrelationships? I prefer to see the glass as half-full. Although we cannot set out a simple algorithm, we can identify certain tendencies that act as signposts for our efforts to design public service organizations. Thus, for example, we should be very cautious about contracting-out to the market sector functions that are highly consequential, politically salient and hard to standardize. On the other hand, if we are dealing with a function whose outputs are both standardizable and visible, and is seldom a matter of party political contention, then putting it at arm's-length may be both feasible and attractive. If efficiency is one of the most desired characteristics, then privatization or competitive tendering may be worth investigating. There will be many mixed cases, where a delicate balance needs to be struck. Perhaps, to attract extra finance, a market partner is attractive but, because of political sensitivity (a city centre property development, a water purification plant) strong transparency and accountability requirements are also present. There is nothing to stop such requirements being built into a contract. Meetings can be made open to the public, other forms of access can be guaranteed, regular provision of certain types of information can be written in and so on. The crucial step in each case is to take a clear view of the service at the beginning, to identify its main characteristics and to engage the responsible politicians (and probably other stakeholders) in giving priority to the key criteria and outlining what is culturally acceptable, and what is beyond the pale. When the big picture has thus been sketched, more detailed design can begin.

To summarize, the message I draw from this complexity is that the design of the organizational form of a public service is a craft, not a science, and should be the work of many, not the work of few. It is a craft because there is no scientific formula that will integrate and balance all the various criteria and functional peculiarities which need to be taken into account. Tradition, skills, politics and experience each play a part. It is the work of many rather than few because rarely is any one manager or politician likely to possess all the necessary information and experience to design the set of arrangements that will give the best chance of success—an acceptable "fit" between our aspirations and our capacities. This approach therefore suggests that we should remove the design of public services from the technocrats and bring it back into the democratic realm of consultation and debate between stakeholders. It makes the choice of form for a public service something distinctively *public*.

Afterword: Public Services and the Legitimacy of the Contemporary State

PROVIDING PUBLIC SERVICES, OR AT LEAST ARRANGING FOR THEIR PROVISION, HAS A special political significance. In most western states it is among the most *popular* of government activities. It also tends to be the most expensive and to employ the most people. Other government activities, such as maintaining public order, regulating business, planning land use or levying taxation tend to be cheaper, smaller scale, less popular, more controversial or some combination of these things. So providing public services—education, health care, the fire brigade, social security—*is central to the legitimacy of the modern state*. When, during the 1940s, 1950s and 1960s, governments built up large welfare states their popularity and legitimacy grew (at first). Instead of being a distant regulator and maintainer of order, the state stepped directly into the everyday lives of most of its citizens, offering them affordable health care, education and social services. As governments have tried to modify, dilute or back away from some of these commitments during the 1980s and 1990s, the citizen trust in politicians has fallen significantly. Yet at the same time citizen trust in public-service professionals who actually deliver services, though diminishing somewhat, has remained relatively high (Canadian Centre for Management Development 1998*a*, *b*; Pew Research Centre 1998, 2). Younger age groups in the most economically advanced societies (postmaterialists) may well have lost respect for the bearers of state authority, such as the police or the armed forces, but substantial majorities still trust their doctors, teachers and nurses (Inglehart 1999; Pew Research Centre 1998).

The reason why I conclude with a consideration of this aspect of public services is because so much of the debate about public service reform has been conducted in other terms. Typically, the discussion has focused on the need to provide more flexible, rapid, integrated, decentralized, high-quality services and all at lower unit cost. In no way do I wish to deny the significance of these criteria, most of this paper has been about them. My final proposition, however, is that these organizational factors, important though they are, always need to be seen within a broader political context, and that context is one where the very existence of public services is one of the principal foundations of the perceived legitimacy of modern government. When we reorganize public services, therefore, we are doing much more than simply improving their management. We are confirming, reinforcing or perhaps even unwittingly undermining notions of citizenship and collective identification. To borrow language from Kymlicka's paper in this volume, we are engaged, if not in nation-*building*, then at least in nation *maintenance*.

Notes

This paper is less inadequate than it would otherwise have been because of the opportunity I had to revise it after the comments it received at the Montebello workshop. There were too many comments for me to be able to acknowledge all the speakers individually, but I owe a particular debt to Ralph Heintzman, whose responses combined constructive criticism and supportiveness in his usual generous proportions. Thank you, also, to Tom Courchene and Donald Savoie, both of whom gave suggestions that improved the paper.

References

Aberbach, J. and T. Christensen. "Radical Reform in New Zealand: Crisis, Windows of Opportunity and Rational Actors." *Public Administration*, Vol. 79, no. 2 (2001): 403-422.

Algemene Rekenkamer. *Tweede Kamer, 1994/95, 24120, no. 3.* Den Haag: Algemene Rekenkamer, 1995.

Audit Commission. *Listen up! Effective Community Consultation.* London: Audit Commission, 1999.

Bardach, E. *Getting Agencies to Work Together: The Practice and Theory of Managerial Craftsmanship.* Washington, DC: The Brookings Institution, 1998.

Behn, R. *Rethinking Democratic Accountability.* Washington, DC: The Brookings Institution, 2001.

Böllhoff, D. "The New Regulatory Regime: The Institutional Design of Telecommunications Regulation at the National Level." Presented to the Conference on Common Goods and Governance across Multiple Arenas, Bonn, June/July 2000.

Bovens, M. and S. Zouridis. "From Street Level to System Level Bureaucracies: How ICT is Transforming Administrative Discretion and Constitutional Control." Presented to the PAT-NET conference, Leiden University, Netherlands, June 21–22, 2001.

Boyne, G. "Bureaucratic Theory Meets Reality: Public Choice and Service Contracting in US Local Government." *Public Administration Review*,Vol. 58, no. 6 (1998): 474-484.

Cabinet Office. *Wiring it up: Whitehall's Management of Cross-Cutting Policies and Services.* London: Performance and Innovation Unit, 2000.

Canadian Centre for Management Development (CCMD). *Citizen/Client Surveys; Dispelling Myths and Redrawing Maps.* Ottawa: CCMD, 1998*a*.

________ *Government at your Service: A Progress Report from the Citizen-Centred Service Network.* Ottawa: CCMD, 1998*b*.

Chancellor of the Duchy of Lancaster. *Next Steps: Agencies in Government, Review 1996*, Cm3579. London: The Stationery Office, 1997.

Clarke, J. and J. Newman. *The Managerial State: Power, Politics and Ideology in the Remaking of Social Welfare.* London: Sage, 1997.

Department of Environment, Transport and the Regions (DETR). *Cross-Cutting Issues in Public Policy and Public Service.* Report produced by a team from the School of Public Policy, University of Birmingham, 2000. Available from http:www.local-regions.dtlr.gov.uk/cross/ccpps/02.htm

Dunleavy, P. "The Globalisation of Public Service Production: Can Government be 'the Best in the World'?" *Public Policy and Administration,* Vol. 9, no. 2 (1994): 36-65.

Elliot, J. "The First Batch of NHS Patients Set for Europe." *Sunday Times*, October 14, 2001, p. 26.

Finland. Ministry of Finance. *Public Management in Finland.* Helsinki: Ministry of Finance and Public Management Department, 2001.

Gains, F. "Next Steps Agencies and Accountability: The Experience of Modernisation." *Public Policy and Administration*, Vol. 17 (2002), forthcoming.

Gore, A. *Businesslike Government: Lessons Learned from America's Best Companies.* Washington, DC: National Performance Review, 1997.

Guyomarch, A. "'Public Service,' 'Public Management' and the Modernization of

French Public Administration." *Public Administration*, Vol. 77, no. 1 (1999): 171-193.

Halligan, J. "The Diffusion of Civil Service Reform." In *Civil Service Systems in a Comparative Perspective*," ed. H. Bekke, J. Perry and T. Toonen. Bloomington, IN: Indiana University Press, 1996.

Hood, C. *The Limits of Administration*. London: Wiley, 1976.

________ *The Art of the State: Culture, Rhetoric and Public Management*. Oxford: Oxford University Press, 1998.

Hood, C. and M. Jackson. *Administrative Argument*. Aldershot: Dartmouth Pub. Co., 1991.

Hughes, O. *Public Management and Administration: An Introduction*, 2d ed. Basingstoke: Macmillan, 1998.

Inglehart, R. "Postmodernization Erodes Respect for Authority but Increases Support for Democracy." In *Critical Citizens: Global Support for Democratic Governance*, ed. P. Norris. Oxford: Oxford University Press, 1999.

Judge, D., B. Hogwood and M. McVicar. "The Pondlife of Executive Agencies: Parliament and Informatory Accountability." *Public Policy and Administration*, Vol. 12, no. 2 (1997): 95-115.

Kavanagh, D. and D. Richardson. "Departmentalism and Joined-up Government: Back to the Future?" *Parliamentary Affairs*, Vol. 54 (2001): 1-18.

Lane, J.-E. *New Public Management*. London: Routledge, 2000.

Ling, T. "Unpacking Partnership: The Case of Health Care." In *New Managerialism, New Welfare?*, ed. J. Clarke, S. Gerwitz and E. McLaughlin. London: Sage, 2000.

Lowndes, V. and C. Skelcher. "The Dynamics of Multi-Organizational Partnerships: An Analysis of Changing Modes of Governance." *Public Administration*, Vol. 74, no. 2 (1998): 313-333.

Lowndes, V., G. Stoker and L. Pratchett. *Enhancing Public Participation in Local Government*. London: DETR, 1998.

Lowndes, V., L. Pratchett and G. Stoker. "Trends in Public Participation: Part 2 — Citizens' Perspectives." *Public Administration*, Vol. 79, no. 2 (2001): 445-455.

May, M. and E. Brunsdon. "Social Services and Community Care." In *Public Management in Britain*, ed. S. Horton and D. Farnham. Basingstoke: Macmillan, 1999.

Micheletti, M. "The End of Big Government: Is it Happening in the Nordic Countries?" *Governance*, Vol. 13, no. 2 (2000): 265-278.

Ministère de la Fonction Publique. *L'accueil dans les services publics*. Paris: Ministère de la Fonction Publique, 1994.

Newman, J. *Modernising Governance: New Labour, Policy and Society*. London: Sage, 2001.

Next Steps Team. *Towards Best Practice: An Evaluation of the First Two Years of the Public Sector Benchmarking Project, 1996-98*. London: Office of Public Service (Cabinet Office), 1998.

Organisation for Economic Co-operation and Development (OECD). *Responsive Government: Service Quality Initiatives*. Paris: PUMA/OECD, 1996.

________ *Managing Cross-cutting Issues*. Paris: PUMA/OECD, 2001. Available from http://www.oecd.org/puma/strat/managing.htm

Osborne, D. and T. Gaebler. *Reinventing Government: How the Entrepreneurial Spirit is Transforming the Public Sector*. Reading, MA: Adison Wesley, 1992.

Peters, B.G. "Managing Horizontal Government: The Politics of Co-ordination." *Public Administration*, Vol. 76, no. 2 (1998): 295-311.

________ *Institutional Theory in Political Science: The 'New Institutionalism'*. London: Continuum, 1999.

Peterson, M. "The Fate of 'Big Government' in the United States: Not Over, but Undermined?" *Governance*, Vol. 13, no. 2 (2000): 251-264.

Pew Research Centre. *Deconstructing Distrust: How Americans View Government*. 1998. Available from http://www.people-press.org/trustrpt.htm

Pierre, J., ed. *Bureaucracy and the Modern State: An Introduction to Comparative Public Administration.* Aldershot: Edward Elgar, 1995.

Pierson, P. "Increasing Returns, Path Dependence and the Study of Politics." *American Political Science Review*, Vol. 94, no. 2 (2000): 251-267.

Pollitt, C. "Improving the Quality of Social Services: New Opportunities for Participation?" In *Towards More Democracy in Social Services*, ed. G. Flosser and H.-U. Otto. Berlin: de Gruyter, 1998, pp. 339-370.

________ "Institutional Amnesia: A Paradox of the 'Information Age'?" *Prometheus*, Vol. 18, no. 1 (2000): 5-16.

Pollitt, C. and G. Bouckaert. *Public Management Reform: A Comparative Analysis.* Oxford: Oxford University Press, 2000.

Pollitt, C., K. Bathgate, A. Smullen and C. Talbot. "Agency Fever? Analysis of an International Policy Fashion." *Journal of Comparative Policy Analysis*, Vol. 3, no. 3 (2001): 271-290.

Premfors, R. "Re-Shaping the Democratic State: Swedish Experiences in a Comparative Perspective." *Public Administration*, Vol. 76, no. 1 (1998): 141-159.

Prime Minister and Minister for the Cabinet Office. *Modernising Government.* Cm4310. London: The Stationery Office, 1999.

Prince, M. "Banishing Bureaucracy or Hatching a Hybrid? The Canadian Food Inspection Agency and the Politics of Reinventing Government." *Governance*, Vol. 13, no. 2 (2000): 215-232.

Rhodes, R. *Understanding Governance: Policy Networks, Governance, Reflexivity and Accountability.* Buckingham: Open University Press, 1997.

Rouban, L., ed. *Citizens and the New Governance: Beyond New Public Management.* Amsterdam: IOS, 1999.

Sahlin-Andersson, K. "National, International and Transnational Constructions of New Public Management." In *New Public Management: The Transformation of Ideas and Practice*, ed. T. Christensen and P. Laegried. Aldershot: Ashgate, 2001, pp. 43-72.

Seargeant, J. and J. Steele. *Who Asked You? The Citizen's Perspective on Participation.* London: Improvement and Development Agency, 1999.

Schiavo, L. "Quality Standards in the Public Sector: Differences between Italy and the UK in the Citizen's Charter Initiatives." *Public Administration*, Vol. 78, no. 3 (2000): 679-698.

Stewart, J. *Managing Difference: An Analysis of Service Characteristics.* Birmingham: Institute of Local Government Studies, 1992.

United Kingdom. National Audit Office. *Government on the Web*, HC. 87. London: The Stationery Office, 1999.

Waldegrave, W. "The Reality of Reform and Accountability in Today's Public Service." In *Reader: Changes in the Civil Service*, ed. N. Flynn. London: Public Finance Foundation, 1994, pp. 81-88.

Walsh, K. *Public Services Go to Market: Competition, Contracting and the New Public Management.* Basingstoke: Macmillan, 1995.

World Bank. *Anti-corruption in Transition: A Contribution to the Policy Debate.* Washington, DC: World Bank, 2000.

The Dialectics of Organizational Design

Introduction

CHRISTOPHER POLLITT IS ONE OF THE MOST ELEGANT, WISE AND, ABOVE ALL, BALanced observers of contemporary public management. As I agree with everything he says here—or perhaps ever has said—I may not be the ideal choice for commentator, if controversy and disagreement were the objectives of the exercise.

Be that as it may, my comments are in four parts. I will begin by noting three virtues of Pollitt's paper, that is to say, three things I agree with. Then I will mention two issues that might have deserved further development or nuance. Next I will touch on two issues on which the chapter is relatively silent. And I will conclude with a few comments on current organizational design issues within the government of Canada.

Before I get to this, however, it may be helpful to say something about the subject of the Pollitt paper, since it may not be immediately obvious to those who do not follow the literature or controversies in public administration. In a word, the paper is about the decision whether and how to deliver programs and services through organizational forms other than the "traditional" unified ministerial department.[1] Against this background, Pollitt reviews the menu of choices for doing so, and the criteria for selection.

Three Virtues

LET ME BEGIN, THEN, BY SUGGESTING THREE STRENGTHS OF THE PAPER, OR THREE things with which I am in strong agreement.

A dialectical approach

The first virtue to which I would call attention is what I will call the paper's *dialectical* spirit. Pollitt begins by noting that the requirements for organizational design in modern governments are likely to involve "if not actual contradictions, than at least some tensions and trade-offs" (Pollitt 2002). The paper then proceeds to explore three of these contradictions, or trade-offs: (i) the dialectic of efficiency and accountability; (ii) the dialectic of efficiency and integration; and (iii) the dialectic of efficiency and participation.

Although Pollitt does not do so, I have called these pairs of contradictory objectives "dialectics" because that is the traditional term in western thought for a pair of linked contraries that are in tension, yet mutually necessary one to another. The conviction that reality has a profoundly dialectical character is rooted in a long tradition of western thought going back well beyond Hegel—its leading modern exponent—to Nicholas of Cusa in the fifteenth century and even to Augustine of Hippo in the fifth century.

The dialectical frame of mind has enjoyed a vigorous revival in recent management literature, primarily related to the private sector. Authors such as Kim Cameron, James Collins and Jerry Porras, Paul Evans, Richard Tanner Pascale and Robert Quinn have all drawn attention to the "paradoxes" and "dualities" of organizational life, and have argued that a central, if not *the* central, challenge of modern organizational leadership is the management and reconciliation of dualities.

Acknowledgement of the role of dualities in public organizations and public administration goes back at least to Herbert Simon's seminal work of the 1940s (Simon 1946), and has been noted by a number of current scholars, including Peter Aucoin (1990), Guy Peters (1998) and Pollitt himself (Pollitt and Bouckaert 2000). But this theme merits more attention in the public management literature, because managing "paradox" is even more central to public than to other kinds of organizations. In fact, one might almost say that what is *in* the public sector—and deserves to *remain* in the public sector—are the very cases where trade-offs between conflicting objectives are most salient and difficult to reconcile. For this reason, public management is inherently dialectical and we get into trouble when we forget this, as we often do (especially in times of major change) and focus on only one side of a particular dialectic. In Canada, for example, a major federal department has been through an undeservedly rough period at the hands of the Auditor General and of the public press because, for a time, it did not pay enough attention to both sides of Christopher Pollitt's dialectic of efficiency and accountability.

A recent report of the UK Select Committee on Public Administration underlined the importance of this particular dialectic:

> Our key theme is the importance of achieving and maintaining combined progress on two key issues: improving the performance of public services at the same time as maintaining or increasing their public accountability. Both goals are crucial for maintaining public confidence in what government does, yet they are too often treated separately (UK. House of Commons 2001).

Of course, it is extraordinarily hard to do two contradictory things at the same time—let alone a whole series of contradictory things—and do them well. As Pollitt rightly points out, this requirement makes service delivery and management in the public sector "even *more* challenging and complex" than in the private sector. Interestingly, over 90 percent of Canadians recognize this fact (CCMD 1998). Yet in the same proportion they still expect that public services should be equal or higher in quality to private sector services. This presents public managers with an enormous challenge. Fortunately, Canadians also think that, in many important cases, public services *are* superior to private services. For example, Canadians give higher service quality ratings to the Canada Customs and Revenue Agency and to Canada Post than they do to Canada's chartered banks (CCMD 2000).

Service characteristics

Another strength of Pollitt's paper is its discussion of how specific organizational circumstances and the nature of the work to be performed should influence organizational design. Pollitt identifies four service characteristics: (i) standardizability (of outputs); (ii) observability (of outputs and outcomes); (iii) political salience; and (iv) consequentiality (the risk to life and safety). This is a good list. It is absolutely critical to identify and understand the role that each of these characteristics plays in the delivery of programs and services, and how they shape what can or should be done, especially concerning organizational form.

Pollitt notes that where services are difficult to standardize, or results are not easily observable, there may be a need for higher levels of trust, long-term relationships, a strong public ethic, a spirit of professionalism and security of tenure. In other words, something close to a traditional public bureaucracy, or public service.

This discussion rightly draws our attention to the importance of the service context for organizational design. Form should follow function. Pollitt himself has put this in a memorable way in an earlier essay:

> I do not want an entrepreneur looking after my state pension (or my aged grandparent), but neither do I want a cautious bureaucrat driving the fire engine or giving pump-priming grants to inventors. The problem is not one of how to apply a set of management techniques right across the public sector, it is much more a question of seeking, in each separate case, a match of function, form and culture. A less rousing sermon no doubt, but a more useful one (Pollitt 1995).

Cultural context

A third virtue of the paper is its emphasis on cultural context. As Pollitt emphasizes, it is very unwise simply to import reforms from elsewhere without taking account of such things as the institutional context, political culture and so on. Reforms which are essential in one context may not be needed and may not work in another. They may even do great harm. Arguably, for example, the new public management reforms, which have been introduced in many developed countries, are not appropriate for and may even have done significant damage in less-developed countries.

In a recent OECD paper, Alex Matheson has noted that "there is a growing body of opinion that in developing and transitional countries, the best practice notion has done considerable harm." Many of the management reforms trumpeted (often mistakenly, or with too little evidence) as best practice in developed countries have proven inappropriate and therefore ineffective in other settings, thus wasting resources, generating cynicism and actually making problems worse.

> For example, privatisation has been pursued in the absence of appropriate legal or governance architecture; decentralisation in the absence of credible reporting and control; managerial delegation in the absence of a rule-compliant administrative culture; or accrual accounting in the absence of a sound cash-accounting system (PUMA 2001).

While the greatest damage has no doubt occurred in developing countries, the same phenomenon can be observed among the developed countries themselves. Reforms that were shaped by the institutional and constitutional setting, administrative patterns and political cultures of one jurisdiction have been cut loose from their original setting and advertised as a recipe for improvement elsewhere. The results have not always been as anticipated, for organizational design as for other aspects of public management. If what we seek in organizational design is the right form for the right function, the organizational forms we need are those that, as Pollitt observes, meet "the specific priorities of a specific service delivered within a specific community."

Implications and consequences

The implication from all of this, I think, is that countries or jurisdictions that have taken an *a priori* or ideological approach to redesign of the state—imposing form on function, instead of the other way around—have often encountered problems down the road. They have subsequently found themselves obliged to rebuild: (i) the "centre" of government; (ii) horizontal linkages, or "joined-up" government; (iii) public service values and ethics, the public service ethos; or (iv) sometimes all three.

The need for these kinds of subsequent adjustments reflects an initial failure to get the balance right between the twin imperatives of cohesion and autonomy. Focusing exclusively or excessively on only one side of the dialectic leads inevitably to trouble down the road. This is true everywhere, as the research on the private sector mentioned above suggests. But it is especially true of the public sector, whose very nature is defined by the need to reconcile and balance competing public goods.

The bottom line for Canada from all of this is that, by being "behind" in public service reform, Canada has actually ended up "ahead." By refusing to adopt a dogmatic or Procrustean approach to public sector reform, by cleaving instead to its traditional incremental and pragmatic methods, Canada has been able to avoid some of the excesses of public sector reform. Canada has been able to maintain, through adjustment, a reasonable balance between competing objectives, and, as a result, a strong, over-all public service institution. As we are now entering a new period of public service reform, potentially major reform, within the Canadian federal government, this achievement now hangs in the balance, something to which I will return at the end of my comments.

Two Issues

As advertised above, I should now like to draw attention to two issues that might have deserved further development or nuance.

Service and legitimacy

The first is the link between service and the legitimacy of the state. One of the deliciously teasing elements in Pollitt's paper is the "Afterword." He suggests, very briefly, that public sector service delivery needs to be seen in a "broader political context," in which the provision of public services is "central to the legitimacy of the modern state." In other words, service delivery in the public sector is never just about service: it is also about democracy, about strengthening confidence in public institutions and convictions about democratic citizenship.

I believe this is an extremely important point, one that deserves much more development than the cursory and tantalizing treatment Pollitt is able to give it here. I sense another paper coming. I hope so, because I believe this will be an important future theme for public administration.

Unfortunately, in this paper, Pollitt does not relate the issue of legitimacy back to the design choices and service characteristics he identifies earlier in the paper. If he had, I think it might have led to a sharper distinction, in the survey of service characteristics, between: redesign *within* the state or the public sector and redesign that involves the transfer of functions *outside* the core public sector—when the state is replaced as service provider.

I believe the issues of legitimacy are more urgently raised by the latter than by the former. Activities that remain within an identifiable public sector continue to build legitimacy for the state; activities located outside a recognizable public sector probably do not. There is an obvious link here with Jane Jenson's comments in her paper in this volume: reducing the state may play a role in reducing citizenship as well.

Fragmentation versus integration

In his exploration of the dialectic of "efficiency and integration," Pollitt notes that "narrow efficiency-oriented reforms have undermined integration." Programs of "agencification" at all costs, and without any reference to context or to competing objectives, have brought about "fragmentation" of the public service, have reduced coherence, have created barriers to more seamless and integrated service delivery and have therefore prompted a subsequent wave of concern for more "joined-up government," as under the Blair government in the United Kingdom.

This is all true and is a very fair warning. But Pollitt omits to notice that "agencies" can also be used to promote service integration. The Canadian Food Inspection Agency, Service New Brunswick and Australia's Centrelink are all examples of single-window service agencies that have been created expressly to *cross* organizational boundaries and to promote more seamless and integrated service delivery.

Of course, it is important to note that the same objectives can be pursued *without* using the agency form. In Canada, similar single-window and service-integration mandates have been given to "traditional" unified ministerial departments in Ontario (Ministry of Business and Consumer Services), Nova Scotia (Service Nova Scotia) and British Columbia (BC Government Agents).

Two More Issues

HAVING NOTED TWO ISSUES COVERED IN THE PAPER THAT MIGHT MERIT FURTHER development and nuance, I should now like to raise two additional issues *not* covered or raised there, but that might have been.

Organizational culture

One of the few things I could find missing from the paper was a discussion of the role of organizational culture in the redesign of the state. This is a very interesting omission for two reasons: first, because organizational culture is the key *driver* for redesign; and second, because, paradoxically, organizational culture is also what is most *at risk* in redesign.

Let me briefly explain these two contradictory statements.

Organizational culture as driver. Something Pollitt does not really discuss in the paper but simply takes for granted, as self-evident, is why redesign or restructuring the state is an issue at all.

I believe the answer lies in the coexistence within the "traditional" unified ministerial department of two antithetical organizational cultures. To use Henry Mintzberg's terms, one is the culture of "managing up"; and the other is the culture of "managing down." The first culture looks upward and inward, to manage the policy process, the senior public service (the deputy minister or permanent secretary), the minister, central agencies and Parliament. The second culture looks downward and out, to manage staff, processes and program delivery to citizens, clients and business. In the Canadian case, to complicate things, the first is largely an Ottawa-based culture, while the second is the culture of the federal public service *outside* Ottawa. And the relationship between them is often a dialogue of the deaf.

The problem for the second culture is that the first is on top. And because its attention and priorities are elsewhere, the first culture can make it more difficult for the second to perform at its optimal level. A simple anecdote may illustrate the problem. I am informed by a number of observers who have participated in the executive committee of a major service delivery department in a Canadian government over a number of years that service delivery issues have only rarely been a subject of discussion by the committee, except in periods of crisis or controversy. The attention of the committee is normally given elsewhere: to large policy issues, to the minister, to Cabinet and Parliament, to managing the relationship with the central agencies and so on. Actual program and service delivery has usually been an afterthought, something taken for granted, except when things go wrong. It is not a focus for performance management on a daily basis. The concerns, perspectives, outlook, values and culture of the largest part of the department never or only rarely make it to the table. Most of the time another culture takes up all the available space.

Proposals for redesign of the state in the past two decades have come largely from the need to fix this problem. The impulse for redesign is the need to establish adequate "organizational space" in order for the service and program delivery parts of government to be more effective. They need the "room to manoeuvre" that will allow them to develop the leadership, systems, practices, values, discourse and culture needed for high performance in the delivery of programs and services to citizens. The establishment of new service agencies, whether inside or outside traditional unified ministerial departments, has been driven by this imperative: by the need to supply this kind of room to manoeuvre, and to allow the development of the leadership, systems and culture required for the tasks of managing down and "out," as opposed to those of managing in and up. Agencies are not an end in themselves, simply a means to an end. In fact the most urgent new frontier for organizational design might well be within traditional unified departments themselves, where many program and service delivery functions may be suffering for lack of adequate organizational space. In other words, to adapt a celebrated circumlocution of a wily Canadian prime minister: agencies if necessary, but not necessarily agencies.

Organizational culture at risk. Organizational culture is thus one of the drivers for the redesign of the state. But, at a higher level, organizational culture is also what is *most at risk* in redesign.

It is important to keep in mind that the issue of organizational culture presents itself at two levels in a public service. On the one hand is the organizational culture of individual public service organizations. These can be many and various and suited to the organizational task. The first issue in redesign is to establish the appropriate organizational space for each of these functions to be carried out as well as they can be.

But, on the other hand, there is the broad organizational culture of the public service at large. This culture is equally important, but it has too often taken a back seat in redesign, until it is too late, until the damage has been done and corrective measures are required. What is at risk in redesign is this broader culture of the public service: the values and ethics that underlie the very idea of public service. In a word, the public service *ethos*.

A culture is sustained by community, by the sense of participating in a community that practices and upholds certain standards and norms. Fragmentation and dispersal of the state threaten to undermine the "community of practice" that sustains public sector values. A degree of unity, mobility and critical mass are important ingredients to sustain a sense of membership in a broad public service community, and an implicit commitment to the values that go with that community (Deputy Minister Task Force on Public Service Values and Ethics 1996).

It is sometimes assumed or argued that public service values can, by themselves, counterbalance or offset the effects of fragmentation. But this is an illusion because values are shaped by institutions as much as by the reverse. What we believe influences what we do, of course. But what we do also shapes, in the end, what we believe. If public service values and culture are important, we need to design the institutions to sustain them, not assume that they will be enough to sustain the institution.

What this means, in practice, is that architects and artisans of redesign need to give just as much attention to the cohesion and health of the overall *public service institution* as they do to the efficiency and effectiveness of the organizations of which it is composed. Redesign is just as much about linkages and relationships as it is about establishing new organizational space to improve organizational performance. A balancing act, once again. And one to which far too little attention has been directed to date. That is why culture is, at one and the same time, the chief driver of the redesign of the state, and also what is most at risk in such restructuring.

A world without frontiers

While Pollitt's paper does touch in passing on the link between the redesign of the state and the theme of this book—the art of the state in a world without frontiers—it is relatively discrete on the actual nature of the relationship between globalization and organizational design in the public sector.

It seems to me that this question might be approached from at least two directions: first, how can organizational design help to respond to the challenges of globalization? And second, what are the implications of globalization for organizational design? Answers to these two questions would, I think, be very different, perhaps—in the paradoxical spirit of this paper—even contradictory.

Responding to the challenges of globalization. As to the first, it strikes me that new organizational forms with an altered relationship to ministerial oversight and accountability have been used, or attempted to be used, *within* federations, to cross political frontiers. In Canada, examples include the Canadian Food Inspection Agency and the Canada Customs and Revenue Agency. The rationale for the creation of both these agencies included the hope and expectation that the agency form would position these new organizations to take on a service-delivery role for more than one order of government more easily than a "traditional" unified ministerial department could do. In Australia, Centrelink delivers human services not only for a variety of Commonwealth (federal) departments but also for other levels of government as well.

It seems at least possible that a similar approach might eventually be used at a transnational level. Between Canada and the United States, for example, it would be possible to imagine new organizational forms that might be used to manage common areas of concern, such as the border and security issues that were a prominent feature of discussion at the conference leading to this book, or some other potential future areas of common concern, such as the currency. The precedent and success of the International Joint Commission is certainly suggestive. Of course whether, and under what conditions, such new organizational arrangements would be appropriate is a matter that would need to be analyzed and debated in a wider public policy context.

Implications of a borderless world. But what about the second question: the implications of a world without frontiers for organizational design in the public sector? Here I fear my answer may be somewhat contradictory.

I believe the advocates of a more open, porous, contractual state and public service—a public service based on the so-called "employability" principle that was fashionable, for a time, during the public sector downsizing of the mid-1990s—such advocates have always gravely overlooked or minimized the degree to which such a public service employment regime would make public institutions vulnerable to malevolent external influences, especially to corruption and bribery, to organized crime and to foreign agents.

Unfortunately, the events of September 11, 2001 now require us to add global terrorism to this list, perhaps at the top of it.

What all of these forces have in common is that they are now organized on a global scale, and can bring immense resources and technical sophistication to their programs of infiltration and undermining of good government. In the foreseeable future, the public interest and its guardians will be under siege as never before. For this reason, among others, September 11, 2001 gives us added incentive to re-evaluate and rediscover the merits of a relatively "closed," professional bureaucracy, characterized by long-term employment, and a strong professional culture and ethos, oriented to the public interest.

Concluding Thoughts: Public Service Reform in Canada

Some of the issues touched on in these reflections are far from "academic" in Canada, because we are in the midst of another round of public service reform and organizational redesign, potentially the most important since 1917.

For the first time in 30 years or so, Canada will substantially overhaul the legislation governing the public service employment regime.

This is long overdue. But frustration with the rigidities, slow pace and cumbersome nature of the old system could well lead the reform effort to extreme rather than balanced solutions.

As I mentioned earlier, the essence of sound organizational design in the public sector is getting the balance right between cohesion and autonomy. The risk is that we might not get this balance right for the challenges that face us in a world without frontiers. By being behind in public sector reform, Canada had ended up ahead. It would be a great irony if we were now to catch up, and then fall behind.

Notes

1 Throughout this paper I have referred to the "traditional" unified ministerial department, in quotation marks. The quotation marks are intended to remind the reader that the unified ministerial department is not something that has existed from time immemorial. This organizational form has its own history and is a relatively new creation, enjoying its heyday in the middle decades of the twentieth century. It was preceded and followed—and indeed accompanied—by a rich variety of other organizational forms. There never was, as Pollitt himself notes, "only one, centralized, hierarchical type of organization ...This makes the past more interesting and, occasionally, may remind us that problems we encounter with what we think of as new forms actually have many precedents." The same point is made in Heintzman (1997, pp. 11-12).

References

Aucoin, P. "Administrative Reform in Public Management: Paradigms, Principles, Paradoxes, and Pendulums." *Governance*, Vol. 3, no. 2 (1990): 115-137.

Canadian Centre for Management Development (CCMD). *Citizens First*. Ottawa: Canada Communication Group Inc., 1998.

________ *Citizens First 2000*. Ottawa: Canada Communication Group Inc., 2000.

Collins, J.C. and J.I. Porras. *Built to Last: Successful Habits of Visionary Companies*. New York: HarperBusiness, 1994.

Deputy Minister Task Force on Public Service Values and Ethics. *A Strong Foundation: Report*. Ottawa: Canadian Centre for Management Development, 1996, 1998.

Evans, P. and Y. Doz. "The Dualistic Organization." In *Human Resource Management in International Firms*, ed. P. Evans, Y. Doz and A. Laurent. New York: St. Martin's Press, 1990, pp. 219-242.

Heintzman, R. "Canada and Public Administration." In *Public Administration and Public Management: Experiences in Canada*, ed. J. Bourgault, M. Demers and C. Williams. Quebec: Les publications du Québec, 1997, pp. 1-12.

Pascale, R.T. *Managing on the Edge: How the Smartest Companies Use Conflict to Stay Ahead*. New York: Simon & Schuster, 1990.

Peters, B.G. "What Works? The Antiphons of Administrative Reform." In *Taking Stock: Assessing Public Sector Reforms*, ed. G. Peters and D. Savoie. Montreal and Kingston: McGill-Queen's University Press, 1998, pp. 78-107.

Pollitt, C. "Management Techniques for the Public Sector: Pulpit and Practice." In *Governance in a Changing Environment*, ed. B.G. Peters and D. Savoie. Montreal: McGill-Queen's University Press, 2000, pp. 203-238.

Pollitt, C. and G. Bouckaert. *Public Management Reform: A Comparative Analysis*. Oxford: Oxford University Press, 2000.

PUMA. *Public Sector Modernisation: A Ten-Year Perspective*. Paris: Organisation for Economic Co-operation and Development, 2001.

Quinn, R.E. 1988. *Beyond Rational Management: Mastering the Paradoxes and Competing Demands of High Performance*. San Francisco: Jossey-Bass, 1988.

Simon, H.A. "The Proverbs of Administration." *Public Administration Review*, Vol. 6, no. 2 (1946): 53-67.

United Kingdom. House of Commons, Select Committee on Public Administration. *Making Government Work: The Emerging Issues*. 7th Report. London: Stationery Office, 2001.

Policy First: Three Case Studies

Introduction

THE CENTRAL LESSON I DRAW FROM EXPERIENCE IS THAT IN GOVERNMENT IT IS IMPOSSIBLE to settle on an appropriate form of organization until what it is intended to do is clear. And then clear in some detail: policy first, then structure.

The fading of public confidence in government is much discussed. The other side of the coin is government's declining confidence in itself, which has a lot to do with the public service's intensifying preoccupation with how to organize itself.

Reorganization is often the product of desperation. It is when a department or agency is uncertain, when it cannot decide what to do about a nasty problem, that it becomes most interested in organization. Perhaps a new structure will turn up something better in policy. The phenomenon has long been familiar for individual units. Declining confidence, in government and of government, is generalizing it. Faced with contemporary complexities, increasingly unsure of what they can do or should do, politicians and officials seek solace in working at how to be better organized. To put it more unkindly: when you are short on policies, fiddling with process and procedure may at least give the spin doctors a better chance to impress the media.

This impetus helps to explain why "make government more like business" is a theme that resonates so strongly among reorganizers. In many areas of business, success is largely a matter of getting the organization right. If the economy is working as it is supposed to do, the famous hidden hand of the market largely determines what individual enterprises can do. The big decisions are about how to do it.

In reality, of course, markets are imperfect and bigger companies do have to make some decisions that can be labelled "policy." Even so the factors to be taken into account are fewer, as well as generally more calculable, than those with which government struggles. In the public sector the tough job is to decide on the lines of action that will best satisfy, on balance, a variety of considerations and interests: get the policy clear first, the organization will then follow.

I do not mean that it follows automatically. There is still plenty of scope for getting it wrong. But the clearer the policy, the better the chances of creating an effective organization. Certainly that was my experience, as the deputy minister responsible in the 1960s for organizing two new federal departments: Manpower and Immigration (M&I) and Regional Economic Expansion (DREE). I think it fair to say that the first went reasonably well. The second did not. While there were several reasons for the difference, one was dominant. In the case of the M&I we knew well what it was for. In the case of DREE, we did not.

Three Case Studies: M&I, DREE and GCHQ

I can never speak of M&I without apologizng for the sexist label, but 35 years ago "manpower policy" was an *avant-garde* phrase; "human resource development" would have been pretentious jargon. What the label of the times covered was clear. Most importantly, it meant employment information and counselling, comprehensively and consistently available across the country, along with extensive training and mobility programs accessible independently from the Unemployment Insurance (UI) program. Such ideas had been developed over a considerable period and were quite widely understood across the country. In Ottawa they were becoming familiar: politically and bureaucratically.

That they called for a new organization was readily accepted: new but not, readily, unconventional. In 1966, federal management was still highly centralized in Ottawa. The effectiveness of M&I's operations required a then unprecedented devolution of responsibility to program directors across the country. One of the toughest battles I fought with Treasury Board was to obtain more senior classification levels for those posts than had hitherto been accorded to officials located away from the majesty of Ottawa.

On the other hand, what was then an unconventional structure lessened the disruption costs of reorganization. Only a few people were diminished by the changes and not many were disappointed in their competing expectations of advancement. The problems of that kind were not within the federal service but in their relations with some provincial departments. The new federal policy involved a considerable change in their way of doing things. There was some use of defensive tactics that provided an early and severe test of the new organization's resilience.

I should add that the department later encountered other problems, economic and political. The original policy idea was strictly concentrated on "hand-up" as distinct from "hand-out" programs. While I have no sympathy with the pejorative view of income supports that the second label often implies, it is important to recognize that the two different kinds of programs call for distinct administrative organizations. I therefore refused to have unemployment insurance linked with M&I, although it had been the basis for such employment services as we inherited.

Later, however, political pressures produced a reunification with UI, and more recently other income support programs were absorbed into what is now Human Resources Development Canada (HRDC). The result, in my view, is a confused as well as a monstrous department. That, however, is another story. It does not detract from the assessment that M&I began, and for quite a long time continued, as a successful reorganization for government functions of major importance.

DREE was a sharply different case. It did not start from a clear idea. True, there were programs, dating particularly from the later 1950s and earlier 1960s, aimed at economic development in a variety of deprived areas, agricultural and industrial, rural and in some respects urban. But they had not led to any formulated idea of regional development as a general function of the federal government. That concept burst on an unprepared Ottawa in the Trudeaumania election of 1968. Removing regional disparities was the nearest thing to a definite commitment that the new prime minister brought to government.

Official Ottawa tried to absorb the shock. My own view was that the "just society" of Mr. Trudeau's eloquence did indeed call for federal help to particularly troubled communities, but for the most part that would involve more specific, case-by-case measures than "regional" development suggested. We had previously given thought to some such action within the ambit of manpower programs, and my response to the election was therefore to propose that "community development" be added to the mandate of M&I.

That could have been a natural fit, but two factors weighed strongly against it. Senior bureaucrats feared that Manpower and Community Development would be too powerful for the comfort of other departments and central agencies. (The creation of the much bigger HRDC, a generation later, is a contrast that tells much about the shrunken influence, on major issues, of senior bureaucrats.) Second, Mr. Trudeau preferred that his then most publicized theme should be identified with a department of its own. The upshot was that I moved from M&I to what became the Department of Regional Economic Expansion.

The clumsy name betrayed the uncertainty of purpose. The first task was to develop some concept of regional policy for which a federal department would be appropriate. What emerged, after much controversy in the offices of Ottawa, was reasonable enough. The emphasis of the departmental legislation was on "special areas" where some special set of actions was required and could be taken in cooperation with the province concerned.

That, however, was a concept only on paper. Neither in Ottawa nor in the provinces was it rooted in prepared ground. Special action on any area basis cuts across the established structure of line departments, each delivering its own kind of programs throughout the country or the province. In Ottawa in 1968 these departments were already losing authority to strengthened central agencies, the new Treasury Board Secretariat and Trudeau's rapid creation of empires in place of the formerly minute Privy Council Office and Prime Minister's Office. DREE, threatening another cut across departmental turfs, was hardly welcome.

DREE also conflicted with what was then still the ideology of official Ottawa, which saw itself as fully responsible for national matters but regarded dabbling in subnational affairs as rarely more than an unavoidable concession to political patronage. In consequence, the existing small agencies that had to be absorbed in the new department—ADA, ADB, ARDA, FRED, PFRA[1]—were all weak, suspected and resented.

Building an effective organization from such beginnings would have been slow, with nasty personnel problems, even if a sound concept of development policy had taken hold in Ottawa politics. In fact, even the basic starting assumption—that most of the country's economy was in great shape, the troubled areas peripheral—was soon shaken. Nationally, employment slackened, creating demands for "special" action in widening areas. That political pressure came to a climax with the 1970 FLQ crisis. The Trudeau Cabinet rationalized Quebec's discontent as having economic causes. Something special must be done, and the instrument at hand was DREE. The fledgling regional development programs were stretched by designating the Montreal area as "special"; it received incentives for industry and a major infrastructure project: the misconceived Mirabel airport. The political motives were strong, but the inclusion of Canada's second largest city in its mandate made nonsense of DREE's supposed focus on the disparities arising from underdevelopment in less central parts of the economy.

In politics, precedent easily confuses purpose. Other claims to special attention soon weakened considerations of special need. In more favourable circumstances DREE would have won eventual acceptance for the policy it had started without. In the event, it did not. This does not mean that the regional development effort was the waste of resources that many academics and business critics allege. It produced no transformations, but without it the economies of the Atlantic provinces and some parts of the Prairies would be significantly weaker. It must also be said, however, that despite the best efforts of my colleagues and successors (I left in 1971) DREE as such remained a confused organization whose end was little lamented.

My third example was both the most successful experience and the craziest of improvisations. I was a very junior recruit in the wartime of the 1940s. The agency's methods of recruitment, operation, command structure and everything else would have driven any respectable organization expert to cries of woe and worse. This was GCHQ, better known as Bletchley Park and—since the release of United Kingdom Cabinet documents 30 years later—as the Ultra Secret. The secrecy was ultra because not only did GCHQ have a high rate of success in breaking the various forms of the "enigma" machine ciphers in which German forces communicated; it did so with such secrecy that the German command remained confident that the ciphers were unbreakable.

This was the result of work led by mathematicians and chess masters and the like, quite a few of whom would undoubtedly now be classified as extreme security risks. Their dedication reflected, of course, the mood of wartime Britain. Their success also owed much to Prime Minister Winston Churchill. No doubt the operation pleased both the romantic and the wily sides of his nature. Certainly his support ensured that, from the early, experimental stages of their endeavour, the weird people at Bletchley Park got the resources they needed. Slashers of environmental and health protection agencies and the like, please note.

Conclusions

To summarize, from the three experiences I have mentioned and a few others, I offer three conclusions. One, the golden rule for particular government functions is "policy first, then organization." Get the purpose clear and in detail; ensure that it is understood and accepted by Cabinet and the senior bureaucracy, as well as by a sufficient constituency outside; then, and only then, start to establish the organization to fit the policy and the circumstances.

Two, these circumstances are more diverse than they usually appear to people whose major interest is organization itself. Beware of patterns for departments or agencies. What fits one set of policy and circumstance is not a model for others.

Three, there is, nevertheless, a qualification to diversity. Individual units in all their variety can work well only if all are compatible with the form of the country's governance. In our case, that is Cabinet government within Parliament. Organizers who do not understand its principles are a menace: foes of democratic accountability, those moles who for 30 years have been helping prime ministers undermine Cabinet.

I can therefore end with a cut I would like to see: improve the Prime Minister's Office by cutting it to a fraction of its present size.

Notes

1 The following agencies were: ADA, Area Development Agency; ADB, Atlantic Development Board; ARDA, *Agricultural and Rural Development Act*; FRED, Fund for Rural Economic Development; and PFRA, Prairie Rehabilitation Administration.

Discussion

THE FLOOR DISCUSSION CENTRED ON THE LEGITIMACY OF GOVERNMENT. PERHAPS because there have been so many experiments with respect to the machinery of government in recent years, the participants generated a flood of questions. Would ensuring legitimacy require that the government itself act as provider as well as organizer? Why could governments not organize what needs to be delivered, but then turn over the delivery responsibility to the private or volunteer sector? Another asked whether the political process itself was not playing havoc with the legitimacy of government, since the adversarial nature of parliamentary government and partisan politics encourages politicians in opposition parties to search for reasons to be critical of public services and government organization. The unfortunate result is that front-line public servants get caught in the crossfire of partisan politics. Still another participant asked why governments insist on creating new agencies to get around stifling administrative processes and rules? Why not simply change these stifling rules for everybody?

Others sought to explore how society could make greater use of the volunteer sector and make civil society an extension of government. Along alternative service-delivery lines, some participants suggested that governments should turn to the agency concept to further broaden their ability to deliver services. The agency concept, it was pointed out, enables departments to break loose from bureaucratic red tape and processes and to be far more responsive to citizens. Because traditional departments and agencies perform different tasks, they require different accountability regimes. It should also be noted that the agency concept has in recent years been promoted in Canada as a "national" organization rather than a federal agency, at least in the tax collection field. A number of participants, notably practitioners, argued that we should explore other opportunities to create "national" rather than federal or provincial agencies. They also argued, however, that we should make every effort to encourage more competition within and outside government.

The floor discussion revealed once again that politics and accountability concerns continue to underpin how governments do things. A former senior federal government official reported that a guiding principle for civil servants is to always avoid doing things that might make their ministers look bad. He added that, in his experience, when briefing ministers he would very often focus on what the opposition would raise to "score political points" rather than on the substance of the issues.

A former federal Cabinet minister asked how public sector unions have responded to new organizational forms and to what extent we can push the envelope further. Another participant questioned whether the not-for-profit sector could be better at delivering government services than traditional departments. Would they, she asked, be better at offering opportunities for public participation?

The pervasive presence of politics and accountability requirements in government operations can colour the type of organizational models that the government may wish to pursue. For example, Tom Kent pointed out that while national agencies may well hold promise, there are policy issues that fall squarely within the sphere of political representatives and one has to be careful not to destroy the doctrine of ministerial responsibility.

Ralph Heintzman, in his wrap-up comments, argued that it was still much too early to assess whether the agencies have been successful. He reported that the new federal government agencies were supposed to save money, but that three of them are more costly to manage than their predecessors. There are some signs, however, that although service delivery is better, the techniques employed to improve performance could have been just as easily implemented by any traditional government department.

Chris Pollitt acknowledged that organization culture matters a great deal more than is generally assumed and that we need to understand it better when initiating organizational change. He applauded the thinking that once you know what you want to accomplish and once you have the policy right, then it becomes a great deal easier to get the organization right. He added: "when you know what you are trying to achieve, it gives you the legitimate political argumentation to prioritize."

Pollitt also sought to establish a difference between in-house and external criticism. It is one thing for a minister to come in to a department and say things have to change for a number of reasons. It is quite another for the minister to go on television and say departmental officials are letting the public down. Politicians, he added, ought to be more careful when they publicly attack government departments and public servants.

Pollitt sees potential with the voluntary sector. But he argues that it is very difficult for governments to harness this potential without bureaucratizing the very organization whose assistance they seek to enlist. The question is not whether we should turn to the voluntary sector for help, but rather how to do it. That is, government can still retain legitimacy even if it does not act as the provider as well as the organizer. The voluntary sector can play an important role but great care must be taken not to turn voluntary organizations into something that is a far cry from what they were when they were first established.

New Forms of Citizenship

New Forms of Citizenship

Introduction

IN CANADA, AS IN THE REST OF THE WESTERN WORLD, WE ARE WITNESSING NEW forms of political agency and political mobilization taking place within new institutional forums, by people with new sorts of political identities. I will discuss some of these novel forms of political agency below. But it would be a mistake, I think, to exaggerate these changes. In many ways, the basic meanings and contexts of citizenship in the West have not changed dramatically. The "new forms of citizenship" are often variants or developments of the "old" forms of citizenship.

My aim in this paper, then, is to trace both the differences and the continuities in our current practices of citizenship. I will begin by exploring what I take to be the main features of the "old" model of citizenship which began to emerge in the late eighteenth century, and which has become gradually entrenched throughout the West. I will then discuss two sorts of challenges which have arisen recently, both in Canada and elsewhere in the West, to this traditional picture of citizenship—the challenge of minority nationalism and of transnationalism.

Citizenship in Liberal Nation-States

THE MODEL OF CITIZENSHIP THAT HAS DOMINATED THE THEORY AND PRACTICE OF western democracies for the last 150 years has rested on two central premises. The first concerns the values of citizenship, which have typically been defined in *liberal-democratic* terms. If citizenship can be understood in part as a package of rights and responsibilities, then this package has been defined by reference to liberal-democratic values. At the heart of our citizenship rights are individual liberties. These include the freedom of association, speech and conscience, and more generally the freedom of choice about how to lead our lives. Similarly, our duties as citizens are quintessentially liberal duties, for example, the duty to be tolerant, to accept the secular nature of political power and hence the separation of church and state, to exercise our individual autonomous judgement and critical reasoning when engaging in voting or public reasoning.

The second characteristic concerns the boundaries of citizenship, which have invariably been defined in *national* terms. If citizenship can be understood in part as membership in a political community, then the traditional model of citizenship emphasizes membership in national political communities. The nation-state has been seen as the privileged locus for political participation, self-government and solidarity. If democracy is the rule "of the people," then it is the nation that defines "the people" who are to rule themselves. We exercise self-determination through electing national legislatures, and our citizenship rights are protected by national constitutions.

This picture of citizenship as based on liberal-democratic values institutionalized in national political communities has been a very powerful one in the recent history of western democracies. Western democracies have had a great deal of success in promoting and inculcating this model of citizenship. The levels of popular commitment to both liberal values and national institutions are surprisingly high in most western countries.

This model has recently come under challenge, as I discuss below, but it is important to consider why it has historically been so successful. There was nothing inevitable or self-evident about this model. After all, very few political communities were either liberal-democratic in orientation or national in scope 200 years ago. Yet we have witnessed two powerful, indeed overwhelming, trends in the last two centuries in the West: first, the nearly-universal reordering of political space from a confusing welter of empires, kingdoms, city-states, protectorates and colonies into a system of nation-states, all of which have embarked on "nation-building" policies aimed at the diffusion of a common national identity, culture and language throughout the territory of the state;[1] and second, the nearly-universal replacement of all forms of pre-liberal or non-democratic forms of government (e.g., monarchies, oligarchies, theocracies, military dictatorships, communist regimes, etc.) with systems of liberal democracy.

Nation-building

Let me briefly describe these two processes, and how they are interrelated. They have both been long-term processes. The process of "nation-building"—that is, of standardizing and diffusing common national languages, laws, flags, anthems, schools, public institutions and identities—was a long and protracted one in most countries. Within a few years of the French Revolution, for example, the elites in Paris had adopted a conception of what language, culture and identity a French citizen should have, but it was not until the twentieth century that these ideas really took hold in much of the rural periphery or in the lower classes (Weber 1976). It was a combination of modern technological innovations, such as trains, cars, telephones, radios and television, combined with an expanded state role in the provision of education, health care and other social services, that finally gave western states the means for establishing a "national" presence throughout the territory of the state, through national transportation systems, national media networks, national legal institutions, national educational and health services, and so on.

In some countries this process of nation-building was strongly contested, particularly if there were sub-state groups that viewed themselves as nations of their own with a history of governing themselves. Where such "nations within" have been strong enough, they have been able to resist these nationalizing policies. This indeed is the first sort of challenge to the traditional model of liberal nation-state citizenship that I will discuss below: the challenge of minority nationalism, of which the Québécois are a prime example, along with the Catalans, Flemish, Scots and others.

But minority nationalisms aside, this sort of nation-building has been strikingly successful. In particular, it has proven effective in integrating members of the working class. Indeed, the need to integrate the working class into a common national community was one of the defining features underlying the development of citizenship in the twentieth century. According to T.H. Marshall's well-known account, the history of citizenship can be seen as a three-stage development, each stage occurring in a different century: citizens acquired civil rights in the eighteenth century; political rights in the nineteenth century; and social rights in the twentieth-century (Marshall 1965). This third-stage extension of citizenship to include social rights was intimately bound up with ideas of nation-building, and in particular with the national integration of the working class.

As Marshall notes, citizenship is not just a certain legal status, defined by a set of rights and responsibilities. It is also an identity, an expression of one's membership in a political community. And his argument for extending citizenship rights to include basic social rights, such as health care and education, was precisely that it would help promote a common sense of national membership and national identity. Ensuring that people had health care and education was important for Marshall not just for humanitarian reasons, that is, to meet basic needs. Social rights would also help integrate previously excluded groups into a common national culture, and thereby provide a source of national unity and loyalty. The goal was to include people in a "common culture" that should be a "common possession and heritage" (Marshall 1965, 101-102). Providing social rights would help secure "loyalty to a civilisation that is a common possession." He was writing in particular about England, and the need to integrate the English working classes, whose lack of education and economic resources excluded them from enjoyment of this national culture, such as Shakespeare, John Donne, Dickens, King James Bible, Cromwell, the Glorious Revolution and cricket.

Marshall felt that a common set of social rights would integrate people into a common national culture, and that this was good from the point of view of both the previously-excluded group and the state. There were fears that if the working class did not identify with and feel loyal to British civilization, its members might be tempted to support "foreign" ideas, particularly communism and Soviet Bolshevism.[2] Moreover, from the point of view of the state, it is easier to govern a society when its citizens share a common national language, culture and identity. All of the major functions of the state—communication and consultations, planning, investment, regulations and enforcement—work better if there is a certain cultural commonality amongst citizens. (I will return to this below.)

In short, extending citizenship to include common social rights was a tool of nation-building, intended in part to construct and consolidate a sense of common national identity and culture. And this helps explain *how* these social rights are implemented in practice. For example, the right to education is not a right to education in any language the child or parent chooses, but rather to education in the national language, since the goal is not just to meet some abstract need for rationality, literacy or knowledge, but also to educate people in a way that will help integrate them into the national culture. Similarly, western countries do not provide health care in separate hospitals for each ethnic group, even though this might be an efficient way of delivering health care, since the goal is not only to meet certain basic needs in the abstract, but rather to create a common sense of citizenship, based on common entitlements and common experiences in the exercise of those entitlements. Social rights are, in general, the right to gain certain common benefits through common public institutions operating in a common national language, so as to meet basic needs while simultaneously creating a common national identity.

Whatever the motives, the development of the welfare state has been quite successful in integrating the working classes into national languages, cultures and loyalties throughout the western democracies. To be sure, there are still many class differences between the popular culture of the masses and the high culture of the well-off. The affluent are more likely to prefer tennis to wrestling; or to read newspapers rather than tabloids. But amongst all classes there is a common language, the core of a common national culture,[3] and a common loyalty to the state as a protector of the nation. Moreover, this core national culture bears the imprint of all classes: while it involves exposing working-class children to the high culture of the elites, it also involves exposing upper-class children to the popular culture of the masses.

Indeed, it is now often the working class which is the strongest defender of ideas of nationhood, resisting efforts by elites to tear down national boundaries. This working-class commitment to preserving the nation-state is sometimes seen as evidence of an illiberal or irrational conservatism, or of the manipulation of the masses by unscrupulous populist demagogues. But it can instead be seen as a commitment to a model of political community that, in theory and to some extent in practice, is open to members of all classes, resting on a national identity, language and culture that is shared by all.

It is important to remember that in earlier periods of European history, elites tried to dissociate themselves as much as possible from "the plebs" or "the rabble," and justified their powers and privileges precisely in terms of their alleged distance from the masses. Aristocrats often spoke a different language from the popular vernacular, viewed themselves as a separate race and would not even have understood the idea that they could or should share the same culture as the peasants or labourers. The rise of nationalism, however, valorized "the people." Nations are defined in terms of "the people"—the mass of population in a territory, regardless of class or occupation—who become "the bearer of sovereignty, the central object of loyalty, and the basis of collective solidarity" (Greenfeld 1992, 14). National identity has remained strong in the modern era in part because its emphasis on the importance of the people provides a source of dignity to all individuals, whatever their class. So it should not be surprising that "the masses" have a deep emotional attachment to political communities that operate in a distinctly "national" political space and cultural milieu.[4]

In short, we have seen a process of nationalizing western societies. It look a long time to reach the lower classes and outlying regions—in some cases, only in the past half-century—but once it took hold, it developed powerful and enduring forms of national identification across class lines.

Liberal democracy

The process of liberalization and democratization has been equally drawn-out. In many European countries, liberal democracy was in a more or less evenly matched battle with both fascism and communism until World War II, and it was not until the 1970s that military dictatorships were overthrown in Portugal, Spain and Greece. And even in those countries that remained stable liberal democracies, like Britain or the United States, they were far from ideal in their actual implementation of liberal-democratic principles. It might be more accurate to say that, until recently, western states were liberal democracies for some groups (particularly white, middle-class Christian men), but quite illiberal and undemocratic for other groups. At various points in the history of these countries, the right to vote or run for office was restricted to those of a particular class, or race, or gender or religion, and even when these restrictions were restricted, there remained various other forms of discrimination in access to educational and economic opportunities or social benefits.

It was really not until the civil rights revolution of the 1960s and 1970s that firm constitutional and statutory protections of equal rights and non-discrimination were developed for women, gays and racial and religious minorities throughout the West. (In Canada, the first important statutory provision was the Bill of Rights of 1960; the constitutional provisions came with the equality rights of the Charter of Rights and Freedoms in 1982.)

To be sure, we are still far from achieving genuine equality in life-chances for many members of these groups, but there has been definite progress in the protection of civil, political and social rights on a non-discriminatory basis. And with these developments, we can plausibly describe western states as liberal democracies for all citizens, not just for privileged groups.

And, here again, this process of liberalization and democratization has been strikingly successful, in the sense that support for the general principles of liberal democracy is hegemonic—over 95 percent in most western states. There is no credible alternative today to the basic principles of constitutional democracy; anyone who questions these principles is almost immediately labelled as an extremist or fanatic. There are debates, of course, about precisely which rights deserve constitutional protection, and about how they should be interpreted and enforced. But the general idea of a constitutional democracy that guarantees certain civil, political and social rights on a non-discriminatory basis is virtually unchallenged in the West.

The liberal-democracy/nationhood tension

So the old model of citizenship is the culmination of two long-term processes: (i) a process of nation-building, in which national languages, cultures, loyalties and institutions were diffused socially downwards from the elites to the working class and geographically outwards to peripheral regions; and (ii) a process of liberalization and democratization, in which disadvantaged groups fought to gain non-discriminatory access to the civil, political and social rights of citizenship. While both processes started in the eighteenth or nineteenth centuries, it is only in the twentieth century, and in some cases only in the last few decades, that they have been more or less fully implemented.

While both these processes were initially contested by rival visions of the appropriate values or scope of political community, the resulting model of liberal/national citizenship eventually triumphed. Indeed, its triumph was so great that, for at least a few decades between the 1950s and 1980s, it was virtually the only model of citizenship present in public debate or academic writings. The assumption that citizenship referred to the exercise of liberal-democratic rights and responsibilities within a context of national political institutions was so widespread that many theorists did not feel the need to defend this assumption, or even to make it explicit. It was just taken for granted that liberal values would be institutionalized in national settings, and hence to talk of citizenship (or justice or rights) was to talk about the nation-state.[5]

But no sooner had this old model been more or less comprehensively implemented than it began to be questioned. Since the 1990s, in particular, we see an increasing number of people who question the necessity or desirability of nation-states as the appropriate scope for citizenship. Many of the "new" models of citizenship rest on the assumption that we can sever the link between liberal democracy and nationhood: that is, that we can and should develop forms of liberal-democratic citizenship that are not institutionalized in national institutions, and that do not require shared national languages, cultures, identities or loyalties. The processes of nationalization and liberalization may historically have gone hand-in-hand in the West, they argue, but the latter can be separated from the former.

Indeed, some people argue that linking liberal democracy to nationhood inevitably leads to a kind of contradiction—liberal democracy is universalistic and individualistic, whereas nationhood is particularistic and collectivistic. Tying notions of democratic citizenship to nationhood, in this view, is inevitably exclusionary, it will involve illegitimately denying rights to those individuals who are not seen as authentic or full-fledged members of the "nation."

This contradiction can certainly be seen in the history of western democracies. It is reflected in the historic denial of the franchise to immigrant groups or religious minorities on the grounds that they were not, and could not become, full members of the nation. It is reflected in notions of "Christian America" or "White Australia," in which the American or Australian nation was defined in terms of particular religious or racial characteristics. It is also reflected in gender-coded notions of nationhood, in which men were defined as the defenders of the nation and women as the mothers of the nation, and accorded different citizenship rights and responsibilities on this basis.

Wherever nations are defined in these ethnically or religiously-exclusive ways, or in gender-coded ways, there is indeed a contradiction between promoting liberal democracy and upholding nationhood. And since nations have often been defined in these illiberal ways, many critics argue that the best way to promote greater liberalization or democratization is to divorce ideas of democratic citizenship from ideas of nationhood.

In practice, however, western states have dealt with these contradictions between liberal democracy and illiberal conceptions of nationhood, not by abandoning the centrality of nationhood, but by liberalizing and democratizing notions of nationhood. Thus the Australian nation has been redefined from a "white" nation to a "multicultural" and multiracial nation; the American nation has been redefined from a Protestant or Christian nation to a multi-faith nation; gender-coded notions of nationhood have been replaced with notions of nationhood that are committed to gender equality.

As a result of these changes, the content of nationhood has been dramatically "thinned" in most western countries, compared to 50 or 100 years ago.[6] We have abandoned earlier assumptions that members of the nation should share the same race, religion or lifestyle. Yet these thinner notions of a "multicultural" or "multi-faith" nation are still very much notions of *nationhood*: citizens are still expected to speak a common national language, share a common national identity, feel loyalty to national institutions and share a commitment to maintaining the nation as a single, self-governing community into the indefinite future. Ethnic and religious minorities have been granted equal citizenship rights, not because it no longer matters whether they are members of the nation, but because they are now seen as (and indeed have become) full members of the nation or "the people."

Rethinking the liberal-national nexus

So it appears that there is no necessary or inherent contradiction in having citizenship that is national in scope and liberal democratic in content. At any rate, this contradiction is not as sharp or as deep as some people have supposed. Notions of nationhood are not inherently exclusionary toward religious or ethnic/racial minorities or women and gays. Notions of nationhood have thinned and expanded to include such groups as full members of the nation.

This points to an important fact about the nature of nationhood in the modern world—namely, it is extremely amorphous and protean. Many commentators in the 1850s or even 1950s would have said that it was inconceivable to imagine a non-racial or multiracial conception of German or Australian nationhood: the idea of "German blood" or "White Australia" seemed foundational to the very idea of the German or Australian nations. So too with Catholicism in France or Italy. But these exclusionary ideas of nationhood were not foundational, they could be and were abandoned when they no longer served people's needs and aspirations. Throughout the West, earlier beliefs that nations were held together by racial purity, religious faith or cultural authenticity have been abandoned, so as to make room for new people, new ideas and new practices. Nationhood has preserved its centrality to modern political life because it has proven capable of adapting to changes such as immigration or secularization.

So the achievement of greater liberal democracy in the West has come, not through abandoning ideas of national citizenship, but by redefining nationhood in more liberal and democratic terms. Indeed, some commentators would go further and claim that this is the only viable basis for liberal democracy in the world today. The only sort of liberal democracy that has ever been achieved, it is argued, is in states that are conceived of as the embodiment or expression of a particular national community and are legitimized by reference to ideas of national sovereignty. The only sort of liberal-democratic political community that is possible is one that is grounded in the idea of the nation as "the bearer of sovereignty, the central object of loyalty, and the basis of collective solidarity," but that thins and democratizes its understanding of nationhood.

What would explain such a tight link between nationhood and liberal democracy? There is obviously no logical link between these two ideas. We all know of nation-states that are not liberal democracies: consider Spain, Portugal or Latin America in the 1970s, during the rule of the military dictators, or countries in post-communist Eastern Europe in the 1990s. These were all nationalizing states, but not liberal democracies. Conversely, there is no logical reason why liberal-democratic values cannot be institutionalized at the supranational level, as we see today in the European Union. We can imagine forms of citizenship that are national but not liberal, or liberal but not national.

Yet many commentators, often labelled as "liberal nationalists," argue that there is an important affinity between nation-states and liberal democracy.[7] We can think of liberal democracy as involving three connected but distinct kinds of principles: (i) social justice; (ii) deliberative democracy; and (iii) individual freedom. Liberal nationalists argue that all three of these principles can best be achieved—or perhaps only be achieved—within *national* political units, and that any attempt to divorce liberal-democratic citizenship from this setting is problematic.

Let me say a few words about each of these linkages: Social justice. Liberal-democratic theorists differ amongst themselves about the precise requirements of social justice. Some left-liberals favour a dramatic redistribution of resources so as to achieve some conception of "equality of resources" or "equality of capabilities." But even those on the centre-right of the liberal spectrum would generally agree that distributive justice requires: equal opportunity to acquire the skills and credentials needed to participate in the modern economy and to compete for valued jobs; and second, a system of social entitlements to meet a person's basic needs, and to protect people against certain disadvantages and vulnerabilities (e.g., health care, pensions, unemployment insurance, family allowances).

Why think that social justice in these senses has any intrinsic connection to nation-states? Liberal nationalists suggest two sorts of reasons. First, a welfare state requires us to make sacrifices for anonymous others whom we do not know, will probably never meet, and whose ethnic descent, religion and way of life differs from our own. In a democracy, such social programs will only survive if the majority of citizens continue to vote for them. History suggests that people are willing to make sacrifices for kin and for co-religionists, but are only likely to accept wider obligations under certain conditions such as: (i) that there is some sense of common identity and common membership uniting donor and recipient, such that sacrifices being made for anonymous others are still, in some sense, sacrifices for "one of us"; and (ii) that there is a high level of trust that sacrifices will be reciprocated: that is, if one makes sacrifices for the needy today, one's own needs will be taken care of later. Liberal nationalists argue that national identity has provided this common identity and trust, and that no other social identity in the modern world has been able to motivate ongoing sacrifices (as opposed to episodic humanitarian assistance in times of emergency) beyond the level of kin groups and confessional groups (Miller 1995; Canovan 1996).

Second, the commitment to equality of opportunity, by definition, requires equal access to training and jobs. As the economy has industrialized, jobs have come to require a high degree of literacy, education and the ability to communicate (compared to work in a peasant economy). According to Gellner, the diffusion of mass education in a common language was a functional requirement of the modernization of the economy. In his view, "nationalization" of education was not initially done in order to promote equality of opportunity for all citizens, but was simply a way of ensuring an adequate labour force (Gellner 1983). However, the nationalization of education was quickly adopted by left-liberals and social democrats as a tool for greater equality in society. National systems of education, providing standardized public education in a common standardized language, succeeded in integrating backward regions and the working class into a common national society, and made it possible (in principle) for children from all regions and classes to gain the skills needed to compete in a modern economy. Indeed, in many countries, equality of opportunity is often measured precisely by examining the success of different groups within these common national educational institutions.

For both these reasons, various "nation-building" policies by states can be seen as promoting social justice, by promoting the solidarity needed to motivate redistribution, and by promoting equal access to common educational and economic institutions.

Deliberative democracy. Liberal democracy is, by definition, committed to democratization. But for liberals, democracy is not just a formula for aggregating votes: it is also a system of collective deliberation and legitimation that allows all citizens to use their reason in political deliberation. The actual moment of voting (in elections, or within legislatures) is just one component in a larger process of democratic self-government. This process begins with public deliberation about the issues that need to be addressed and the options for resolving them. The decisions that result from this deliberation are then legitimated on the grounds that they reflect the considered will and common good of the people as a whole, not just the self-interest or arbitrary whims of the majority.

Why think deliberative democracy in this sense has any intrinsic connection to nation-states? Here again, liberal nationalists suggest two sorts of reasons. First, as with social justice, deliberative democracy requires a high level of trust. People must trust that others are genuinely willing to consider one's interests and opinions. Moreover, those who lose out in one election or debate are only likely to abide by the results if they feel that they might win next time, and that others will abide by the results if and when they do win. And, as we have seen, liberal nationalists argue that only a common national identity has succeeded in securing this sort of trust.

Second, collective political deliberation is only feasible if participants understand one another, and this seems to require a common language. In principle, one could imagine extensive translation facilities amongst people of different languages, but this can quickly become prohibitively expensive and cumbersome. When nation-states promote a common national language, therefore, they can be seen as enabling a more robust form of deliberative democracy. For liberal nationalists, national political forums with a single common language form the primary locus of democratic participation in the modern world, and are more genuinely participatory than political forums at higher levels that cut across language lines.

Why? For one thing, most citizens only feel comfortable debating political issues in their own tongue. As a general rule, it is only elites who have fluency with more than one language, and who have the continual opportunity to maintain and develop these language skills and who feel comfortable debating political issues in another tongue within multilingual settings. So there are practical reasons why politics conducted in the national vernacular is likely to be more democratic.[8] Moreover, there is an important symbolic value to using the language of the people in political life. As I noted earlier, one of the most powerful attractions of nationalism is its claim that the political community belongs to the people, and not to the elite. The use of the language of the people is confirmation of this central democratic idea.

Individual freedom. The link between individual freedom and nationhood is more complicated than that of social justice and deliberative democracy. The latter two are collective enterprises, and it is clear why they might require some sense of bounded community. By contrast, it may be less clear how nationalism can be seen as promoting liberal principles of individual freedom. After all, nationalism tends to assume that people's identity is inextricably tied to their nation, and that people can only lead meaningful lives within their own national culture. Is this not in conflict with the liberal ideal of autonomy, which rejects attempts to imprison people in ascribed group identities?

According to liberal nationalists, however, the relationship between individual autonomy and national culture is more complex. Participation in a national culture, they argue, far from inhibiting individual choice, is what makes individual freedom meaningful. The basic idea is this: modernity is defined (in part at least) by individual freedom of choice. But what does individual choice involve? People make choices about the social practices around them, based on their beliefs about the value of these practices. And one's national culture not only provides these practices, but also makes them meaningful. As Avishai Margalit and Joseph Raz put it, that membership in a national culture provides meaningful options, in the sense that "familiarity with a culture determines the boundaries of the imaginable." Hence if a culture is decaying or discriminated against, "the options and opportunities open to its members will shrink, become less attractive, and their pursuit less likely to be successful" (Margalit and Raz 1990, 449).

For this reason, the foundational liberal commitment to individual freedom can be extended to generate a commitment to the ongoing viability and flourishing of national cultures. This does not explain why people need access to their *own* national culture, rather than integrating into some other, perhaps more flourishing, national culture. Liberal nationalists offer a number of reasons, however, why it is difficult for the members of a decaying culture to integrate into another culture. According to Margalit and Raz, for example, the option of integrating is difficult not only because it is "a very slow process indeed," but also because of the role of cultural membership in people's self-identity. Cultural membership has a "high social profile," in the sense that it affects how others perceive and respond to us, which in turn shapes our self-identity. Moreover, national identity is particularly suited to serving as the "primary foci of identification," because it is based on belonging, not accomplishment. Hence cultural identity provides an "anchor for [people's] self-identification and the safety of effortless secure belonging." But this in turn means that an individual's self-respect is bound up with the esteem in which their national group is held. If a culture is not generally respected, then the dignity and self-respect of its members will also be threatened (Margalit and Raz 1990, 447-449). Similar arguments about the role of respect for national membership in supporting dignity and self-identity are given by Charles Taylor (1992) and Yael Tamir (1993, 41, 71-73).

Tamir also emphasizes the extent to which cultural membership adds an "additional meaning" to our actions, which become not only acts of individual accomplishment, but also "part of a continuous creative effort whereby culture is made and remade." And she argues that where institutions are "informed by a culture [people] find understandable and meaningful," this "allows a certain degree of transparency that facilitates their participation in public affairs." This in turn promotes a sense of belonging and relationships of mutual recognition and mutual responsibility (Tamir 1993, 72, 85-86). James Nickel emphasizes the potential harm to valuable intergenerational bonds when parents are unable to pass on their culture to their children and grandchildren (Nickel 1995). Benedict

Anderson and Chaim Gans emphasize the way national identity enables us to transcend our mortality, by linking us to something whose existence seems to extend back into time immemorial, and forward into the indefinite future (Anderson 1983; Gans 1998). For all of these reasons, liberal nationalists argue, people's sense of individual freedom and meaningful autonomy is typically tied up with participation in their own national culture.

All of these arguments can be disputed. Indeed, none of them would even be remotely plausible if national cultures were themselves static or hermetically sealed. It is quite clear that modern individuals do not want to simply reproduce the way of life of their ancestors, but rather want the right to question and revise them and also to learn from and adopt whatever is interesting and attractive from other national cultures. People would not support national movements that cut them off from the larger world of ideas, goods and practices.

Many commentators have concluded from this that modern freedom-loving citizens are abandoning (or will soon abandon) ideas of bounded nationhood in favour of some notion of "cosmopolitanism." But here again, we must not underestimate the protean character of nationalism. Ideas of nationhood have adapted to accommodate this desire for cultural openness. It is no longer considered "un-American" to eat Italian food, practise Chinese meditation techniques, buy German automobiles, or listen to African music. (This is related to the "thinning" of ideas of nationhood discussed above.) Indeed, ideals of openness to the world—whether in terms of immigration, free trade or cultural interchange—have become part of the very self-definition of many nations. Nations pride themselves on being open. Yet this is very much a *national* pride. It is "we," as a nation, who have made this transition to a more open society, through our self-governing decisions adopted in our national political institutions. And it is our national culture that is thereby enriched, as we incorporate new ideas and practices and pass them on to our children through our national institutions (schools, media, museums, etc.). The fact that the boundaries of our nation are permeable to goods and ideas and people, and that our national cultures are now multicultural and multi-ethnic, does not change the fact that the nation remains the "the bearer of sovereignty, the central object of loyalty, and the basis of collective solidarity."

Put another way, people want their nation to be "cosmopolitan," in the sense of embracing cultural interchange, without accepting the political ideology of cosmopolitanism which denies that nations should be self-governing, or that people have any deep bond to their own national language and society.[9] Freedom for modern individuals requires a degree of cultural cosmopolitan*ism*, but this is not necessarily inconsistent with political nationalism, which privileges (open and permeable) nations as the prime locus of self-government and democratic citizenship.

In sum, liberal nationalists give a variety of reasons why nation-states provide the appropriate units of liberal democracy. Liberal-democratic values of social justice, deliberative democracy and individual autonomy, they argue, are best achieved in a nation-state: that is, in a state that has diffused a common national identity, culture and language amongst its citizens. This helps explain the puzzle that "liberalism is the most universal of ideologies yet, paradoxically, it is the most national in form" (Sakwa 1998). As Margaret Canovan puts it, nationhood is the battery that makes liberal democratic states run (Canovan 1996, 80). Insofar as these liberal nationalist arguments are sound, it helps explain why, as Tamir puts it, "most liberals are liberal nationalists" (1993, 139), and why the liberalization and nationalization of political life have gone hand in hand in the West.

Some people argue that this seemingly happy marriage of liberal democracy and nationhood is becoming less and less sustainable as the definition of nationhood becomes "thinned." Perhaps co-nationals were likely to trust and feel solidarity for each other 50 or 100 years ago, when they all shared the same race or religion, and when members of racial or religious minorities were denied citizenship. But as the meaning of nationhood becomes thinner and thinner, so that co-nationals share less and less in common in terms of descent, religion or way of life, can it still generate feelings of trust and solidarity and mutual understanding?

The answer appears to be "yes," thinned national identities are still strong national identities and loyalties. Indeed, there is little evidence that the liberalizing of nationhood has diminished the attachment to or significance of national identities or loyalties anywhere in the West.

We can now see why the imminent demise of nationalism has often been predicted, and why these predictions failed. Some commentators have assumed that nationalism would disappear because it was tied to illiberal or pre-modern ideas of racial purity, religious orthodoxy or cultural authenticity, all of which were inconsistent with the mobility and autonomy desired in the modern world. Other commentators argued that, even if nations were able to liberalize in this way, a liberal form of nationhood would be too thin to sustain bonds of social cohesion or solidarity or trust. In other words, nationalism has often been seen as caught on the horns of a dilemma: a "thick" form of nationalism, it is argued, can sustain trust and solidarity, but cannot be liberalized; a "thin" form of nationalism, by contrast, can be liberal, but cannot sustain trust and solidarity. Yet it appears that this dilemma is not as severe as commentators supposed. Nations have been able to adapt to the modern needs for mobility and autonomy, by thinning and liberalizing the definition of nationhood, and these liberalized nations have been capable of sustaining social cohesion. Thin national identities have nonetheless proven to be strong and stable identities, capable of serving as the "battery" for cohesive political communities.

This combination of flexibility and resilience is, I believe, one of the keys to the success of the liberal nation-state model, and explains why it has been taken for granted by most recent political theorists of citizenship. Today, however, the link between liberal-democratic citizenship and the nation-state is being questioned from a number of angles. I will examine two of them: minority nationalism and transnationalism. I should emphasize that these are both challenges to the *scope* of citizenship, not to the values or principles of liberal-democracy per se. As I noted earlier, there is no credible alternative to liberal democracy in contemporary political debates, and support for the general principle of a constitutional democracy is virtually unanimous in the western democracies. Support for the basic values of liberal democracy has probably never been higher, now that the last vestiges of communism, fascism and military dictatorship have been thoroughly discredited.

To be sure, there is growing disaffection with some of the institutional embodiments of these principles. In particular, there is declining identification with political parties, and declining confidence in or deference to political elites and the media.[10] This is, I think, an inevitable result of the growing levels of education and political literacy of citizens. Fifty years ago, university education was still more or less restricted to elites, and many voters only had a minimal education. Under those circumstances, it made sense that many voters formed an uncritical attachment to a particular party, and simply deferred to its political elite. Today, most voters are well-educated and feel that they are as competent to understand political issues as their elected members of Parliament or bureaucrats, and see no reason to defer to the judgements of people who are often no better educated than they are. Today's citizens do not like being told what they should think by political elites, and resent the sort of old-fashioned authoritarian paternalism which they associate with traditional political parties or bureaucracies. Citizens are more interested than before in political issues, and feel more competent to understand them, but feel they are not getting the information they need from the media, and are not given the opportunity to participate by traditional political parties or bureaucracies.

Political parties, governments and bureaucracies today are scrambling to catch up to the demands of educated and competent citizens for information and participation. But these demands rarely question the basic idea of a liberal democracy. If these demands are frustrated for too long, they can result in periodic populist outbursts against political, judicial or media elites, and in favour of more "direct democracy," such as referenda. Taken to the extreme, these populist demands could question the foundations of liberal democracy, since they imply that people's fundamental constitutional rights might be vulnerable to being overriden by majoritarian voting. But in fact there is relatively little support in Canada for the idea that the protection of fundamental rights should be subject to referenda or other forms of direct democracy. Canadians want a more open and accessible form of parliamentary liberal democracy, not its replacement with a non-liberal direct democracy.

How to accommodate the demands for greater information and participation is an enormous issue, ably discussed in the paper by Guy Peters. But it is primarily a matter of institutional reform which does not by itself question either the basic scale or basic values of citizenship. In the rest of the paper, I want to focus on these new forms of citizenship which challenge the privileging of the nation-state as the locus of citizenship, either in the name of a narrower *sub-state* political community (minority nationalism) or in the name of a broader *supra-state* political community (transnationalism).

The Challenge of Minority Nationalism

THE FIRST OF THESE CHALLENGES—AND THE MOST IMPORTANT HISTORICALLY IN Canada—is that of minority nationalism. As I noted earlier, the attempt to construct mononational political communities has been strongly resisted by certain groups that view themselves as "nations within," and mobilize to maintain or regain their historic rights of self-government, with their own public institutions, operating in their own national language and culture.[11]

The Québécois are a paradigm case of such a group, and their successful nationalist mobilization has prevented or precluded any attempt to turn Canada into a traditional nation-state. Other successful cases of minority nationalism in the West include the Flemish in Belgium or the Catalans in Spain. But the phenomenon of minority nationalism is a truly universal one. The countries affected by it

> are to be found in Africa (for example, Ethiopia), Asia (Sri Lanka), Eastern Europe (Romania), Western Europe (France), North America (Guatemala), South America (Guyana), and Oceania (New Zealand). The list includes countries that are old (United Kingdom) as well as new (Bangladesh), large (Indonesia) as well as small (Fiji), rich (Canada) as well as poor (Pakistan), authoritarian (Sudan) as well as democratic (Belgium), Marxist-Leninist (China) as well as militantly anti-Marxist (Turkey). The list also includes countries which are Buddhist (Burma), Christian (Spain), Moslem (Iran), Hindu (India), and Judaic (Israel) (Connor 1999, 163-164).

Indeed, some commentators describe the conflict between states and national minorities as an ever-growing "third world war," encompassing an ever-increasing number of groups and states (Nietschmann 1987).[12]

The centrality of Québécois nationalism to Canadian history hardly needs explaining or recounting. The need to accommodate the existence of "the French fact" has been at the heart of many of the most important moments in Canadian history, and it was and remains the only major threat to the stability of the country. Nor is Canada unique in this respect. Every case of state break-up in the twentieth century has been associated with minority nationalism, as is every current case of a political mobilization to break up states in the West.

While minority nationalism is a profound challenge to the nation-state, in another sense it simply confirms the unrivalled importance of ideas of nationhood to the legitimacy of states. Where states have been able to diffuse a common sense of nationhood throughout their territory, there is essentially no possible basis to challenge its right to exist and to govern itself in that territory. A state that truly is a nation-state has a virtually unchallengeable right to exist. There may, of course, be conflicts, even civil wars, over *how* such a nation-state should govern itself—witness the civil wars in Algeria between secularists and fundamentalists, or in Nicaragua between leftists and rightists. But neither side in these conflicts contests the right of Algeria or Nicaragua to exist as sovereign states, or seeks to break up the state, since both sides agree that there is an Algerian and Nicaraguan nation or people, and that it should govern itself through the apparatus of a nation-state.

Conversely, the only way to delegitimize the existence of a state, and to seek to break it up, is to argue that it is not a nation-state, but rather is a multinational empire which has incorporated or imprisoned sub-state national groups whose distinctive national identities, languages, cultures and institutions are suppressed. That is to say, the only legitimate basis for demanding a new state is to appeal to the idea of national liberation or national self-determination, that is, to argue that a new state is needed to embody and express the will of a distinct nation.[13]

So minority nationalism is the most serious challenge to the model of a liberal nation-state, both in Canada and around the world. Yet, in another sense, it is not really a challenge to that model of citizenship at all. After all, minority nationalism appeals to the very same arguments and principles that underlie the model of liberal nationalism. It is a reiteration or replication, rather than a repudiation, of the idea that citizenship should be national in scope and liberal in content. Indeed, all of the historical trends and moral arguments I discussed earlier in relation to the construction of liberal nation-states can be applied to minority nationalisms.

If we consider Quebec, Catalonia, Flanders, Puerto Rico or Scotland, we see the same long-term processes at work that we saw earlier at the level of nation-states: first, a process of (minority) nation-building, by which a common national identity and culture is extended to all classes and outlying regions; and second, a process of liberalization, by which the (minority) nation has been redefined and "thinned" so as to be more ethnically and racially inclusive and less gender-coded. Moreover, these two processes have often been very successful, generating high levels of support in these sub-state regions for both a sense of distinct nationhood and for liberal-democratic values.

As with nation-building at the central level, some critics of minority nationalism have argued that there is a contradiction between these two processes of nation-building and liberalization. The former is said to preclude the latter, since minority national identities are said to be inherently exclusionary, and hence inconsistent with the liberal imperative to construct inclusive political communities. And we can easily find cases where minority nations have historically been defined in religiously or racially exclusive ways (e.g., religious definitions of Québécois nationhood; racial definitions of Basque nationhood). But, as at the central-state level, liberalization at the sub-state level has been achieved not by disavowing ideas of minority nationhood, but precisely through liberalizing these conceptions of nationhood, by making them thinner, and more open to the world.

In short, we see the same powerful combination of political nationalism, liberal democracy and cultural cosmopolitanism at the level of minority nations that we saw earlier at the level of nation-states. And, as with nation-states, this process of constructing liberal/national political communities at the sub-state level has been defended as the best way of promoting cohesive political communities capable of achieving justice, deliberative democracy and individual freedom.

So, in one sense, there is little new here, in terms of the underlying idea of citizenship. Minority nationalisms in the West typically appeal to the same basic picture of citizenship, according to which citizenship involves the institutionalization of liberal-democratic values within national political contexts.

Of course, this underlying similarity in models of citizenship does not by itself remove the problem of how to accommodate minority nationalisms, and does not provide any concrete guidance about how to resolve difficult issues about the division of powers, the sharing of revenues, language rights, veto rights and so on. Some of these institutional issues involved are discussed in the papers by Ronald Watts and Michael Keating in this volume. But I do think that a crucial first step in addressing these issues is recognizing that the conflict between states and minority nationalisms in the West is not typically a clash of "values" or "world views." For example, there is a tendency amongst some English-speaking Canadians to say that the Québécois are nationalists whereas we are not; or that we are liberals and they are not. In reality, as public opinion surveys have shown, anglophones and francophones in Canada share the same western enlightenment values of popular sovereignty and liberal citizenship. The same is true of minority nationalisms in Catalonia, Scotland or Flanders as well, there is little or no difference in underlying values between members of the national minority and citizens of the larger state. Indeed, in some areas, national minorities are more liberal than the dominant groups.[14]

This suggests that the only feasible and morally defensible response to the phenomenon of minority nationalism is to accommodate, rather than suppress, the minority's national identities and aspirations, through some form of self-government. And this indeed is what we see throughout the western democracies. There has been a clear trend toward the adoption of federal or quasi-federal forms of self-government which create territorial jurisdictions in which the national minority forms a local majority. The national minority can then use its *de facto* control over these territorial jurisdictions to construct its own forms of liberal/national citizenship at the sub-state level. We can see this not only in Canada, Spain, Belgium and the United Kingdom, but also in several other cases of territorially-concentrated national minorities, such as Puerto Rico in the United States, German-speaking South Tyrol in Italy, or the Swedish-speaking Aland Islands in Finland. Many of these experiments in minority self-government are still new, and contested, but I would argue that this trend toward the adoption of federal or quasi-federal forms of self-government for national minorities has been successful. It has been a prudential success, in the sense of reducing the potential for violent conflict or political instability that often accompanies the problem of conflicting nationalisms within a single state. But it is also morally successful, in the sense of constituting a fairer response to the problem, promoting greater equality between the members of different national groups within the same state, while simultaneously promoting processes of liberalization and democratization at both the central state and sub-state levels.[15]

Minority nationalism, then, raises a difficult political challenge to the nation-state, but the difficulty does not arise from any deep disagreement over the underlying model of citizenship. Both majority and minority endorse the idea that citizenship is exercised within territorially-bounded political communities which are simultaneously national in scope, liberal in values, and open to the world culturally and economically. Indeed, the challenge of minority nationalism often becomes greater the more that the national minority shares this vision of liberal/national citizenship. It was precisely when Québécois nationalist leaders abandoned ideas of economic autarky, cultural purity and racial exclusivity that the old *modus vivendi* broke down, and Québécois nationalism started to compete with English-speaking Canada for immigrants, foreign investment and trade, cooperation with international organizations, cultural exchanges and so on.

So too with Catalan, Scottish or Flemish nationalisms. They pose a challenge to the larger state precisely because they have proven to be capable of adapting to the pressures and imperatives of immigration, free trade and cultural globalization, and of satisfying the aspirations of an increasingly educated and mobile citizenry for democratic participation, economic opportunities, and cultural exchanges. If, as some critics like to pretend, national minorities formed pockets of inward-looking pre-modern communities, defined in racially and religiously restrictive ways, cut off from the world at large, they might be a source of embarrassment to the larger state, but they would not pose an effective threat to displace the central state and take over its functions and powers. Yet that is precisely the challenge of minority nationalism in the West today, and it is a challenge that arises because minority nationalisms draw upon the same successful and powerful formula of nationhood and liberalism. Sub-state nationalisms, like nation-states, can draw upon the cohesiveness, legitimacy and solidarity of a bounded national community, without sacrificing the inclusiveness and openness of liberalism, and without cutting themselves off from the larger world.

Transnational Citizenship?

SO MINORITY NATIONALISM CAN BE SEEN AS SIMPLY REPLICATING, RATHER THAN CHALLENGING, the model of liberal-democratic citizenship within territorially-bounded national political communities. If we want to find a real challenge to this model, we need to look elsewhere. And the most obvious candidate is the set of ideas or trends lumped together under the heading of "transnationalism." Transnationalism does not simply challenge the nation-state in the name of some other nation, but rather challenges the very idea that citizenship should be tied to a territorially-bounded national political community.

But the term transnationalism covers a range of ideas and trends, and we need to carefully distinguish them, since at least some of them may turn out, on inspection, to be derivative of the continued existence of the liberal/national model. I will briefly discuss five different forms of political activity that have been presented in the literature as forms of "transnational citizenship." I will suggest that, of these five, only one poses a genuine alternative to the liberal/national model, and it is by far and away the least significant, at least to date.

Immigrant transnationalism

In many recent discussions, immigrants are viewed as the vanguard of a new transnationalism. Immigrants are said to have rejected the old model of immigrant integration, in which they were expected to abandon their previous national identity and assimilate into their new country's national culture. The act of immigration, in this old view, was seen as a decision to replace membership in one nation with membership in another. That old model probably never really worked in practice, but in any event it is clearly now obsolete. Aided by modern technology,which has made it easier to travel to and communicate with their homeland, many immigrants today remain active in the economic, social and political life of their country of origin.

This phenomenon of enduring immigrant participation in homeland politics, while not new, is probably growing in scope, and is increasingly accepted as legitimate. And this does reflect a change in our traditional notions of liberal/national citizenship, which typically viewed nationality as mutually exclusive, that is, people could (or should) be members of one and only one nation. The idea of being a "dual national" or "double national" was widely viewed with apprehension until quite recently, and this was reflected in legal requirements in most western democracies that immigrants renounce or abandon their previous citizenship in order to naturalize in their new country. Too great an interest in homeland politics was seen as unpatriotic, and perhaps even disloyal.

This idea of nationality as mutually exclusive has been more or less effectively repudiated in the West.[16] The desire of immigrants to maintain links with their homeland is increasingly accepted as normal and natural, and is being legally facilitated by the increasing acceptance of dual citizenship. In many western countries (including Canada), immigrants are no longer required to abandon or renounce their original nationality in order to naturalize and become citizens of their new country.

So we now accept dual nationality. But is this really a challenge to the model that politics should be organized through bounded national political communities? After all, dual nationals are precisely dual *nationals*, that is, they participate in, and feel loyalty to, two bounded national communities. That some people participate in two national political communities does not, by itself, explain why politics can or should be organized on some non-national or non-territorial basis.

Yet some commentators insist that immigrants today are really the vanguard of a "post-national" form of political membership, rather than just being "dual nationals." According to Yasemin Soysal, for example, immigrants today reject the expectation that their rights should depend on their inclusion or integration into the "nation," and instead appeal to post-national norms of human rights which are divorced from any assumptions about how long immigrants have lived in a nation's territory, or whether they have integrated into its national culture (Soysal 1994). Since nation-states oppose this attempt by immigrants to avoid national integration, immigrants pursue their claims at a transnational level, such as the European Union (EU). Immigrants, then, are seen as harbingers of a new model of political agency in which people demand the right to participate wherever they live, independently of national identity or membership, and look to transnational bodies and transnational norms for the protection of this right. Citizenship in territorially-bounded national communities, in this view, will increasingly fade into irrelevance as more and more people link their political agency to transnational norms of human rights backed up by transnational institutions.

The difficulty with this "post-national" interpretation of immigrant claims is that there is little empirical support for it (Joppke 2001; Koopmans and Stratham 1999). On the contrary, public opinion remains overwhelmingly supportive of the idea that immigrants should meet some minimal test of national integration (e.g., residency period, knowledge of state language) before acquiring full political rights, *and immigrants themselves share this view* (Labelle and Salée 2001). Indeed, on some issues, immigrants are actually in favour of tightening access to citizenship—demanding longer residency periods or stronger language requirements. Moreover, immigrants today in most countries are in fact integrating as quickly if not more quickly than earlier generations of immigrants, in terms of learning the national language, taking out citizenship, participating in national elections, marrying outside their own ethnic group and so on.[17] Immigrants still overwhelmingly aspire to some level of national integration, and accept that this is a legitimate condition for the exercise of full citizenship.

Defenders of the post-national view often note that western democracies have extended the rights guaranteed to various categories of non-citizens (e.g., Turkish guest-workers in Germany), which they interpret as evidence of the triumph of international human rights norms over national laws or national imperatives. But in fact these changes in the rights of aliens have been the result of domestic courts interpreting national constitutions, with international law or the EU being "plainly irrelevant" (Joppke 2001, 58). Moreover, expanding the rights of aliens has been justified, not in terms of universal human rights, but precisely in terms of (and in proportion to) the immigrants' participation in the communal life of the host country. The rights of aliens are defended as "protocitizen" rights, in recognition of partial integration, and as a step toward fuller national integration.[18]

In short, immigrants today are still expected to integrate into their new national community, they accept the legitimacy of this expectation, and in fact are integrating. There is little evidence that the old model of the integration of immigrants into a national society is breaking down, either in law or in practice. To be sure, these immigrants still retain an active interest in the politics of their country of origin. But their participation in homeland politics is very "national"—if anything, diasporas are often more nationalist than their co-nationals in the homeland. It is precisely as members of the nation, born and raised in the homeland, that they assert the right to participate in homeland politics and work to defend its national sovereignty, often against what they perceive as "foreign interference" by international agencies. There is nothing "post-national" about the way diasporas participate in homeland politics, it is nationalist politics in every recognizable sense.[19]

So it is implausible, I think, to view the increasing significance of diaspora politics and dual nationality amongst immigrants as an example of the transcending of territorially-bounded national communities. These immigrants are literally dual nationals, not post-nationals, and the evidence to date suggests that they are as committed as anyone else to the view that politics should remain organized through bounded national political communities, both in their new home and their country of origin.

Transnational advocacy networks

If we want to find genuinely transnational political activities, that is, people exercising political agency in forums beyond those of the nation(s) they belong to, we need to look elsewhere. One relevant phenomenon is the growth of what we call transnational advocacy networks—the recruiting of allies, usually non-governmental organizations (NGOs), in other countries to help put pressure on one's own government. For example, indigenous peoples in Canada have recruited allies around the world to pressure the Quebec government to change its policies on development in James Bay, or to pressure the Canadian government to change its policies regarding the Lubicon Lake band (Jenson and Papillon 2000). Similarly, environmental groups have sought international allies to put pressure on Canada to stop the seal hunt and on British Columbia to stop clear-cut logging. These international allies may write letters of protest to the Canadian government, organize boycotts of Canadian products, or pressure their own governments to protest to the Canadian government.

Of course, the same process also works in the other direction— Canadian NGOs are often recruited to put pressure on governments in other countries. Thus, Canadian NGOs have been active in pressuring Brazil to change its policies in the Amazon.

These are examples of what Jenson and Papillon call "weak" transnational political agency, since the ultimate goal is still to pressure *national* decision-makers, and the appeal to international allies is instrumental to this domestic goal. As they put it, "transnational networks and alliances are used strategically in a political struggle that remains focused on local or national controversies and in which the main opponent remains the state" (Jenson and Papillon 2000, 248-249; see also Keck and Sikkink 1998).

This sort of transnational activism is an important and growing phenomenon, and often beneficial, I think, in forcing governments to reconsider some of the harmful or unjust effects of their decisions. It enables citizens who have only limited political voice within national political systems to amplify their voice, and to highlight harms and injustices that might otherwise be neglected.

However, this does not, by itself, lead to the creation of any sort of self-governing transnational political community, nor is it intended to do so. When Canadian NGOs seek European allies to stop the seal hunt, they are not suggesting or hoping that jurisdiction over the seal hunt be shifted from the Canadian government to some new transnational Euro-Canadian parliament. When Brazilian NGOs seek Canadian allies in fighting deforestation in the Amazon, they are not hoping or suggesting that Canadians and Brazilians should elect or appoint representatives to a joint Brazilian-Canadian agency that will decide on the development of the Amazon.

Transnational advocacy networks, at least in this "weak" form, still assume that the ultimate locus of decision-making is territorially-bounded national legislatures. It does not offer any alternative model or theory for determining how political authority should be allocated, or how political communities should be defined. In the end, the weak transnationalism of advocacy networks is predicated on, even parasitic on, the ongoing existence of bounded political communities whose existence and legitimacy rests on their claim to nationhood, and to be the expression of the sovereignty and self-determination of a particular nation or people. Transnational advocacy networks are an attempt to influence how nations exercise their sovereignty, not an attempt to offer an alternative post-national or non-territorial forum for political decision-making.

International legal authority

So the mere fact that people have strategic reasons to engage in political activism or alliances beyond the borders of their nation does not, by itself, imply that political decision-making can or should be transferred away from bounded nation-states to some post-national or non-territorial structure. To find genuine alternatives to the liberal/national model of citizenship, we need to find cases, not only of transnational activism, but also of transnational decision-making and transnational governance that is replacing or contesting the power of nation-states, and whose legitimacy is not parasitic in the exercise of citizenship at the national level.

I will briefly discuss three forms of transnational authority: international law, particularly human rights law, intergovernmental regulatory bodies, from the international aviation authority to the World Trade Organization (WTO) or the World Bank, and international parliaments or legislatures, such as the European Parliament of the European Union. In my view, only the third offers a serious alternative to the liberal/national model of citizenship, and it is the least feasible and perhaps even the least desirable.

Let me start, however, with international law, particularly human rights laws. In the postwar period, there has been a substantial growth in international human rights law, such that respect for human rights is now widely seen as a requirement for a country to be a member in good standing of the international community. Until recently, these declarations were largely hortatory—violation of human rights "law" led to international criticism, perhaps, but no real international sanction or intervention. But we now see movements to develop stronger international monitoring and enforcement mechanisms. These include new international courts, such as the international war crimes tribunal, or giving existing international courts, like the European Court of Justice, jurisdiction over human rights issues. Or it may involve other forms of sanctions for human rights violations, such as the denial of international loans or even with the withdrawal of international recognition for a government.

All of these developments are often seen as undermining the liberal/national model, since they challenge old assumptions of the inherent or unconditional sovereignty of nation-states. These developments assert that there is a legitimate international interest in how nations treat their own citizens, and that the legitimacy of governments requires meeting certain international standards of human rights.

But this challenge to unconditional state sovereignty is not really a challenge to the liberal/national model of citizenship, for it too asserts that the legitimacy of governments is conditional and depends on respect for the rights of citizens. This is precisely what makes it a *liberal*/national model. Indeed, if we examine the rights being codified at the international level, we will see that they essentially correspond with the liberal/national view of the rights citizens hold against their own governments. There is nothing in international human rights law that conflicts in any way with the liberal/national view of how political authority should be organized and exercised.

There would be a conflict if international law promoted a post-national model of citizenship, if, for example, international law said that people have rights to full political participation independent of their national membership, and so precluded domestic laws that required people to learn the national language and/or to have lived a certain period of time in a country before acquiring citizenship. There would also be a potential conflict if international law mandated the construction of transnational or post-national political communities whose legitimacy was not tied to ideas of nationhood. But, as I discussed earlier, international law does not in any way promote a post-national form of citizenship. On the contrary, it implicitly assumes that the world is organized into nation-states which tie citizenship to nationhood. Indeed, it explicitly endorses the structuring of the world into national political communities, through its endorsement of the principle of the self-determination of peoples.

In short, international law offers no alternative to the model of national political communities and no conflict with the liberal/national citizenship. On the contrary, it can be seen as universalizing that model. It is saying, in effect, that the only legitimate form of political community is one that respects the self-determination of nations; and secondly, respects the rights of individuals within the nation. To be sure, the definition of civil and political rights in international law is often weaker than that provided by domestic constitutions in the West—international law does not require all countries to be as liberal or democratic as the most developed western, liberal democracies.[20] But there is widespread hope and belief that pressuring countries to meet the minimal requirements of international human rights law will inevitably lead to their more comprehensive liberalization and democratization, so that they become more "like us."

And this helps to explain the ambivalent view of international law which we find in the West. There is widespread support for the idea of international human rights norms, but virtually no public support for the idea that our *own* laws should be subject to international review. Most Canadians think that our constitution provides fully adequate protection of our human rights, and that our courts are fully competent to interpret and enforce those rights in an independent and impartial way. We do not need international law or international courts to uphold our human rights. On the contrary, if anything, we think our constitution is superior to that of the United Nations declarations on human rights, and that our judicial system is better than any international court stocked with people from Latin America, Asia or Africa. Most Canadians (or Americans) have little interest in what the UN Human Rights Commission says about our laws, and no desire to give it or any other international body the jurisdiction to overturn our legislation based on international human rights norms.[21]

In short, people in western, liberal democracies support international human rights norms, not because "we" need them, but because "they" need them, that is, people in those countries that are not (yet) liberal democracies. International human rights norms are needed for those countries that have illiberal constitutions, undemocratic political traditions, and corrupt judicial institutions, and who therefore need help in defining, interpreting and enforcing human rights.[22] We hope that international institutions, including international human rights law, will pressure such countries to start moving down the road toward becoming liberal-democratic nation-states, like us.[23]

In short, international human rights law, far from challenging the liberal/national model, can be seen as exporting and universalizing it. It does put limits on state sovereignty, but the limits it places are consistent with those already implicit in liberal models of nationhood. Far from seeking to transcend the liberal/national model of political community, it is largely an attempt to pressure or cajole non-western states to adopt that model.

So we have not yet found any real challenge to the liberal/national model of citizenship. Whether it is minority nationalism, or dual citizenship, or transnational advocacy networks, or international human rights norms, none of these offers any alternative model for organizing political communities except as territorially-bounded national polities.

This shows, I think, how pervasive ideas of nationhood are in the modern world. Yet this is not to deny the obvious fact that we need international regulatory institutions that transcend national boundaries. We need such institutions to deal not only with economic globalization, but also with common environmental problems and issues of international security, or simply to coordinate air-travel, Internet domain names, or the mail. This fact is widely accepted even by those who continue to emphasize the centrality of nationhood and national identities in the modern world.[24]

Such international organizations are proliferating, both at the global level (e.g., the WTO), or at regional levels (e.g., the institutions established by the EU or the North American Free Trade Agreement [NAFTA]). At present, these transnational organizations exhibit a major "democratic deficit," and have little public legitimacy in the eyes of citizens. They are basically organized through intergovernmental relations, with little if any direct input from individual citizens. Moreover, these institutions have evolved in an ad hoc way, each in response to a particular need, without any underlying theory or model about the kinds of transnational institutions we want, or how they should be governed, or how they should relate to each other, or what sorts of principles should regulate their structures or actions.

In short, while we have an increasing number of transnational institutions, which exercise an increasing influence over our lives, we have no political theory of transnational institutions. We have well-developed theories about what sorts of principles of justice should be implemented by the institutions of the nation-state; well-developed theories about what sorts of political rights citizens should have vis-à-vis these national institutions; and well-developed theories about what sorts of loyalties and commitments citizens should have to these institutions. By contrast, few people have any clear idea what principles of justice or standards of democratization or norms of loyalty should apply to transnational institutions.

It is increasingly clear, therefore, that we need to extend or adapt our conceptions of democratic citizenship to include these transnational institutions. To oversimplify, we can imagine two broad strategies for doing so. The first is to construct a genuinely transnational form of democracy—to create elected parliaments or legislatures at a transnational level that would have jurisdiction over these transnational institutions. The other strategy is to increase the extent to which transnational institutions are indirectly accountable to national political communities. Let me briefly discuss these two options in turn.

Transnational legislative/parliamentary bodies

One option, then, is to create some form of directly-elected transnational legislature or parliament to make decisions about the creation and operation of transnational institutions. Just as democratically-elected national legislatures oversee national regulatory institutions, like the CRTC in Canada or the Bank of Canada, so there would be democratically-elected transnational legislatures to oversee transnational regulatory institutions like the WTO.

The idea of constructing a democratic transnational parliament at the global scale is utopian in the foreseeable future, if only because many countries do not have democratic elections for their own national governments, and so are unlikely to permit democratic elections for transnational parliaments.[25] But many people believe it is feasible and desirable on a regional level, such as the European Union or North America, where all the countries are democratic, and where there is already a high degree of economic interdependence and common political values. And indeed, we see the outlines of such a development in the European Parliament of the EU.

This strategy—endorsed by many proponents of "transnational" or "cosmopolitan" citizenship—seems at first glance to be the most obvious and appropriate one. If we need transnational institutions, and if we believe in democracy, then why not establish transnational democracies to govern them? And yet it is striking that there is virtually no public support for such an idea, particularly in North America. The idea of creating a common North American parliament to make decisions regarding NAFTA-based institutions, for example, is not even on the radar screen of public opinion, let alone a subject of any popular mobilization. No political party or social movement in any of the three NAFTA countries is pressing to create such a transnational legislature.

Even in the EU, where the idea of constructing a transnational democracy is certainly on the radar screen, there is almost no popular mobilization behind it. The mass of citizens in EU countries are apathetic or indifferent to the EU Parliament, with low rates of voting in EU elections. The idea of a popularly-elected EU Parliament was supposed to promote the "democratization" of the EU, but it is unlike any other form of democratization in the past century. In other cases of democratization, disenfranchised groups have fought long battles to gain democratic rights, which ruling elites grudgingly conceded. In the case of the EU Parliament, by contrast, there was no popular mobilization, it was an attempt by ruling elites to generate legitimacy for the EU by granting democratic rights that were not requested.[26] Public opinion polls show repeatedly that the mass of citizens of EU member states look to their elected representatives in the national legislature, rather than their representatives in the EU Parliament, as the appropriate persons to debate and defend their interests, *even regarding European-wide policies*. If citizens of the UK or France dislike EU agricultural policy, for example, they protest to their national governments, not to their EU representatives.

In short, the idea of a transnational democracy is met with hostility in North America and indifference in Europe. The prospects for transnational democracy are even poorer in other parts of the world. What is the explanation for this striking phenomenon?

At first glance, one might think it is a problem of size: people worry that transnational democracies will simply be too large to govern effectively or democratically. But that cannot be the explanation. After all, a North American parliament governing 400 million people would still be less than one-half the population of India, which is a functioning democracy. In fact, it would only be one-third larger than the current population of the United States. A European parliament governing 370 million people is even smaller. India and the United States show that it is perfectly feasible to democratically govern hundreds of millions of people.

Why is an American legislature for 300 million perfectly viable, but a North American parliament for 400 million seemingly inconceivable? The answer is obviously not size, but rather the fact that Americans share a common national identity which tells them that they form a single people who belong together in a single, self-governing state. By contrast, they do not feel that Mexicans or Canadians belong to the same "people" or "community of fate," and hence have no desire to govern together with them (and vice versa, Mexicans and Canadians have no desire to govern together with Americans in a common legislature).

Where this sense of nationhood is strong, political communities can be enormous—hundreds of millions, even over a billion. Conversely, where people do not share a common national identity, then even very small states can be "too big" to govern effectively or democratically. Czechoslovakia, with 15 million, split in two; the Cameroons, with 13 million, may split in two; what's left of Yugoslavia, with 10 million, may split again in three; Georgia, with 5 million, may split in three; Macedonia, with under 2 million, may split in two; Sri Lanka, with

18 million, may split up. In these countries, many people are pushing to reduce the size of the political community, not because it is "too big" in a purely numerical sense, but because there is no sense of common nationhood.

In short, size has nothing to do with people's perceptions about the appropriate boundaries of political community. What matters is a feeling of belonging together, of being a "nation," "people" or "community of fate." Some defenders of transnational democracy recognize this problem, but respond that it should be possible to socialize people in Europe or North America to feel a sense of belonging together, and to see themselves as a single community of fate.[27]

David Held, for example, argues that globalization is undermining the sense that each nation-state forms "a political community of fate," since "some of the most fundamental forces and processes which determine the nature of life chances" cut across national boundaries (Held 1999, 102-103). But this is a misunderstanding, I believe, of what it means to form a community of fate. What determines the boundaries of a community of fate is not the forces people are subjected to, but rather how they respond to those forces, and, in particular, what sorts of collectivities they identify with when responding to those forces. People belong to the same community of fate if they *care* about each other's fate and want to *share* each other's fate, that is, they want to meet certain challenges together, so as to share each other's blessings and burdens. Put another way, people belong to the same community of fate if they feel some sense of responsibility for one another's fate, and so want to deliberate together about how to respond collectively to the challenges facing the community. As far as I can tell, globalization has not eroded the sense that nation-states form separate communities of fate in this sense.

For example, as a result of NAFTA, North Americans are increasingly subjected to similar economic "forces and processes." But there is no evidence that they feel themselves part of a single community of fate whose members care about and wish to share each other's fate. There is no evidence that Canadians now feel any special sense of responsibility for the well-being of Americans or Mexicans (or vice versa).[28] Nor is there any evidence that Canadians feel any moral obligation to respond to these challenges in the same way that Americans or Mexicans do (or vice versa). On the contrary, Canadians want to respond to these forces *as Canadians*, that is, Canadians debate amongst themselves how to respond to globalization, and they do so by asking what sort of society Canadians wish to live in, and what sorts of obligations Canadians have to each other. Americans ask the same questions amongst themselves, as do the Mexicans.

The economic forces acting on the three countries may be similar, but the sense of communal identity and solidarity remains profoundly different, as has the actual policy responses to these forces. Despite being subject to similar forces, citizens of western democracies are able to respond to these forces in their own distinctive ways, reflective of their "domestic politics and cultures" (Banting 1997, 280). And most citizens continue to cherish this ability to deliberate and act as a national collectivity, on the basis of their own national solidarities and priorities.

Why do citizens of national political communities continue to cherish their sense of being distinct communities of fate? In part for the reasons I discussed earlier: nations have proven to be effective in creating forms of solidarity and forums of democratic participation across lines of class, race and religion. The "masses" in a (liberal-democratic) nation have the cultural capital and institutional means to hold national elites accountable; they are connected by a common language, common media, common education system, common myths, symbols and loyalties. Most citizens fear that they will have no corresponding ability to hold transnational political elites accountable. If an Italian farmer dislikes what a minister in the Italian parliament does, he or she knows what national television stations or newspapers to complain to, what national political parties and NGOs to contact, and can do so because the same national language is shared with all of these organizations. But how would an Italian farmer complain to a minister from Denmark in the EU Parliament? There is no pan-European media, no pan-European political parties, and no pan-European language, let alone more intangible issues of common loyalties or solidarities.

As I discussed earlier, part of the success of national democracy is the dense web of connections that bind the elite to the masses. The elite govern in the name of the people, speak the language of the people, share a common media and education system that inculcate common national narratives (or myths, if you prefer) and core elements of a common national culture. All of this was a profound change from pre-national forms of government, in which the elites were cut off culturally, linguistically and institutionally from the masses. Transnational democracy threatens to return us to this pre-national phase, in which the masses will be governed by elites who do not share their own language and culture, and in which politics is conducted in a language and in a media that is "foreign" to the masses. It should not be surprising, then, that ordinary citizens are unenthusiastic about transnational democracy, and view national politics as inherently more democratic than transnational politics.[29]

Intergovernmental regulatory authorities

If the prospects for the construction of transnational democracy are dim for the foreseeable future, certainly in North America, does that mean we are condemned to live with the "democratic deficit" in our growing number of transnational institutions? Not necessarily. In the absence of transnational democracy, these international bodies will remain primarily *intergovernmental* in form, that is, they will emerge from negotiations between states, be administered by people appointed by states, and have an agent-principal relationship to states: they are delegated power by states to exercise in accordance with the interests of these states.

It is notoriously difficult to ensure proper accountability of such agent-principal relationships, even at the domestic level. Regulatory organizations are vulnerable to the "reversal of control," by which agents begin to exercise their delegated power in their own interests, rather than on behalf of the principals (Bohman 2001, 10-11). This problem is even more serious in the case of international regulatory organizations.

But there are ways in which citizens can exercise greater indirect control over these institutions. We need to find ways to hold international institutions more accountable through nation-states. For example, one could imagine giving nation-states stronger veto powers over certain decisions of transnational institutions, so that citizens know what their country could or could not change in those decisions. Or one could require that certain decisions of transnational institutions be debated and approved publicly within each national context, particularly if they involve the imposition of new obligations. According to James Bohman, a minimal condition of a successful agent-principal relationship is that citizens be able to avoid unwanted obligations as a consequence of the decisions of their transnational agents (Bohman 2001, 13).

In any event, more could be done to ensure greater openness and transparency in these organizations, such as requiring that draft agreements or conventions be publicly released before being signed. (This was one of the major goals of protestors regarding the Free Trade Agreement of the Americas.) Also, various NGOs and international non-governmental organizations (INGOs) be given a "seat at the table" of these international organizations. Even if not given a vote, or not the same weight of vote as states, the mere presence of these organizations would ensure that citizens would learn more about how the representatives of their nation-state behaved.[30] These NGOs and INGOs could then work together in the sort of transnational advocacy networks discussed earlier, to pressure national governments to reconsider their stance on various international issues, if they have ignored important harms or injustices. Various proposals in this regard are discussed in the paper by Pierre Marc Johnson and Karel Mayrand.[31]

In these and other ways, citizens could feel that they had greater control over transnational institutions through the pressures they can bring to bear on their elected national representatives. Citizens would know more about what sort of power their governments exercise in transnational institutions, what sorts of positions they have taken, and how well or badly they have represented their national interests. The ability to effectively represent and defend national interests or values in transnational institutions would then become an important criterion for electoral success at the national level. And indeed, we already see a trend in this direction. Questions about the ability of different leaders and parties to defend Britain's interests in the EU, for example, were a part of the most recent British election.

This may seem like an unsatisfactory response to the growing problem of the democratic deficit of transnational institutions. But I believe that this is the sort of response most citizens themselves want. They look to their elected national representatives to defend their principles and interests within transnational institutions. What we need to do, therefore, is to give elected national representatives the power to evaluate how well international organizations live up to their agent-principal responsibilities, and to give citizens the tools to hold elected national representatives accountable for how well they exercise that power. This indirect form of democratic accountability through nation-states is obviously limited, but to jump over this problem by seeking a more direct form of transnational democratic accountability may be neither feasible nor, paradoxically, democratic. There is no democratic mandate for creating new forms of transnational democracy, in part because ordinary citizens feel (probably correctly) that they would be less able to participate in an equitable and effective manner at the transnational level than at the domestic level.

So we may be stuck with the complex task of enhancing indirect accountability. The sorts of measures needed to do this, like increased publicity and discussion of draft agreements, increased representation for NGOs, increased veto powers, will undoubtedly slow up the work of some international organizations. They will require more time, more discussion, more publicity, more voice, more representation. But, in my view, this is not necessarily a bad thing. Apart from issues of international security, the issues confronting international organizations rarely require urgent decisions. There is no necessity to sign a free trade agreement this month, as opposed to next month or next year, and no reason not to take the time needed to discuss trade or environmental agreements in depth within national political settings. Democracy is worth it.

Conclusion

According to Robert Dahl, the great American theorist of democracy,

> Supporters of democracy should resist the argument that a great decline in the capacity of national and subnational units to govern themselves is inevitable because globalization is inevitable. To be sure, the forces leading to greater internationalization of the economic, political, military, social and cultural spheres of human life appear to be extremely powerful. However, I do not see how we can know with confidence the extent to which globalization is inevitable or contingent. The last three centuries are a graveyard packed with the corpses of "inevitable" developments (Dahl 1999, 34).

He suggests that "instead of yielding to triumphal claims of inevitability," we should examine each case on its merits, to see whether the robust forms of democracy developed at the national and subnational level can be retained and employed in dealing with the challenges of globalization.

Like Dahl, I think that the quality of democratic citizenship achieved in modern liberal-democratic national political communities, while imperfect and inequitable in many ways, is nonetheless a significant human accomplishment. Any successful response to the challenges of globalization should seek to take advantage of this accomplishment, and to preserve it and build on it. Newly emerging forms of transnational political agency will work best, I believe, if they appeal to, rather than seek to erode or replace, the conceptions of popular sovereignty and nationhood that underlie modern western liberal democracies. And, as I have tried to show, that is indeed what we see with most of the "new forms of citizenship." Whether it is minority nationalism, immigrant dual-nationalism, transnational advocacy networks, or international human rights law, the underlying model of democratic citizenship and political legitimacy remains tied to territorially-bounded national political communities. This "old" model of citizenship remains the touchstone from which new forms of citizenship depart, and eventually return.

Notes

1 For example, in the eighteenth century, the Holy Roman Empire consisted of 1,800 distinct territories, ranging from large states like Austria to tiny ecclesiastic and princely estates (Gagliardo 1980, p. 4).

2 It also provided a rationale for elites to channel public funds to support their culture, on the grounds that this culture was now the "national" culture, available to all citizens regardless of class.

3 In Britain these core elements might include the BBC, Shakespeare, historical events (Waterloo) and figures (Churchill), soccer and contemporary politicians.

4 It may seem paradoxical that elites would try to diffuse theories of nationhood that valorize "the people." Why would elites promote a model of political community that ties their legitimacy to how well they reflect and represent the masses? See Greenfeld (1992) for an exploration of this question, which she ties to inter-elite conflict. In the English case, for example, Henry VIII invoked ideas of nationhood to justify breaking with the Pope. In other countries, aristocrats invoked ideas of nationhood to justify disobeying the King. In yet other countries, later on, nationhood was invoked because it had proven to be the most effective means of mobilizing people and resources for war against rival empires or monarchies.

5 According to John Rawls, for example, a theory of liberal justice should apply to "the basic structure of society." But what is the relevant "society"? For Rawls, "society" is defined in terms of the nation-state. Each nation-state is said to embody one (and only one) "society and culture" (Rawls 1993, 277), and Rawls' theory applies within the boundaries of each nation-state. He is hardly alone: most modern political theorists have taken for granted that the theories they develop should operate within the boundaries of the nation-state. When theorists develop principles of justice to evaluate economic systems, they focus on national economies; when theorists develop principles of rights to evaluate constitutions, they focus on national constitutions; when theorists develop an account of the appropriate virtues and identities required for democratic citizenship, they ask what it means to be a good citizen of a nation-state; when theorists discuss what "political community" can or should mean, they are asking in what sense nation-states can be seen as political communities. This focus on the nation-state is not always explicit. Many theorists talk about "the society" or "the government" or "the constitution" without specifying what sort of society, government or constitution they are referring to. But on inspection, they almost always have nation-states in mind. The assumption that political norms apply within nation-states, conceived as single integrated "societies," is so pervasive that many theorists do not even see the need to make it explicit. This is remarkable given that liberal values are often defended as universalistic, so that the restriction of their application to national settings would seem to be in some need of justification (see Black 1991). I return to this below.

6 For more on the thinning of national cultures, and how it distinguishes liberal from illiberal forms of nationhood and nationalism, see Kymlicka and Opalski (2001).

7 For discussions of liberal nationalism, see Miller (1995); Tamir (1993); Canovan (1996); Beiner (1999); McKim and McMahan (1997); Couture, Nielsen and Seymour (1998); Gilbert (1998); Poole (1999).

8 Or so I argue in Kymlicka (2001, ch. 10).

9 For more on the difference between cosmopolitanism in the sense of cultural openness and cosmopolitanism as a political ideology which rejects the nation-state, see Kymlicka (2001, ch. 10).

10 For the evidence, see Nevitte (1996, 2000).

11 By national minorities, I mean groups that formed complete and functioning societies

in their historic homeland prior to being incorporated into a larger state. The incorporation of such national minorities has typically been involuntary, due to colonization, conquest, or the ceding of territory from one imperial power to another, but may also arise voluntarily, as a result of federation.

12 Gurr (2000), however, notes that the violence associated with these conflicts started to decrease in the late 1990s, mainly due to a greater willingness by states to accommodate the key demands of minority nationalism.

13 The extent to which sub-state national groups have rights of self-determination under international law is quite unclear and contested. So there is no clear legal right to self-determination under international law. But in the broader public debate, this is the only argument that has any resonance or effectiveness in challenging the existence of states, or in seeking to break them up.

14 This is true, for example, of issues regarding gender equality or sexual orientation in Quebec and Scotland. For the more general convergence in political values between national minorities and dominant groups in the West, see Kymlicka (2001, chs. 10-15). The situation with indigenous people is more complicated: in at least some cases, the conflict between the state and indigenous nationalisms is also a conflict over values and world views.

15 For a defence of the success of these accommodations of minority nationalisms, see Kymlicka and Opalski (2001). See also Gagnon and Tully (2001); Keating and McGarry (2001); and Tully (1995).

16 Attempts to force everyone into the "one nationality per person" box never worked, particularly for children of mixed marriages.

17 For the evidence from Germany and Britain, see Koopmans and Statham (1999); for Canada, see Kymlicka (1995, ch. 1); see also Aleinikoff and Klusmeyer (2001).

18 As Joppke puts it, "Postnationalists have misjudged not only the locus of alien rights, but also their logic. In a postnational reading, alien rights are universal human rights which protect abstract human personhood irrespective of an individual's communal boundedness and involvement. Regarding migrants, however, the only such personhood right is probably the right of asylum. For all other migrants, a different communitarian logic is at work: the scope of rights increases with the length of residence and the development of ties to the receiving society" (2001, 59).

19 See, for example, Skrbis (1999) on "long-distance nationalism." Diasporas that are long-settled in the West tend to internalize liberal-democratic values, and so often promote a more liberal model of nationalism in the homeland (see Shain [1999] on the way immigrant groups in the United States are used by the government to market the American liberal creed abroad). Nonetheless, these immigrant groups are still very much committed to the defence of the nationhood and national rights of their ancestral group.

20 In the areas of social and economic rights, international human rights instruments are often stronger than domestic western constitutions. But these parts of international human rights law are almost entirely ignored in the West, and often dismissed as a regrettable compromise needed to gain the support of communist countries for the "real" human rights, that is, civil and political rights.

21 I am not, of course, endorsing this rather cavalier attitude toward international law. On the contrary, I think international law can and should play a larger role in our political life in North America. But I think it is important to realize how little international law enters into the everyday views of Americans or Canadians, and how little most people think we need it. The most important exception to this generalization concerns the indigenous peoples in Canada and the United States, many of whom have looked to the UN as a protector of their

rights. But this is an exception that proves the rule, since indigenous people do not regard the US/Canadian constitutions or courts as their own, but rather as the constitutions/courts of their conquerors.

22 The one exception to this general opposition in the West to international scrutiny of domestic laws is the European Court of Justice, which has asserted the right to overturn the domestic laws of EU states that violate the European Convention of Human Rights. This remains controversial in many EU countries, and was partly adopted because some EU countries were until recently military dictatorships (Spain, Portugal, Greece) with little or no tradition of liberal democracy, and because prospective EU countries in Eastern Europe have very weak traditions of liberal democracy or judicial independence. Here again, the international monitoring and enforcement of human rights norms is endorsed by the citizens of western democracies primarily to help "them," not to create an international monitor over "us."

23 Why do people in the West want to assist in the liberalization and democratization of non-western countries? Probably for a mixture of humanitarian reasons (to prevent oppression) and prudential reasons (non-democratic states are more prone to violence and aggression, with "spillover" effects on other countries in terms of refugee flows, arms smuggling, etc.).

24 For defences of the need for transnational political institutions, see Held (1995, 1999); Archibugi and Held (1995); Carter (2001); Heater (1996); Robbins (1998); Hutchings and Dannreuther (1999); and Bosniak (2000).

25 Also, the differences in values between various parts of the world may be too great to sustain feelings of legitimacy. People in the West would probably not accept as legitimate decisions premised on non-western values, even if endorsed by a majority of the world's population. The minimal level of shared values needed for a cohesive political community may not be present at the global level.

26 For popular resistance to elite-led campaigns in support of the EU, see Dahl (1999, 29); and Wendt (1999, 129).

27 For debates about how to democratize the EU, and how to create a feeling of a pan-European "demos," see Lehning and Weale (1997); Nentwich and Weale (1998); and Eriksen and Fossum (2000).

28 I say "special" responsibility since Canadians feel some sense of humanitarian concern for people wherever they live, even half-way around the world. But a "community of fate" is bound together by feelings of special responsibility which go beyond this universal humanitarian concern. And there is no evidence that Canadians feel stronger concern for Mexicans than, say, Guatemalans.

29 For similar concerns about the difficulty if not impossibility of democratizing international institutions, see Dahl (1999).

30 See the proposals in Held (1999); Franck (1997); Archibugi and Held (1995); and Bohman (2001), amongst others.

31 The ability of citizens to form NGO advocacy networks to contest government decisions, either at the domestic level or in international organizations, is important in ensuring greater justice and inclusiveness in decision-making, and appropriate rules of publicity and representation should be adopted to enable this. But it is worth restating that this sort of transnational advocacy, while vital, is no alternative to traditional territorial models of political community. NGOs should be able to object to decisions, but in the end we need some account of who has the legitimate authority to assess the merits of those objections, and the only credible answer to that question remains "the people," as embodied in democratic national polities.

References

Aleinikoff, A. and D. Klusmeyer. "Plural Nationality: Facing the Future in a Migratory World." In *Citizenship Today: Global Perspectives and Practices*, ed. A. Aleinikoff and D. Klusmeyer. Washington, DC: Carnegie Endowment for International Peace, 2001.

Archibugi, D. and D. Held. *Cosmopolitan Democracy: An Agenda for a New World Order*. London: Polity Press, 1995.

Anderson, B. *Imagined Communities: Reflections on the Origin and Spread of Nationalism*. London: New Left Books, 1983.

Banting, K. "The Internationalization of the Social Contract." In *The Nation State in a Global/Information Era*, ed. T. Courchene. Kingston: John Deutsch Institute for Policy Studies, Queen's University, 1997.

Baubock, R. *Transnational Citizenship: Membership and Rights in Transnational Migration*. Aldershot: Edward Elgar, 1994.

Beiner, R., ed. *Theorizing Nationalism*. Albany, NY: SUNY Press, 1999.

Black, S. "Individualism at an Impasse." *Canadian Journal of Philosophy*, Vol. 21, no. 3 (1991): 347-377.

Bohman, J. "Cosmopolitan Republicanism: Citizenship, Freedom and Global Political Authority." *Monist*, Vol. 84, no. 1 (2001): 3-21.

Bosniak, L. "Citizenship Denationalized." *Indiana Journal of Global Legal Studies*, Vol. 7, no. 2 (2000): 447-509.

Canovan, M. *Nationhood and Political Theory*. Cheltenham: Edward Elgar, 1996.

Carter, A. *The Political Theory of Global Citizenship*. London: Routledge, 2001.

Connor, W. "National Self-Determination and Tomorrow's Political Map." In *Citizenship, Diversity and Pluralism: Canadian and Comparative Perspectives*, ed. A. Cairns et al. Montreal and Kingston: McGill-Queen's University Press, 1999.

Couture, J., K. Nielsen and M. Seymour, ed. *Rethinking Nationalism*. Calgary: University of Calgary Press, 1998.

Dahl, R. "Can International Organizations be Democratic? A Skeptic's View." In *Democracy's Edges*, ed. I. Shapiro and C. Hacker-Cordon. Cambridge: Cambridge University Press, 1999.

Eriksen, E.O. and J.E. Fossum, eds. *Democracy in the European Union: Integration Through Deliberation?* London: Routledge, 2000.

Franck, T. "Tribe, Nation, World: Self-Identification in the Evolving International System." *Ethics and International Affairs*, Vol. 11 (1997): 151-169.

Gagliardo, J. *Reich and Nation: The Holy Roman Empire as Idea and Reality*. Bloomington, IN: Indiana University Press, 1980.

Gagnon, A. and J. Tully, eds. *Multinational Democracies*. Cambridge: Cambridge University Press, 2001.

Gans, C. "Nationalism and Immigration." *Ethical Theory and Moral Practice*, Vol. 1, no. 2 (1998): 159-180.

Gellner, E. *Nations and Nationalism*. Oxford: Blackwell, 1983.

Gilbert, P. *Philosophy of Nationalism*. Boulder, CO: Westview, 1998.

Greenfeld, L. *Nationalism: Five Roads to Modernity*. Cambridge, MA: Harvard University Press, 1992.

Guéhenno, J.-M. *The End of the Nation-State*. Minneapolis, MN: University of Minnesota Press, 1995.

Gurr, T. "Ethnic Warfare on the Wane." *Foreign Affairs*, Vol. 79, no. 3 (2000): 52-64.

Heater, D. *World Citizenship and Government: Cosmopolitan Ideas in the History of Western Political Thought*. London: St. Martin's Press, 1996.

Held, D. *Democracy and the Global Order: From the Modern State to Cosmopolitan Governance*. Cambridge: Polity Press, 1995.

________ "The Transformation of Political Community: Rethinking Democracy in the Context of Globalization." In *Democracy's Edges*, ed. I. Shapiro and C. Hacker-Cordon. Cambridge: Cambridge University Press, 1999.

Hutchings, K. and R. Dannreuther, eds. *Cosmopolitan Citizenship*. London: St. Martin's Press, 1999.

Jenson, J. and M. Papillon. "Challenging the Citizenship Regime: The James Bay Cree and Transnational Action." *Politics and Society*, Vol. 28, no. 2 (2000): 245-264.

Joppke, C. "The Evolution of Alien Rights in the United States, Germany and the European Union." In *Citizenship Today: Global Perspectives and Practices*, ed. A. Aleinikoff and D. Klusmeyer. Washington, DC: Carnegie Endowment for International Peace, 2001.

Keating, M. and J. McGarry, eds. *Minority Nationalism and the Changing International Order*. Oxford: Oxford University Press, 2001.

Keck, M. and K. Sikkink. *Activists Beyond Borders: Advocacy Networks in International Politics*. Ithaca, NY: Cornell University Press, 1998.

Koopmans, R. and P. Statham. "Challenging the Liberal Nation-State? Postnationalism, Multiculturalism, and the Collective Claims-Making of Migrants and Ethnic Minorities in Britain and Germany." *American Journal of Sociology*, Vol. 10, no. 3 (1999): 652-696.

Kymlicka, W. *Multicultural Citizenship: A Liberal Theory of Minority Rights*. Oxford: Oxford University Press, 1995.

________ *Politics in the Vernacular: Nationalism, Multiculturalism, Citizenship*. Oxford: Oxford University Press, 2001.

Kymlicka, W. and M. Opalski, eds. *Can Liberal Pluralism be Exported? Western Political Theory and Ethnic Relations in Eastern Europe*. Oxford: Oxford University Press, 2001.

Labelle, M. and D. Salée. "Immigrant and Minority Representations of Citizenship in Quebec." In *Citizenship Today: Global Perspectives and Practices*, ed. A. Aleinikoff and D. Klusmeyer. Washington, DC: Carnegie Endowment for International Peace, 2001.

Lehning, P. and A. Weale, eds. *Citizenship, Democracy and Justice in the New Europe*. London: Routledge, 1997.

Linklater, A. *The Transformation of Political Community: Ethical Foundations of the Post-Westphalian Era*. Columbia, SC: University of South Carolina Press, 1998.

Margalit, A. and J. Raz. "National Self-Determination." *Journal of Philosophy*, Vol. 87, no. 9 (1990): 439-461.

Marshall, T.H. *Class, Citizenship and Social Development*. New York: Anchor, 1965.

McKim, R. and J. McMahan, eds. *The Morality of Nationalism*. New York: Oxford University Press, 1997.

Miller, D. *On Nationality*. Oxford: Oxford University Press, 1995.

Nentwich, M. and A. Weale, eds. *Political Theory and the European Union: Legitimacy, Constitutional Choice and Citizenship*. London: Routledge, 1998.

Nevitte, N. *The Decline of Deference*. Peterborough, ON: Broadview Press, 1996.

________ "Value Change and Reorientations in Citizen-State Relations." *Canadian Public Policy/Analyse de Politiques*, Vol. 26 supplement (2000): S73-94.

Nickel, J. "The Value of Cultural Belonging." *Dialogue*, Vol. 33, no. 4 (1995): 635-642.

Nietschmann, B. "The Third World War." *Cultural Survival Quarterly*, Vol. 11, no. 3 (1987): 1-16.

Poole, R. *Nation and Identity*. London: Routledge, 1999.

Rawls, J. *Political Liberalism*. New York: Columbia University Press, 1993.

Raz, J. "Multiculturalism: A Liberal Perspective." *Dissent* (Winter 1994): 67-79.

Robbins, B., ed. *Cosmopolitics: Thinking and Feeling Beyond the Nation*. Minneapolis, MN: University of Minnesota Press, 1998.

Sakwa, R. "Liberalism and Postcommunism." Presented at a conference on "Liberalism at the Millennium." Gregynog, Wales, February 1998.

Shain, Y. *Marketing the American Creed Abroad: Diasporas in the US and their Homelands*. Cambridge: Cambridge University Press, 1999.

Skrbis, Z. *Long-Distance Nationalism: Diasporas, Homelands and Identities*. Aldershot: Ashgate, 1999.

Soysal, Y. *Limits of Citizenship: Migrants and Postnational Membership in Europe*. Chicago: University of Chicago Press, 1994.

Spinner, J. *The Boundaries of Citizenship: Race, Ethnicity and Nationality in the Liberal State*. Baltimore, MD: Johns Hopkins University Press, 1994.

Tamir, Y. *Liberal Nationalism*. Princeton, NJ: Princeton University Press, 1993.

Taylor, C. "The Politics of Recognition." In *Multiculturalism and the "Politics of Recognition,"* ed. A. Gutmann. Princeton, NJ: Princeton University Press, 1992.

Tully, J. *Strange Multiplicity: Constitutionalism in an Age of Diversity*. Cambridge: Cambridge University Press, 1995.

Weber, E. *Peasants into Frenchmen: The Modernization of Rural France 1870-1914*. London: Chatto and Windus, 1976.

Wendt, A. "A Comment on Held's Cosmopolitanism." In *Democracy's Edges*, ed. I. Shapiro and C. Hacker-Cordon. Cambridge: Cambridge University Press, 1999.

Young, I.M. *Justice and the Politics of Difference*. Princeton, NJ: Princeton University Press, 1990.

The Frontiers of Citizenship: Reflections

SINCE SEPTEMBER 11, 2001, FRONTIERS HAVE BECOME EVEN MORE VISIBLE THAN PREviously, and indeed we have witnessed the emergence of efforts to re-establish, strengthen and create boundaries that will protect Canadians from the threats of international terrorism. Therefore, our world is obviously a world *with* frontiers. This is a world in which issues of citizenship have become the stuff of everyday discussion as well as debate among academics and policy-makers.

It would be a mistake, however, to attribute all the attention to borders and to citizenship as simply the fall-out of the events of September 11th and the subsequent war. These serve only to remind us that citizenship is *always*, and always *has been*, about tracing borders between "us" and "them," a way of identifying who belongs and who is an outsider. Internal frontiers have also been characteristic of all citizenship regimes. Therefore, one of the ways of distinguishing among different regimes is to map these internal frontiers and to observe how they shift in response to actions of states and citizens.

To understand the forms of citizenship, then, there is a need for a working definition that allows us to identify such borders between and within. This is provided by seeing citizenship as involving two relationships: the status of members of a political community in the face of political authority, and the relationships of mutual support and solidarity that exist among such members because they are part of that community. Full citizenship involves, then, being recognized as a member of a community, having access to its rights and responsibilities as well as to participation in it. This membership includes the feeling of belonging and of sharing a common destiny.[1] These practices establish the *boundaries of citizenship*.[2]

As Will Kymlicka makes very clear in his analysis, the creation of new forms of citizenship, the title of the paper, has involved the extension over the last two centuries of citizenship rights to all categories of the population. Such decisions have had nation-building effects. In addition to setting the geographical borders of countries in a Westphalian world of national sovereignties, granting full citizenship to workers, to women, to ethnic minorities and religious minorities, as well as to immigrants, broke down the internal borders of class and gender relations, pushing them in the direction of greater equality. Such reforms transformed persons already living within the country's borders from outsiders to insiders. Through such actions, countries created themselves in the image of—always to a greater or lesser extent—pluralistic societies, open to a variety of experiences and ways of being.

Will Kymlicka's paper makes the important point that it has been a combination of flexibility and resilience that has been key to the success of the liberal nation-state model. The definition of citizenship has "thinned" such that it is no longer necessary to have a common religion, culture or lifestyle to be counted within the ranks of the citizenry. Indeed, as Yasmin Soysal's work, *inter alia*, teaches, categories such as migrant workers may share many of the benefits of citizenship status without actually bearing the nationality of the country.[3] Almost everywhere, however, boundaries have been stretched to provide equal rights to groups previously excluded, such as non-property owners, women and national minorities.

The vision thereby generated in Canada, whose definition of citizenship is one of the most pluralistic and flexible, has been of a multicultural or intercultural society, in which citizenship is open to those who accept basic human rights and liberal democratic political forms, and who are willing to define themselves as belonging to a single country, even when they do not necessarily share the same sense of national identity because they do not belong to the same "nation." Canada has not been built by "nation-building" in the ways that Kymlicka describes typical liberal democracies. In the place of an appeal to a single nation, there has been an insistence on a shared commitment to a limited but important set of key values and practices, and allegiance to a political community.[4]

There have been two results of such citizenship practices that I will raise here. The first is that, because citizenship and national identity are not coterminous, the *practices* of citizenship provide its primary grounding. The way that citizenship is lived, the expressions of solidarity and belonging that it implies, are the base on which it is built. Therefore, practices with respect to rights, responsibilities and access, more than expressions of values or common sentiments of belonging, sustain commitments to solidarity. Second, and again because citizenship involves something other than national identity, the way the *state* practises citizenship must be taken into account.

In his paper, Kymlicka describes citizenship practices in recent decades in liberal democracy in the following way:

> Some people argue that this seemingly happy marriage of liberal democracy and nationhood is becoming less and less sustainable as the definition of nationhood becomes "thinned." Perhaps co-nationals were likely to trust and feel solidarity for each other 50 or 100 years ago, when they all shared the same race or religion, and when members of racial or religious minorities were denied citizenship. But as the meaning of nationhood becomes thinner and thinner, so that co-nationals share less and less in common in terms of descent, religion or way of life, can it still generate feelings of trust and solidarity and mutual understanding?

He concludes that the answer to this question is that such fears are misplaced, in other words, because there is little evidence that even in a globalizing world, liberal-democratic political forms are threatened, that sub-state (or minority) nationalism threatens the basic principles of liberal-democratic citizenship and that transnationalism is undermining the national state.

I agree with these propositions, and much that is said in the paper about the continuing importance of national borders and national state forms for the future, despite the dual challenges of minority nationalism in many places and transnationalism as political practice in the face of globalization. This said, however, I think it is important to pay more attention than Kymlicka does to the *architecture of citizenship* and the state actions that are redesigning its own citizenship practices. These practices may be weakening ties of citizenship by creating new *internal borders* of difference and inequality.

In general then, in the next sections I will argue that citizenship is being redesigned as a result of choices being made by Canadian governments and that many of these choices are presented as the necessary or desirable consequences of globalization. Therefore, they merit more attention than Kymlicka gives them, if his goal is truly to understand "new forms of citizenship." Secondly, I will argue that some state responses to globalization are fashioning a weaker kind of citizenship, because states sometimes act to diminish their own capacities. Indeed, in several ways the key actor in any citizenship regime—that is the state that confers recognition, establishes rights and responsibilities, provides access to political participation and helps fashion feelings of belonging—has withdrawn from centre-stage. In doing so, new patterns of social differentiation have generated patterns of exclusion rather than incorporation. Social exclusion, as a threat to social cohesion, is now recognized in Europe and increasingly in Canada as the greatest social danger we face. Policies to foster *inclusion*, and thereby to regenerate access to full citizenship, motivate the social and cultural policies of many countries as well as the European Union and Council of Europe. *These* are the "new forms of citizenship" practice, and as such they also deserve attention.

The New Architecture of Welfare[5]

IN THE FIRST SECTION OF HIS PAPER, WILL KYMLICKA DESCRIBES A PROCESS OVER THE last 50 years that has generated stronger feelings of solidarity. In many ways the practices he describes go against the supposed trend of "thinning" citizenship that is the focus of his paper. They actually resulted in a thickening of citizenship, as the shift of responsibility for well-being to the public sector took place.[6]

Following T.H. Marshall, Kymlicka concludes that by the 1950s and 1960s there had been an extension of social rights of citizenship to all classes, such that incorporation of the working class into the nation had occurred. Solidarity across classes was expressed in regimes of social protection, education and health care. Thus, in the same years that citizenship recognition practices were becoming more accepting of differences in language, religions, culture and lifestyle habits, that is, they were "thinning," there was simultaneous "thickening" of feelings of solidarity and common destiny associated with the extension of social rights. With the latter, the "benefits" of common citizenship became visible, as risks were shared.

The conclusion he draws is, again using Marshallian language, that the working class was incorporated into citizenship. This process is then treated as an "accomplishment," an *acquis*, that merits no further attention. Yet, when we actually examine new forms of citizenship, there has been a significant "thinning" of it, as the "responsibility mix" is altered. The responsibilities of states, markets, families and communities have been significantly altered in the last decades, as a consequence of neo-liberal ideologies (Maxwell 2001, 6-7). These idea sets are themselves one of the elements of what we term "globalization."

In particular, the state has reduced its own role by a process of off-loading to families and the voluntary sector, as well as markets. In this process, the boundaries of citizenship have shifted; less can be expected as a right of citizenship. There has been a redesign of the architecture of welfare, as responsibilities have been reassigned among:[7]

- markets (purchased welfare),
- families (reciprocity of kin),
- voluntary associations (private solidarity), and
- governments (solidarity among citizens).

The postwar citizenship regime to which Kymlicka refers was one that had a responsibility mix in which the government role was prominent, and in which solidarity among citizens had pride of place. We can no longer take for granted that citizenship rights and responsibilities will be at the core of the future welfare architecture. Nor can we assume that the only threats to citizenship practices come from minority nationalisms or transnational political practices. New forms of citizenship are being constructed in ways that may constitute more of a danger for social cohesion than either of the two phenomena upon which Will Kymlicka focuses.

Redesigning the Responsibility Mix

HISTORICALLY, THE NOTION OF CITIZENSHIP WAS CLOSELY ASSOCIATED WITH THE individualization of society, and elimination of traditional ties of obligation, derivative for the most part from feudal and patrimonial representations of social relations. Nonetheless, this individualization has never meant that theories of citizenship did not include attention to social ties and social cohesion. The French revolutionaries, for example, clearly sought to rework traditional ties of social solidarity into modern ones, by giving fraternity the same standing as liberty and equality. By fraternity they meant what we call solidarity.

Because citizenship has so long been imbued with notions of solidarity, it was not surprising that T.H. Marshall identified in the politics of the interwar and immediate postwar years, the emergence of a new set of rights: social ones. Whereas in the nineteenth century, during the heyday of classical liberalism and its nightwatchman state, "dependency" had brought a loss of citizenship, by the twentieth century access to certain public supports in time of need was a citizenship right and recognition of belonging.

The capacity to be self-supporting and fully responsible was redefined to mean that it was possible to receive some supports from the state and remain a "full citizen." With the expansion of social programs in conjunction with the broadening of political rights to new groups (the working class and women), a major shift occurred in notions of economic autonomy. Mobilization by social reformers, Social Democrats, the organized working class, promoters of positive liberalism, Christian Democrats and so on all gradually transformed "poor relief" into "income security," and charity (both public and private) into social programs. The individual no longer had to be economically autonomous in order to participate politically (with the elimination of property restrictions and the Poor Laws) or to enjoy full civil rights. By 1945 women in most countries had finally gained the vote, although it did take until the mid- to late 1960s before married women enjoyed full civil rights with respect to contracts and many financial matters.

Social citizenship, within the mixed economies of the postwar years, generated rising expenditures on education, health, children and the poor. People often made explicit links to citizenship, as did the post-1945 Labour government in the United Kingdom and Canada's Liberal government in the postwar years. In the 1940s when Newfoundlanders were enticed into Confederation and in the constitutional politics of the 1960s, the notion that social programs provided the glue of common belonging was widespread (Banting 1999, pp. 112-113).

Since then, however, a number of political and economic actors have sought a substantial narrowing of the terms of citizenship. In some cases, there are proposals that citizenship be reduced to the civil and political rights identified by Marshall and the liberty and political equality identified by the French revolutionaries. Markets, rather than collective choices exercised through political institutions, have been identified as the locale most appropriate for the exercise of consumer sovereignty. Indeed, the liberal paradigm of citizenship finds public good in private decisions, particularly those organized by markets.

The result has been the appearance of a new architecture of citizenship, and in particular to the internal borders that differentiate full citizens from "second class" citizens, that is those people who have not yet assumed all their responsibilities, and therefore rights. Two examples of redesign will be sketched here.

Expressions of social solidarity limited to the excluded

Increasingly, there is a redesign of the architecture of social welfare that limits expressions of social solidarity to those "at-risk" of social exclusion, that is the poorest, the least skilled, the "truly needy." On the other hand, "ordinary citizens" are left to their own resources and they are responsible for their own well-being, finding it in the family or in markets. All of the programs put in place to share risk in the first decades after 1945 have been redesigned to become targeted, or "clawed back" when an income threshold is passed, or simply eliminated.

This has produced a perspective on social policy that envisions no more than "social safety nets" for those parts of the population most at-risk. Thus, if Canadians have proudly believed that their welfare state was more universal than that of their southern neighbours, the reality of current program design does not match the belief. Since the late 1970s there has been a significant shift from universal programs to selectivity (Myles and Pierson 1997). Secondly, governments have engaged in a reassignment of the responsibilities of the state, markets and families. They now put greater emphasis on individuals' (and therefore their family's) responsibility for their own well-being, their own life chances, and their own income security, as well as on the market as the mechanism for delivery of life chances and conditions.

Universal family allowances, for example, were created in 1946 as an expression of solidarity among those with children and those without, that is, a form of horizontal equity. They were first transformed into targeted programs with income testing in the 1980s, and then eliminated. Nor are their replacements, the Canada Child Tax Benefit and the other components of the National Child Benefit designed to be universal. The commitment is, as the government clearly says, to "improving support to low-income families with children." With the cut-off for low-income occurring near the poverty line, most Canadian families are left to themselves and their own resources.

In a similar way, low-cost university education in public universities, instituted in the 1960s, is being transformed into a much more expensive system, access means that students and their families must pay significantly higher fees, incur debt, and so on. The result is that access to university education is again being limited to those who can afford it, or those who qualify for bursaries. Universal health care, the jewel in the crown of Canada's post-1945 citizenship regime, is also under threat, with debates about user fees, private provision, two-track access and so on. Access to a full range of services depends upon having private insurance or a provincial health card, available as part of social assistance.

These three examples follow the same pattern. Solidarity remains a commitment within the Canadian citizenship regime; the poorest and most at-risk of exclusion receive support as an expression of solidarity among citizens. Beyond that, however, the new architecture is one in which the *rest* of the citizenry has been reassigned responsibility, as it was before 1945, for buying welfare in *markets* (private insurance, fees, etc.), relying on the *family* for redistributing resources across generations, and so on.

Redefining the model citizen

Instead of the adult worker-as-citizen—the ideal type in Marshall's mind—there is an ongoing process to transform the child as the "model citizen." This redesign of the definition of citizenship means that a new frontier is being generated: between those who have children and those who do not. Social benefits and spending are accessed *because* one has children, rather than because of one's relationship to the labour force (Beauvais and Jenson 2001).

The architecture of social investment states and human capital approaches to social policy all focus on children. Investing in children is the goal, because the long-term payoff is high. In the 1980s and even more rapidly in the 1990s, new programs with "child" or "children" in the title have proliferated, especially in conjunction with the Social Union Framework Agreement, which is presented as the up-dated version of intergovernmental relations for the era of globalization.

In all of this, the "citizen" has been reconstructed with reference to a central image, that of the "child," while the state's responsibility for fostering equality of opportunity is limited to this child, or at most young people. Adults are left to fend to themselves "responsibly" in the neo-liberal world of individualization and market relations, unless they are parents of young children. In such cases there are employability programs available to help them enter and remain in the labour force, so that they will be able to provide for their children.[8]

This new emphasis on equality of opportunity for children in the social union discussions and Agreement (signed in 1999), while clearly benefiting some children and their families, has come with a cost. It has made other dimensions of equality among citizens, such as equal access to democratic institutions or fostering gender equality in the economy, the society and the family somewhat more difficult to pursue. Such a redesign of welfare and income redistribution does nothing to address the income security needs, assure equity or promote equality for adults whose children are grown or who have no children. In particular, employment policies focused on parents of young children render virtually invisible the needs of older workers, whether they are women returning to the workforce or male workers who have lost their employment in traditional industries.

These categories of adults have become virtually invisible in social policy as well as having very few forms of support available to them. The shunting of the disabled, adults as well as children, from social assistance regimes to their own programs, as well as the "removal" of children from social assistance has meant that those adults who need income supports are at risk of simply being classified as "undeserving" and without any claim on collective resources.

Third, there is the issue of gender equality. It is true that much of the focus on children has had the happy consequence of bringing the need for child care to the fore. However, beyond the mantra that women or families must be able to balance work and family life, we are actually experiencing declining attention to matters of gender equality in Canada.[9] For those with a right to paid parental leave, the transition from Unemployment to Employment Insurance (EI) substantially reduced eligibility. Thus, the recent extension from six months to one year, while welcomed by those parents who are still eligible for EI paid leave, does nothing for the more than 50 percent of new mothers who are not. Questions of gender power in the workplace, in politics and even in everyday life are more and more difficult to raise, as adults are left to take responsibility for their own lives.

Finally, there is the matter of democracy. Children may be symbolically citizens in my analysis, but they are not full citizens in fact. They remain minors. Therefore, they cannot, as real citizens must, employ the force of democratic politics to insist on social reform in the name of equality. A child-centred definition of equality and citizenship is, then, also one that renders less visible the need for collective action by citizens mobilized to make claims and thereby use the state against all forms of unequal power, particularly the power of market forces.

What Happens to Citizenship When the Architect Steps Down?

IF ONE OF THE DEFINING RELATIONSHIPS OF CITIZENSHIP IS THE STATUS HELD BY MEMbers of a political community in the face of political authority, it is obvious that political authority capable and willing to confer this status is necessary. To the extent that states, as we have seen, redesign the responsibility mix among markets, families, communities and themselves, they are reducing their own capacity to maintain the second relationship. They are less able to design and manage the relationships of mutual support and solidarity that exist among members of the community. To the extent that such support exists, it will be designed by other institutions, such as markets (in the social economy, for example) or churches (as expressions of private solidarity, for example). Therefore, the question for the new forms of citizenship is whether we can still speak of "citizenship" when the responsibility mix had been modified and privatized such that the architect is shutting up shop.

Notes

1. The differential distribution of these three dimensions of citizenship—rights and responsibilities, access and belonging—provide the characteristics of a citizenship regime and permit analysts to distinguish among them. See Jenson and Phillips (1996).
2. On the concept of shifting boundaries of citizenship, see Jenson and Papillon (2000).
3. For the classic study of how migrant workers in Western Europe came to acquire some of the rights of citizenship, via the application of the principles of international human rights codes, see Soysal (1994).
4. For an elaboration of this argument and a comparison of the Canadian citizenship regime with that of Quebec, see Jenson (1998).
5. This terminology is adopted and adapted from Esping-Anderson et al. (2001).
6. On the Marshallian notions of social citizenship see Jenson and Papillon (2000) and Banting (1999).
7. These are adapted from Esping-Andersen et al. (2001). A fourth domain of responsibility is added, that of community. Neglect of this domain is endemic of this tradition of analysis, and merits more attention. See Mahon (2001).
8. For example, welfare to work programs focus almost exclusively on families with children. Quebec's APPORT (parental work assistance program) provides an income supplement if any income at all (a monthly minimum of $100) is earned. The target of NB Works, a six-year experimental program mounted with the federal government, was overwhelmingly for single parents. An adult without a dependent child has little support even for efforts to get into the labour force or recognition for doing so.
9. This is in significant contrast to the European Union, where gender equality remains at the heart of political discourse in considerations of the new welfare architecture. See Esping-Andersen et al. (2001).

References

Banting, K.G. "Social Citizenship and the Multicultural Welfare State." In *Citizenship, Diversity and Pluralism*, ed. A.C. Cairns et al. Montreal and Kingston: McGill-Queen's University Press, 1999.

Beauvais, C. and J. Jenson. *Choices and Investments in Policies for Families with Children*. Ottawa: CPRN, 2001.

Esping-Andersen, G., D. Gallie, A. Hemerijck and J. Myles. *A New Welfare Architecture for Europe?* Report submitted to the Belgian Presidency of the European Union, September 2001, available at http://vandenbroucke.fgov.be/Europe%20conf2%20report%20summ.htm

Jenson, J. "Recognizing Difference: Distinct Society, Citizenship Regimes and Partnerships." In *Out of the Impasse and Towards Reconciliation*, ed. G. Laforest and R. Gibbins. Montreal: IRPP, 1998.

Jenson, J. and M. Papillon. "The Changing Boundaries of Citizenship: A Review and a Research Agenda." In *Modernizing Governance: A Preliminary Exploration*. Ottawa: Canadian Centre for Management Development, 2000.

Jenson, J. and S.D. Phillips. "Regime Shift: New Citizenship Practices in Canada." *International Journal of Canadian Studies*, Vol. 14 (1996): 111-136.

Mahon, R. "Theorizing Welfare Regimes: Toward a Dialogue?" *Social Politics*, Vol. 8, no. 1 (2001): 24-35.

Maxwell, J. *Toward a Common Citizenship: Canada's Social and Economic Choices*, CPRN Reflexion. Ottawa: CPRN, 2001.

Myles, J. and P. Pierson, "Friedman's Revenge: The Reform of 'Liberal' Welfare States in Canada and the United States." *Politics and Society*, Vol. 25, no. 4 (1997).

Soysal, Y. *Limits of Citizenship: Migrants and Postnational Membership in Europe*. Chicago: University of Chicago Press, 1994.

Discussion

NORMAN MOYER OF HERITAGE CANADA, IN HIS ROLE AS THE DESIGNATED PRACTITIONER for the session, began the floor discussion by reminding us of some key aspects of Canadian citizenship. Noting that Will Kymlicka referred to "a community of fate," Moyer stressed that our fate as Canadians is to be part of a community of searching. In this sense, Canadian citizenship is, importantly a "work in progress." Some of this is due to the fact that we do not have a set of unifying myths/experiences to build upon, as other countries do (although the Charter is now a powerful unifying force). Part also is that we have a multiplicity of histories, languages and cultures. Beyond this, among all nations Canada is probably the foremost immigration society (relative to population). Moyer went on to note that in Kymlicka's terms we have a "thinned national identity," with the good news being Kymlicka's view that thin national identities can still be strong national identities. He concluded with a quote from Amin Malouf's *Les Identités Meurtrières* relating to the requisite of reciprocity:

> C'est dans cet esprit que j'aurais envie de dire, aux uns d'abord: plus vous vous imprégnerez de la culture du pays d'accueil, plus que vous pourrez l'imprégner de la vôtre. Puis je dirais aux autres: plus un immigré sentira sa culture d'origine respectée, plus il s'ouvrira à la culture du pays d'accueil.
>
> (It is in this spirit that I am tempted to write to new citizens—the more you embrace the new culture, the more it will embrace your own culture. I would write to the others—the more you accept new citizens and their culture, the more they will embrace your own culture.) Translated by the editors.

Michael Keating then addressed some issues relating to the transnational dimension of citizenship in the context of the Europeanization of rights. Here one of the key documents is the European convention of rights, which speaks in a language of "denationalized" human rights. They are incorporated in different ways into different national constitutions. Indeed, Keating notes that as a Scot he now has rights that have nothing to do with British citizenship, and are not mediated by the British state. While Europe may be an exception here, it does represent an area where Kymlicka's analysis needs to be nuanced.

Also in need of some qualification is the suggestion that Europe can only work as a democratic-liberal polity if it moves in the direction of a nation-state. It is true that the European Parliament is not a great success in mobilizing public opinion and participation, but this is because its role is more about accountability than about mobilization. The more relevant observation is that there is a process of democratization taking place at all levels in Europe. While Europe is admittedly not becoming a nation, it is nonetheless becoming an increasingly significant political space. This "Europeanization process" is facilitating the Northern Ireland peace process, the Spanish and UK internal asymmetries, and it may well provide the backdrop where Belgium could come apart peacefully.

Kymlicka responded by noting that one of the social successes of the European Union (EU) has been the stabilizing and deepening of the democracies of some of its member states (Portugal, Spain), a process that is likely to spread to central Europe as well. Thus, the relationship between the EU on the one hand and national political communities on the other has been very successful and important. Kymlicka reasserted his position that accepting this achievement is quite different than holding out hope that the Europeanization will be in the vanguard of a post-national order that will lead to the disappearance of national identities.

Several participants raised the relationship between citizenship and territory. We are accustomed to thinking that citizenship necessarily involves territorial relationships. Federalism can handle different sorts of rights across various subnational divisions, but these typically remain based on territory. Yet the approach of the Nisga'a Treaty (and the Yukon Indians' agreements) point in the direction of rights being assigned in terms of *who* you are, not *where* you are. In the case of the Nisga'a, a member of the band not resident in the defined territory can enjoy the rights, privileges and duties of Nisga'a citizenship. Kymlicka agreed with the comment, especially since territorial forms of rights tend to be both over- and under-inclusive. But the intriguing question is: Why have western democracies been so prone to adopting territorial forms of accommodation of minority rights? Part of the reason has to do with the nature of cultural groups and their institutional preconditions to maintain themselves over time. Moreover, part has to do with the nature of democratic governments and their desire to have territorial solutions. This is an area that needs more probing and more research.

The discussion then focused on how to close the existing democracy deficits. One obvious way, in the European context, would be to strengthen the European Parliament. Another is the Kymlicka approach to strengthening *indirect* representation—have nation-states carry their citizens' priorities to supranational decision-making fora. Might not citizen movements provide a third option, since citizens are arguably the principal beneficiaries of the information revolution. The mobilization of like-minded citizens across national boundaries is a very powerful force: it stopped the MAI and it triggered the "battle in Seattle." Jane Jenson responded to this question from the perspective of democracy and participation, noting initially that while democracy is about participation, not all participation is democratic or is a form of citizenship. Her view is that the demonstrations in Seattle were not democratic because there was no institutional access. Thus, this participation is not an exercise in international citizenship, nor does it serve to close democracy deficits. Rather, it is international participation in search of a new space for addressing the democratic deficit, not the means of closing such deficits, although the way in which the system responds to the demonstrations may open the way for the creation of a new space for democratic expression.

In his closing comments, Kymlicka agreed with Jane Jenson's comments, namely that he did not devote enough attention to the "internal barriers" to citizenship. He added that there is a permanent tendency for the advantaged to attempt to distance themselves from the less well off. Nationalism, along the lines of his analysis, has historically served as one of the effective counterweights to this tendency. Nationalism will not, of and by itself, solve this problem, but we would be much worse off if we were not able to appeal to nationalism as a way of trying to mutually connect the less well off with the wealthy.

Finally, Kymlicka agreed with Moyer's vision of Canada's uniqueness and its open and diverse and undefined and dynamic models of citizenship. But he added that we also have to understand the reality of the two extremely powerful and successful nation-building projects in Canada—the federal government has been extremely successful in promoting a certain kind of pan-Canadian identity in most of English-speaking Canada, and Quebec has been extremely successful in building national identity within Quebec. Our fate, therefore, is as a country dealing with contending nationhoods.

Subnational Communities

The Territorial State: Functional Restructuring and Political Change

The Transformation of the State

THERE IS A BURGEONING LITERATURE ON THE FUNCTIONAL TRANSFORMATION OF THE state. Opinions differ as to the extent and causes of this and about whether there is anything new, but the broad outlines of the argument are familiar. The consolidated nation-state as we knew it in the twentieth century represented a coincidence within defined territorial boundaries of a set of functional systems, a national identity and culture, and a set of decision-making institutions. These were bounded and underpinned by national sovereignty, which referred both to a principle of international law, and to the effective ability of states to make policy autonomously. Within these bounds, national politics could be practised and social compromises, such as the welfare state, made. The debate centres on the degree to which this package has been unraveled by the globalization, economic change and functional restructuring and, to the extent that it has, whether politicians are capable of doing anything about it.

One aspect of this, which has perhaps received less attention, is the spatial articulation of the sovereign nation-state and the extent to which this too is under pressure in contemporary conditions. For most of the twentieth century, at least in the developed countries of the West, the territorial nation-state was taken for granted to the point that comparative politics referred almost exclusively to comparisons among states; social science data sets were almost always aggregated at state level; and examples of territorial discontent were taken not as forms of normal politics, but as a pathology of the body politic. In recent years, however, the territorial state has been treated as a phenomenon to be explained, rather than taken for granted. Historians have explored the various forms of territorial polity that existed in the past and asked why some triumphed in some times and places and others elsewhere (Tilly 1975, 1990; Osiander 1994; Spruyt 1994). Sociologists have sought other levels of analysis that might prove useful correctives to state-centrism; and political scientists have come to see the maintenance of the territorial integrity of the state as a "problem" equally worthy of explanation as its occasional disintegration (Keating 1988, 1998).

States were often, if not always, constructed through military force, diplomacy and other forms of coercion. They have maintained their territorial integrity and unity under conditions of democracy in three ways: through normative integration, through functional integration and through territorial management. All three are proving more difficult. Modernization theorists for much of the twentieth century put the emphasis on normative and functional integration and tended to regard the process of national integration, except in certain catastrophic and limiting cases, as a one-way process. States were based on core areas, which expanded their cultural influence to incorporate peripheries through education and other socialization measures, the extension of the bureaucratic apparatus, and the displacement of traditional particularistic values with the universal values. In fact, national integration was taken as a part of modernity itself. At the same time, market structures and industrialization broke down traditional roles and status forms in the periphery, incorporating the whole into the national economy. So industrialization too became almost synonymous with national integration. In this way peripheries were functionally incorporated into national economic and administrative systems; and their populations were normatively assimilated, adopting the language, culture and values of the centre.[1] With the creation of a national population or *demos*, the way was prepared for democratization, in which sovereignty could be transferred from pre-democratic institutions to democratic ones. National sovereignty, the principle that the state has no external superior, could thus take on an internal dimension, in which the unitary people could brook no internal obstacle.

There was always a question as to why functional and normative integration should take place on the basis of nation-states and, indeed, many of the theories of European integration rely on more or less the same set of processes at a supra-state level. There is an even bigger question mark over the identification of state-level integration with modernity and progress itself, as minorities across Europe and North America have long complained. Another perspective puts the emphasis not on a one-way process of functional and normative integration but on the ability of state elites to maintain the state through an array of institutional and policy measures summed up under the label of territorial management. Institutional mechanisms include federal systems, political parties and intergovernmental arrangements. Policy measures include economic management, spending policies and cultural concessions. Somewhere between the institutional and the policy-type are clientelist mechanisms for resource allocation, sustaining reliable collaborators on the periphery, who can maintain their local legitimacy by their ability to redirect state resources to their dependants. In the nineteenth century, tariff policy was perhaps the most common device for territorial management, allowing for territorial-sectoral coalitions within national politics. Examples are the alliance of iron and grain in Germany, or of the southern agrarian landowners and northern industrialists in post-unification Italy. In the United Kingdom, the dominant coalition from mid-century was free trading but it too had both sectoral and territorial components. There is no need to labour this issue for a Canadian audience. From mid-twentieth century, regional policies were a vital instrument in territorial management in industrialized states.[2] During the *trente glorieuses années*, diversionary regional policy, steering development away from wealthy areas and into needy ones, appeared as the ideal non-zero-sum policy instrument. Needy areas gained from the new investment; booming areas gained from the relief of inflationary and development pressures; and national economies gained from bringing into production otherwise idle resources. A similar logic underlay fiscal transfers and spending as the "donor" regions could rest assured that most of the money would return in the form of orders for their goods. Territorial redistribution could further be defended as a contribution to the welfare state principles of equality and solidarity and as a concrete manifestation of the principle of shared nationality.

The institutional manifestation of this differed in important ways between unitary and federal states, but the logic was similar as policy-making came to take on both sectoral/functional and territorial dimensions. Federal states tended to evolve in consequence toward cooperative federalism, with a high degree of collaboration in common functions across institutional boundaries; while unitary states moved to systems of regional planning in which the territorial perspective was integrated into the national functional one.

Forces for Change

ARRANGEMENTS FOR TERRITORIAL MANAGEMENT HAVE ALWAYS BEEN OPEN TO change, from either internal or external forces, which can destabilize old patterns and give rise to new challenges. The consolidation of national markets in the nineteenth century made peripheries of former centres and vice versa. Globalization in its first manifestation, in the late nineteenth century, altered the political economy of territory. Manchester and Glasgow became bastions of free trade, while the industrialists of northern Italy, supported in due course by their workers, sought national protectionism. The bourgeoisie of Catalonia, competitive within Spain but not against British, German or northern Italian exporters, pressed the rather discordant demands of Catalan home rule and protectionism within the Spanish market. The collapse of the international trading system between the wars similarly affected territorial management.

Present-day challenges to the territorial state have come from functional restructuring, especially as mediated by dominant ideological discourses; from a recomposition of political identities and frames of reference; from the rise of other forms of democratic legitimation and claims to authority challenging the old doctrines of sovereignty; and from institutional change above, below and alongside the state. Functional restructuring is a complex process, widely credited with having eroded the territorial principle or even heralding "the end of territory" (Badie 1995). My interpretation is that this has weakened certain forms of the territorial system (notably the nation-state) while encouraging a re-territorialization in other ways. So it has become more difficult to model national economies or to use them as discreet units of analysis, but while this is due partly to global integration, it has also to do with the rise of regions as production systems in their own right, a matter on which there is now a huge literature (Scott 1998; Storper 1997) but still a lot of controversy (Lovering 1999). In this new paradigm, place becomes important not merely as a location but as a socially constructed space in which distinctive productive models emerge based on networks of interdependence and reciprocity. Regions and cities thus constructed are portrayed as engaged in competition in world markets for investment, markets and know-how, thus moving the focus from inter-firm competitiveness to interregional competition. Some observers have taken the analysis further, arguing that these new territorial production systems are potentially the basis for a different model of capitalism, more socially integrative and generally benign.

Critics have complained that this is to reify the place, that the whole idea of competition is the product of neo-liberal ideology, and that the prophets of the new regionalism are generalizing wistfully from a few atypical and often misunderstood cases. Whatever the truth of the matter, the new regional development paradigm has become well-established within governments at all levels at a time when traditional forms of diversionary regional policy are more difficult to sustain. In an age of global competition for investment, states cannot steer investment within their own territories as in the past, while transfer payments are more difficult to keep up when they are no longer part of a nationally-bound bargain in which all component territories can gain. Faced with the "imperative" of global competition, wealthy regions in Europe as in Canada are demanding a retrenchment of equalization and transfers toward their poorer compatriots.

Functional restructuring may also be seen in the cultural field. Ironically, at a time of instant and almost costless communication, territory seems ever more important for movements of cultural and linguistic defence. This is because of the territorialization of economic and other functions, which means that linguistic use is a territorial matter and institutions on which linguistic promotion is based are themselves territorially constituted. So in countries like Canada, Belgium or Spain, the politics of language is becoming more linked to territorial control and regulation. Matters are less clear in the field of social solidarity, although it may be that the weakening of national and class solidarities may be promoting territorial forms of solidarity and support for welfare. This would be another factor undermining support for inter-territorial transfer payments. Another striking example is that of human rights, which are increasingly being taken out of the framework of the nation-state, expressed in universal terms, and lodged in transnational institutions.

Normative integration has, in one sense, continued, in that across Europe and North America there is a convergence on basic economic and social values, often spurred by secularization. Yet at the same time there has been a reassertion of local and regional identities, based in some cases on historic units and in others on more recent imagined communities. This combination of normative convergence and differentiated identities causes some puzzlement to national majorities who often seem to believe that, to exist let alone to exercise self-governing rights, the minorities must somehow be "different." Then, in a double bind, it is claimed that if the minorities are espousing distinct values, they must not be observing universal liberal norms, and thus should not be entitled to self-government. Yet, as Will Kymlicka also observes in this volume, the minorities are usually behaving no differently from the majorities, just choosing a different territorial or communitarian framework in order to express and realize these common values. This, at one level, makes territorial management easier but, at another it actually makes it more difficult, since territorial minorities are now competing on the same political ground as the state itself and making claims for powers of general social regulation rather than advancing particularist claims which might be met by policy differentiation. This, which goes to the heart of the Canada-Quebec dilemma, is an issue found also in European countries like the United Kingdom, Spain or Belgium.

Institutional change has involved a transfer of functions downwards to regional units in both federal and unitary states in industrial countries. The United States has seen a revival in state governments, while all the major European countries now have an intermediate or *meso* tier of government. At the same time there has been a shift of functions to transnational regimes of various types, as other chapters show. This is taken furthest in the emerging European space which, in a variety of institutional forms, now embraces market integration, a range of regulative policy spheres, human rights and defence and security matters. There is a debate over whether this really represents a loss of power by the nation-state or merely a device for states to retain their power and freedom to manoeuvre, a debate whose contours have hardly changed in the last 40 years.

Sovereignty and the State

THERE IS A LIVELY DEBATE NOW ABOUT THE EROSION, HOLLOWING OUT OR RETREAT of the state, captured in other chapters of this volume. There are those who deny that the state has lost power and authority, pointing to the share of state spending in gross domestic product (GDP) or the range of tasks still performed by modern states, or noting that states are free to withdraw from transnational bodies at their discretion, albeit perhaps at some cost. Others distinguish between the amount of work that states do and their functional autonomy in deciding what to do and how. So they recognize that the state does a lot, but claim that it has lost much of its functional autonomy under the influence of global economic forces and institutional interdependence.

Some people have concluded that, as it loses functional autonomy the sovereign state as we have known it is on the way out, to be replaced by new and more complex forms of authority and regulation. This has become a very contentious matter. For supporters of the state-sovereignty model, sovereignty is a formal principle that cannot be surrendered and is independent of the actual exercise of power and autonomy. It is above all a normative principle of *legitimate* authority. I do not think that we can really separate out power and sovereignty in this way since, while they may be conceptually distinct there must be a point at which the loss of functional autonomy makes formal sovereignty meaningless. In any case, the formalistic argument that, despite functional change, sovereignty itself can never be attenuated has always rested upon a certain ideological mystification. State elites have used the doctrine of state sovereignty, with its democratic overlay of popular sovereignty, to erect powerful systems of social regulation and control. Now, after its explicit or implicit glorification in the social sciences, the nation-state has suffered a certain ideological demystification in recent years. The spell broken, sovereignty has been made banal or even treated as no more than a power resource. This causes real problems for traditional sovereignty theorists for whom sovereignty is absolute or is nothing. Yet new legal thinking is beginning to provide a way out.

Legal scholars have started a debate on legal pluralism, based on the idea that there might be multiple sources of original normative laws, which do not have to be reduced to a single principle of sovereign statehood and which may not be in a hierarchical relationship to each other. This provides a counterpoint to the functional and institutional changes discussed above, but also rests on older traditions of divided, shared or contested sovereignty (MacCormick 1999). International law and European law are presented as legal systems in their own right and not merely emanations of state law. Those of an historical bent have also unearthed sources of original law beneath and within states. Scottish scholars have refurbished the argument that the British Parliament lacks absolute sovereignty in Scotland and that the *Acts of Union* of 1706–07 represent a pact between nations that cannot be changed merely at the whim of the larger party.[3] Basque scholars and politicians insist that the traditional rights or *fueros* of the Basque provinces are original law, the product of Basque sovereignty, and not the gift of the Spanish constitution. These arguments, and similar ones in Catalonia or Quebec, sustain the theory that the state is the product of a pact among peoples and not of a single sovereign will. Miguel Herrero de Miñon (1998*a*,*b*) has revived a more general debate in Spain about historic rights, based partly on the ideas of the nineteenth-century German Georg Jellinek (1981). Rokkan and Urwin's (1983) concept of the "union state" in which some parts have entered by a distinct path, retaining elements of original law and institutions, points in the same direction, as does Elazar's (1987) identification of unions as a distinct form of territorial state. Some Scottish scholars are now claiming that the revived Scottish Parliament embodies the (limited) sovereignty claims of its pre-1707 predecessor. Certainly hardly anyone in Scotland believes the official Westminster doctrine that the Scottish Parliament is no more than the expression of the sovereign will of the UK Parliament and is therefore entirely its creature. None of this makes for a complete alternative doctrine of sovereignty but it certainly brings into question old state-centred doctrines and generates a whole new set of sovereignty claims.

The impact of these changes on territories has been very uneven, as has the political response. Some territories are economic/functional spaces, cultural spaces and the location of historic traditions and sovereignty claims. In other places, the various meanings of place do not coincide, or there is no distinct spatial articulation below the level of the state. Some places are the location of political movements seeking to pull together the various elements in order to construct new systems of political action and social regulation or even to forge alternative nation-states. Gradually, there is an acceptance that the old categories may be inadequate and that territories, in so far as they can be constructed as social entities, are caught in new patterns of interdependency. While the old territorial management game could be presented as a dyadic relationship between the state and the regions, the new dispensation finds regions managing a dependency on the international market and on the emerging transnational regimes. This gives a whole new meaning to the idea of regional autonomy. A region may become more autonomous of its parent state but, by losing state protection, be rendered more dependent on the international market. This dependence in turn may be offset by seeking the protection of a transnational and then becoming an actor within it. The number and type of strategies to be played to manage these interdependencies is legion, as we can see from the huge literature about the role of regions within the European economic and political space.

The regional state

One intellectual response is represented by Kenichi Ohmae's (1995) "regional state." Ohmae's formulation is economically determinist and thoroughly reductionist, presenting a world of competing regional systems of production locked in battle for competitive advantage.[4] The analysis and prescription are a curious mixture of neo-liberalism, in which government is seen as an obstacle to market-driven growth, and neo-mercantilism, in which regional states seem to have a moral imperative to do everything they can to promote competitive advantage. A more sophisticated version is presented by Courchene (1999, 2001) who draws on the literature on the new regional development paradigm and on trends in the international economy to argue that regions must adapt to their external environment. Since this entails keeping their cost structures in line with those of their immediate competitors, there are large implications for politics and public policies. The "state" in this formulation does not carry the implications of sovereign authority which are its defining characteristics in political science and law, but refers rather to a system of regulation and public policy-making within a looser federal-type arrangement.

There is also a social democratic version of the regional state or "new regionalism" paradigm. Scott (1998) sees the region as the locus of new production systems in conditions of globalism and post-Fordism but broadens the agenda of regionalism to include issues of worker rights, gender, the environment and political representation. Avoiding the term regional state he sees a need for new forms of regional regulation in the shape of "regional directorates" in order to integrate these diverse concerns in the face of weakened nation-states. Cooke and Morgan (1998) follow similar reasoning about the rise of regional economies, placing the emphasis on associationalism, which they see as a new form of regulation distinct from the neo-classical market and the interventionist state mode. This associationalism can both enhance economic efficiency, by coping with collective action problems and externalities, and foster social solidarity. This sounds almost too good and their findings, along with the new regionalism in general, have in turn been criticized from a leftist perspective by Lovering (1999), who seems to suggest that the whole thing depends on a degree of wishful thinking bolstered by local boosterism. Certainly, we have to ask whether the forms of social interaction necessary for a regional production system are the same as those underpinning solidarity and about the conditions under which this might and might not be true. I have also argued against economic or functionalist reductionism in explaining regionalism, insisting on the need to bring together the elements of functional restructuring, especially in the economy; culture and its uses; and political change (Keating 1998). Regional development coalitions are built differently in different places and the motivations of actors are sometimes not linked to economic competition at all, but to political advancement or stateless nation-building (Keating 2001*a*). Gagnon (2001) similarly broadens the concept of the regional state in its application to Quebec, presenting it as an alternative both to status quo federalism and to independence. His notion of the regional state encompasses economic regionalism but also includes cultural and social dimensions.

What the social democratic critics have in common is an insistence that there is more than one equilibrium point for a regional system of production and social regulation, allowing multiple strategies—all of which can succeed; and that regions, like states before them, need to forge social compromises and integrate the social dimension with that of economic growth. Some have argued for a distinction between a "low road" to success, based on low-wage costs, taxes and social overheads, and a "high road" which involves large investments in human capital and social stability, in pursuit of higher value-added products and production technologies (Cooke, Boekholt and Tödtling 1999). I have tentatively categorized this still further, distinguishing between the low road and three other models. The "bourgeois regionalist" model[5] is a high-cost model, emphasizing investment in collective goods, research and development and human capital, in order to get on the high road of development, but does not necessarily emphasize social solidarity for its own sake. The "social democratic" model stresses social solidarity and distributive issues directly as part of the regional welfare function. The "nation-building" model gives priority to political autonomy and culture, although using the new regionalist economic paradigm as an instrument to gain more functional autonomy and build a distinct system of social regulation in the face of global markets and transforming states. These are merely ideal types and many strategies involve a combination of elements.

For example, Quebec has combined nation-building with elements of social democracy, while Flanders has combined it with bourgeois regionalism.[6]

The rise of city regions

Another form of territorial restructuring focuses on city regions, especially the phenomenon of global city regions (Scott 2001). The argument for the rise of city regions is normally expressed in economic terms, seeing the city as a unit of production, particularly in relation to post-Fordist forms of economic activity including high technology and financial services. In the global city-region version, these are penetrated by external influences and linked in global chains of production and competition. Despite their reliance on high technology communication, these cities provide economies of agglomeration in activities requiring face-to-face contact and learning (Sassen 2001). These include company headquarter services, hence the concentration of control. Like the related regional-state paradigm, the global city has often been presented as a form of economic reductionism, but there is also a literature emphasizing the importance of cities as refractors of class relations and, above all, as the site of distinctive social movements opposed to the commodification of space. These include neighbourhood groups, environmental movements, users of public services and cultural movements that invest space with important symbolic meanings. There is a recurring tension at the heart of urban politics over the use of scarce land, and global competition has in many cases exacerbated it. Central cities, previously often written off in North America and the United Kingdom, if not elsewhere in Europe, have become key sites for high value-added activities, as well as for modern living. This has revived old tensions between these uses and the needs of low-income residents who may be displaced from the employment market and from affordable accommodation.

Cities have also become the focus of new forms of democratic impulse and reform, and bases for political power. Decentralization reforms in France, while slightly enhancing the status of regions, have greatly increased the standing of city governments and mayors. The power vacuum in Italy following the collapse of the old political class in the 1990s has been partly filled by a new generation of activist mayors with their own power bases. Direct election and a gradual expansion of their functions and autonomy have helped this process. In some cases, there is a tension between political movements or development coalitions based in cities and those in the wider regional framework. The rivalry between

Catalonia and the city of Barcelona has been notorious and there are tensions in some of the French and Spanish regions. In England, proposals to elect city mayors directly have collided with a movement for larger scale regional government. There has also been a revival of the idea of consolidated metropolitan government after a period in which the virtues of fragmentation were preached. While the emphasis in the past tended to be on the need to expand service provision, now it is on the need for effective planning and investment to sustain economic growth, and to curtail competition within metropolitan areas in order to enhance the competitiveness of the area against outsiders. Experience in Canada is paralleled in several European countries, although the new metropolitan and consolidated structures tend to be lighter than those of the past.

Competitive federalism

These changes have had a major impact on federal systems of government as well as in federalizing states like Spain or the United Kingdom. Scholars of federalism have traditionally recognized two modes: coordinate federalism, in which each tier has its own distinct competences exercised independently; and cooperative federalism, in which the two levels cooperate on common problems and tasks. It is generally recognized that the twentieth century saw a move toward cooperative federalism under the impact of the expansion in the size and complexity of government and the social and economic problems it thought itself capable of addressing. In particular, Keynesian economic management and the welfare state cut across previous lines of functional demarcation. In recent years, there has been a further move, toward competitive federalism, in which federated governments compete against each other and against the federal state. One form of this is market competition for advantage as identified by the regional-state school discussed above, and involves policies of investment attraction, marketing and a generally neo-mercantilist orientation.

There has also been something of a revolt of the rich regions against fiscal equalization and transfer payments, now that these can no longer be presented as matters of enlightened self-interest within bounded national economies. As noted above, the economic rationale for transfers is undermined in open economies, while national and other forms of solidarity are weakening. So the wealthier regions of Germany, Belgium, Italy, Spain and the United Kingdom, as well as Canada, are complaining about the burden.[7]

Another dimension, however, concerns policy innovation, with governments competing to demonstrate their ability to deal with social and economic problems, to learn from best practices elsewhere and to impress their electorates with their ability to take the lead. Federated governments may use their powers in new ways to produce new programs, while federal governments may seek to get back into key areas of domestic policy and bolster their political bases through innovations of their own. Federated governments may also seek to impress their electorates by demonstrating superior policies to those pursued by neighbouring jurisdictions. While much of this may be wasteful or redundant, it can also be a force for innovation and renewal in the system as a whole as governments are obliged to innovate and to learn from others. Bruno Dente (1997) has argued that this reflects the needs of modern conditions of government. Coordinate federalism, he argues, was appropriate in a era when both problems and solutions were known and it was merely a matter of applying resources and regulations. Cooperative federalism was appropriate in an era where the problems were known but the solutions were not, prompting cooperation in the search for new answers across jurisdictional boundaries. Competitive federalism is appropriate in an era where neither the problem nor the solution is known, calling for experimentation and action research.

We can see these trends at work not just in Canada but in the United States, where state governments have revived and become more innovative, as well as in Europe. In the United Kingdom, for example, the decision of the Scottish Parliament to abolish up-front university tuition fees and to provide free long-term care for the elderly theoretically has no implications for the rest of the state, since they must be accommodated within the Scottish budget. Yet the example has placed heavy pressure on the other two devolved administrations and on the central government (which doubles as the government of England) to follow suit or demonstrate why they are not doing so. Autonomous communities in Spain are beginning to show some policy innovation, with some much more active and inventive than others (Fundación Encuentro 1997). There are also signs of policy competition among Italian regions, as central control of their activities is relaxed.

Competitive federalism, together with the rise of national regions also favours increasing asymmetry either *de jure* or *de facto* as different governments interpret their role differently. Policy differentiation is perfectly compatible with traditional federalism—indeed it is part of its essence—but when governments adopt radically different attitudes to common issues like the welfare state then the role of government in relation to society is changed. It is likely that as competition increases, regional governments will formulate their role in different ways and may seek constitutional change to recognize this. Regions seeking to play the new regionalist game of competing in the global economy will also seek to loosen ties with their states and fellow regions. Recent governments of Flanders, increasingly uncomfortable with the Belgian interventionist welfare state, have sought ever greater powers, against the resistance of Wallonia, which not only has different economic interests, but sustains a different political culture and attitude to the role of government generally. The United Kingdom has responded to distinctive pressures in its various peripheries with a highly differentiated pattern of asymmetrical devolution. Scotland has a national parliament with general competence, Wales has a national assembly with defined administrative powers and Northern Ireland has a devolved assembly constructed on consociational lines to ensure power-sharing between the two communities. Proposals for England, on the other hand, respond to the desire for more effective regional planning and economic promotion. The Spanish devolution process also has asymmetrical features as a result of competition between the historic nations, pressing their *hechos diferenciales*, and the central state which seeks uniformity.

Stateless Nation-Building

WE HAVE ALSO SEEN A RISE IN NATIONALIST MOVEMENTS IN THE STATELESS NATIONS of advanced industrial democracies, notably in Canada, the United Kingdom, Spain and Belgium. Now this is a very old issue but nationalist movements have taken on new characteristics in conditions of state transformation and transnational integration (Keating and McGarry 2001). They have generally embraced free trade and transnational integration, seeing these as providing new opportunities for autonomy and action. This is not merely because they are rich regions and feel that they would be better off on their own, although that is an element in some cases. More often, nationalism is the prior force, with the strategy of playing in the global market providing a new opportunity.[8] Secondly, nationalist movements have generally moved from a vision of ethnic exclusivity to a broader, civic or territorial conception of the nation (Keating 2001*a*) in which the entire population is included in the national project. This is not as surprising as it often appears to critics of nationalism since it merely reflects trends in the wider society and nation-states of the developed West. Nation-builders in Quebec, Scotland, Catalonia and the Basque Country have been at pains to stress that all can be members of the national community, although not everyone has bought into this idea.[9] Thirdly, nationalists have, in various ways, largely abandoned the idea of creating a separate nation-state. We are familiar with 30 years of debate among Quebec nationalists about forms of sovereignty-association or partnership which would allow Quebec to determine its own fate without breaking all links with Canada. The Catalan *Convergència i Unió* is quite explicit about not wanting to separate from Spain, but to establish a looser confederal state within a united Europe—indeed this strategy has a long history going back over a hundred years. Basque nationalism is divided between traditional *independentistas* and those who would prefer the Catalan strategy. The Scottish National Party officially favours independence within the European Union but contains divisions running from those who would prefer a Danish strategy of being within the European Union (EU) but resisting further integration, to those who would go for the Catalan line of playing for autonomy in multiple fora without worrying too much about formal independence. Another group of nationalists within Europe favours independence in some form in a distant future when the existing states have given way to a new transnational European order. This utopian "Europe of the Peoples" vision can be seen in the Welsh *Plaid Cymru*, the *Esquerra Republicana de Catalunya* or the former Flemish *Volksunie*.

Analysis of public opinion in the stateless nations[10] shows varying but generally strong levels of support for greater autonomy and national affirmation, but a profound ambivalence on the implications of this. It is not only in Quebec that large bodies of opinion can be found apparently wanting independent statehood and to remain within the host state at the same time. Similar apparent contradictions are visible in the United Kingdom and Spain. It is tempting to conclude that the electors simply cannot understand the question or do not know the differences between devolution and independence, but I think that these responses contain something more interesting. Electors are simply refusing to adopt the categories of statehood framed for them by lawyers, social scientists and politicians, and are open to new forms of political order. This is particularly notable in Quebec and Scotland, where voters have been exposed to the debate over nationalism, self-government and independence almost continuously for a generation. These are also societies in which many people have always regarded their membership of the state as, to some degree, conditional and the result of a pact among peoples that ought to be renegotiable from time to time.

These societies also show evidence that individuals are adopting multiple identities, equipping them to operate in the emerging order. The local identities are tending to predominate, but state identity remains a factor. Divided societies like Northern Ireland and, in different ways, Quebec and the Basque Country, present further questions, as here different sectors of the population identify with different territorial levels and national communities.

These strategies share in common a concept of authority beyond the familiar categories of the sovereign state. All are making claims based on nationhood, which in turn is founded on two quite distinct principles: the existence of the nation as an historic community with original rights; and on the nation's self-recognition as a self-determining community, as shown in support for nationalist movements and demands. Self-determination in this sense is taken, not as a synonym for independence, but as the right of the nation to negotiate its own position within the emerging state and transnational order. The implications of this are far from clear since there is as yet no recognized status for a territory wishing to be more than a region or federated unit but less than a state, although there are multiple opportunities within the emerging European order (Keating 2001*b*).

Trapped in the old categories of statehood and nationality, we often lack the conceptual tools to analyze these identities and demands, hence the tendency to dismiss them as meaningless or confused. I have, with some trepidation, used the term "post-sovereignty" to capture this phenomenon, which is both new and old. Social scientists are given to resolving this type of terminological conundrum by resorting to the prefixes "neo" and "post," not abandoning the old terms but incorporating them into the new. The term "post-industrial," for example, does not denote the abandonment of industry—all post-industrial societies are industrial—but refers to a stage in which industrialism no longer provides the sole or main social paradigm. Post-modern, according to the *Cambridge English Dictionary*, "includes features from different periods in the past or in the present and past." So, unable to find a better alternative, I have been using the term post-sovereignty not to denote an era in which sovereignty has disappeared but rather to denote its transmutation into other forms. Sovereignty is no longer lodged in a single place, but nor is it nested within fixed or hierarchical forms as in classical federations. Rather, there are multiple sites of sovereign authority, often drawing on different forms of legitimacy and which must be linked through political means.

Challenges of the New Territorial Politics

THE NEW TERRITORIAL DISPENSATION PRESENTS OPPORTUNITIES AND PROBLEMS FOR regions, states and the transnational order. While the new regionalist literature stresses the positive aspects of the regional perspective on economic development, there are also dysfunctional ones. The idea of comparative advantage, in which all regions can find their place in the global division of labour, has given way to the notion of competitive advantage, implying a zero-sum game with winners and losers.[11] This in turn has fostered a neo-mercantilist form of politics, in which regions seek to gain at each others' expense, tapping into what is seen as a fixed pool of mobile investment or technological opportunities. The resulting proliferation of investment grants and incentives, and the generalization of low taxation regimes, can then lead to the under-taxation of business, the starvation of social programs, without any overall benefit, since the various incentives merely cancel each other out. The focus on the region as a production system can lead to a certain reification and the construction of a shared territorial interest in opposition to that of neighbouring regions. It is this that has proved the main obstacle to cross-border cooperation, especially in North America, even where shared problems and opportunities exist. External effects of development policies are thus neglected and external benefits unrealized. This is not merely an objective result of economic restructuring and changing modes of production. The theme of shared regional interests in opposition to neighbouring regions is a tempting one for politicians seeking to establish a broad basis of support, especially in the context of weakened class and other loyalties. So the imperative of competition may be as much a creation of ideology and political strategy as a response to facts on the ground, closing off political debate in favour of a *pensée unique*.

Competitive federalism may be creative in fostering innovation and a certain amount of redundancy may be an inescapable part of this (Dente 1997), but it also encourages governments to adopt "boutique policies," highly visible initiatives outside or on the margins of their own jurisdiction, in order to establish a political presence in policy fields. These may represent a serious waste of resources.[12] There are also problems in the maintenance of national welfare states, although it should be said that these have tended to hold up rather well in the face of pressures to retrenchment.

All of this may call for new forms of supra-regional regulation not relying on the hierarchical authority of a strong state. The Canadian social union process seems to be an effort to realize this, although judgement would at this stage have to be reserved. In Europe, by contrast, the situation is quite different given the construction of a new and rather comprehensive system of regulation through the European Union. So while NAFTA would seem to reinforce the market effects of globalization, exposing regions more directly to international competition without the protection of the old state form, in Europe this is mediated by continental institutions. For example, there is a much more constraining regime to regulate zero-sum regional economic competition.[13] Although some of the wealthier regions have complained about this, it is generally a way to enhance regional autonomy, since it frees regions from the pressures to spread indiscriminate subsidies before investors. There is a weaker commitment to maintain high standards of worker protection and welfare provision through the Social Chapter, which aims to combat what the Europeans call "social dumping" by competitive undercutting of the social costs of production. This does not provide a European welfare state but does sustain the conditions for the survival of national welfare states in their various forms. The EU also has a system of redistribution through the Structural Funds but, while these are now the second most important item in the budget, they amount to only 0.41 percent of GDP, falling to 0.31 percent in 2006 (Keating and Hooghe 2001). In any case, it is by no means clear how much of the money goes to the designated regions, rather than being kept by national governments as compensation for spending that they would have incurred in any case. European monetary union presents further problems by depriving governments of an instrument they could use to cope with asymmetrical shocks. While Europe will now have a single currency, it lacks the automatic stabilizers in the form of national taxation and spending programs which spread the burden of adjustment in federations like Canada and the United States.

Another problem is the "democratic deficit" that appears as policy-making is detached from national states and disappears into intergovernmental and public-private networks. A return to the integrated state is sometimes presented as the answer to this problem, bringing functional systems back in line with institutions of popular representation and accountability (Dahrendorf 2000). It is not, however, so easy to put the genies of globalization and decentralization back into the bottle. In any case, as Jáuregui (2000) notes, the old nation-state model achieved democracy within the state only at the cost of its complete denial in the international system. Democratic and accountable government is a complex matter, but there would seem to be two basic requirements. The first is the existence of deliberative spaces for the formation of a democratic will. I am assuming here, against the Public Choice school, that citizens' democratic preferences are not the mere sum of individual desires, which could be left to the market or to referendums, but result from deliberation and exchange. It is these deliberative spaces that need to correspond to a sense of common or shared identity, or to a *demos*, if not an exclusive one. The second requirement is a system of accountability corresponding to the areas of decision-making in the emerging functional systems. In a complex system with functional and territorial divisions, these can no longer always be done by the same institutions.

For example, the European Parliament is probably as good as most national parliaments (admittedly not a difficult test) in scrutinizing executive institutions and holding them to account. It does not, on the other hand, sustain a pan-European deliberative community or help form a pan-European democratic will. It probably never will, and possibly never should. We may therefore need to delink these activities. Accountability and scrutiny may take a variety of forms—audit, legal control, parliamentary investigation, adversary politics—and work at various levels. The extension of legal regulation and of the courts into more areas of social and economic life, deplored by many traditional democrats, may be a necessary concomitant of growing governmental complexity and fragmentation. The growth of human rights law is particularly important in this respect, both in Canada and in Europe.

Deliberative democracy and will formation can similarly occur at multiple levels. These may include national states, especially in the smaller and more homogeneous states of Europe. Elsewhere, the pressures for participation and democratization have favoured deliberative communities at the city level. This is notably the case in France, where decentralization has strengthened the local level as a political arena, and in Italy, where the crisis of the central state has coincided with a re-valorization of the local level. In other cases again, the deliberative community might be a large region, beyond a city but without the characteristics of a stateless nation. In the limiting cases, democratic will and identity may be located at a very small scale, as in the small communes of many countries, and are too small to correspond to any functional system. It is this extension and deepening of democracy in multiple arenas that I have referred to as plurinational democracy (Keating 2001*b*). These remarks are even more relevant outside Europe, where there is less by way of a transnational political or democratic order.

Finally, there are serious questions about equity. Social solidarity within regions may be undermined in a world where economic competitiveness is equated with a low-cost model of development and an emphasis on growth at all costs. On the other hand, this effect can be greatly exaggerated, since there is also evidence that the emerging regional spaces are also the basis for new forms of social solidarity. This may be especially true where there is a shared "national" or regional identity to underpin the idea of shared destiny, although such a shared destiny might in some circumstances be used to justify social discipline and subordination to supposed global market imperatives. More serious, perhaps, is the issue of inter-territorial equity in a world of weakened states. Rich regions no longer see the need to redistribute as a form of enlightened self-interest. Upper-tier governments, for their part, are less keen to act as conduits for intergovernmental transfers, either because they lack the resources or because they wish to take political credit for programs emerging from their own tax efforts. More broadly, some regions are well-equipped to compete in the new order, possessing economic resources and a degree of social and political organization enabling them to mount a coherent development project. Others face being reduced to new forms of dependence on both the state and the international market.

Conclusion

PROPONENTS OF THE END OF TERRITORY AND THE END OF HISTORY HAVE BEEN equally confounded. Space and time remain key elements of political structuring, even as their impact is modified by the new global context. Social science, growing up with, and in the framework of, the consolidated nation-state, has had difficulty in accommodating other forms of political order. Yet, in historical perspective, the consolidated nation-state was perhaps an interlude rather than the culmination of modernity. Complex forms, both functional systems and of legitimate authority, have been the norm in history. Social scientists have now produced a substantial body of work mapping the new forms of disaggregated power and authority in the modern polity, but we still lack a new paradigm to replace the old state-centric one. There is also a need for more work on the normative dimensions of the new complexity, and how to address the challenges both of functional efficiency and of multi-level democracy.

Notes

1 The term "periphery" is used in this literature in a rather general way, and is not confined to places at the territorial margins of the state.

2 With the exception of the United States, where the allocation of federal construction and military projects provided the wherewithall for territorial pork barrels.

3 The idea that the British Parliament does not have absolute sovereignty in Scotland was upheld in *MacCormick v. Lord Advocate* in 1953 but, while most Scots would agree with the proposition, it remained for many years little more than an intellectual curiosity.

4 His list of dynamic regions, apart from demonstrating a shaky grasp of geography, suggests that he has fallen for the propaganda of regional boosters in places like Wales. For the invention of Wales as a dynamic regional state, see Lovering (1999).

5 A term I borrowed from Harvie (1994) who uses it in a slightly different way.

6 There was also a bourgeois regionalist element in Quebec, especially under Liberal governments.

7 Interestingly, the argument, in Italy, Germany, Belgium and Spain as in Canada, is the same. Wealthy regions insist that they are not against solidarity in principle, they just want to know how much is being transferred and for the amount to be justified. The problem is that once transfers are truly transparent and have to be justified by reference to general principles, they become extremely difficult to sustain.

8 It is worth emphasizing this point, as there are still those who reduce nationalism to economic self-interest, claiming that Scots are interested only in North Sea oil, or Catalans in getting rid of the burden of transfer payments. Economic viability is a conditioning factor in nationalist movements, but it is not the prime cause, otherwise we would find them in other places.

9 There are still some Basque nationalists who cling to the ideas of Sabino Arana, with his ethnic and racial definition of Basqueness. Flemish nationalists have not embraced the immigrant community. In Quebec, as we know, civic nationalists are routinely embarrassed by outbursts of ethnic exclusiveness by fellow nationalists.

10 Again we are bedeviled by terminological problems here. There are those who insist that Quebec and Scotland are not stateless, since they have their own political institutions, albeit embedded within a federation or union. My point is that this is different from sovereign statehood in the classic mode. The debate on Quebec sovereignty is whether Quebec should shift from one to the other. If it further objected that the distinction has in practice been greatly eroded, then I can only agree.

11 There is a great deal of confusion about this. Porter (2001) seems to suggest that regions are indeed in competition but to conclude that somehow they can all win. This is to make the idea of competition meaningless.

12 There are Canadian examples such as the federal scholarship plan. One might also include in this category some of the smaller EU initiatives on urban and regional development.

13 This is managed not through the EU's regional policy, but through its competition policy. The relationship with EU regional policy remains problematic.

References

Badie, B. *La fin des territoires: Essai sur le désordre international et sur l'utilité sociale du respect.* Paris: Fayard, 1995.

Cooke, P. and K. Morgan. *The Associational Economy: Firms, Regions, and Innovation.* Oxford: Oxford University Press, 1998.

Cooke, P., P. Boekholt and F. Tödtling. *The Governance of Innovation in Europe: Regional Perspectives on Global Competitiveness.* London: Pinter, 1999.

Courchene, T. "Ontario as a North American Regional State." *Regional and Federal Studies*, Vol. 9, no. 3 (1999): 3-37.

________ *A State of Minds: Toward a Human Capital Future for Canadians*. Montreal: Institute for Research in Public Policy, 2001.

Dahrendorf, R. "La sconfitta della vecchia democrazia." *La Repubblica*, January 12, 2000.

Dente, B. "Federalismo e politiche pubbliche." In *Terzo rapporto sulle priorità nazionali. Quale federalismo per l'Italia*, ed. A. Martinelli. Milan: Fondazione Rosselli and Mondadori, 1997.

Elazar, D.J. *Exploring Federalism*. Tuscaloosa: University of Alabama Press, 1987.

Fundación Encuentro. *Informe España*, Vol. 5. Madrid: Fundación Encuentro, 1997.

Gagnon, A.-G. "Le Quebec, une nation inscrite au sein d'une démocratie étriquée." In *Repères en mutation : Identité et citoyenneté dans le Québec contemporain*, ed. J. Maclure and A.-G. Gagnon. Montreal: Québec Amérique, 2001.

Harvie, C. *The Rise of Regional Europe*. London: Routledge, 1994.

Herrero de Miñon, M. *Derechos Históricos y Constitución*. Madrid: Tecnos, 1998*a*.

________ "Estructura y Función de los Derechos Históricos: un problema y siete conclusiones." In *Foralismo, Derechos Históricos y Democracia*, ed. M. Herrero de Miñon and E. Lluch. Bilbao: Fundación BBV, 1998*b*.

Jáuregui, G. *La democracia planetaria*. Barcelona: Ariel, 2000.

Jellinek, G. *Fragmentos de Estado*, translation of *Uber Staatsfragmente*. Madrid: Civitas, 1981.

Keating, M. *State and Regional Nationalism: Territorial Politics and the European State*. London: Harvester-Wheatsheaf, 1988.

________ *The New Regionalism in Western Europe: Territorial Restructuring and Political Change*. Aldershot: Edward Elgar, 1998.

________ *Nations Against the State: The New Politics of Nationalism in Quebec, Catalonia and Scotland*, 2d ed. London: Macmillan, 2001*a*.

________ *Plurinational Democracy: Stateless Nations in a Post-Sovereignty Era*. Oxford: Oxford University Press, 2001*b*.

Keating, M. and J. McGarry, eds. *Minority Nationalism in the Changing State Order*. Oxford: Oxford University Press, 2001.

Keating, M. and L. Hooghe. "Bypassing the Nation-State? Regions in the EU Policy Process." In *European Union. Power and Policy-Making*, ed. J. Richardson. London: Routledge, 2001.

Lovering, J. "Theory Led by Policy: The Inadequacies of the 'New Regionalism'." *International Journal of Urban and Regional Research*, Vol. 23 (1999): 379-390.

MacCormick, N. *Questioning Sovereignty: Law, State and Nation in the European Commonwealth*. Oxford: Oxford University Press, 1999.

Nairn, T. *After Britain: New Labour and the Return of Scotland*. London: Granta, 2000.

Ohmae, K. *The End of the Nation State: The Rise of Regional Economies*. New York: Free Press, 1995.

Osiander, A. *The States System of Europe, 1640-1990: Peacemaking and the Conditions of International Stability*. Oxford: Clarendon, 1994.

Porter, M. "Regions and the New Economics of Competition." In *Global City-Regions: Trends, Theory, Policy*, ed. Allen J. Scott. New York: Oxford University Press, 2001.

Rokkan, S. and D. Urwin. *Economy, Territory, Identity: Politics of West European Peripheries*. London: Sage Publications, 1983.

Sassen, S. "Global Cities and Global City-Regions: A Comparison." In *Global City-Regions: Trends, Theory, Policy*, ed. Allen J. Scott. New York: Oxford University Press, 2001.

Scott, A. *Regions and the World Economy*. Oxford: Oxford University Press, 1998.

________ *Global City-Regions: Trends, Theory, Policy*. New York: Oxford University Press, 2001.

Spruyt, H. *The Sovereign State and Its Competitors*. Princeton: Princeton University Press, 1994.

Storper, M. *The Regional World: Territorial Development in a Global Economy*. New York: Guildford, 1997.

Tilly, C. *The Formation of National States in Western Europe*. Princeton: Princeton University Press, 1975.

________ *Coercion, Capital and European States, AD 990-1990*. Oxford: Blackwell, 1990.

Is Quebec a North American Region State? A Preliminary View

Introduction

Michael Keating's excellent paper on the transformation of the nation-state, especially in its "Regional State" and "Stateless Nation-Building" sections, struck me as particularly relevant to a topic on which I have some interest and knowledge, namely the recent evolution of Quebec. Drawing, in addition, from the work on Courchene and Telmer (1998) on the emergence of Ontario as a North American region state, I have centred my discussion on subnational communities and specifically on the evidence pointing in the direction of the emergence of Quebec as a North American region state.

My thesis is threefold: that Quebec's economic and political elites, with strong popular support, *wanted* Quebec to become a region state, that is, to act increasingly as an autonomous entity whether or not it became independent from Canada; that Quebec *needed* to become a region state in order to achieve optimal growth; and that it was further *pushed* into becoming a region state by virtue of the particular political context. In what follows, the principal emphasis will centre on the first two of these.[1]

Foreshadowing a Region State: The FTA and the GST

In the late 1980s and early 1990s, Quebec's elites made two macroeconomic decisions that prepared the way for the transformation to come and provided the first signal of their awareness of Quebec's need to become a region state operating in the North American Free Trade Agreement (NAFTA) economic space. The first of these was Quebec's bipartisan support for the Canada-US Free Trade Agreement (FTA) in the 1988 election. Intriguingly, at that point in time more of Quebec's exports were destined for the rest of Canada (and particularly Ontario) than to the rest of the world. Yet, Quebec's new entrepreneurs were enthusiastic in favouring free trade with the United States. Politically, as early as 1984, the then-premier, René Lévesque delivered a pro-FTA speech in the US. Later, Liberal Premier Robert Bourassa joined the free trade movement, even though the federal Liberals campaigned against the FTA. In the election of 1988, Quebec and Alberta were the only provinces to give an overwhelming majority of seats to Brian Mulroney's Conservatives, thus enabling the FTA to become a reality.

The second was the goods and services tax (GST). The Quebec Liberal government, supported by the Parti Québéçois opposition and the Quebec business class, quickly realized the comparative advantage arising from converting the Quebec provincial sales tax to a value-added tax (VAT). The export-neutral features of a VAT (or a GST) made Quebec's international exports that much more competitive. There was some loss of short-term revenue—about $2 billion—but this was seen as a critical investment in the expansion of exports, as well as a comparative advantage gained on Ontario, where this type of tax harmonization was and still is politically out of the question. Important to the conception and implementation of a region state, this combined provincial/federal GST is collected by Quebec.

International Exports: Time of Harvest

Spurred on by FTA/NAFTA and Quebec's GST, among other factors such as the fall in the value of the Canadian dollar, the international export expansion arrived. From figure 1, in 1989 Quebec's exports to the rest of Canada (ROC) exceed its international (ROW) exports. A decade later, Quebec's ROW exports were twice as large as its ROC or interprovincial exports. Indeed, by 2000, Quebec was the sixth most important trading partner of the US, larger than the United Kingdom, France, Germany, Brazil or Russia. As noted by Courchene and

Telmer (1998), Ontario's "cross-over" point (where international exports exceeded interprovincial exports) was roughly a decade earlier than Quebec's (1981 versus 1990) and Ontario now has a ROW-ROC ratio approaching three.

Table 1 presents further data on export trends for Quebec, Ontario and the all-provinces average. What is striking about Ontario and Quebec is the magnitude of the growth of their international exports in the decade of the 1990s. The provinces' average export growth is 180 percent. Quebec achieved 190 percent and Ontario 192 percent. Corrected for population growth, Quebec's performance surpasses that of Ontario: 173 percent versus Ontario's 153 percent. Furthermore, the change in both provinces' international trade ratio (relative to their gross domestic product [GDP]) is well above the all-provinces' average: 90 percent and 94 percent for Ontario and Quebec respectively, relative to 74 percent for all of Canada (row 4).

Row 5 compares the ROW-ROC ratios for 1989 and 1999. The all-provinces average value was 1.2 in 1988 and 1.9 a decade later. In 1989, Quebec's ratio was 0.9 (below the all-province average) whereas in 1999 the ratio is 2.1 (above the 1.9 all-provinces average) with Ontario's ratios being 1.3 and 2.9 respectively. However, the increases in the ratios for Quebec and for Ontario are fairly equal: 128 percent for Ontario, and 124 percent for Quebec, in comparison with an 85 percent for all-provinces' ratios (row 6). One should note in passing (although not presented in table 1) that the row 5 ratios for Newfoundland and British Columbia topped the numbers in 1989 and they remain among the top three in 1999. However, the decade of the 1990s did not "transform" the BC and Newfoundland economies in terms of the destination of exports since their ratios, although high, only increased by 18 and 13 percent respectively, far below the 85 percent increase for the all-provinces average. Nonetheless, this demonstrates that these criteria alone cannot be the bar for what constitutes a region state.

A final relevant set of observations from table 1 are the row 3 ratios of exports to GDP. Again Quebec goes from under the all-provinces ratio in 1989 (21 percent versus 29 percent) to slightly above it in 1999 (41 percent versus 40 percent) and as already noted, Quebec surpasses both Ontario and the provincial average in terms of the growth of exports over the decade (see row 4). Were one to combine ROC and ROW exports and express this as a percentage of GDP (as a definition of openness), Ontario and Quebec would rank fourth and fifth respectively in terms of countries of the Organisation for Economic Co-operation and Development.[2]

Quebec Exports, 1989–2000

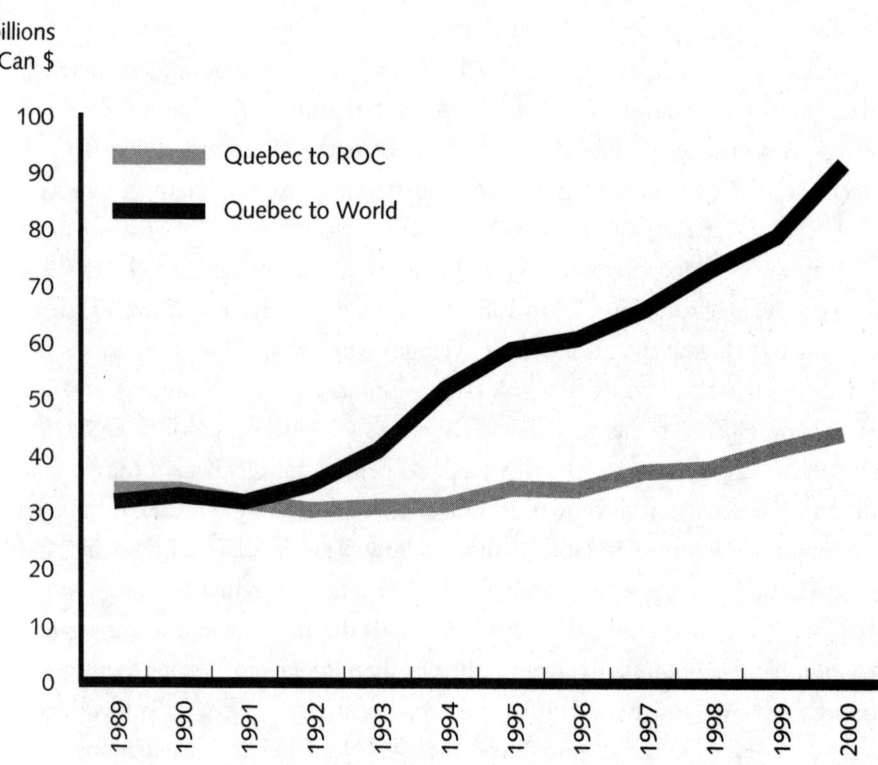

Source: Statistics Canada; Lisée (2001).

International Trade Trends, Provincial (or Canadian) average, Ontario and Quebec, 1989–2000

	Provincial Average	Ontario	Quebec
Growth of exports to the world	180%	192%	190%
Growth of exports to the world/per capita	152% (Canada)	153%	173%
Ratio 1989–2000 world exports/GDP	23/40%	29/54%	21/41%
Growth of world exports/ GDP ratio	74%	90%	94%
Ratio 1989–99 world exports/ROC exports	1.2/1.9	1.3/2.9	0.9/2.1
Growth of world exports/ ROC export ratio	85%	128%	124%

Notes: ROC = rest of Canada;
GDP = gross domestic product.

The *volume* of trade tells only part of the story, although an essential one. For Quebec, the *composition* of exports also changed dramatically. Raw materials exports have been overtaken by aerospace production and telecommunications, although both were hard hit by recent events. Quebec has moved from pulp and paper and aluminium (although remaining a world leader there) to building and selling fully one-half of all the civilian helicopters in the world. In the process, Quebec has become a a net importer of raw materials, to a greater extent than Ontario.

Interestingly, the structure of intra-industrial trade sets Quebec apart from its Canadian neighbours, and this can be viewed as a marker for region-state status. Pierre-Paul Proulx (1999) has shown that the intra-industrial commerce that Ontario (and the rest of Canada) have with the US outweighs their intra-industrial commerce with the rest of the world. In Quebec, the reverse is true, largely thanks to Quebec's greater European connections. Proulx (1999) writes that the history and role of Montreal and of Quebec as a transit point with Europe continues.

North-South Investment

IF THE FLOW OF GOODS IN QUEBEC SHIFTED FROM EAST-WEST TO NORTH-SOUTH IN THE 1990s, what can be said about the flow of cross-border investment? Data on investment are notoriously hard to break down into foreign and interprovincial private investment. However, relying on the set of acquisition figures compiled by Crosbie & Co. for its *Mergers & Acquisitions in Canada* series, we note (see figure 2)[3] that over the 1994–99 period (and especially from 1996 onward) the dollar value of Quebec-US acquisitions mushroomed relative to the Quebec-ROC value. While this trend held for all of Canada, it was more marked for Quebec.

Although Quebec's share of Canada's GDP is in the range of 22 percent, Quebec's share of US acquisitions reached 33 percent over this period. Even more striking, Quebec's share of Canadian acquisitions in the United States registered 49 percent. In part, this may be due to the fact that of the $63 billion of acquisitions in Canada and US made by Quebec corporations, 82 percent were in the US. Over the same period, US acquisitions in Quebec were almost three times as important as those from the rest of Canada ($27 billion versus $10 billion), a gap that is growing. This is further evidence that the Quebec economy is increasingly repositioning itself in North American economic space.

Acquisition Flows, to and from Quebec 1994–1999

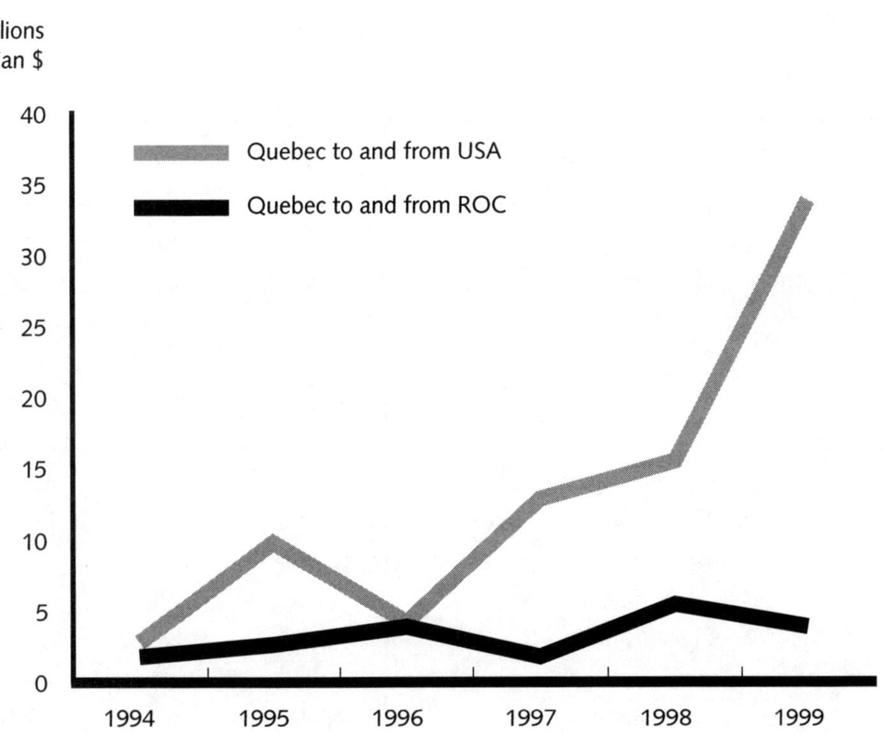

Source: Mergers & Acquisitions in Canada, MICQ; Lisée (2001).

Indicators/year	Rank		
	1	2	3
1 GDP Growth (1997–1998)	USA	France	Canada
2a Schooling level (postsecondary-96)	Canada	Quebec	USA
2b Schooling level (university-96)	USA	Quebec	Canada
3 Technological level (HighTech-96)	Japan	Quebec	France
4 Private R&D spending 97	USA	Japan	Germany
5 Private R&D staff 97	Japan	Germany	Quebec
6 Scientific + technical staff (97)	Japan	USA	Quebec
7 Investment, machinery + equipment (97)	Japan	Italy/USA	
8 Exports to GDP ratio (97)	Canada	Quebec	UK
9 Exports by technological level (96)	USA	UK	Japan
10 Number of patents (95)	USA	Japan	Germany
11 Industrial funding of univ. research (97)	Canada	Quebec	Germany
12 Education spending (95)	Quebec	Canada	USA
13 University research spending (97)	Quebec	Japan	Germany
14 Number of scientific publications (95)	Quebec	Canada	UK

* Missing data for some countries. Source: Conseil de la science et de la technologie du Quebec, *Rapport de conjoncture 2001: pour des régions innovantes*, mars 2001, p. 78.

Quebec's Position in the World—G7 Countries

4	5	6	7	8
Germany	Quebec	UK	Italy	Japan
UK/Germany		France	*	*
UK/Germany		France	*	*
USA	UK	Germany	Canada	*
France	Quebec	UK	Canada	Italy
France	Canada	UK	Italy	*
Germany	Canada	France	UK	Italy
France	Germany	UK	Canada	Quebec
Italy/France/Germany			USA	Japan
Quebec	France	Germany	Canada	*
Canada	France	UK	Italy	*
UK	USA/Italy		France	Japan
France	Germany	Japan/Italy		*
France/USA		UK	Canada	Italy
USA	France	Germany	Japan	Italy

Quebec in G7 Comparative Perspective

Although not usually viewed in global perspective, Quebec is becoming an economic powerhouse. Its GDP is the fifteenth largest in the world, the sixth in the Americas.[4] In the spring of 2001, the Conseil québécois de la science et de la technologie produced a report (*Rapport de conjoncture 2001: pour les régions innovantes*) that included table 2, which presents Quebec's per capita performance in G7 perspective in terms of 14 indicators of innovation. For eight of the 14 indicators, Quebec ranked in the top three, ahead of Canada as a whole. Only the US fared better. Obviously, Ontario would have fared very well in this exercise. However, Quebec's recent export transformation in the direction of a region state is being accompanied by a corresponding and more fundamental transformation of the Quebec economy in the direction of donning the mantle of a knowledge-based economy and society.

Conclusion

To date, much of the focus on Canada-Quebec relations has been couched in political terms: independence, sovereignty, etc. The purpose of this brief discussion has been to emphasize that Quebec is also maturing as an economic region state, one whose economic, trade and commercial linkages are of an international nature. Along with fellow region states like Lombardy, Catalonia, Baden-Wurttenberg and Scotland in Europe, and Ontario and perhaps BC and Alberta in Canada, these region states (or, in some case, stateless nations as well) will progressively complicate governance for their own central or federal states.

Notes

1 Aspects of the politics of Quebec's becoming a region state are dealt with in a related article (Lisée 2001) as well as the longer work from which both of these are drawn. Found under a similar title at www.vigile.net/auteurs/1/liseejf.htm

2 If we were to compare Ontario and Quebec's export ratios to other states, it would result with this listing for 1998:

	(%)		(%)
1. Luxembourg	91	Next G7 countries	
2. Ireland	80	18. Germany	29
3. Belgium	75	21. UK	27
4. ONTARIO	70	22. Italy	26
5. QUEBEC	57	23. France	26
6. Netherlands	55	28. USA	11
7. Austria	44	29. Japan	11
8. Canada	43		

3 These calculations were undertaken by Stéphane Comeau, Sylvain Carpentier and Christian Trudeau of the Ministère de l'Industrie et du Commerce du Québec, on the basis of *Mergers & Acquisitions in Canada* data. The merger and acquisition figures are not scientifically satisfactory because the values of a number of investments are not reported. However, they are reliable in terms of identifying trends. The values of acquisitions reported in figure 2 amount to 10 percent of the full amount of US direct investment in Canada and 17 percent of the full amount of Canadian direct foreign investment in the US, as compiled in Statistics Canada's *International investment position* figures, data unfortunately not broken down by province.

4 It is important to recognize the precise nature of this comparison: Quebec is being compared with other countries. Obviously, if the comparison also included other subnational jurisdictions such as New York, California, or Ontario, Quebec would be further down in the rankings.

References

Conseil de la science et de la technologie du Québec. *Rapport de conjoncture 2001: pour des régions innovante*, 2001. Available at www.cst.gouv.qc.ca/ftp/conjoncture2001/chap_3_ang.pdf.

Courchene, T.J. and C.R. Telmer. *From Heartland to North American Region State: The Social, Fiscal and Federal Evolution of Ontario.* Toronto: Rotman School of Business, distributed by University of Toronto Press, 1998.

Lisée, J.-F. "Is Quebec a North American Region State?" *Policy Options*, Vol. 22, no.10 (2001): 25-32.

Proulx, P.-P. *Les effets de l'Ale et de l'Aléna sur les économies canadiennes, québécoises et américaine: examen des études récentes.* Montreal: L'Institut de la statisque du Québec, 1999.

Discussion

SOME PARTICIPANTS INSISTED THAT GLOBAL CITIES, NOT REGION STATES, CONSTITUTE the important development in the new economy and that we have concentrated too much of our research efforts on the rise of region states. One commentator argued that Toronto, not Ontario, is the successful economic motor in the global economy and pointed to the economic problems of northern Ontario to make the case. This, in turn, prompted others to ask about multiple identities and one participant questioned, for example, whether people in Montreal consider themselves to be Montrealers first, or Quebecers, or Canadians.

Other participants asked whether supra or multinational institutions such as the European Community make it more or less desirable for regions to become an independent nation-state. For example, does the existence of the European Union make it less or more attractive for Scotland to be independent of Britain? The verdict: multinational organizations make it easier for regions to become independent, but it also makes it less necessary for them to become independent.

Several participants challenged the notion that the new economic order is breaking down traditional ties between have and needy regions. One European participant insisted that transfers from rich countries to needy ones still enjoy a priority status in Europe. She reported that one-third of the European budget is earmarked for a regional redistribution policy known as the "cohesion policy." Another argued that, in Canada, public opinion surveys reveal support for regional policies though some provincial governments may be raising questions about the continued viability of federal transfer payments. Yet it appears that Ontarians and Albertans remain committed to transfers from rich regions to needy ones.

Participants discussed at some length the role of Quebec in the Canadian federation, whether it had become a "stateless nation" and how economic growth played an important role in the national unity debate in Canada. One noted that the sovereignists insisted that economic growth was good for their cause because it would establish preconditions for sovereignty, that it would lower the government deficit, and ultimately give Quebecers confidence that they could build their own country. Federalists, meanwhile, insisted that economic growth was good for their cause because Quebecers would see that they would have more to lose if their province became independent. Some observers insisted that Quebec has already effectively attained nation-state status and that we ought not refer to Quebec as a "stateless nation." One participant, however, responded by asking what Quebec would look like after a successful referendum. He added "Quebec keeps having referenda about something. There is something that it is not but wants to be."

In his response to points made by participants, Jean-François Lisée agreed with the observation that global cities are now the key sites for value-added activities. He pointed to Montreal which, in economic terms, now represents half of the Quebec economy. With respect to identity, he reported that Anglo-Montrealers consider that they are Montrealers first, Canadians second, and Quebecers third. Regarding transfer payments, he insisted that it was still in the interests of have-regions to have neighbouring regions with strong economies.

Keating concluded his observations by pointing out that cities are increasingly important in the global economy. He explained: "We are seeing new regional development coalitions, territorial restructuring and new systems of regulations emerging at the urban level." Global cities, he added, should not be viewed strictly in economic terms. They are becoming the focus for new "democratic impulses" and "bases for political power."

International Governance and Canada

Citizens, States and International Regimes: International Governance Challenges in a Globalized World

Introduction: The Rising Crisis in Global Governance

THE TRAGIC DEATH OF CARLO GIULANI AT THE JULY 2001 GENOA G7/8 SUMMIT SENT shock waves throughout civil society, international organizations and governments. The young demonstrator became the first victim of the sustained and growing conflict between elements of civil society and official international governance. Symptoms of this global governance crisis have become common front-page news since the Seattle events of December 1999. Indeed, the street blockade strategy was used for the first time in Seattle, leading to hostilities that have since been repeated in the streets of Washington, Prague, Nice, Quebec City, Genoa and many other cities. But the processes that led to these events were initiated long before that; the first examples of the disconnect between economic governance processes and civil society were apparent in the debates that surrounded the negotiation of the North American Free Trade Agreement (NAFTA) in 1993, and in the last stages of negotiations of the failed attempt to conclude a Multilateral Agreement on Investment (MAI) in 1998.

In all those cases, civil society groups used the new information technologies and a growing sense of citizen awareness in western countries to successfully mobilize wide networks of activists and significant portions of public opinion against economic liberalization. Governments and international organizations have responded to that challenge in two ways. The first strategy has been to open channels of dialogue with civil society at various levels, supported by a systematic approach attempting more transparency and tentative participation of civil society organizations in international negotiations. A second reaction has been the establishment of a siege mentality: it pushed host governments in the direction of establishing larger security perimeters surrounded by fences and thousands of anti-riot police forces. More recently, it appears to be evolving into the hosting of international meetings in remote areas where public dissent cannot effectively take place.

It is perfectly legitimate and appropriate for host governments to use the means necessary to ensure the security of heads of states and members of delegations against assaults from highly organized and violent anarchist groups. These groups have shown that they are willing and able to take over otherwise impressively peaceful and sometimes joyful gatherings of street dissent. One casualty here is the normal, democratic and often constitutionally protected collective voicing of dissenting opinion, disrupted initially by the actions of these anarchist groups and often later by the consequential repression by public security forces.

Clearly this phenomenon poses a fundamental challenge to our democratic institutions. As already noted, temporary solutions have taken the form of hosting meetings in remote areas (Doha - Kananaskis): longer term solutions will require a deeper analysis of the causes of the malaise affecting global governance. In the interim, the hyper-polarization has given way to mass media coverage concentrating essentially on the violence-repression aspect of the interaction between civil society and the international institutional structures. In turn, this focus masks the fundamentals of what is really going on in western democratic societies. The voices of dissent are expressing concern about a variety of social, economic, environmental, human rights and equity issues that usually take the route of participation in open and transparent processes in domestic, democratic institutions. If international gatherings of governments cannot address and be seen to address these issues, they will lose domestic public opinion support essential to further trade liberalization.

The role of this paper is to attempt to identify strategies to resolve the current crisis through the integration of global governance into a coherent scheme and through the development of meaningful channels for civil society participation. In order to arrive at these strategies, we begin by defining the concept of governance and its relevance as a conceptual framework for analyzing and understanding the current crisis. We then direct attention to the implications of globalization on and among citizens, states and international regimes which in turn provides the needed theoretical and practical backdrop to address the above-mentioned strategies.

A snapshot of global governance in 2001

Governance can be defined broadly as a "framework of rules, institutions and established practices that set limitations and give incentives for the behaviour of individuals, organizations and firms" (UNDP 1999, 8). Operationally, governance is a dynamic, interactive, multi-centred and integrative concept that builds both on formal and informal structures and power relationships (Commission on Global Governance 1995, 8). As a result, global governance is a moving target to the analyst, and any analysis of the concept is merely a snapshot of global governance at a given point in space and time.

It is useful at the outset to differentiate between governance and government, in order to understand the tension between the two concepts that is at the core of the current crisis. Governance is a far more flexible and dynamic form of power than is government, since it is based on changing patterns of social behaviour and transversal power relationships. This is in contrast to the classical Weberian conception of government which is static and organized along vertical lines of control (Von Moltke 2001*a*). As a result of this rigidity, governments adapt with difficulty to the changing governance environment, especially in periods of rapid change and transition.

Along the lines of David McGuinty (2001) and Thomas Courchene (2001), the current changing nature of global governance lies in a series of three concerted, non-mutually-exclusive shifts of power: upwards to powerful economic actors, downwards to local authorities and civil society, and laterally through the development of networks. Nation-states are therefore currently facing the challenge of adapting their practices and institutional structure to this dynamic change in the paradigm of global governance, from a Westphalian, state-centred system to an information age, multi-centred system.

This picture of global governance at the beginning of the twenty-first century allows one to understand the tensions that have been building over the last decade in the triangular relationship between the nation-state, civil society and international regimes. In order to begin the process of designing innovative solutions to the current challenges of governance, it is necessary to gain a deeper understanding of the underlying forces that are shifting its patterns.

States, Citizens and Regimes in a Globalized World: Players in the New Governance Paradigm

THE PHENOMENON OF GLOBALIZATION HAS BEEN DESCRIBED IN SOME DETAIL ELSEWHERE (Johnson 2000*b*; Courchene 2001), so we will limit our analysis of this process to understanding how its underlying forces impact on the structure of global governance. The core drivers of globalization are trade and investment on the economic side, and the development of information and network technologies on the scientific side. These two fundamental changes, combined with increased movements of population, are contributing to the porosity of borders and the creation of a new social fabric which is empowering transnational networks. In addition, globalization is accompanied by social inequities and environmental externalities that require strong collective intervention. As a consequence, it is empowering international regimes and raising substantive issues of wealth distribution and environmental protection in a context of international relations over which traditional democratic political constructs have little bearing.

The socio-economic forces unleashed by globalization have profoundly changed the roles of the main players in the global governance system. These players are rapidly adapting to this new governance context and in the process are elaborating innovative and flexible strategies to address both substantive and procedural issues that are being forced onto the democratic political agenda. The following section will assess the impacts that globalization has had on three fundamental players in governance: citizens, nation-states and international regimes.

The rise of an international civil society

The changing role of the citizen in the globalized governance system is closely linked to the perception of the evolving roles of the nation-state and international regimes. As a socio-political actor, the citizen seeks to maximize his or her interest by participating in democratic decision-making. Citizens therefore want to influence societal orientations that bear upon their real or perceived interests, based on objective or suggestive assessments of the impacts of globalization on their daily lives. Several recent phenomena have transformed the perceptions of citizens and their capacity to articulate their interests and to voice them in an organized fashion. This is particularly true in the developing world where more than a hundred developing countries and countries in transition have abandoned military or one-party rule during the past ten years (UNDP 2001), thereby allowing citizens to express their interests and participate in domestic and international governance. In the developed world, many factors come together to transform the classic citizenry into a global civil society; immediate and cheap access to communications have allowed the development of powerful transborder lateralities among actors of globalization.

The declining confidence in the state. Intensification and deepening of globalization over the last 15 years has generated many phenomena that have contributed to modifying citizens' perception of the state and international regimes. First and foremost, the nation-state has faced a vertical loss of sovereignty; it has delegated some of its sovereignty to international regimes in an upward fashion and, in a downward fashion, has done the same in favour of local entities in the context of both the fiscal crisis and the implementation of the subsidiarity concept in most countries of the Organisation of Economic Co-operation and Development (OECD) (Johnson 2000*b*). Combined with this loss of sovereignty, the voluntary restraint of state intervention as a result of the adoption of the neoliberal economic doctrine has led the state to lose influence in terms of traditional socio-economic management. For significant segments of the population, this has nurtured a sense of loss of relevancy of state activism and interventionism. This declining confidence in the state, combined with a growing awareness of the need for public participation in governance, has fuelled the development of an extensive civil society (World Commission on Global Governance 1995, 23).

The end of the permissive consensus. As globalization intensifies, citizens have been increasingly affected by international events and decisions taken within the framework of international regimes. For example, the 1997–98 Asian financial crisis had a direct impact on the commodities markets and affected many sectors of the Canadian economy, including the Canadian currency. More recently, the

September 11, 2001 terrorist attacks sent shockwaves through world financial markets and affected civil aviation and tourist and insurance industries worldwide. In both cases, the net result for citizens has been increased socio-economic and political insecurity. In addition, several core values shared by citizens in many jurisdictions are increasingly affected as international regimes deepen and enter into sensitive areas of public policy such as culture, agriculture or services.

Not surprising, this constellation of factors is raising issues of legitimacy, transparency and accountability in international policy-making; the traditional *permissive consensus* that used to characterize international economic governance is eroding. Sylvia Ostry (2000) argues that such a permissive consensus existed for decades in the post-World War II era. During that period nation-states benefited from strong public support in favour of foreign policy and trade policy, allowing them significant leverage and flexibility in international negotiations. The erosion of this traditional support creates a new context that calls for replacing this *permissive consensus* with a *participatory consensus*.

The development of networks. The 1990s have also seen tremendous technological change, especially in the field of information and network communications. The rise of the Internet and the development of telecommunications have greatly reduced the costs of international communications and have made them available to the masses. For example, a data transfer that used to cost $150,000 in 1970 cost only 12¢ in 1999. Sending a 40-page document from Chile to Kenya costs $50 by courier, $10 by fax and less than 10¢ by email (UNDP 2001). This phenomenon, combined with movements of populations that are unprecedented in human history, is creating a new context for the development of transnational social movements.

The development of information technologies and the decreasing costs of networking have been fundamental drivers in the transformation of national citizenries into a truly global civil society that is informing and shaping the new governance context. Indeed, as Curtis (2000) argues, horizontal networks tend to replace classic hierarchical democratic networks in the new information age. Consequently, the number of civil society organizations (CSOs) has risen from 6,000 to 26,000 in the last decade of the twentieth century (Keohane and Nye 2000). These structural changes have produced a better-educated, more informed and highly networked citizenry which is perfectly able to understand the causal links between international events undertaken in remote centres of decision and their local impacts. Furthermore, citizens have also augmented their capacity to articulate clearly their interests and to organize at the international level through CSOs and specialized networks.

In the words of Peter Drucker (1989, 204-205), the new international civil society has the potential for generating new bonds of community and for creating new spheres of citizenship. Ensuring transparency, legitimacy and accountability of states and international regimes are high on the agenda of international civil society. Thus far, international governance processes have not been able to satisfactorily integrate this movement, perhaps because international regimes and nation-states are themselves undergoing profound globalization-triggered transformations.

The changing nature of the nation-state

The nation-state used to be the central, unique, almost omnipotent player of the old Westphalian world order. In a similar manner, the classic Weberian nation-state used to exert rigid hierarchical control within its own borders. These characteristics of the state are still operating, but they now face new challenges as the world becomes multi-centred and horizontal networks shape internal and international dynamics alongside the traditional hierarchical lines of control. The state is rapidly adapting to these new conditions and its role in the new world governance system is profoundly altered by this changing nature.

The transformation of the Weberian model. The classic Weberian model of the nation-state, inspired by the functioning of the Prussian army, was based on hierarchically defined lines of command and a powerful bureaucratic capacity to treat information in a systematic way in order to circumscribe issues and define adequate strategies through compartmented administrative structures. It is now impossible to isolate and control issues within clearly delimited geographical or administrative borders. Consequently, state control must now be developed in partnership with local authorities, the private sector, communities and civil society. Whereas the nation-state used to assert direct control within its borders, it now needs to act as a leader and a convenor by using a series of innovative tools and strategies (Clarkson 2000*b*, 10).

The increased pace of change and rising uncertainties also entail a transition from the traditional command and control approach to an adaptation and resilience strategy. This new flexibility in socio-economic management must be built on horizontal networks, partnerships and stake-holding by a diversity of actors. State flexibility and institutional resilience relies on the capacity to treat information and to adapt to changing circumstances, two aspects that point to the importance of human resources in information-age organizations. But, as Curtis (2000) points out, as the world was becoming more complex in the 1990s, governments were downsizing and reducing their capacity to treat information and understand this complexity. It is clear that states are still experiencing a transitional period and are building new capacities at the same time that they are reforming and downsizing their Weberian structures.

Decentralization and the rise of subnational entities. The decentralization of the modern state is the result of two concurring pressures: the fiscal crisis that pushed central governments to delegate responsibilities to subnational entities and local governments on the one hand, and the associated pressures with a globalized economy favouring subsidiarity. Indeed, adaptation to the world economy requires specific strategies for each economic region. In addition, regions and major cities are now interacting directly on the world scene without necessarily using the traditional interstate interface. This profoundly alters the distribution of power and responsibilities within nation-states. This phenomenon also challenges uniformity and calls for more flexibility in the development of subnational socio-economic strategies.

As a federal and decentralized state, Canada is a clear example of this phenomenon. This new context calls for new cooperative strategies in Canadian federalism that recognize the expertise of all levels of government and allow for a flexible interpretation of constitutional jurisdictions. Moreover, Courchene (2001) makes the point that the different economic conditions of the various regions in Canada calls for decentralization and asymmetry.

The end of the Westphalian paradigm: an opportunity for middle-sized powers? The post-Westphalian global governance both places constraints and provides opportunities for a middle-sized country like Canada. While the state is confronted with a loss of control both internally and externally, the rise of a multicentred world offers opportunities to build influence and assert leadership through coalition-building. Indeed, as Clarkson (2000*b*, 6) argues, the loss of internal sovereignty can be compensated with increased influence on global governance. Canada has long been supporting multilateralism in international regimes as a way of promoting its interests and compensating for the overwhelming power of its southern neighbour. The new global governance context allows it to identify specific niches and become a leader or convenor in specific issue-areas. Examples of this are the campaign to ban land-mines and the Canadian leadership at the last Summit of the Americas.

Middle-sized countries like Canada see their influence and leadership enhanced by the development of a multi-centred world. In addition, strong regimes protect middle-sized countries from the consequences of unilateral, arbitrary action by stronger players in world governance. Consequently, Canada has a long-standing interest in the orderly, coherent expansion of multilateral regimes and global governance systems. International regimes are becoming key elements of global governance in this new context.

The extension and deepening of international regimes

The rise of international trade in goods and services and the exponential growth of foreign direct investment (FDI) in recent years were made possible through the development of an extensive economic regime, supported by numerous bilateral and multilateral agreements. Stephen Krasner defines regimes as a set of implicit or explicit principles, norms, rules and decision-making procedures around which actors' expectations converge (1983). The strongest and most extensively developed regime is the trade, investment and macroeconomic-management complex which is centred on the General Agreement on Tariffs and Trade (GATT)-World Trade Organization (WTO) system and the Bretton Woods institutions. As it extended and deepened its field of application over the last decade, the regime has been facing increasing criticism from developing nations and western civil society.

The deepening of the global economic regime. The economic regime that was created half a century ago was initially focused on reducing tariffs and supporting the post-World War II reconstruction and macroeconomic restructuring effort. The World Bank, International Monetary Fund (IMF), OECD, GATT and several other regional agreements and institutions were created in that context. Over the next half-century, these regimes slowly extended to new areas of economic policy and increasingly brought nation-states to impose upon themselves limits to the exercise of their own sovereignty. This is especially true in the field of trade policy which was first concentrated on tariff structures and involved trade-offs between sectors of the economy. As trade policy moved into the field of non-tariff barriers to trade and the regulatory systems of nation-states, it started to erode national sovereignty and to impact more directly on societies (Ostry 1997). Nowadays, as international trade policy moves into such issues as investment, services, agriculture or culture, it is reaching the very core of national sovereignty and involving major societal choices that need to build on democratic processes.

The Uruguay Round package, which contained the Agreement on Trade-Related Aspects of Intellectual Property Rights (TRIP), the General Agreement on Trade in Services (GATS), the Agreement on Sanitary and Phytosanitary Measures (SPS), and the Agreement on Agriculture, penetrated deeper into domestic policy than any other economic agreement in history. As Dymond and Hart argue: "Taken together these agreements, combined with the positive obligation to ensure conformity with WTO rules, the new powerful dispute settlement system, and the trade policy review mechanism, institutionalize a degree and intensity of intervention into domestic governance which exceeds anything possible or contemplated under the GATT" (2000, 23-24).

The constitutionalization of trade law. These legally binding agreements, in tandem with their dispute-resolution panels, are considered by many as an embryonic world economic constitution with which nation-states need to comply. Many observers emphasize the fact that the appointed panels are in effect making law by interpreting ambiguous trade rules, thereby redefining the frontiers of national sovereignty (Ostry 2000).

It is understandable in that context that trade policy is encountering more and more opposition from civil society which characterizes this new economic constitution as suffering from a democratic deficit and as imposing unacceptable limitations on the state's capacity to protect health, the environment and social programs. On the other hand, some analysts argue that this legal framework does not affect nation-states' overall capacity to regulate and intervene in these matters, but only that it places constraints on the nature and design of the instruments that can be used legally. This field is still open to debate, and interesting further evidence can be found in an analysis of the investment regime.

The challenges of investment regimes. Bilateral and multilateral treaties on investment, which have been proliferating in recent years, also raise contentious issues related to the deepening of economic regimes. In the last decade, the number of Bilateral Investment Treaties (BITs) quintupled from 385 to 1,857 (Peterson 2001). The overarching objective of investment treaties is to create a stable and predictable environment for investing in foreign countries, especially in developing countries where transnational corporations (TNCs) have regularly been confronted with discriminatory or arbitrary practices. However, these agreements seem to infringe on nation-states' legitimate regulatory capacity, a perception that is largely responsible for the overwhelming opposition to the MAI in 1998. In fact, BITs have raised so many concerns that some have argued in favour of the negotiation of a framework convention on investment outside the WTO or OECD frameworks. This convention would establish general principles on investment and BITs would fall under its umbrella (Von Moltke 2001*b*).

BITs build on classic GATT rules such as the most-favoured nation, national treatment and non-discrimination principles. In addition, they include a series of rights that are designed to protect investors from discriminatory and unfair practices by host governments. In the case of NAFTA's chapter 11 on investment, these provisions include a corporate investor-state litigation procedure and a global protection against state measures that are tantamount to expropriation. These much-criticized provisions have generated a growing number of private challenges to environmental regulations in Canada, Mexico and the United States. As a result of these challenges, governments have faced the obligation of compensating corporations for enacting environmental regulations.[1]

According to many analysts, this has led governments to reconsider the introduction of new regulations they feared would be challenged by corporations. Signs of this *regulatory chill* can already be observed in governments, according to the proponents of this analysis. This situation is even more unacceptable for civil society since litigations are conducted under strict secrecy and do not provide for the consideration of independent environmental expertise. Acknowledging the existence of this problem, the three parties to NAFTA issued an interpretive statement to the chapter 11 provisions in July 2001 that restricts the possibility for private corporations to initiate litigation against states, and somewhat improves the overall transparency of the process.[2]

The economic regimes' effective capacity to regulate the global market. In addition to concerns raised by the deepening of economic regimes, the issue of the capacity of national and international economic regulatory frameworks to effectively manage an increasingly globalized world economy is also questioned by many observers. For example, a recent WTO report (2001) questioned the capacity of the current regime to maintain competitive markets in the context of the increasing size and number of cross-border mergers. Many are also questioning the capacity of an overburdened and under-resourced WTO to support the implementation of Uruguay Round agreements in the developing world, a situation that raises serious concerns about the capacity of developing countries to effectively implement their commitments of the last round before entering into a new one.

But it is probably in the financial sector that the weakness of national and international regulatory frameworks is causing the most concern. Both the 1994 peso crisis and the 1997–98 Asian financial crisis raised serious concerns about the stability of international financial markets. The UNCTAD *Trade and Development Report* (2001) observes that a strengthening of international financial regulatory systems is essential in order to reduce the threat of financial crises. In that context, recent work by the G20[3] under the leadership of Canada constitutes an encouraging step in the direction of improved financial governance and stability.[4] These observations all point to the need to consolidate and strengthen international economic regimes before continuing their deployment.

Imbalances between the implementation of trade and non-trade regimes. The last criticism raised about international regimes is the imbalanced implementation of trade and non-trade instruments. Parallel to the deepening and extending of the legally binding economic regime, several other non-legally-binding regimes have been built over the last 50 years in the fields of human rights, social development, environment, culture and many others. The elaboration of action plans and declarations was especially intense during the 1990s with seven world summits and conferences on issues ranging from children to human settlement (Johnson 2000*b*). Yet the commitments taken under these regimes are characterized by poor implementation, insufficient resources and low-grade political attention. For example, the UN plan to fight AIDS in Africa would require $10 billion in funding, a sum equivalent to only ten days of agricultural subsidies in dollar terms (Moore 2001*c*). This example highlights the different levels of priority given to economic and non-economic regimes in the current governance framework.

The global environmental regime is the most extensively developed of these regimes, with more than 500 multilateral environmental agreements (MEAs), including 323 of regional scope (UNEP 2001*b*). Overall, implementation of environmental conventions remains weak and the resources devoted to the sustainable development regime are insufficient to reverse current trends of environmental degradation. In addition, 20 MEAs currently in force include trade-related measures (Ciuriak 2000), a situation that raises serious concerns about the coherence and relationship between the trade and environmental regimes (Johnson 2000*b*). While trade policy is not the appropriate place to deal with environmental issues, it has become clear that progress on sustainable development will only be possible through coherent and concerted action between the two regimes.

The imbalanced world governance system currently fails to deliver significant results in areas other than economic, trade and investment policy. In order to meet the broader challenges of global governance, including environmental protection, trade policy should not hinder the development of other regimes, nor should it take precedence over other legitimate, democratically determined, social and environmental objectives. The challenge then is to integrate world governance and open new channels for the expression of democratic participation in the international arena. This is the challenge we address in the remainder of the paper.

Strengthening World Governance: Integration and Participation

THE DEVELOPMENT OF THE GLOBAL GOVERNANCE SYSTEM RAISES TWO DISTINCT, interrelated challenges at the start of this new century. The first one is the consolidation of existing regimes, in terms of institutional coordination, substantive coherence and capacity for implementation. The second is the series of democratic and procedural issues raised by the need to involve civil society in the various regimes and instruments that comprise the global governance system. The crisis of global governance, which has been expressed in the streets of so many cities, finds its source in the incapacity of existing regimes to deliver in terms of socio-economic development and non-economic issues such as environmental protection. There is also the failure of these regimes to integrate the powerful networks of civil society in their decision-making and consensus-building processes. Since we appear to be entering a pause in regime creation, the context is ripe for the consolidation of existing instruments and the identification of new strategies that will rebuild bridges between civil society, nation-states and regimes in the form of a *participatory consensus*.

The consolidation of regime structure: environment and economy

The parallel and extensive development of the economic and environmental regimes over the last 15 years, as well as the numerous linkages between them have made the environment-economy nexus a complex governance challenge. It is characterized by the imbalance between a fragmented, under-resourced and low implementation environmental regime and a strong, deepening, legally-binding economic regime. To address this situation, two interrelated strategies must be developed: consolidate the environmental regime and build stronger inter-regime coherence and cooperation.

Intra-regime consolidation: integrating environmental governance. The global environmental regime has grown step by step over the last 30 years, with a significant acceleration in the last 15 years. As noted above, there are now more than 500 MEAs in force in the world (UNEP 2001*a*) and it is estimated that the number of bilateral agreements could be higher than 1,000 (Von Moltke 2001*a*). In addition, there are 30 bodies in the United Nations system with some environmental component to their mandates, including such agencies as the World Meteorological Organization (WMO), the World Health Organization (WHO) and the Food and Agriculture Organization (FAO).[5]

The fact that the environmental regime is so diversified, fragmented and complex is both an asset and a liability for environmental governance. The environmental regime was built to respond to specific environmental issues which are in most cases specialized and transversal in nature, therefore requiring comprehensive collective action integrating CSOs, the academic community and the private sector. The current regime structure thus allows better adaptability and focused intervention (Von Moltke 2001*a*; Le Prestre 2001). This is not to say, however, that there is no place for increased inter-convention coordination. Linkages and coordination must definitely be built in this constellation of instruments and organizations and it now appears that environmental governance needs to be given a more integrated and coherent structure.

The architecture of global environmental governance has become a major theme of the upcoming World Summit on Sustainable Development (WSSD), to be held in Johannesburg, South Africa in 2002. Supporting this orientation, the Malmö Declaration of the Global Ministerial Environmental Forum (May 2000) suggested that the WSSD "should review the requirements for a greatly strengthened institutional structure for international environmental governance based on an assessment of future needs for an institutional architecture that has the capacity to effectively address wide-ranging environmental threats in a globalizing world" (UNEP 2001*a*, 27).[6]

MEAs are the primary instruments on which the environmental governance system is built. Many question the effectiveness of this myriad of decentralized instruments and have proposed the creation of a global environmental organization (GEO) to integrate MEAs into a single framework. Others suggest that the current governance system is adequate and would not be strengthened by such an attempt at centralization. Le Prestre (2001) argues that MEA regimes, or as he calls them, convention governance systems (CGS), constitute the optimal instrument around which the environmental governance system should be built. In his view, CGS are

> adaptive and innovative responses to the complexity of environmental challenges and the evolution of international politics … In particular, they can play a key role in enhancing transparency of implementation and compliance efforts, building policy capacity, developing issue-networks, establishing a set of coherent knowledge, reducing competitive pressures among UN organizations, fostering convergence between international expectations and local practices, facilitate reconciliation of government priorities, and foster learning and regime change (Le Prestre 2001).

Indeed these are key functions of the MEAs governance system. However, some argue that compliance mechanisms must be strengthened to improve their effectiveness.

A key strategy to strengthening the global environmental regime is to improve inter-convention and inter-institutional collaboration on issues such as research, reporting or joint implementation among other areas. The Millennium Global Ecosystem Assessment is an example of the potential of such cooperation. Under this initiative, UNEP, UNDP, the World Bank, the World Resources Institute and other organizations have collaborated in the realization of one of the most ambitious environmental scientific ventures in history. Data and knowledge institutions gained in that project will feed into the work on environmental governance for years.

UNEP (2001*b*, 5) has developed an innovative approach to inter-convention collaboration by dividing environmental instruments into five clusters: the biodiversity-related conventions, the atmosphere conventions, the land conventions, the chemical and hazardous waste convention and the regional seas conventions and related agreements. Grouping the conventions in such clusters eases the identification of possible cooperative activities and allows for the generation of synergies. UNEP remarks that the best inter-convention cooperation has been observed in the biodiversity and regional seas clusters. Also, it seems that there has been a remarkable rise in the number of memoranda of understanding signed between the MEAs' secretariat in the last two years (UNEP 2001*a*). These types of collaborations will likely multiply over the next decade.

Capacity-building is another strategy that needs to be placed at the centre of the environmental governance system in order to realize intra-regime consolidation.

It needs to become the *modus operandi* at all levels of the environmental regime. This means first and foremost building institutional capacity at the state level for the implementation of environmental conventions. In addition, attention should be given to the issue of coordinating implementation of MEAs at the national level, in order to generate synergies and efficiencies in a context of scarce financial and institutional resources. In that regard, OECD countries must provide sufficient financial resources to developing countries to allow them to implement these agreements.

For developing countries, capacity-building in the implementation of the environmental regime is not only a critical approach to protecting the global commons and building national regulatory frameworks to protect the national resource base, but, as well, it constitutes a key strategy to fight poverty. There are two ways in which the environmental regime is an effective tool for alleviating poverty. The first is through the environment-health nexus where significant progress can be made in the sanitary field, through water treatment and sanitation, the reduction of pollution sources and the elimination of hazardous substances. A global improvement of public health is surely one of the key basic elements of development.

The second is that the environmental regime can be an effective tool to combat poverty by introducing better practices for the sustainable and equitable management of natural resources. The Convention to Combat Desertification constitutes the best example of this environment-development approach. Indeed, this convention adopts an integrated approach to environmental protection and poverty alleviation as a means to reverse the downward spiral of poverty and environmental degradation. As a result, the convention is a key instrument for both development and environmental protection since it establishes a framework to provide an integrated strategy for the social, economic and environmental development of local dryland communities.

The environmental regime needs to catch its breath after 15 years of frantic expansion. A pause is needed in the development of this regime to consolidate institutions and processes, to tie loose ends and to plan orderly and harmonious future development. If the 1990s was the decade of regime development, this decade should be one of regime consolidation and implementation. The WSSD therefore generates great expectations and will have to deliver significant integrative reforms backed by strong commitments in order to succeed.

Inter-regime cooperation: the economy-environment nexus. The articulation of the trade-investment and environmental regimes into a coherent and balanced governance structure constitutes a daunting, yet inevitable challenge. Massive amounts of literature have addressed the impacts of trade on the environment (Nordstrom and Vaughan 1999) and the issue of the articulation between the WTO and environmental instruments (Johnson 2000*b*). Several authors have also analyzed how regional trade agreements such as NAFTA address the trade-environment nexus.

Trade policy is certainly not the place to address environmental issues, yet the cross-cutting and far-reaching impacts of trade and investment regimes render their adaptation necessary to make them compatible with the objectives of sustainable development. In fact, it is becoming essential to develop a strong interface between the two regimes to address the trade and environment agenda. Several substantive and procedural issues need to be addressed in that context. They can be summarized in terms of the following five sets of issues:[7]

> *Environmental Regulations.* Many developing countries consider environmental regulations as green protectionism applied by OECD countries. The trade and investment regimes need to draw the line between what constitutes non-trade barriers to trade or discriminatory practices and what is in intent and practice a legitimate intervention to protect human health and the environment. In order to do so, it applies provisions requiring, among other things, that such interventions be based on sound science and constitute the least-trade-restrictive measures available. This approach is under increased pressure as it also raises issues of sound science, risk assessment and precaution. This pressure was observed in the biotech industry over the last five years as the biosafety protocol was being negotiated. Tensions are also observed between eco-certification processes and trade provisions that forbid distinctions between like-products on the basis of production processes and methods (PPMs). Clearly the trade regime will need environmental expertise to establish appropriate distinctions and to establish credible and legitimate criteria to address these issues.

Economic Instruments. The market economy is generating important externalities in the form of environmental degradation. The use of economic instruments is fundamental in reversing these negative trends. A series of triple-win strategies is available, that is, strategies that would benefit trade liberalization, environmental protection and development such as the removal of trade-distorting, environmentally damaging subsidies in the fisheries sector, or the liberalization of trade in environmental services. In addition, many MEAs are using trade-related provisions to implement their regime, a situation that raises issues of compatibility between the environmental and trade regimes. For example, the Montreal Protocol on Substances that Deplete the Ozone Layer provides for trade sanctions to be adopted against countries that are not complying with the convention. Again, this points to the need for a rapprochement between the two regimes.

Intellectual Property. TRIPs, designed to protect intellectual property, have supported the patenting of biological diversity, including seeds and plants. The articulation of this regime with the Convention on Biological Diversity raises problems of equity, sharing of benefits, and the protection of traditional knowledge since many cases of so-called bio-piracy have been reported. The long-term challenge here is to build a regime that will allow the sustainable and equitable exploitation of biological diversity, will bring benefits to local populations and biodiversity rich developing countries and will protect traditional cultures.

Inter-Regime Coherence and Articulation. As the number of potential conflicts between the trade-investment and the environmental regimes rises, the need to clearly articulate their relationship is becoming more urgent. So far, this relationship has been dealt with on a case-by-case basis. For example, NAFTA establishes the paramountcy of measures taken pursuant to a list of MEAs over its trade provisions. The biosafety protocol, which considers a series of trade issues in the biotechnology sector, has an equal "and mutually supportive" relationship with trade agreements. The WTO founding texts are silent on this issue. In this context, the risk of a collision between the two regimes is rising.

Procedural Issues. A series of procedural issues also arises in the articulation of the two regimes. Among the most pressing of these issues is the need to establish a forum that would integrate trade and environmental policy and include the expertise of the WTO, MEA secretariats, UNEP, states, CSOs and the private sector. The International Institute for Sustainable Development and the International Union for the Conservation of Nature and Natural Resources have proposed the creation of a standing conference on trade and environment.[8] In the Americas, a proposal has been put forward to create a Hemispheric Roundtable on Trade and Environment to generate policy options for the Free Trade Area of the Americas (FTAA) (see Johnson, Leff and Runnalls 2001). In addition, the issue of how to bring environmental expertise into dispute-resolution processes has been raised in both the WTO and NAFTA regimes. This issue has been especially controversial. The functioning of dispute-settlement panels should be reformed to make them more transparent and allow such expertise to inform the dispute-resolution process.

In light of the above, it is evident that the trade-investment governance system and the environmental governance system need to clarify their relationship and build an appropriate interface between themselves. In addition to ensuring regime coherence, it would also release some pressure from the WTO. Some have suggested that the creation of a global environmental organization would provide the WTO with a unique interlocutor and constitute an appropriate inter-regime interface. While this proposal is conceptually appealing, it raises several institutional questions and it is far from certain that such an organization could adequately be transplanted in the environmental regime.

In fact, the two regimes have significant differences in their characteristics and approaches that need to be acknowledged in the development of the appropriate interface. The challenge of inter-regime cooperation therefore places us at the heart of a fundamental change in the structure of global governance that will require both time and innovation. In that context, effective and credible strategies will have to be elaborated in order for the next round of negotiations at the WTO to draw public support, let alone to succeed.

Building participatory governance: balancing democracy and effectiveness

Along with substantive issues, procedural issues linked to the participation of civil society in the international governance system lie at the core of the current global governance crisis. Indeed, the rise of a transnational civil society, combined with the new transversal, multi-centred form of global governance *raise* questions of democratic representation in international regimes. As fundamental decisions affecting citizens of the world are negotiated and adopted in international forums (essentially by the executive branches of governments), the accountability issues rise to the fore. Intriguingly, there is an important divide between national and international approaches to participation and accountability. Most developed democracies provide for substantive civil society participation in all levels of government decision-making. Indeed, having meaningful and effective participatory processes for civil society is viewed as important for maintaining the legitimacy of government policy.

When it comes to supranational decision-making or global governance, however, matters are very different. Participation of civil society, so important within nation-states, is typically less than virtual. Issues such as representation, participation, accountability, equity and transparency need to be resolved as part of enhancing and legitimizing global governance. These core democratic principles must inform the evolution of global governance if it purports to integrate civil society into its deliberative processes. This will require both flexibility and adaptability from governance processes, especially in the trade and investment complex.

The role of civil-society organizations in global governance goes beyond providing more democratic legitimacy to governance processes. CSOs can also provide a series of services that can contribute to the strengthening of the global governance system. This role is especially important in the environmental regime and is becoming increasingly relevant to global governance. In that perspective, CSOs should not only be conceived of as issue-identifiers and democratic stakeholders, but as fully competent actors in the world governance system that can contribute both to the identification of issues and strategies, and in the implementation of various instruments of governance.

Selecting which among the 26,000 existing CSOs and networks to collaborate with surely constitutes a puzzle for governments and international organizations alike. All CSOs do not have the same capacity to analyze issues and generate knowledge and policy options, and there are extremely important differences between them in terms of size, membership, policies, practices and orientations. Therefore, principles and criteria must be elaborated to systematize the selection process. Mike Moore (2001*c*) proposes that an understanding be reached between governments, CSOs and international institutions on a code of conduct that would include:

- The rejection of violence
- Greater internal transparency from non-governmental organizations (NGOs) as to their membership, their finances, their rules of decision-making
- Insistence by governments, business and foundations on external rules of transparency and the adherence to an agreed "code" of conduct on the part of NGOs, before they provide funding.

Pursuant to the acceptance of this code by CSOs, governments would give them a stake in the process, while preserving their essential negotiation prerogatives. It is clear that such a code of conduct will be needed if CSOs are to be increasingly involved in the global governance decision-making system.

Approaches to civil society participation. CSO participation at the international level was pioneered at the Stockholm Conference in 1972 (Stairs 2000), and was developed to its fullest extent at the Rio Summit in 1992. Various models for CSO participation have been "tested" over the last three decades. One widely used model is to integrate CSOs into national delegations participating in international conferences. Another one is to establish parallel processes such as information meetings, symposia, conferences, or public forums either upstream in a domestic process led by governments and bureaucrats, or during international conferences. These two approaches allow for a good flow of information and they can generate some useful dialogue, but they remain far from a systematic process that ensures productive and effective dialogue. This is so because several layers of isolation remain in place between these national or international consultations and formal processes. Along similar lines, these approaches are essentially discretionary in nature and lack institutionalization.

An innovative approach has been developed in the North American Agreement on Environmental Cooperation (NAAEC) among Mexico, the United States and Canada which established the Commission for Environmental Cooperation (CEC). The CEC is composed of three bodies: the Council of Ministers, the Secretariat and the Joint Public Advisory Committee (JPAC). The JPAC comprises five participants from each member state. These people are usually well-known, credible members of the civil society who are appointed by governments in their individual capacity. Their mandate is to conduct consultations with the broader civil society and issue recommendations to the council on the work plan of the CEC. The JPAC derives its legitimacy and effectiveness from both a legally defined mandate in NAAEC and from a strict transparency and openness policy. This type of subsidiary body with a legal mandate seems to offer a much more legitimate and systematized input into policy-making than the traditional parallel processes.

Another interesting, but untested approach is the creation of subsidiary multipartite forums where civil society, governments, international secretariats and the private sector can discuss issues and build consensus. The IUCN-IISD proposal to create a Standing Conference on Trade and Environment goes in that direction (Johnson 2000*b*, 19). A similar proposal has been made in the context of the FTAA negotiations, for the creation of a Hemispheric Council on Trade and Environment that would comprise representatives of governments, CSOs, the private sector and hemispheric institutions (Johnson, Leff and Runnalls 2001). If not backed by a legal mandate in this model, the forum's strength and effectiveness will be dependent on the renewed expression of national political support to maintain its credibility.

The Canadian approach and the Summit of the Americas. Canada has a long experience of public participation in foreign policy articulation and occasionally implementation, and a Canadian model of civil society involvement has been developed over the last 15 years. Many channels have been created to provide public input and allow a permanent dialogue on foreign-policy issues. Stairs (2000) has analyzed the consultative process that took place *within* Canada before the Seattle WTO ministerial meeting. The consultative process he describes is transversal in nature and involves multiple channels of communication and dialogue, through departments and parliamentary processes. It includes interdepartmental consultations; direct departmental consultations with stakeholders from the private sector, civil society and labour unions; extensive web-based information systems; and a parliamentary consultations process through the work of the House of Commons Standing Committee on Foreign Affairs and International Trade (SCFAIT).

The Quebec Summit of the Americas provided an opportunity to develop and refine this model. Indeed, the Canadian government invested considerable energy in stakeholders' consultations and supported several parallel events, including the People's Summit of the Americas, the Hemispheric Trade and Sustainability Symposium, an Indigenous People's Summit and events related to cultural diversity. More than 125 Canadian NGOs were involved in various pre-summit consultations (Lortie 2001). As the summit host, Canada was also in a good position to promote its transparency and participatory practices. Canada's leadership, with the support of several countries, was instrumental in the earlier Buenos Aires ministerial meeting decision to release the negotiating texts of the FTAA in early April 2001. Canada also took active leadership in promoting new participatory and transparency standards at the Organization of American States (OAS) in the last few years. But, most importantly, Canada organized a roundtable of selected members of civil society with two dozen ministers of trade and foreign affairs from 20 countries of the Americas under the chairmanship of Bill Graham, chairman of SCFAIT. In effect, this was a formal tripartite process involving civil society, the executive branch and parliamentarians/legislators. The result will create precedents that will influence future hemispheric policy processes. Canada should build on its expertise and continue to systematically seek to export this model in other forums and governance processes.

Civil society participation at the WTO. As the centre of global trade governance, the WTO constitutes a core institution of global governance. It is the forum *par excellence* for international trade negotiations. Consequently, the organization is subject to intense pressure to integrate civil society into its deliberations. The WTO has responded to these demands by developing website communications and a series of symposia and parallel events to its formal processes. These activities focus more on responses to transparency concerns, although they do allow some form of consultation. But so far they have fallen short of offering a systematic, well-defined framework for CSO participation that would offer a degree of stability and consistency, and would give some assurance of a formal and meaningful input into the intergovernmental process.

This situation is, to a degree, understandable. One reason for this relates to the sensitivity of the issues addressed in the negotiations, and the interstate bartering of interests. Negotiations of this sort command a high degree of discretion (it is the very nature of the exercise of diplomacy). Another reason is that developing countries tend to oppose increased participation of CSOs since they believe it will open the doors to a northern labour/environment protectionist coalition that will be detrimental to the expression of their own needs and interests. As a result, there is much confidence-building work to be done and part of this lies in the development of a balanced and equitable process. Increased support for developing countries' governments and NGO participation would do much to generate support for such an opening of WTO processes.

The challenge is thus to allow, both at the domestic *and* the international level, significant, substantive input upstream and possibly during the negotiations, while preserving a context that is comfortable for interstate negotiation. The creation of a Standing Conference on Trade and Environment (SCTE) could support such a strategy as a multipartite, transparent deliberative forum on trade policy issues that are environmentally-related. It would not only increase the legitimacy of the WTO, but would also bring it significant institutional capacity for the identification of options and the implementation of its provisions in a way that is consistent with sustainable development.

In addition to the creation of a SCTE, many analysts have proposed that the expertise of CSOs could inform the dispute-settlement processes in the form of Amicus Briefs. It appears that WTO panels are slowly opening their deliberations to improved participation, but so far decisions on a case-by-case basis have been left to each panel, and a systematic pattern of increasing third-party participation is still missing. In the meantime, CSOs should be systematically given an observer status to dispute-settlement panels.

An enhanced role for parliamentarians. Increased participation from civil society organizations generates concerns of legitimacy and accountability, both at the domestic and international levels. While CSOs are truly representative of certain interests and segments of the broader public, they do not have the same legitimacy and are not accountable to the public in the same way as are democratically elected parliamentarians.

Most western democratic systems are representative in nature and accommodate participatory concerns of citizens by the institutionalization of the consultation, often parliamentary-led, process. To the opposite, for most of the past half-century, economic globalization processes have been dominated by bureaucracies and the executive branch of government. The MAI and Seattle failures showed the limits of this practice as parliamentarians began to harness the beginning of the movement of public opinion. This context calls for the elaboration of new participatory and consultative processes.

While an important bureaucratic role cannot be avoided, Stairs (2000) argues that too much focus on bureaucratic consultations is fundamentally inconsistent with the articulation of foreign policy by democratically elected governments, and is undermining legitimate democratic processes. In addition, he observes that consultations and dialogue with civil society tend to work better with parliamentarians than with officials who are not used to communicating directly with the broader public. In both these situations, the preferred approach would be to involve officials in information sessions and conduct parliamentary consultations either through permanent committees or ad hoc commissions. It is important to understand, however, that these consultations will be credible and draw civil society participation only if they are supported by a stronger role for parliaments in the formulation of foreign policy. Moreover, the legitimacy of the executive in global governance issues can be strengthened through greater transparency and accountability to parliaments.

The same can be true for international institutions and processes. The Commission on Global Governance (1995) took a stance in favour of a stronger involvement of parliamentarians in the work of the United Nations. Recently, Mike Moore, who was at the Inter-Parliamentary Union (IPU) meeting on international trade, developed the following position: "Elected parliamentarians are the measurable and accountable representatives of civil society. Parliamentarians have a vital role to play in bringing international organizations and people closer together and holding us and governments accountable. Parliamentarians need to engage in the critical global issues and be perceived by the public to be doing so" (Moore 2000*a*).

Consequently, he suggests that parliamentary committees play a more aggressive role in scrutinizing the work of international institutions, including the WTO. This could be supported by the creation of a clearinghouse on trade negotiations and trade-related legislations. Moore also favours collective parliamentary action at the international level through parliamentary unions such as the IPU. In his perspective, the WTO could hold an annual one-week meeting with parliamentarians, Chambers of Commerce and unions to discuss issues of trade liberalization and global governance. Others have proposed the creation of an official parliamentary assembly at the WTO that would act as a bridge between civil society and the intergovernmental process.

These proposals find echo in parliamentary unions which are determined to assert their role and leadership in the global governance system:

> Parliamentary oversight at home keeps governments accountable, and through them, the international trade agreements they negotiate. Parliamentary involvement can also help make the trading system more transparent and inclusive, and more widely understood and supported. This could be matched at the international level where parliamentary involvement can help Governments and international organizations ensure that trade negotiations reflect the aspirations of all citizens (Heptulla 2001).

Parliamentarians therefore have a key role to play in bridging the gap between the international governance system and civil society, both at the national and international level. By bridging this gap, parliamentarians can reverse the democratic deficit that has been building over the last decade. Parliaments and parliamentary associations constitute key assets and key actors in the global governance system and they must be allowed a role in rebuilding the social consensus for globalization. Parliamentarians could become major players and important catalysts in building a participatory consensus, thereby fostering the furthering of economic globalization.

Conclusion: The Opportunity for Canadian Leadership

THE TIME HAS COME TO ADDRESS THE CHALLENGES OF INTEGRATION AND OPENNESS in the global governance system. Global governance must be consolidated in a coherent, balanced and mutually supportive set of regimes that will respond to the current problems of inequitable sharing of wealth and environmental externalities. In addition, the global governance regimes must be based on a new participatory approach that will be rooted in increased parliamentary oversight and institutionalized participatory processes. The realization of this agenda will require vision, leadership and political will.

Canada is well positioned to significantly contribute to the reform of the global governance system. Indeed, we have a strong interest in doing so. As a trading country with a natural-resource-based economy, Canada has a fundamental interest in maintaining both a strong multilateral trade and investment regime and a strong environmental regime where both operate under a coherent governance system. In addition, Canada needs to maintain public support in favour of globalization through the development of a participatory consensus. By supporting regime integration and participatory processes, Canada can contribute to maintaining public support for trade liberalization, to increasing the stability and predictability of the current economic governance system, and to strengthening its reputation as a sustainable producer on world markets. Moreover, Canada has developed expertise in integrative and participative processes that it can export to the international sphere.

Looking forward, there are three upcoming meetings/processes where Canada can exercise its influence and utilize its expertise in promoting an integrated approach to international governance.

> First, beyond promoting a focused trade-related environment and development agenda for the next round of multilateral trade negotiations, Canada should seek institutional reform at the WTO to make this intergovernmental process more transparent and accountable. It should consider the establishment of a WTO-related parliamentary committee with a strong mandate to systematize CSOs participation;
>
> Second, Canada should actively seek to consolidate and strengthen the environmental governance system with a view to using it as a tool to alleviate poverty at the 2002 World Summit on Sustainable Development, thus addressing important concerns emanating from the developing world;

> Third, Canada should use its chairmanship of the next G8 Summit, as well as its leadership in the G20 to promote the effective integration of these agendas into a coherent set of G8/G20 orientations that would support a more effective and more open global governance system.

In summary, the international community must abandon the reactive, self-protection strategy it has adopted so far and accept that the new governance context requires significant changes in the way international relations need to be conducted. It is only through building stronger democratic processes and pursuing a more balanced globalization agenda that the global governance processes will begin extricating themselves from the conceptual and physical barricades in which they are now imprisoned.

Notes

1 For a detailed discussion of NAFTA's chapter 11, see International Institute for Sustainable Development and World Wildlife Fund (2001).

2 See "Notes of Interpretation of Certain Chapter 11 Provisions by the NAFTA Free Trade Commission," July 31, 2001.

3 The G20 comprises the following 18 countries: Argentina, Australia, Brazil, Canada, China, France, Germany, India, Italy, Japan, Mexico, Russia, Saudi Arabia, South Africa, South Korea, Turkey, the United Kingdom, and the United States, along with the European Union (EU) and Bretton Woods institutions.

4 For a detailed discussion of the G20 see Kirton (2001*b*).

5 Source: Environment Canada.

6 Canada put forward an interesting approach to conduct this task, namely to orient the reform of the environmental governance system around four "Cs": compliance, coordination, coherence and capacity-building.

7 This list is essentially a summary of Johnson, Leff and Runnalls (2001); and Johnson (2000*a*, 2001).

8 For a more detailed analysis of the proposal for the Standing Conference on Trade and the Environment, see Mercer (1999).

References

Agnew, D. "Presentation to the Couchiching Institute on Public Affairs 70th Annual Summer Conference, Globalization and Democracy: Whose World is it?" Synopsis by Melanie Martin. Orillia, Ontario, August 9-12, 2001.

Ciuriak, D. "The 'Trade and…' Agenda: Are We at the Crossroads?" Paper prepared for the National Policy Research Conference, Ottawa, December 1, 2000.

Clarkson, S. *The Multi-level State: Canada in the Semi-Periphery of both Continentalism and Globalization*. Toronto: University of Toronto Press, 2000*a*.

________ *The Multicentered State: Canadian Government Under Globalizing Pressures*. Toronto: University of Toronto Press, 2000*b*.

Commission on Global Governance. *Our Global Neighbourhood: The Report of the Commission on Global Governance*. Oxford, New York: Oxford University Press, 1995.

Courchene, T.J. *A State of Minds: Toward a Human Capital Future for Canadians*. Montreal: Institute for Research on Public Policy, 2001.

Curtis, J.M. "Trade and Civil Society: Toward Greater Transparency in the Policy Process." Paper prepared for the National Policy Research Conference, Ottawa, December 1, 2000.

Drucker, P. *The New Realities*. New York: Harper Press, 1989.

Dymond, W.A. and M.M. Hart. "Post-Modern Trade Policy: Reflections on the Challenges to Multilateral Trade Negotiations after Seattle." *Journal of World Trade*, Vol. 34, no. 3 (2000): 21-38.

Heptulla, N. "Summary of the Debate by the President of the Council of the Inter-Parliamentary Union." Inter-Parliamentary Union meeting on international trade, Geneva, June 8-9, 2001.

Howse, R. and K. Nicolaidis. "Legitimacy and Global Governance: Why Constitutionalizing the WTO Is a Step Too Far." Presented at the Conference on Efficiency, Equity and Legitimacy: The Multilateral Trading System at the Millennium. Cambridge: Center for Business and Government, Harvard University, June 1-2, 2000.

International Institute for Sustainable Development (IISD) and World Wildlife Fund (WWF). *Private Rights, Public Problems: A Guide to NAFTA's Controversial Chapter on Investor Rights*. Winnipeg: IISD & WWF, 2001.

International Organization for Migration (IOM). *World Migration Report 2000*. New York: IOM and United Nations, 2000.

Johnson, P.M. "Le Libre-Échange et l'environnement." *ISUMA: Canadian Journal of Policy Research*, Vol. 1, no. 1 (Spring 2000*a*): 62-69.

Johnson, P.M. with Karel Mayrand. "Beyond Trade: The Case for a Broadened International Governance Agenda." *Policy Matters*, Vol. 1, no. 3 (June 2000*b*).

Johnson, P.M. "Creating Sustainable Global Governance." In *Guiding Global Order: G8 Governance in the Twenty-First Century*, ed. J. Kirton, J.P. Daniels and A. Freytag. Aldershot: Ashgate, 2001.

Johnson, P.M., E. Leff and D. Runnalls. *The FTAA and Hemispheric Integration: Building a Triple-Win Strategy for Trade and Sustainability in the Hemisphere.* Policy recommendations document presented at the Third Summit of the Americas by the Chairs of the Hemispheric Trade and Sustainability Symposium, Quebec City, April 2001.

Keohane, R. and J. Nye. "The Club Model of Multilateral Cooperation and the WTO: Problems of Democratic Legitimacy." Delivered at the Conference on Efficiency, Equity and Legitimacy: The Multilateral Trading System at the Millennium. Cambridge: Center for Business and Government, Harvard University, June 1-2, 2000.

Kirton, J. *Globalization, Global Governance and Canadian Leadership in the Twenty-First Century*. Toronto: University of Toronto, 2000*a*.

________ *Creating Coherence in Global Environmental Governance: Canada's 2002 Opportunity*. Toronto: University of Toronto, 2000*b*.

________ *Embedded Ecologism and Institutional Inequality: Linking Trade, Environment and Social Cohesion in the G8.* Toronto: University of Toronto, 2001*a*.

________ "The G20: Representativeness, Effectiveness, and Leadership in Global Governance." In *Guiding Global Order: G8 Governance in the Twenty-First Century*, ed. J. Kirton, J.P. Daniels and A. Freytag. Aldershot: Ashgate, 2001*b*.

________ "Bringing Civil Society in: The Advances of the Americas Democracy Summit in Quebec." University of Toronto, April 21, 2001*c*.

Krasner, S., ed. *International Regimes.* Ithaca, NY: Cornell University Press, 1983.

Le Prestre, P. "Releasing the Potential of Emerging Trends: For a Canadian Initiative on Strengthening Convention Governance Systems." Paper presented at a Workshop on International Governance, Vancouver, Canada, August 13-14, 2001.

Lortie, M. "Presentation to the Couchiching Institute on Public Affairs 70th Annual Summer Conference, Globalization and Democracy: Whose World is it?" Synopsis by Melanie Martin. Orillia, Ontario, August 9-12, 2001.

McGuinty, D.J. "Presentation to the Couchiching Institute on Public Affairs 70th Annual Summer Conference, Globalization and Democracy: Whose World is it?" Synopsis by Melanie Martin. Orillia, Ontario, August 9-12, 2001.

Mercer, M. "International Trade and the Environment: Addressing the Co-ordination Challenge." Paper presented at International Conference on the GEO, Montreal, IUCN Canada Office, October 1999.

Moore, M. "Promoting Openness, Fairness and Predictability in International Trade for the Benefit of Humanity." Presentation at the Inter-Parliamentary Union meeting on international Trade, Geneva, June 8, 2001*a*.

________ "Changes in the Multilateral Trading System: Challenges for the WTO." Presentation at the Winconference 2001, Interlaken, Switzerland, July 5, 2001*b*.

________ "Open Societies, Freedom, Development and Trade." Presentation at the WTO Symposium on Issues Confronting the World Trading System, Geneva, July 6, 2001*c*.

Nordstrom, H. and S. Vaughan. *Special Studies 4: Trade and Environment.* Geneva: World Trade Organization, 1999.

Ostry, S. "Globalization and the Nation State." In *The Nation State in a Global/Information Era: Policy Challenges*, ed. T.J. Courchene. Kingston, ON: John Deutsch Institute, Queen's University, 1997.

________ "WTO: Institutional Design for Better Governance." Presented at the Conference on Efficiency, Equity and Legitimacy: The Multilateral Trading System at the Millennium. Cambridge: Center for Business and Government, Harvard University, June 1-2, 2000.

Parliamentary Conference of the Americas (PCA). *Report of the Meeting of the Executive Committee of the Parliamentary Conference of the Americas*, Quebec City, April 20-21, 2001.

Peterson, L. "Changing Investment Litigation, Bit by BIT." In *Bridges Between Trade and Sustainable Development*, Year 5, no. 4 (2001): 11. Geneva: International Center on Trade and Sustainable Development.

Pettigrew, P. "Address to the Couchiching Institute on Public Affairs 70th Annual Summer Conference, Globalization and Democracy: Whose World is it?" Orillia, Ontario, August 9-12, 2001.

Stairs, D. "Foreign Policy Consultations in a Globalizing World: The Case of Canada, the WTO and the Shenanigans in Seattle." *Policy Matters*, Vol. 1, no. 8 (2000).

United Nations Conference on Trade and Development (UNCTAD). *World Investment Report – Promoting Linkages – Overview.* New York: United Nations, 2001.

________ *Trade and Development Report 2001.* New York: United Nations, 2001.

United Nations Development Programme (UNDP). *Human Development Report 1999.* New York: UNDP, 1999.

________ *Human Development Report 2001.* New York: UNDP, 2001.

________ *Least Developed Countries 2000 Report.* New York: United Nations, 2000.

United Nations Environment Programme (UNEP). *International Environmental Governance.* Report of the executive director presented at the first meeting of the Open-ended Intergovernmental Group of Ministers or their Representatives on International Environmental Governance, New York, April 18, 2001*a*.

________ *Multilateral Environmental Agreements: A Summary.* Background paper presented by the secretariat at the first meeting of the Open-ended Intergovernmental Group of Ministers or their Representatives on International Environmental Governance, New York, April 18, 2001*b*.

Von Moltke, K. *Whiter MEAs? The Role of International Environmental Management in the Trade and Environment Agenda.* Winnipeg: International Institute for Sustainable Development, 2001*a*.

________ *An International Investment Regime? Issues of Sustainability.* Winnipeg: International Institute for Sustainable Development, 2001*b*.

World Trade Organization (WTO). *International Trade Statistics 2000.* Geneva: WTO, 2000.

Worldwatch Institute. *Vital Signs 2000.* New York: Norton, 2000.

________ *Vital Signs 2001.* New York: Norton, 2001.

Citizens, States and International Regimes

In their paper, "International Governance and Canada," Pierre Marc Johnson and Karel Mayrand had the courage to raise a centrally important, but dauntingly difficult, set of questions. They have carefully scrutinized a great deal of the pertinent academic and governmental literature and have emerged with a rich array of practical proposals for dealing with the problems they identified. The result is a "packed" paper, thoughtfully argued and presented, and it leaves little room for serious challenge, much less a total demolition of what they have to say. There may be room for a quarrel with a nuance here, a conceptual definition there, or a minor point of emphasis somewhere else. But this would be to dance angels on the heads of pins. At its core, the paper is comprehensive, stimulating and constructive, and it goes to the heart of an intensifying modern dilemma.

Nonetheless, the obligation of the critic is to cast stones, and in this case the critic will begin with a brief declaration of personal prejudice and then move on to a discussion of the paper itself.

The declaration of prejudice asserts that we may be in some danger of assuming that the changes that are addressed in the paper, and indeed in some of the other contributions to this volume, are much more fundamental than they actually are. It suggests that we have come to think that we are facing a systemic upheaval, a kind of "paradigm shift," rather than a simple variation on a fairly traditional form of politics that happens to be hard to recognize because it manifests itself in some mildly novel tactical techniques. This is an intellectually conservative premise—some might think unreasonably so—and it may result from lack of imagination, professional inertia or some unhappy combination of the two. But the basic foundations of politics are ultimately much the same in every era and the discussion that follows rests accordingly on a standing disposition to think that the essentials do not change a great deal, even if surfaces are transformed.

Turning from this vantage point specifically to the paper, I have no quarrel with the authors' account of recent historical events. Nor do I have a problem with their discussion of the concept of "governance," although I think they may treat the term itself a little too kindly. It is a "weasel" word, after all—a word that allows its users to avoid the term "government," and hence to duck some inconvenient and complicated problems in the distinction between *authority* on the one hand, and *power* (or *influence*) on the other. Its attractiveness, not least to those who are engaged in democratic rule, results partly from the fact that governing authority is thought to require concealment in an inclusivist age. Talking about "governance," as opposed to "government," facilitates the concealing. But the paper's discussion captures accurately enough the essence of the chatter in the literature, and it therefore has plenty of company. There is little to be gained by quarrelling over definitions.

Much the same can be said of the authors' account of what is meant by "globalization," and of the way in which the more dysfunctional of its consequences arouses civil society to political action. This happens not least because of various kinds of disappointment over the apparent incapacity of states to act in ways that will prevent or repair the damage. In effect, liberal capitalism is perceived to have been made more brutish by the abusive exercise of a freedom it has acquired by going transnational, and the state seems unable or unwilling to perform its traditional task of smoothing out the rough edges—of restoring to the capitalist experiment a benign and smiling face.

But something else has happened here, as well, or so the argument implies. For the states, in losing their capacity to do their traditional job, have lost their specialness, too. It follows that governance (not government, remember) becomes an exercise in partnership. *Everyone* does it—states, non-governmental organizations (NGOs) or civil society organizations (CSOs), the private sector, local authorities, communities, metropoles, regions. The actors, all of them now equally legitimate participants in the new governance process, are diverse. The Weberian model of the state goes away. There is no hierarchy, and certainly not one with the state at the top. We have instead a motley crew of heterogeneous performers.

Still, all is not quite lost, because a *smart* state, with the right (i.e., middle power) credentials, and the appropriate seasoning and experience (a state like

Canada, in fact), can seize the opportunity to orchestrate the politics—to *lead* it, even—by building coalitions with the new partners, as well as with other states of like mind and capacities comparable to its own. Canada has done this already. It did it with the Land Mines Treaty.

Now, I will pause here to protest just a little.

In the first place, I do not think for a minute that there is no hierarchy of actors out there, or that the states are not at the top of it, with the intergovernmental organizations (IGOs) coming a close, albeit derivative, second. Among other things, the states have *authority*, whereas the CSOs, the corporations, and all the rest have only *influence*, along with the right to try to exercise it. In addition, only the states have the power to tax, and without the resources that taxation brings, the objectives of the CSOs can never be realized. Corporations, it is true, often have very substantial financial assets at their disposal, but except for the charitable donations that they make for public relations purposes, they are neither free, nor motivated, to deploy them for the procurement of public goods. Their obligation, both legally and morally, is to their shareholders, and their shareholders expect them to generate private profit in the end.

The states have some other things going for them as well. For example, they alone carry the responsibility for making the necessary trade-offs between competing and sometimes incompatible demands. This is a job that the CSOs can never do.

But the first two of the states' attributes—their unique authority and their taxing power—are together enough to make them special, and to put them at the top of the actor hierarchy. It is useful to remind ourselves of the fundamentals. If the citizen refuses to do what the state demands, then in the extremity the state can toss him, or her, into jail. This the corporations cannot legally do (although they sometimes find themselves doing it in places where the state has "failed").

In the second place, we can overdo the assumption that the CSOs (or NGOs) are *new* players on the block, and that their presence changes the fundamentals of the game. There are more of them, I agree. They have more political assets (among them communications assets), I agree. They work more commonly now in the company of coalitions, I agree. They can help governments with expertise and program delivery, I agree. But they are not different in kind from what we used to call "pressure groups," or public service interest groups, and their appearance in strength is not in itself a reason to argue that the conduct of international politics (the process of international governance) has been fundamentally transformed as a result.

Nor are the CSOs new in being "transnational." Consider, in the nineteenth century, the campaign against slavery, the campaign to give women the vote, the campaign against the opium trade, the campaign to stop the binding of women's feet in China, and the campaign to come to the aid of the Christians in Armenia. Or consider, again, in the period between the wars, the campaign for general disarmament, and the campaign in support of collective security by the world's League of Nations societies. All of these were transnational political enterprises. Some of them were politically inconvenient to governments. Most of them were ultimately successful. But we did not conclude from that experience that the state was in decline.

In short, the bottles may have some new labels, but the wine itself is well and truly aged.

In the third place, I am not sure that we can assume that Canada will be able, as a matter of normal routine, to form and influence coalitions with the other players—especially the CSO players—in the way that Johnson and Mayrand seem to think. They point to the Land Mines Treaty as the prototypical example. But so does everyone else. This is because other examples are hard to find (although Lloyd Axworthy usually adds the International Criminal Court to make a list of two). In short, the Land Mines Treaty may be a *sui generis* case.

Even more important, it is not clear that Canada will always *want* to lead such coalitions, and least of all in the environmental field, the field that emerges in the paper as the authors' central concern, but which produces in Ottawa policy responses that are clearly given more to hypocrisy and cant than to serious remedial action. (It is hard, after all, to conclude otherwise, when one of the government's key strategies in international environmental negotiations is to claim that Canada needs to do less than others to reduce unwanted emissions because it grows a lot of trees.)

But perhaps these are all relatively minor lamentations, of interest more to political scientists in their faculty lounge debates than to practitioners who are responsible for "real world" decisions. In any case, the paper's most important contributions come with its practical proposals.

Some of these have to do with the need to consolidate the plethora of regimes that are currently in place for dealing with environmental issues, and for integrating them in particular with the *economic* regime (mainly the World Trade Organization, WTO). At the very least, there is a need to develop a constructive interface between the two. This will have to go hand-in-hand with capacity-building at all levels, but especially at the state level.

I would certainly agree with most of this, but with one minor caveat, which is that we can overdo our search for comprehensive rationality, and in the process overload the system. It may well be the case that a certain amount of untidy eclecticism is unavoidable in a field like this, and that trying too hard to make things more coherent will lead to less productive results in the end. It could even bog the process down. There is obviously a case for having an environmental equivalent of the WTO, and even for linking the two together, but it seems to me that the environmental problem is in some ways a much more complex and variegated challenge than regulating world trade, and it might be wise not to complicate it further with unreasonably high expectations of consistency and coherence.

Finally, the paper comes back to the question of process, and to what the authors call "Building Participatory Governance: Balancing Democracy and Effectiveness." Under this heading, they address at some length the various mechanisms, actual and potential, that can be used to involve the CSOs in particular in the global governance project. I do not have any great difficulty with this (which is just as well, since it is happening all over the place whether I like it or not), *provided*, however, that it is clearly understood that the CSOs are not quasi-governmental actors, but (as I have already argued) interest groups seeking to influence what governments do. They are "public service" interest groups, perhaps, but they are interest groups all the same. They are certainly entitled to make representations, and within reason (I think myself that in Ottawa the thing has now gone *beyond* reason, but that is another matter) they have a right to an audience, that is, to opportunities to be heard. But the fact remains that they are not elected. They are self-appointed. And not infrequently they are obsessively single-minded. The more they are treated as if they are the representatives of *demos* at large, moreover, the weaker becomes the position of those who are really supposed to represent demos at large—namely, the elected members of Parliament.

This leads me to one final comment. Johnson and Mayrand want to strengthen the role in their global project of parliamentarians. With this, I could not agree more. I wish only that they had given greater prominence to the suggestion in their paper. I realize, of course, that we have now come to the point at which such notions are widely regarded in Ottawa as quaint at best, and as naive at worst. But this is an attitude that is self-fulfilling, and in being self-fulfilling, it flies in the face of the core premise of our system of government. It also has the side-effect of intensifying the public's disaffection from our political institutions and from the political process.

It is possible that we are gradually moving in the direction of a kind of "pluralistic corporatism," and perhaps we should reconstruct our system of government accordingly. But that would be a large and uncertain undertaking, and clearly it should not be done by stealth. In the meantime I think we would do well to encourage the notion that political communications ought to be channelled as much as possible through political places, and not through the public service (which is ill-equipped to do the job).

Discussion

BARBARA MCDOUGALL, PRESIDENT OF THE CANADIAN INSTITUTE OF INTERNATIONAL Affairs and former minister in the Mulroney government, began the floor discussion by echoing concerns raised by Denis Stairs, namely that the growth and importance of the non-governmental organizations (NGOs) is tending to undermine the legitimacy of the political process. McDougall also noted that NGOs (or civil society) have been given too much credit for the failure of the Multilateral Agreement on Investment (MAI) and for the World Trade Organization (WTO) stalemate in Seattle. The truth of the matter is that both of these situations represented a failure of leadership. But to the extent that the media assign credit and influence to the role of civil society, this serves to further the challenge faced by democratically elected politicians in encouraging society at large to work through the politically accountable processes. In terms of the role for Canadian leadership in international governance, McDougall noted that Canada belongs to more multilateral organizations than any country in the world, in part because we are members of both the Commonwealth and the Francophonie and because we border three oceans. Spreading our expertise this broadly makes it difficult to take leadership on too many files. Where we can have an important influence is in our role as host for the G8 summit in Kananaskis in 2002. The obvious window of opportunity here is for the recently formed G20, under the leadership of Canada's Paul Martin, to inform the G8 summit process since the G20 is a much more representative forum for addressing the Johnson/Mayrand range of issues (north vs. south, developed vs. developing, as well as transparency, accountability and participatory issues relating to global governance). In this, McDougall lends support to the final recommendation of the Johnson/Mayrand paper.

The question period latched onto the significant role of NGOs—"astonishing influence" in the words of one participant, a "tremendous distortion of the pendulum," verging on a "parallel government" in the words of others. Denis Stairs began his response by asking why Ottawa pays so much attention to the NGOs since (i) they do not represent a great deal of electoral power; (ii) they are typically committed to one or other political party so that it would seem costless for the ruling party to take a hard line with them; and (iii) they do not have much in the way of financial assets, apart from what governments themselves give them. His answer, from a small sample of MP responses, was the fear of receiving unfavourable press commentary. Pierre-Marc Johnson weighed in on this media relationship as well, noting that the media discovered global economic regimes and the NGOs in the context of the MAI and Seattle. He also levelled a broadside at TV reporting at the Summit of the Americas in Quebec City, where journalists donned gas masks to cover a struggle between the police and a few hundred thugs. Meanwhile a few thousand people—heads of states, unionists, members of cooperatives, and civil society—were meeting and making meaningful progress on real issues. No coverage! But his message was not so much to scold the media as to argue that there will never be much in the way of meaningful media coverage of real substantive issues unless governments find avenues for civil society to participate in these summits in ways other than rock throwing.

At a related but more fundamental level, the decline of perceived legitimacy and influence of legislatures was suggested by participants to be linked with the possibility that this might be the result of the inability of our legislatures to serve as effective intermediaries for the views of NGOs. Hence, it may be more effective for them to direct attention to the upper echelons of the bureaucracy. Denis Stairs offered the observation that interest group pluralism probably does not fit very well in the context of an executive-dominant parliamentary system. When the Americans created their Constitution they had a very clear understanding of interest group pressures, so that the American checks and balance system appears more able to accommodate interest groups without undermining Congress, in the way that these same pressures might undermine Parliament. Stairs adds that this is not a particularly useful comment since Canada and Canadians are not likely to switch from a parliamentary to a congressional system. But if our underlying institutions are immutable, then the challenge becomes one of finding creative alternative instrumentalities that can accommodate the changing nature of domestic and global governance.

In his wrap-up comments, Pierre Marc Johnson addressed the CSO or civil society issue head on. Agreeing that legitimacy in western democracies can only reside with elected officials, he nonetheless notes that we do listen to citizen and citizen groups through parliamentary hearings, consultative processes, through the executive responding to the legislature, etc. Given that we allow and encourage this in the context of domestic governance, the key issue is why we should preclude this in international/global governance. He then adds that with 40 percent-plus of our gross domestic product going to exports, we had better take a leadership role in the liberalization and stability of the global economic/trade regime, because the costs to Canada of system failure will be quite dramatic.

Johnson concluded his remarks (and the session) by downplaying the oft-heard complaint that many CSOs or NGOs are ideological and/or self-interest groups. How about the pulp and paper industry? Or the energy industry? Or the Canadian Manufacturers' Association? The key here is to ensure that the groups appear in front of parliamentary committees or other bodies that are open, transparent and accountable. No one doubts that the corporate sector in Canada has considerable clout in the corridors of power. Why then, Johnson wonders, shouldn't the NGO community and citizens who have social concerns, environmental concerns, developmental concerns and human rights concerns have at least one international venue where they can publicly, simply and legitimately air their views and visions?

Conclusion

Conclusion: Looking Forward

THE AUTHORS OF THE PAPERS IN THIS BOOK HAVE REVIEWED EMERGING POLITICAL AND economic forces and addressed important challenges confronting Canada and indeed all nation-states. As we conclude this volume, we attempt to look ahead and speculate on "what next." Understanding change, and especially predicting it, is a particularly difficult task for social scientists. We are much better at explaining why things are the way they are than predicting the future or coming forward with prescriptions for how things ought to be. Still, we believe that it is important to consider what the future will look like, and try as best we can to prepare for it.

To be sure, a world without borders is not easy to contemplate and we have precious little experience to draw from. Indeed, borders have always shaped our community, province and nation. They also have shaped our workplace and our identity. When you draw boundaries or borders you draw a visible understanding of how things work and one can more easily plan and implement change. When you remove them, you remove that understanding and you create uncertainty. O.C. McSuite writes that without boundaries "we end up with a big conceptual mess and we cannot have a reasoned approach to life" (1997, 243). The question then is how we can make sense of this big conceptual mess. We believe that the best way to proceed is to identify issues that require further research and reflection.

Accordingly, we have identified a number of issues that we argue should be pursued to strengthen our system of governance and to promote economic development. We were able to draw from the papers tabled at the conference and the roundtable discussions to identify issues that could well dominate the public policy agenda in the years ahead. In so doing, we need to bear in mind that the information revolution and global economic integration are both still in their infancy.

The state of the environment will continue to dominate the public policy agenda. It knows no boundaries and any and all solutions will need to have a regional, if not a global perspective. Among other things, we need to reflect not only about how governments identify solutions, but also how they are held to account by their electors for their actions. One need look no further than to the Kyoto Protocol on climate change and global warming. The United States and Canada, among others, signed the Protocol which required them to reduce emissions of certain kinds of gases. President George W. Bush, in assuming office, simply stated that the United States would withdraw from the Protocol. Canada has yet to take firm steps to reduce emissions. If rich countries, like the United States and Canada, can have a change of heart on environmental issues, then what is to prevent less-developed countries from ignoring these issues altogether? We have a difficult enough time keeping our national and provincial political leaders to account for their actions in delivering national programs. How then can we possibly hold them accountable on regional or global issues?

It is already evident that the new global order is having considerable impact on income distribution. This is because the information revolution is privileging skills and human capital. In turn, we know that high level human capital has become increasingly mobile internationally. Income polarization could well give rise to new political tensions both at home and abroad and all orders of government will need to address this issue.

Global economic integration, at least in Canada, is redefining the traditional relationships that regions have had with one another and the long-term impact will likely be substantial. Relatedly, there is growing evidence, for example, that Atlantic Canada is looking to New England to identify and pursue new economic opportunities. There is also growing evidence that Atlantic Canada is forging tangible political and economic ties with its neighbours to the south. This is true, for example, in the energy sector. What will north-south economic integration mean for Canada's national political and administrative institutions?

Global cities are also forging economic ties with one another. New York, London and Tokyo are the new reference points for Toronto, not Saint John, Winnipeg or Edmonton. What does this mean for nation-states and provincial or state governments? We know, for example, that global cities are expanding as they consolidate metropolitan areas to create new mega-cities. They are integrating their hinterlands to promote more effective planning to secure economic growth by curtailing competition from within their regions in order to strengthen their competitiveness against other global cities. But this too is not without important consequences for nation-states and provincial governments. We will need to redefine in a fundamental fashion how national institutions work and the constitutional agenda of the past will have to give way to a new emphasis on the role of local government in relation to the two senior orders of government.

As we address governance issues, we will need to recognize at the outset that scholars and practitioners have been searching for ways to strengthen democracy and to hold political power to account since the early Greek philosophers and no doubt the search will continue as long as civil society exists. There is no magic bullet, and it seems that every reform brings on not only new approaches that offer promise, but also new problems. Above all, we need to recognize that there can be no *one* final solution. It is invariably a work in progress as our national political institutions adjust to changing circumstances.

Changes to our system of government in the years ahead are likely to occur on three fronts. First, new organizational forms are likely to be designed to manage common areas of concern between trading partners. We may, for example, create a new organization to manage one or more of border, security and common currency issues between Canada, the United States and Mexico. We are slowly coming to terms with the fact that a number of issues simply cannot be understood and acted upon from a national perspective and a North American, if not a global perspective, is now needed. The question is how to manage these issues in absence of multinational or regional political institutions. One conference participant suggested that we could look to the precedent and success of the International Joint Commission. The difference, of course, is that the International Joint Commission deals with fairly technical, non-controversial and low profile issues that generate limited political interest.

Given economic integration and the need for close regional cooperation, we need to ask if the next step is to move in the same direction as the European Union (EU). The EU has set the pace in creating formal institutions to cover a wide agenda of public-policy issues dealing with political, economic, social and cultural integration. It may be that we should consider establishing a North American Commission and assign to it responsibilities that national governments are no longer able to deal with.

But citizens will also need to be more demanding of their political leaders at the national and provincial levels if we are to develop democracy further in the global economy. For one thing, they need to find ways to resist closed-door decision-making at the international level. Citizens may also need to identify new ways to extend their political activity beyond their provincial or national borders. Indeed, this may well be the most effective approach to deal with the resulting "democratic deficit" when policy decisions increasingly detach themselves from national and provincial governments only to disappear in international agreements.

The second area of change to our system of governance is to improve how our domestic, political and administrative institutions work. These institutions will also need to change because of emerging North American regional institutions and the impact of regional trade agreements. Given that North America is home to 90 state or provincial governments and three national governments and the global economy as well, there is an obvious need for regional cooperation in defining or redefining how they relate to one another. Federalism itself will also likely be taking new forms. These 90 state and provincial governments will be reaching out to one another, to foreign governments, and to international bodies to protect their interests. It will be recalled, for example, that Mexican federal authorities agreed to meet with the premier of Quebec despite the objections of the Canadian government.

The pressure to make government operations and programs more transparent and accessible will continue. To be sure, the pressure has been felt for some time. However, few are satisfied with the progress. Indeed, it appears that major and ambitious public service reforms are introduced every five years or so only to fall far short of expectations a few years later. As one senior practitioner observed at the conference, there is evidence that frustration is setting in. The risk, as he explained, is that this will lead to extreme rather than balanced solutions. Unless tangible progress can be documented in the near term, others with more radical solutions could well transform our national institutions beyond recognition with ill-conceived measures.

We need to explore how the voluntary sector can play a role in delivering public services. But as we do so, we also need to consider carefully how it can play this role without losing its distinct characteristics. Phrased differently, how can we involve the third sector in program delivery without introducing a bureaucratic culture in its organizations. Relatedly, we also need to explore how neo-governmental organizations can be created and made to operate in a public environment. Neo-governmental organizations could take many forms. They could be community groups, public-private networks or even government-university research endeavours of one kind or another. They could be fully funded or partially funded by government. They could be guided by an independent board or by boards made up of elected representatives, career government officials and community or business representatives. Indeed, if there is one area where we need to think outside the box, it is how governments can better organize their approach to program delivery.

We also need to rethink our accountability mechanisms in light of the requirements of the global economy and new information technologies. How, for example, should governments now deal with interest groups, given the growing interdependence of public policies and the information revolution? Perhaps because of the increasingly complex nature of policy- and decision-making, accountability in government has become highly personal and come to mean the search for political scandals to feed "gotcha" politics rather than deal with substantial policy and program issues. Our democratic system of government requires more accountability to ensure its continued legitimacy.

The third area of change to our system of government has already been highlighted in an earlier context, namely the role of large cities in the new economy. We know that large cities play an increasingly important catalytic role in the global economy. The unanswered question is how this will influence their existing role, their relations with other levels of government and their relations with foreign states and cities. The other unanswered question is what kind of political power should be decentralized to cities and whether or not these powers are best delivered via political/institutional or constitutional avenues.

These then are some of the challenges we see looking forward. They hardly constitute a full list. New ones will surface in the months ahead and existing ones may well take new forms. Nonetheless, searching for state-of-the-art policies in these and similar areas will be the key to rethinking the art of the state in a world without frontiers.

We want to conclude by again expressing our sincere thanks to the authors, the discussants and the practitioners for their insights and for their contributions to making this book a reality.

Reference

McSuite, O.C. *Legitimacy in Public Administration: A Discourse Analysis*. Thousand Oaks, CA: Sage, 1997.

AIT	Agreement on Internal Trade (Canada)
APC	Annual Premiers' Conference
ASEAN	Association of Southeast Asian Nations
BITs	Bilateral Investment Treaties
CARICOM	Caribbean Common Market
CEC	Commission for Environmental Cooperation
CFIA	Canadian Food Inspection Agency
CGS	Convention governance system
COAG	Council of Australian Governments
CRTC	Canadian Radio-Television and Telecommunications Commission
CSO	Civil society organization
EU	European Union
FAO	Food and Agriculture Organization
FDI	Foreign direct investment
FMC	First Ministers' Conference
FTAA	Free Trade Area of the Americas
GATS	General Agreement on Trade and Services
GATT	General Agreement on Tariffs and Trade
GDP	Gross domestic product
GEO	Global environmental organization
GPTs	General purpose technologies
GSP	Generalized system of preferences
IGO	Intergovernmental organizations
IMF	International Monetary Fund
INGOs	International non-governmental organizations
IPU	Inter-Parliamentary Union
IT	Information technology
JPAC	Joint Public Advisory Committee
KBE	Knowledge-based economy
LBD	Learning-by-doing
M&E	Machinery and equipment
MAI	Multilateral Agreement on Investment
MEAs	Multilateral environmental agreements
MNE	Multinational enterprise
MOU	Memorandum of understanding
NAAEC	North American Agreement on Environmental Cooperation
NAFTA	North American Free Trade Agreement
NAIRU	Non-accelerating inflation rate of unemployment
NEO	New economic order
NGO	Non-governmental organizations
NPM	New public management
OAS	Organization of American States
OECD	Organisation for Economic Co-operation and Development
PPMs	Production processes and methods
PPP	Public-private partnerships
PUMA	Public Management Service of the OECD
R&D	Research and development
SAARC	South Asian Association for Regional Co-operation
SCFAIT	House of Commons Standing Committee on Foreign Affairs and International Trade
SCTE	House of Commons Standing Committee on Trade and Environment
SOAs	Special operating agencies
SPS	Agreement on Sanitary and Phytosanitary Measures
SUFA	Social Union Framework Agreement
TFP	Total factor productivity
TNCs	Transnational corporations
TRIPs	Trade-Related Aspects of Intellectual Property Rights
UNCTAD	United Nations Conference on Trade and Development
UNDP	United Nations Development Programme
UNEP	United Nations Environment Programme
WEO	World environmental organization
WHO	World Health Organization
WMO	World Meteorological Organization
WSSD	World Summit on Sustainable Development
WTO	World Trade Organization

Is It Time for Canada to Embrace Monetary Union?

THE FOLLOWING DISCUSSION ABOUT A COMMON CURRENCY FOR NORTH AMERICA took place between Gordon G. Thiessen, Executive in Residence in the School of Management at the University of Ottawa and former Bank of Canada governor, and three prominent Canadian academics, Thomas Courchene, Richard Harris and Pierre Fortin, as part of the Montebello Conference, "The Art of the State: Governance in a World Without Frontiers."

Thiessen opened the currency discussion and was followed by Richard Harris, Telus Professor of Economics at Simon Fraser University; Thomas Courchene, Jarislowsky-Deutsch Professor of Economics and Financial Policy at Queen's University and Senior Scholar at the IRPP and Pierre Fortin, Professor of Economics at the Université du Québec à Montréal and a Fellow of the Royal Society of Canada. This is a slightly edited version of their remarks, reproduced earlier in the *Financial Post*, November 16, 2001.

Gordon Thiessen

Some of the interest in a common currency comes out of the European experience with the euro. I think it is important to remember what lay behind that experience, which is 50-some years of increasing economic cooperation and increasing political cooperation of various sorts. And in the end, even with all of that, the final decision to go for monetary union was basically a political judgement, rather than one that came out of pure economics.

The real argument for currency union has to do with transaction costs. For cross-border movements, if you do not have to change currencies, then obviously there is a lower transaction cost, and if you do not have to worry about the fluctuations in those currencies, then there is less uncertainty than there otherwise might be. But it is very important to remember that to get the full benefit of all of that, you do not just want a fixed exchange rate. You really do have to have something that is stronger than that—some kind of common currency.

On the other side of the argument, a floating exchange rate offers flexibility and the benefits of assisting adjustments to economic shocks. And if your economy is rather different than your major trading partner's, in our case, the United States, then it is likely that those shocks are going to affect you differently.

The classic example in Canada is commodity price shocks. If commodity prices go up, Canada is better off and because the Americans are net importers of commodities, the Americans are worse off and vice versa. For example, after the Asian financial crisis when commodity prices went down by some 20 percent (weighted in terms of Canada's production of primary commodities), we as a country were worse off. The Americans as net importers were better off.

We have these two closely integrated economies, but at times they go in different directions. It seems to me that in order to make that system work well, some kind of shock absorber is needed between those two economies. That is what the flexible exchange rate does. It provides a shock absorber.

The other thing a flexible exchange rate does is that it allows us to pursue a Canadian monetary policy. The interesting case is recent fiscal policy, where Canada got into some fiscal difficulty, having built up a lot of public debt. Then, once that public debt reached the stage where it worried investors and taxpayers, something had to be done about it, and fairly quickly. In those circumstances, we followed an extremely tight fiscal policy, both federally and provincially, beginning around 1994–95. That meant that we had a major fiscal drag on our economy.

How do you compensate for that? You make up for it with a monetary policy that is easier than it otherwise would be. Now, if you did not have that ability to pursue an independent monetary policy, the adjustment to that fiscal cutback would have been very severe indeed. And the only way to have an independent monetary policy is to have a floating exchange rate.

There has recently been much concern because the Canadian dollar has tended to be weak relative to the US dollar, resulting in a couple of things that worry people about the weak Canadian dollar. One of them is that somehow we end up losing on the productivity side because the Canadian dollar is weak, the cost of capital goods is higher since typically they are imported from the US and priced in US dollars. Therefore, Canadian companies will not invest as much in machinery and equipment, and we will not get the productivity growth that we would otherwise.

But the question is why has the Canadian dollar been weak in US dollar terms? It is usually because of differing economic developments between Canada and the US. And most recently, that difference has tended to be in the commodity price area with commodity prices going down. There has also been a differential in productivity growth and economic growth generally between Canada and the US.

Take the recent situation where US growth has been strong and Canadian productivity and commodity prices have been relatively weak. If we had tried to prevent the exchange rate from depreciating in those circumstances we would have ended up with very high interest rates and a much weaker economy. Is that going to lead to more investment than otherwise? I don't think it will.

Finally, there is the issue of a weak Canadian dollar causing a fire sale of Canadian firms. It seems to me that if a company is selling internationally traded goods, those goods tend to be priced internationally in US dollars. The company then translates that into Canadian dollars, in terms of its income, revenue, and so on. The problem is that if that is the way it works for internationally traded goods output, how is it that the assets that are used to produce those goods do not get looked at in the same way? It is highly unlikely that somehow the weak Canadian dollar makes those assets really cheap internationally, and makes them subject to foreign takeover, but does not affect the international price of the product they produce.

In the case of Canadian companies generating products only sold in Canada, then those products are priced in Canadian dollars. A foreign investor might think that the price of the company is very low, because the Canadian dollar is low, but if the company is producing goods only sold in Canada and only generating Canadian dollars, then the foreign company is not going to be any better off as it takes its profits and translates them back into US dollars. Unless a foreign company is speculating that the Canadian dollar is going to go up one day. Is there any reason to think that foreigners are better at speculating in the Canadian dollar than Canadians? I don't think so.

Professor Rick Harris

I think the next step in this debate is going to be when Britain makes the decision to use the euro or not because I do not see the debate here in Canada moving much until that happens. Gordon Thiessen emphasizes the role of commodity shocks in defining an optimal currency area, but this misses the important question regarding the optimal size of a currency area. If commodity price shocks are that important then that logic would suggest that Alberta should have its own currency. You can push the commodity price argument to these illogical extremes without coming to the only reasonable conclusion: it makes no sense for Alberta to have its own currency.

Let me ask an alternative question for Canada. If we had been in a monetary union with the US, it is absolutely clear that the macro adjustment mechanism that took place within Canada, which was a substantial real depreciation of the currency, would not have occurred. There would have been another set of adjustment mechanisms that would have taken place. I suggest that if you want to look at what those adjustment mechanisms would be, look to US states and industries that are similar to ones in Canada. Look at the automobile industry in Michigan, which is just next to Ontario, or the lumber industry in Washington and Oregon and compare it to BC, or the oil industry in Texas and compare it to Alberta. The big difference is that in Canada, all of those industries and regions experienced large real depreciation of the currency while similar US industries and regions did not. Is it the case that the macroeconomic adjustment mechanism was that much better in Canada? Clearly not, because the fact of the matter is that our growth performance was much worse than in comparable US regions.

A more general argument about the questionable wisdom of accommodating commodity price declines with currency depreciation is somewhat deeper. I think that we made a mistake. Commodity prices have been steadily falling for a very long time, even though we occasionally get periods in which energy prices blip up. But real commodity prices are going down. One of the things we did, probably inadvertently, was that by accommodating weak commodity prices with the currency depreciation, we locked ourselves into an old pattern of comparative advantage, which has resulted in relatively low productivity growth. In our high technology and non-resource-based industries, productivity growth would have been higher, and they would have expanded faster had they faced the same set of relative prices that prevailed in the United States.

In the absence of the exchange-rate depreciation, would those resource industries have had adjustment problems? Absolutely, but no more so than in comparable US regions. What about the issue of exchange-rate-induced fire sales? The fire-sale issue is partially an empirical puzzle. Take two firms, for example, one located in the

United States and one in Canada, each doing more or less the same thing in the same industry. One could be called MacMillan Bloedel and the other Weyerhaeuser. A substantial currency depreciation should not have led to a substantial depreciation in US dollar terms of the market value of the Canadian firm. But it did.

For whatever reason, there is some cross-border segmentation in capital markets, not only in the non-traded or service sector but also in the traded goods sector and this is in part due to the existence of separate national currencies. Of course, the consequence of the weak Canadian dollar was that Weyerhaeuser took over MacMillan Bloedel, as opposed to the opposite. I agree that it is a puzzle, but what are the longer run consequences for an open economy like Canada when most of the country's valuable corporate assets are marked down for substantial periods of time due to currency depreciation? It is indeed an open question and one that needs a great deal more research.

Professor Tom Courchene

Let me begin with a few plaudits directed toward the Bank of Canada. From a central banking perspective, we can be proud of the Bank of Canada. The Bank demonstrated, admittedly at some considerable cost, that in addition to achieving lower inflation than in the US it could also achieve the so-called "interest-rate crossover," namely Canadian nominal interest rates lower than US nominal interest rates (consistent with our lower inflation rates). In central banking jargon, the Bank of Canada has "credibility." Thus, the fact that I favour a North American common currency has nothing to do with the inability of the Bank of Canada to operate as central banks are supposed to operate. Nor has it anything to do with the reason why some other nations—for example, Mexico—might want to be part of a common currency of the Americas, namely to achieve a low and stable domestic inflation rate. Canada has done this. Rather, the case for a North American Monetary Union (NAMU) lies elsewhere.

Let me begin where Governor Thiessen did: with Europe and the euro. The governor is clearly right, the factors that led to the creation of the euro have few counterparts in North America. But once the euro is up and working, its origins are no longer that important. What is important is that the euro is a supranational currency and is triggering a major drive toward currency consolidation. While the formal euro area encompasses 12 nations, this will double soon and probably triple in terms of the outer countries that link themselves to the euro area. Hence, there will be many fewer currencies in the world in the near future and I doubt whether the Canadian dollar will be one of them. But even if I am wrong, good old Canadian prudence suggests that we ought to begin thinking and researching the range of alternatives for Canada's floating dollar.

I now turn to what is arguably the key analytical rationale for flexible exchange rates—the role for the exchange rate to act as a buffer or a shock absorber. I think that this role is way overrated. To see this, consider the following (realistic I would suggest) scenario. Canada is composed of a series of quite different economies: Atlantic, Quebec/Ontario, Manitoba/Saskatchewan, Alberta and Pacific-Rim British Columbia. Each of these economies is integrated north-south with its US counterpart. Assume that Ontario/Quebec is in cost equilibrium with the US Great Lakes states, that Alberta is matching policies with the Texas Gulf, that BC is in competitive harmony with the Pacific Northwest, etc. Now there is a sudden increase in resource prices (i.e., a commodity shock). Initially, nothing different happens to either side of these cross-border economies, the shock affects Windsor and Detroit the same way, and similarly for Houston and Calgary and for Vancouver and Seattle. But if the Bank of Canada "accommodates" or "buffers" this commodity price increase by appreciating the exchange rate, then every Canadian region becomes offside *vis-à-vis* its US counterpart. Why would we do this? It is much better to keep these cross-border exchange rates fixed. The only way to do this is to have a fixed rate with the US, which means, in effect, that Ontario will adjust to the shock the same way as Michigan does. Two caveats are in order. First, the real shock is not cross-border but rather between Ontario and Alberta or between Texas and Michigan, that is, it is an internal east-west shock. Changing the Canada-US exchange rate does not buffer this. Second, because resources are a larger component of the Canadian economy than the US economy, we have to have policies in place to accommodate this "macro" shock. But we do have such policies: fiscal policy, Employment Insurance, equalization, etc. Arguably, the "buffering" mechanism under a fixed rate regime or a currency union is every bit as effective as the flexible rate version. And as the north-south integration intensifies, the common-currency adjustment mechanism is progressively preferable.

However, the really problematic aspect of the Bank's buffering argument is that it appears to be a not-very-disguised policy for offsetting the longer term downward trend in commodity/resource prices. To this extent, we are effectively providing subsidies to keep labour and capital in the "old economy" and providing disincentives for investing in the new economy, that is, a fall in the Canadian dollar means that information technology and equipment become more expensive since they are typically priced in US dollars. Arguably, this is why Canadian productivity has been lagging US productivity.

On a related point, flexibility itself may be a problem. The wild swings in the Canadian dollar—from US$1.05 in the mid-1970s to 70 cents in 1986 to 89 cents in 1991, to 62½ cents in the summer 1998 currency crisis, then back to the 67-cent range before falling back again to historic lows—are anything but salutary in a progressive human-capital era where cost predictability is more important than it was when we were a resource-based economy. Moreover, some market analysts predict a further falling dollar while others suggest that a return to the mid-70-cent range is likely. This is simply too much in the way of uncertainty for us to maximize our economic prospects in NAFTA economic space.

A word, finally, about sovereignty: under the version of a common currency that Rick Harris and I favour, some Canadian symbolism could still remain on the currency. But the more important sovereignty issue is that those policies that Canadians value most highly—medicare, equalization, CPP/QPP, the Canada Assistance Plan, even regional development—were put in place (or finalized in their current form) during the 1960s. Yet the 1960s was the only period in the postwar period where Canada had a fixed exchange rate with the US. Therefore, tying ourselves to the US monetary policy did not lead to a decline in our ability to legislate in our likeness and image elsewhere in the policy arena. Indeed, what sovereignty is there in a 62-cent dollar if this leads to US/foreign purchases of our assets? More speculatively, how long will it be before the US begins to question our low dollar, especially in light of our large trade surplus with the US? And would we have a softwood lumber problem on our hands if our dollar were 80 cents rather than 63 cents?

It is hard to predict the next episode that will trigger some further evolution toward a common currency. In terms of US interests, I expect that the presumed success of the euro currency launch in 2002 and the number of non-euro countries whose citizens will want to hold euros will cause the US Federal Reserve to wish that the formal dollar area were also expanded. On the domestic front, Canadians will be influenced by the British decision toward the euro. Since the British want no part of a political union with European nations, adopting the euro would send a message that a common currency is all about economics and market access and not about sovereignty. I think Canadians are increasingly sensing this.

Professor Pierre Fortin

In discussing the future of the Canadian dollar, we ought not to forget that the Canadian dollar could appreciate sharply in the not too distant future. The Canadian-US exchange rate is so low that a representative basket of goods and services worth US$100 in the US currently costs C$160 to buy in that country, but only around C$117 to buy in Canada, according to purchasing power parity calculations done by Statistics Canada and the OECD. This means it is 35 percent more expensive to buy goods in the United States than in Canada. The only game in town is to buy Canadian and sell American. As long as this situation persists, our export-to-GDP ratio and our trade and current account surpluses will go only one way—up. This will not only result from Canadian firms exporting more to, and importing less from, the US, but also from US and other foreign firms producing in Canada for the US market. A large fraction of recent foreign acquisitions of Canadian firms and foreign start-ups in Canada are part of this process.

In 1994, Canada had a $330 billion external debt. It has since been reduced to $220 billion and in the past two years, we have begun to generate huge trade and current account surpluses. This has had our external debt falling at a rapid rate. If the Canadian dollar remains low, our external debt will likely continue to fall as our trade surplus continues to forge ahead. Moreover, the debt will decline at a faster and faster rate. This is because less debt means less interest and dividends to pay, and therefore an even larger surplus, which in turn means that the debt will fall even faster.

At one point, the financial-market herd will suddenly realize that Canadians are becoming net lenders to the rest of the world for the first time since Leif Erikson. The Canadian dollar will instantly become extremely popular and could appreciate rapidly from 63 cents to 75 or 80 cents. This will send our exporting firms berserk. The behaviour of world financial markets is extremely difficult to predict in the short run, but over the medium to long run, they cannot get around economic fundamentals. This is something we should bear in mind if we continue to allow the Canadian dollar to float.

Final Remarks, Gordon Thiessen

Well, I do not know how this should be summed up. The European experience is interesting here. The adoption of a common currency caused many people to think about it here. However, that did not necessarily make it relevant to us. The long period of economic integration in Europe needs to be examined. That period was long and increasingly had political elements attached to it. If we imagine that we are going down that same road in North America, then the notion of a common currency may become more plausible. But monetary union is something that should only be contemplated at the end of the process, or very close to the end, just as in Europe. And it surely should only be contemplated after some kind of political accommodation has been made with the United States. I do not think a common currency is the place to start. When adjusting to increasing economic integration, a flexible currency is very helpful. Or if the Canada-US exchange rate is to be locked in, it should be at the end of the process, when some kind of political accommodation has been made, and most of the economic adjustment has been done.

In the end, the problem of any kind of currency union here without political union implies that Canada adopts the US currency. We have none of the comparable arrangements that they have in Europe. If, for example, the British accept the euro, they will be another large country along with France, Germany and Italy in the European Central Bank. They are going to have a lot of influence relative to those other countries in making European monetary policy. The North American situation is just not comparable. And the Americans really do make it quite clear that they are not about to make any comparable accommodation. Thus, if you are talking about currency union, remember you are talking about adopting the US dollar. If you are contemplating a decision to adopt the US dollar, then I think you had better think very hard about what kind of political arrangements with the United States you want to go along with that decision.

André Blais is a Professor in the Department of Political Science and Research Associate with the Centre de recherche et de développement en économique at the Université de Montréal. His research interests include elections and voting behaviour, electoral laws, public opinion and public policy. He is the principal co-investigator of the 1997 Canadian Election Study, and was on the editorial board of the *International Encyclopedia of Elections*. His most recent book is *To Vote Or Not To Vote? The Merits and Limits of Rational Choice*. Professor Blais received the Prix Marcel-Vincent for his contribution in social science from the Association canadienne-française pour l'avancement des sciences in 1996 and was elected a member of the Royal Society of Canada in 1999. Last year, he was named a Canada Research Chair in Electoral Studies.

Thomas J. Courchene was born in Wakaw, Saskatchewan and educated at the universities of Saskatchewan, Princeton and Chicago. Professor Courchene is the Jarislowsky-Deutsch Professor of Economic and Financial Policy at Queen's University and is a Fellow at the Institute for Research on Public Policy in Montreal. Tom is a Fellow of the Royal Society of Canada, an Officer in the Order of Canada, holds honorary degrees from the universities of Western Ontario and Saskatchewan and in February 2000 was awarded the prestigious Canada Council Molson Prize for Lifetime Achievement in the Social Sciences. Tom and Margie Courchene live by the St. Lawrence River in Kingston, Ontario.

Ron Daniels is Dean and Professor at the Faculty of Law, University of Toronto. He was appointed to the Faculty of Law in 1988, where he teaches corporate law, securities and finance, mergers and acquisitions and regulation of financial institutions. He has been Dean of the Faculty since 1995. He is the author (or co-author) of numerous scholarly articles on topics as diverse as corporate and securities law, federalism and financial institution regulation, privatization and government reform. Dr. Daniels is active in public policy formulation, and has contributed to several policy-related task forces, including: Chair of the Ontario Task Force on Securities Regulation, member of the Toronto Stock Exchange Committee on Corporate Governance (the Dey Committee), and Chair of the Ontario Market Design Committee, the committee that was charged with the task of developing the market rules for the new Ontario electricity market. Currently, Professor Daniels is Chair of the Ontario Law Deans and past President of the Canadian Law Deans.

Don Drummond first joined the federal Department of Finance upon completing his studies at Queen's University. During almost 23 years at Finance, Mr. Drummond held a series of progressively senior positions in the areas of economic analysis and forecasting, fiscal policy and tax policy. His last three positions were respectively, Assistant Deputy Minister of Fiscal Policy and Economic Analysis, Assistant Deputy Minister of Tax Policy and Legislation and most recently, Associate Deputy Minister. In this latter position Mr. Drummond was responsible for economic analysis, fiscal policy, tax policy, social policy and federal-provincial relations. In particular, Mr. Drummond coordinated the planning of the annual federal budgets. He joined the TD Bank in June 2000 as Senior Vice President and Chief Economist and leads the TD Economics' work in analyzing and forecasting economic performance in Canada and abroad. For Canada, this work is conducted at the city, provincial, industrial and national levels. TD Economics also analyzes the key policies that influence economic performance, including monetary and fiscal policies.

Pierre Fortin is Professor of Economics at the Université du Québec à Montréal (UQAM), which he joined in 1988 after teaching at Université Laval and the Université de Montréal. He is a Fellow of the Royal Society of Canada. He holds a MSC in mathematics from l'Université Laval and a PhD in economics from the University of California at Berkeley. His research interests include wage and price dynamics, economic fluctuations and growth, taxation, fiscal and monetary policies, social policy and population economics. He was awarded the Purvis Prize in 1997 for the best book or article recently published on economic policy in Canada. He is past President of the Canadian Economics Association and is a member of the Board of Directors of the Centre for the Study of Living Standards.

Richard G. Harris is the Telus Professor of Economics at Simon Fraser University, and Senior Research Fellow at the C.D. Howe Institute. Prior to 1990 he had spent most of his professional career in the Department of Economics at Queen's University with visiting appointments at Berkeley, MIT and the University of New South Wales, and was a former director of the John Deutsch Institute for the Study of Economic Policy at Queen's University. His major area of specialization is international economics, competitiveness and economic growth. During the 1980s he worked extensively on economic modelling of the impact of the

Canada-US Free Trade Agreement and subsequently on NAFTA. Dr. Harris has served as consultant to a number of Canadian government departments, international organizations, including the World Bank and OECD and corporations in the area of international economics. In addition to a number of technical articles, he has published policy-oriented books and articles on Canada-US free trade, international macroeconomics, economic growth, the Asia-Pacific region, exchange rate regimes and Canadian public policy. He is currently involved in research on the determinants of innovation and productivity growth, North American monetary integration and the New Economy. He is a Fellow of the Royal Society of Canada and a former president of the Canadian Economics Association.

Ralph Heintzman is Assistant Secretary (Strategic Policy and Planning) in the Treasury Board of Canada Secretariat. Prior to this appointment, in April 2002, Mr. Heintzman served as Assistant Secretary (Service and Innovation) since February 1998. Previous to holding these posts, Dr. Heintzman was a faculty member and Vice-Principal, Research at the Canadian Centre for Management Development, concurrently serving as Vice-Chair of the Deputy Minister Task Force on Public Service Values and Ethics. From 1987 to 1989, Dr. Heintzman served as Executive Director of the Social Sciences and Humanities Research Council of Canada. He was a chercheur invité at the Centre de recherche en civilisation canadienne-française at the University of Ottawa while on leave from the Federal-Provincial Relations Office from 1984 to 1986. Earlier, Dr. Heintzman had held governmental posts concerning federal-provincial relations and cultural policy. His involvement in academia includes ten years as associate editor and editor of the *Journal of Canadian Studies* and as a contributor to the *Canadian Historical Review* and *Canadian Journal of Political Science* and the *International Review of Administrative Sciences*.

Jane Jenson, has been the Director of the Family Network of Canadian Policy Research Networks since June 1999. She is also Professor of Political Science at the Université de Montréal and Director of the Université de Montréal/McGill University Institute of European Studies. In 2001 she was awarded a Tier 1 Canada Research Chair for Governance and Citizenship at the Université de Montréal. She is also editor of *Lien social et Politiques—RIAC*, a social policy journal. Dr. Jenson earned her BA from McGill University and her PhD from the University of Rochester in 1974, and then taught at Carleton University until 1993, when she moved to the Université de Montréal. In addition, she has been a visiting professor at a number of European universities and at Harvard University, where she held the Mackenzie King Chair in Canadian Studies. She was elected to the Royal Society of Canada in 1989. Her work in recent years has focused on social policy and she currently holds two grants from the Social Science and Humanities Research Council of Canada for an individual project on Citizenship Regimes and New Social Unions: Learning from Caring and a Strategic Grant for Fostering Social Cohesion: A Comparison of New Policy Strategies.

Pierre Marc Johnson is a lawyer, physician, former Premier of Quebec and former professor of Law at McGill University. Mr. Johnson has been Senior Counsel with the offices of Heenan Blaikie since 1996 and serves on numerous corporate boards as a Director and sits on the Board of IRPP. He acts in commercial negotiations, international partnerships and foreign investment ventures related to new information technologies, entertainment, real estate and financial products. He has a wide experience in international negotiations with the United Nations on environmental and developmental issues. Vice-Chairman of the National Round Table on the Environment and the Economy and Chair of its Foreign Policy Committee from 1990 to 1997, he is an advisor to the Commission for Environmental Cooperation (a NAFTA parallel institution). He is the author of many essays and a textbook on international trade law, *The Environment and NAFTA: Understanding and Implementing the New Continental Law* (1996) and "Beyond Trade: The Case for a Broadened International Governance Agenda," a *Policy Matters* published by IRPP in 2000. Mr. Johnson has an honorary doctorate from Claude Bernard University in Lyon, France. He is a Fellow of the Royal Society of Canada and a Grand Officier de l'Ordre de la Pléiade.

Michael Keating is Professor of Regional Studies at the European University Institute, Florence and Professor of Scottish Politics at the University of Aberdeen. From 1988 until 1999 he was Professor of Political Science at the University of Western Ontario and before that was Senior Lecturer at the University of Strathclyde, Glasgow. He gained his BA at the University of Oxford (1971) and PhD at Glasgow College (1975), and has published widely on urban and regional politics and nationalism. His recent books include *The New Regionalism in Western Europe* (1998); *Nations against the State* (second edition, 2001), *Minority Nationalism and the Changing International Order* (2001, edited with John McGarry). *Plurinational Democracy*, which analyzes the politics of the United Kingdom, Canada, Belgium and Spain in a post-sovereignty era, appeared from Oxford University Press in 2001.

Tom Kent was responsible as a Deputy Minister for organizing two new federal departments. He also served as Policy Secretary to Prime Minister Pearson. In a diverse career he has been a newspaper editor, corporation president, university dean and Royal Commission chairman. He was the founding editor of *Policy Options politiques* and is now Fellow of the School of Policy Studies of Queen's University, a lifetime Fellow of IRPP, and a Companion of the Order of Canada.

Will Kymlicka received his BA in philosophy and politics from Queen's University in 1984, and his PhD in philosophy from Oxford University in 1987. He is the author of five books published by Oxford University Press: *Liberalism, Community, and Culture (1989), Contemporary Political Philosophy* (1990; second edition 2002), *Multicultural Citizenship* (1995), *Finding Our Way: Rethinking Ethnocultural Relations in Canada* (1998) and *Politics in the Vernacular: Nationalism, Multiculturalism, Citizenship* (2001). He is also the editor of *Justice in Political Philosophy* (1992), and *The Rights of Minority Cultures* (1995), and co-editor of *Ethnicity and Group Rights* (1997), *Citizenship in Diverse Societies* (2000), *Alternative Conceptions of Civil Society* (2001), and *Can Liberal Pluralism be Exported? Western Political Theory and Ethnic Relations in Eastern Europe* (2001). He is currently a Professor of Philosophy at Queen's University, and a visiting professor in the Nationalism Studies Program at the Central European University in Budapest. His works have been translated into 23 languages.

Jean-François Lisée—Foreign correspondent and reporter in Paris and Washington for Quebec and French media in the 1980s, he published in 1990 *Dans l'oeil de l'aigle: Washington face au Québec* (Governor General's award for non-fiction) followed by three books on Quebec politics, among them *The Trickster* on the post-Meech situation in Québec. In 1994, he became special advisor to Premier Jacques Parizeau and a key strategist for the 1995 referendum campaign, then went on to advise Premier

Lucien Bouchard. Resigning in late 1999, he published in 2000 *Emergency Exit—How to Avert Québec's Decline,* which sparked an important debate on the future of Quebec. Born in Thetford Mines, Quebec in 1958, Mr. Lisée has degrees in Law, Journalism and Communications. Now a researcher in public policy, member of the Montreal-based Centre de recherche sur les politiques et le développement social, he is currently guest researcher at the Centre d'études et de recherches internationales in Paris. His work focuses on social policy and globalization.

Donald G. McFetridge is a Professor in the Department of Economics at Carleton University in Ottawa. Professor McFetridge has been teaching both undergraduate and graduate courses and supervising doctoral research in industrial economics and competition policy since 1971. He has published numerous articles and books on various aspects of industrial economics and policy, the economics of innovation, industrial policy and competition policy.

B. Guy Peters is Maurice Falk Professor of American Government at the University of Pittsburgh and Honorary Professor at the City University of Hong Kong. He also continues to be a Senior Fellow of the Canadian Centre for Management Development. Among his publications are *The Politics of Bureaucracy* (fifth edition), *Institutional Theory in Political Science, Administering the Summit* (with R.A.W. Rhodes and Vincent Wright) and *Governance in the 21st Century* (with Donald J. Savoie). He was also founding co-editor of *Governance: An International Journal of Policy and Administration*.

Christopher Pollitt took up his position as Professor of Public Management at Erasmus University, Rotterdam in January 1999, after having taught as Professor of Government and Dean of the Faculty of Social Sciences at Brunel University (London), 1990-1998. His current research includes a comparison of central government public management reforms in ten countries and an analysis of performance management systems in Dutch, Finnish, Swedish and UK agencies. Dr. Pollitt has published many books and academic articles, including *Managerialism and the Public Services*, *Decentralising Public Service Management*, *Performance or Compliance? Performance Audit and Public Management in Five Countries* (with others) and, most recently, *Public Management Reform: A Comparative Analysis*, which reviews the experiences of ten countries with *Public Management Reform Since*

1980 (with Geert Bouckaert). Between 1980 and 1989 Dr. Pollitt was editor of the journal *Public Administration*, and from 1996 to 1998 he was President of the European Evaluation Society. As a consultant, he has worked for the OECD, the European Commission, the World Bank, the UK Treasury, the Finnish Ministry of Finance and many other public authorities. Dr. Pollitt holds an MA from Oxford (modern history) and a PhD in government from the London School of Economics.

Donald Savoie holds the Clément-Cormier Chair in Economic Development at l'Université de Moncton and has degrees in politics and economics from l'Université de Moncton, the University of New Brunswick and Oxford. He has extensive work experience in both government and academia. He held senior positions with the government of Canada, including Assistant Secretary, Corporate and Public Affairs with the Treasury Board (1987-1988) and Deputy Principal of the Canadian Centre for Management Development, Ottawa (1988-1990). He founded the Canadian Institute for Research on Regional Development at l'Université de Moncton in 1983 where he was also appointed Professor of Public Administration. He has served as an advisor to a number of federal, provincial and territorial government departments and agencies, the private sector, independent associations, OECD, the World Bank and the United Nations. He was made an Officer of the Order of Canada, elected Fellow of the Royal Society of Canada, and awarded the Vanier Gold Medal in public administration. He has also been awarded several national and international prizes for his published work.

Denis Stairs—McCulloch Professor in Political Science at Dalhousie University, Stairs attended Dalhousie, Oxford and the University of Toronto. A former President of the Canadian Political Science Association, he was the founding Director of Dalhousie's Centre for Foreign Policy Studies from 1970 to 1975. He served as Chair of his department from 1980 to 1985, and as Dalhousie's Vice-President (Academic and Research) from 1988 to 1993. A Fellow of the Royal Society of Canada, he specializes in Canadian foreign and defence policy and Canada-US relations.

Ronald L. Watts is Principal Emeritus and Professor Emeritus of Political Studies at Queen's University where he has been a member of the academic staff since

1955, and was Principal and Vice-Chancellor from 1974 to 1984. He is a Fellow and former Director of the Institute of Intergovernmental Relations at Queen's University. He was President of the International Association of Centres of Federal Studies 1991-1998, and is currently a member of the Board of the International Forum of Federations. He is a former Board member and chairman of the Research Committee of the Institute for Research on Public Policy. On several occasions he has been a consultant to the Government of Canada during constitutional deliberations, most notably 1980 to 1981 and 1991 to 1992, and has been a constitutional advisor to governments in several other countries. As a political scientist, Professor Watts has worked for over 40 years on the comparative study of political systems and on Canadian federalism, and has written or edited over 20 books, monographs and reports and over 60 articles and book chapters. His most recent book is *Comparing Federal Systems.* The second edition was published in 1999. He has received five honourary degrees, and became an Officer of the Order of Canada in 1979 and was promoted to Companion of the Order of Canada in 2000.

Robert Young is Professor of Political Science at the University of Western Ontario, where he was Chair of the department from 1996-2000 and is Co-Director of the Political Economy Research Group. He took his BA and MA at McGill and his PhD from Oxford, and also studied at the University of Michigan and l'Institut d'Études Politiques in Paris. He has written on public policy and development in the Maritimes, and contributed many articles and commentaries during the Canadian debate about free trade. Recently he has focused again on Canadian federalism, Quebec and secession more generally. His works in these areas include *The Breakup of Czechoslovakia* (1994), *The Secession of Quebec and the Future of Canada* (1995) and *The Struggle for Quebec* (1999).